Masked Voices

SUNY series in Queer Politics and Cultures

Cynthia Burack and Jyl J. Josephson, editors

Masked Voices

Gay Men and Lesbians
in Cold War America

CRAIG M. LOFTIN

Figure 3 courtesy of Phyllis Lyon; figures 14 and 15 reprinted with permission by Bob Mizer Foundation; all other figures courtesy of ONE National Gay and Lesbian Archives.

An earlier version of Chapter 10 appeared in the *Journal of Social History* XL, 3 (Spring 2007).

Published by State University of New York Press, Albany

© 2012 State University of New York

For information, contact State University of New York Press, Albany, NY
www.sunypress.edu

Production by Eileen Meehan
Marketing by Anne M. Valentine

Library of Congress Cataloging-in-Publication Data

Loftin, Craig M.
    Masked voices : gay men and lesbians in cold war America / Craig M. Loftin.
        p. cm. — (SUNY series in queer politics and cultures)
    Includes bibliographical references and index.
    ISBN 978-1-4384-4014-9 (pbk. : alk. paper)
    ISBN 978-1-4384-4015-6 (hardcover : alk. paper)
    1. Homosexuality—United States.   2. Gays—United States   3. One (Los Angeles, Calif.)   I. Title.

    HQ76.25.L64 2012
    306.76'6097309045—dc22   2011013328

10 9 8 7 6 5 4 3 2 1

For Mom and Dad,
who have always encouraged and supported my curiosity.

Contents

List of Illustrations

Figures

Tables

Acknowledgments

I am deeply grateful to many people who have helped make this book a reality. First and foremost, I thank Lois Banner and Steve Ross in the history department at the University of Southern California for serving as co-chairs of my dissertation committee, for reading countless chapter drafts over many years, and for their unceasing encouragement and inspiration throughout graduate school. I also thank Phil Ethington in history and Michael Messner in sociology for serving on my dissertation committee and providing invaluable feedback and support throughout the process.

Many people at USC made important contributions to this specific project and my development as a scholar and teacher. I thank Elinor Accampo (and Sophie, for being such a good dog), Alice Echols, Terry Seip, Richard Fox, George Sanchez, Lynn Spigel, Philippa Levine, Carole Shammas, Drew Casper, Marjorie Becker, Judith Grant, Rick Jewell, Carla Kaplan, Julie Nyquist, and Walter Williams. Thank you to my fellow graduate students at USC, especially Tillman Netchman, Karin Huebner, Matt Newsome-Kerr, Stacy Newsome-Kerr, Vicki Vantoch (and Misha), Pete La Chapelle, Shirley Brautbar, John Bradshaw, Ian Livie, Chris West Y Jimenez, Liz Willis-Tropea, Treva Tucker, Joseph Wright, Marion Umeno, Jeff Montez de Oca, James Thing, Michael Carter, James Bell, and Jon Acevedo. A special thank you to Jeff Kosiorek for being such a good friend and for playing all those Monopoly games with me. A sincere and heartfelt thank you to the USC history department staff: Lori Ann Rogers, Laverne Hughes, Brenda Johnson, Sandra Hopwood, and, of course, Joseph Styles.

Thank you to the USC College of Letters, Arts, and Sciences for generous funding over the years. Thank you to the Ford Foundation and Social Science Research Council for additional funding through the Sexuality Research Fellowship Program. Thank you to Diane Mauro, Lissa Gundlach, and the talented scholars I had to privilege to meet and get to know at the Kinsey Institute in 2005.

This book would not exist if not for the graciousness and generosity of the volunteers and staff at the ONE National Gay and Lesbian Archives in Los Angeles. I thank everyone for making my years there as a researcher and volunteer so rewarding. I especially thank Joseph Hawkins for his superb leadership of the archive as well as his academic camaraderie and friendship. A special thank you to Pat Allen for pointing me in the direction of the *ONE* magazine correspondence back in 2000. Thank you to the many scholars, volunteers, staff, and stewards of the archive who I have had the pleasure to know, including Stuart Timmons, Michael Quinn, Yolanda Retter, James Morrow, Dan Luckenbill, David Hensley, David Kaiser, Misha Schutt, Ashlie Midfelt, Matt Knowlton, Daniel Rivers, Bud Thomas, John Master, and Fred Bradford. A very special thank you to Lee McEvoy, a longtime ONE volunteer who tutored me extensively about gay history and its complex interplay with the history of classical music.

I am indebted to my study group of gifted historians for reading chapter drafts and offering such an abundance of helpful suggestions. Thank you Steve Ross (once again), John Laslett, Leila Zenderland, Frank Stricker, Nancy Fitch, Hal Barron, Bob Slayton, Jan Rieff, Becky Nicolaides, Allison Varzally, Karen Brodkin, Toby Higbie, and Jennifer Luff. I have benefited from our monthly meetings in more ways than I can describe.

Thank you to my colleagues in the American Studies Department at California State University, Fullerton. Thanks especially to Jesse Battan and John Ibson for professional guidance and wisdom over the years. Thanks to fellow instructors Sharon Sekhon, Randy Baxter, Kristin Hargrove, Tracy Sachtjen, Karen Kidd, Casey Christensen, Trista O' Connell, Amanda Perez, Shawn Schwaller, and Sam Sousa for creating such an intellectually invigorating working environment. Thank you Carole Angus and Karla Arellano for such superb work every day. A big thank you to CSUF's undergraduates for their talents, energy, and enthusiasm.

Thank you to SUNY Press for being so supportive of my research. Thank you to editors Larin McLaughlin and Andrew Kenyon for guidance throughout the submission process and for so promptly answering all my emails and questions. Thank you series editors Cynthia Burack and Jyl Josephson for your professionalism, encouragement, and wisdom. Thank you to the anonymous reviewers for such constructive and thoughtful feedback. Thanks also to Doug Mitchell for initial interest in the project.

Thank you to the many individuals who have inspired me over the years. At the University of California, Santa Barbara, I profusely thank Richard Flacks, who gave me the confidence to pursue graduate studies, and Albert Lindemann, for his tireless copyediting of my senior honors thesis many years ago. Thank you Kenneth Plummer, Rich Appelbaum,

John Baldwin, and Johan van der Zande. I sincerely thank Leila Rupp for her generous time spent with my manuscript and invaluable suggestions, and to the staff at the Davidson Library Special Collections. At the University of Oregon, thank you Dan Pope, Ellen Herman, John McCole, Glenn May, Peggy Pascoe, Alex Dracobly, Julie Hessler, Gail Unruh, Christopher Phelps, and James Mohr. And, of course, thank you Manuel and Nora.

A big thank you to all of my colleagues in history as well as in gender studies, women's studies, and gay, lesbian, and queer history. I especially thank Leisa Meyer, Martin Meeker, Marc Stein, Ian Lekus, Marcia Gallo, and Karen Krahulik for their work with the Committee on Lesbian, Gay, Bisexual, and Transgender History and for their feedback on my research, guidance in maintaining the Committee on Lesbian, Gay, Bisexual, and Transgender History website, and intellectual mentorship over the years. Thank you Lillian Faderman, John D'Emilio, George Chauncey, Chris Stansell, Daniel Hurewitz, David Johnson, C. Todd White, Jonathan Katz, Jeffrey Escoffier, Gilbert Herdt, Susan Stryker, Gayle Rubin, Elizabeth Armstrong, Vern Bullough, Martha Vicinus, Marjorie Garber, Joanne Meyerowitz, James Sears, and countless others for your personal generosity and for conducting such inspiring and important research.

Thank you to my family for their generous support over the years. Thank you to my parents for their kindness and love throughout my life.

Finally, thank you to my husband Daniel. Thank you for suffering with me through a bleak academic job market, the uncertainties of California's state budget—and every other crisis that has come our way in the ten years we have been together. Thank you for your insightful and careful editing of my research and thoughtful feedback at every stage of the process. Thank you for making my lunch for me when I go to work and for taking such good care of our pug, Maggie. Thank you for being my number one fan, and please know I am your number one fan.

Craig M. Loftin
November 2011

Introduction

In the spring of 1954, a man named John walked by a newsstand in downtown Los Angeles and spotted something he had never seen before. It was a small magazine called *ONE: The Homosexual Magazine*. *ONE* was the first, and at that time, the only American magazine directly marketed to gay and lesbian readers. Browsing the pages with curiosity, John was impressed by the magazine's pro-gay and lesbian tone. He saw the address for the magazine's headquarters inside the front cover. Realizing it was just a short bus ride away, he decided to visit *ONE*'s offices and share a personal story with *ONE*'s staff.

Upon arriving at 232 South Hill Street, he entered the shabby building and proceeded upstairs to room 328. "ONE, Inc." was stenciled on the door. He entered to find a stuffy, cramped office, and a balding, middle-aged man sitting at a typewriter surrounded by books. The man was Dorr Legg, *ONE*'s business manager. John, who suffered from a stuttering disability, described a harrowing experience to Legg. He had worked as an orderly at a veteran's hospital. One day, unexpectedly, hospital officials had announced a new policy forbidding the employment of homosexuals, and that all gay and lesbian employees would be fired. Investigators reviewed hospital personnel records and conducted interviews to determine which employees were gay. Several of John's friends lost their jobs. Eventually the investigators interviewed John, asking him a series of questions about his personal life. After establishing that John was gay, the investigators told John that he could keep his job if he told them the names of other gay men and lesbians working at the hospital. Under duress, John gave investigators the names of other gay employees. The assurance about his job, however, was a trick—because he had admitted he was gay and because hospital policy dictated his dismissal, John was fired.[1]

John explained to Dorr Legg that when he searched for a new job after being fired, he faced a difficult dilemma. He could be honest to prospective employers about his homosexuality and almost certainly not be hired. Or, he could lie about why he lost his previous job and hope his new employer would not check references and, therefore, never discover the real reason for his previous dismissal. Months passed without finding a new job. His savings dwindled. He became overwhelmed with guilt because he had identified other gay people to the hospital investigators. Legg wrote years later in *ONE* magazine that John was "abysmally ashamed of himself, utterly debased at the thought of the disasters he had brought down upon so many others. At the same time he was choking with rage and contempt at those who had taken advantage of his honesty to entrap him, and with loathing for the Senator who was the apparent cause of it all."[2] Readers of *ONE* magazine knew that the "Senator" referred to was Joseph McCarthy of Wisconsin.

Eventually, John found another job, regained his savings, and became a lifelong volunteer for ONE, Inc.[3] A 1961 editorial in *ONE* posited John as a symbol of the anxieties, indignities, and repression afflicting gay people since the end of World War II. Yet John also symbolized the perseverance of gay people to work constructively toward a better future. The cover illustration of John (Figure 1: *ONE* cover, August 1961, "I Was Fired") reflects both aspects: his facial expression is serious with no hint of a smile, suggesting bitterness. He appears down beaten, yet resiliently tough. It is the face of a victim as well as a survivor.

This book is about people like John: ordinary gay men and lesbians in the 1950s and early 1960s caught between dissonant forces operating in American politics, culture, and sexuality. As a Los Angeles resident, John was able to easily visit *ONE*'s office and share his story in person. Thousands of other gay people throughout the country (and the world) shared their stories, opinions, anxieties, and joys with *ONE* magazine through written correspondence. This book is an analysis of letters to *ONE* written from 1953 to 1965. Most of these letters were not published in *ONE* magazine. *ONE* published only a small sample of the letters it received. As the letter volume increased over the years, *ONE* published only short excerpts and omitted personal information. I accidentally uncovered the full collection of letters while working as a volunteer at the ONE National Gay and Lesbian Archives in Los Angeles organizing unprocessed archival material. I read several thousand letters for this study and ultimately based my analysis on 1,083 letters representing 735 individuals. The letters chosen for this study were ones that provided autobiographical narratives or personal information, described gay communities and patterns of social interaction, or offered thoughts and opinions about the meaning of sexuality, gender, and politics. I skipped

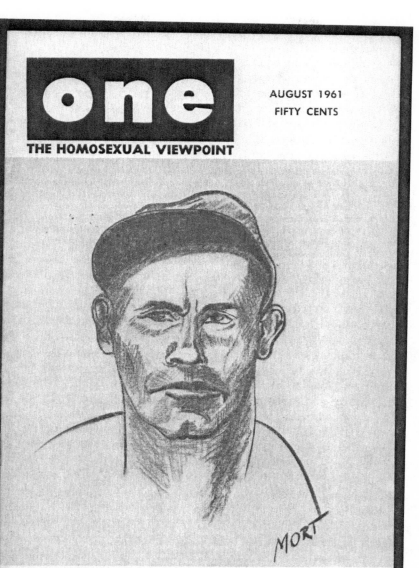

one

AUGUST 1961
FIFTY CENTS

THE HOMOSEXUAL VIEWPOINT

MORT

I Was Fired . . . a case history

Figure 1. *ONE* cover, August 1961, "I Was Fired."

letters that were merely subscription renewals or routine business with the magazine. The letters are not necessarily representative of all gay Americans during these years. Nevertheless, the letters offer an unusually rich glimpse into the collective mentality of postwar lesbians and gay men across the country. This study also draws from a wide variety of primary sources, including newspaper clippings, personal papers, oral histories, publications, and rare books, in order to contextualize the letters within a broader spectrum of postwar homosexual discourses.

These letters describe the myriad ways that lesbian and gay Americans negotiated the social, political, and cultural forces that threatened their livelihoods, reputations, and family relations. The letters contradict the prevalent belief that most gay Americans spent the 1950s and early 1960s cowering fearfully "in the closet."[4] Labeling gay people as "closeted" in these years represents an ahistorical oversimplification and is contradicted by the language gay people used to describe themselves. In addition, the letters refute the thesis that only a handful of exceptional, anomalous individuals were interested in advancing the collective status of gay and lesbian people during these years. Scholars often point to the "brave few" individuals active in the small 1950s gay civil rights movement (known as the "homophile movement") as the only evidence of a gay civil rights consciousness after World War II.[5] In fact, the homophile movement represented the tip of a much larger iceberg of collective discontents and shared desires to improve the status of gay people as a national minority. In every corner of the country, significant numbers of gay people challenged their stigmatized status in creative—albeit limited—ways.

The letters touched on a wide variety of topics, such as employment, police harassment, family life, gay bars, and religion. Employment was the most frequently discussed topic. Many letters described getting fired due to homosexuality; others expressed worry about the possibility of getting fired. This rampant job anxiety highlights the influence of cold war politics on the lives of everyday gay men and lesbians in the 1950s and early 1960s. Similar to individuals suspected of communist loyalties, gay men and lesbians suffered from blacklists that prevented them from working in government, the defense industry, education, and a range of other professions. Like suspected communists, gay people underwent invasive investigations into their personal lives that resulted in public humiliation and institutional ostracism. Gay persons in high-level white-collar professional jobs worried most acutely, but John's case shows that lower status workers such as hospital orderlies were also vulnerable to antigay job purges conducted in the name of cold war national security.

In referencing Joseph McCarthy, John understood that his firing was inextricably linked to the cold war. The cold war resulted from a collapse in diplomatic relations between the United States and the Soviet Union as each nation vied for economic power after World War II. Historians have disagreed over the years whether the Soviet Union or the United States was ultimately responsible for this diplomatic breakdown; the opening of Soviet archives in the 1990s revealed that blame could be shared by both sides. President Harry Truman used inflammatory and exaggerated rhetoric in announcing his 1947 Truman Doctrine to the nation, which was designed to contain communism where it already existed and use U.S. military force to prevent communism's expansion (leading to proxy "hot" wars in Korea, Vietnam, Central America, and elsewhere—evidence of an expansionist American Empire to some scholars). The Soviet Union, meanwhile, had its own expansionist agenda as a hegemonic communist superpower under the authoritarian grip of Joseph Stalin.[6] As diplomacy collapsed between the United States and Soviet Union in the late 1940s, a powerful anticommunist sentiment permeated U.S. politics and society. In October 1947, the House Committee on Un-American Activities (HUAC) investigated whether communist agents had infiltrated Hollywood movie studios to brainwash the nation into communism via the silver screen. The following year, a high-level State Department official, Alger Hiss, was publicly accused of being a Soviet spy. In 1949 the Soviet Union developed its own atom bomb, and shortly thereafter, China became a communist nation. In 1950 Julius and Ethel Rosenberg were executed for suspected treason, and the Korean War commenced. In the wake of such a rapid series of alarming events, nuclear warfare between the United States and the communist world seemed imminent to millions of Americans. Fear and paranoia flourished in such a political climate.

Within this climate of fear emerged the political phenomenon called McCarthyism. The word "McCarthyism" derived from the right-wing Senator from Wisconsin who dominated American media from 1950 to 1954 with his ongoing anticommunist investigations. McCarthyism refers to the exploitation of anxiety over communism in order to expand political power and attack political foes whose actual connections to communism were minimal, insignificant, or nonexistent. At the height of McCarthyism in the early 1950s, thousands of Americans were followed by Federal Bureau of Investigation (FBI) agents, summoned before Kafkaesque investigating committees, and declared subversive by the national press. McCarthyism destroyed lives, stifled free speech, and trampled civil liberties. Even after the 1954 political downfall of Senator Joseph McCarthy, an aggressive, virulent anticommunism lingered in U.S. politics well into the 1960s.[7]

Dozens of books have been written about McCarthyism, but only recently have historians analyzed McCarthyism's devastating impact on gay people.[8] David Johnson's *The Lavender Scare*, for example, describes how investigations of homosexuals under national security auspices allowed McCarthyites to bolster claims that their political opponents were "soft" on communism, thus jeopardizing national security. In the process, thousands of gay people were fired and blacklisted from government jobs. From 1947 to 1953, twice as many individuals were fired from the State Department for suspected homosexuality than for suspected loyalty to communism.[9] Antihomosexual sentiment in Washington, D.C., peaked in 1950 when a U.S. Senate committee conducted a full-scale investigation of "homosexuals and other sex perverts" working in the federal government.[10] Gay governmental firings jumped from five to sixty a month in 1950. In 1951 the FBI launched a Sex Deviate Program to monitor gay people more effectively.[11]

As Johnson explains, Senator Joe McCarthy's personal involvement in these antihomosexual purges was limited.[12] Nonetheless, to gay people he symbolized the political and social forces working against them. "Ever since the Grand Inquisitor from Wisconsin got under way," wrote George from Daly City, California, to *ONE* in 1955, "I have strongly resented the implication that because of what I am, I am also a traitor to my country, if not an avowed communist. . . . Benjamin Franklin, I believe, once made the statement that if we don't hang together we shall surely hang separately. And the climate of this country is such that this could well apply to our own minority group."[13] McCarthy lurked in the postwar gay imagination as a proto-fascist bogeyman, an evil icon of antigay repression and intolerance.

While scholars have documented the devastating impact these purges had on gay and lesbian federal government workers, the *ONE* letters demonstrate the broader ripple effect of these government purges throughout the American workforce. The growth of the military-industrial complex during the 1950s embedded the government's harsh policies against gay people into many large, private companies. The federal government also encouraged state, county, and city governments to follow its lead, thus impacting a broader range of professions. Teachers became especially vulnerable.

The letters demonstrate the ways this pernicious job anxiety interacted with family life. Many letter writers explained that the main reason they feared being fired from their jobs was because family members might find out the circumstances. The same is true regarding homosexual arrests. In both cases, family was a paramount concern, be it parents, relatives, siblings, an opposite-sex spouse, or children.

The dominant image of American family life presented in magazines, television programs, and advertising after World War II was an idealized white middle-class suburban family consisting of a genial patriarchal breadwinning father and a contented domesticated housewife with two or three well-behaved children. No serious problems, such as poverty, racial bigotry, substance abuse, or marital infidelity, affected their lives. According to Elaine Tyler May, such an idealization reflected how family and home represented sanctuaries from cold war anxieties for middle-class Americans.[14] Politicians and psychologists in the 1950s argued that healthy and stable nuclear families were an important home-front defense against the communist threat. In their view, marriage and family were not merely sources of personal fulfillment, but the very glue holding together a patriotic capitalist society. The realities of postwar family life, however, were far more complex than this ideal. Most families faced difficult problems that eluded Ozzie and Harriet Nelson or the Cleavers on television. The dissonance between the sanitized ideals and sobering realities of postwar family life created strain, and throughout American culture, anxiety and frustration seethed behind the smiling façade of the idealized postwar American family.[15]

The letters show that gay people were not immune to the lure of the postwar idealized family despite the multiple ways they challenged mainstream postwar conceptualizations of family life. Even though family life was a common source of anxiety for gay people in the 1950s and early 1960s, gay people, like heterosexuals, sought sanctuary from their anxieties in their family lives. They worked hard to maintain bonds with their heterosexual family members. The letters show that when a person's homosexuality was revealed to family members, the reactions were varied and complex, not monolithically hostile as is commonly assumed about these years. While some unfortunate gay people were kicked out of their families once their homosexuality was revealed, the more common reaction involved compromise, accommodation, and sometimes, outright acceptance. Similarly, gay people went to great lengths to participate in the institution of marriage in different ways. The letters suggest that gay people have long been among the institution's most creative and dedicated practitioners.

The prejudices of the era, whether in the form of job discrimination, police harassment, or family ostracism, sparked anger, outrage, and ultimately, a civil rights impulse among individual gays and lesbians. Scholars have explored post–World War II gay civil rights by analyzing the origins, development, key personalities, and internecine conflicts of the three major 1950s homophile organizations: The Mattachine Society (founded in Los Angeles in 1950); ONE, Inc. (also from Los Angeles, founded in 1952); and the lesbian-oriented Daughters of Bilitis (founded in San Francisco in 1955). The letters to *ONE* allow us to go beyond the small network of devoted homophile activists and analyze the multiple and varied expressions of a civil rights impulse among a broad cross-section of gay men and lesbians across the country who were not part of the inner circles of homophile activism and whose connections to homophile organizations were minimal. The letters serve to bridge social movement history (specifically, scholarship on the homophile movement) with a social history approach focused on everyday people (exemplified in the many urban case studies published in gay and lesbian history since the early 1990s.)[16] Whereas the social movement historiography has tended to relegate the civil rights impulse to a small clique of activists, the urban case study approach has frequently portrayed the 1950s as a dark age. The letters suggest that gay people across the country, not just in homophile activist circles, were thinking about their sexuality in a political manner, and that despite the serious challenges gay people faced, these years were not exactly a dark age.

The civil rights impulse is demonstrated in the numerous letters that explicitly express the right to live one's life as a homosexual as well as a desire to change social attitudes about homosexuality. These letters were a striking contrast to the more stereotypical letters from people who were miserable, isolated, self-pitying, conflicted, or ashamed about their sexuality. Significantly more correspondents used their letters to ONE as opportunities to unambiguously assert their right to live a gay or lesbian life rather than wallow in the decade's McCarthyite miseries.

ONE magazine encouraged such a pro-gay outlook, so the correspondents are probably biased to some extent. A random national sample of gay people in 1958 (which of course was never conducted), as opposed to a sample of people who voluntarily wrote letters to ONE or voluntarily responded to homophile questionnaires, might reveal a less positive mindset. ONE undoubtedly politicized some of its readers for whom a pro-gay attitude might have been unimaginable before encountering the magazine. At the same time, the magazine's influence over its readers' attitudes should not be overstated. Many letters expressing a civil rights impulse imply that ONE magazine did not so much introduce this impulse to them as it helped articulate, clarify, and reinforce this impulse. Many correspondents stated that they had already come to comfortable terms with their homosexuality before encountering the magazine. ONE's pro-gay approach thus reflected an existing mentality circulating throughout the country in these years. Not everyone shared this mentality, but it was much larger than just the homophile organizations. The correspondents' affirmative ethic influenced the magazine's character just as the magazine's calls for dignity, equality, and justice influenced its readers. The letters' prideful tone reflected the dynamic interplay of the magazine's political goals and its readers' personal experiences.

The 1950s black civil rights movement also influenced the civil rights impulse of many gay and lesbian Americans, but this influence should not be overstated either. Surprisingly few letters mentioned the black civil rights movement. Early gay activists drew their models and inspiration from a broad range of social movements throughout American history, such as women's rights, left-wing radicalism, and bohemian traditions, not to mention the European gay rights movement described in chapter 3.[17] There were, however, important shared experiences between black Americans and gay Americans as distinct (yet overlapping) social groups that triggered simultaneous calls to activism. Most important was World War II, which inspired both groups to question their second-class status because such status seemed to negate the whole purpose in fighting the war. Despite their patriotic sacrifices, black veterans were still being called "boy" after the war, and gay men and women who had risked their lives found themselves demonized as criminally insane national security threats. Thus black Americans dramatically accelerated a long-running struggle for dignity and equality, and gay Americans for the first time sustained their own civil rights movement.[18] The letters suggest that these World War II experiences were more influential in shaping a gay rights consciousness than the concurrent black civil rights struggle, even though homophile activists paid close attention to the black movement and tried to learn from it.

ONE magazine was part of a broader cultural rethinking of American sexuality in the years following World War II. Within a year of ONE's debut in January 1953, for example, two other notable magazines made their debuts: Robert Harrison's Confidential magazine, which reveled in the tawdry sexual hypocrisies of American celebrities, and Hugh Hefner's Playboy, which promoted a sexually liberated "playboy lifestyle" for heterosexual men.[19] All three publications—ONE, Confidential, and Playboy—were deeply influenced by Alfred Kinsey's famous two reports on human sexuality from 1948 (male) and 1953 (female), both of which were national bestsellers widely discussed among American media and society. Kinsey's research demonstrated the wide gulf between sexual ideals and practices in American society. Kinsey's data showed, for example, that homosexuality was far more prevalent than commonly believed—more than one-third of surveyed men admitted to adult homosexual behavior.[20] Kinsey's groundbreaking research reverberated throughout American popular culture during the 1950s, and many of the decade's most popular playwrights (especially Tennessee Williams) and novelists (particularly Grace Metalious, whose Peyton Place was the best-selling novel of the 1950s) further explored themes of sexual hypocrisy in American society.[21]

Thus, while McCarthyism sought to reinforce conventional sexual morality by cracking down on homosexuals, a separate cultural current was nudging gay people in a more liberating direction. The dissonance between these conflicting strains in American life was at the heart of gay people's anxieties. It is a cliché to describe the 1950s as an "age of anxiety," yet "anxiety" offers a useful concept for understanding the general mood of gay men and lesbians in these years.[22] At a practical level, gay people experienced anxiety because so many faced instant ruin if their sexuality was discovered. An existential void loomed over their lives. Yet, as Søren Kierkegaard argued in his groundbreaking philosophical work on anxiety, anxiety was not merely a negative feeling or emotion, but also a teacher that could push individuals toward greater manifestations of freewill. Anxiety provided motivation for adaptation, overcoming crises, and ultimately reaching a more authentic sense of what it meant to be a human being.[23] The *ONE* letters capture the collective anxieties of postwar homosexuals as well as gay people's efforts to channel these anxieties into the constructive process of creating a national subculture.

To manage their day-to-day anxieties, most *ONE* correspondents "passed as heterosexual." Through omission, implication, or outright dishonesty, they presented themselves as heterosexual to mainstream society. Many gay writers, activists, and historians in later decades have interpreted this behavior as evidence that most gay people were "in the closet" in the 1950s, but the letters conclusively show that postwar gay men and lesbians did not use the "closet" metaphor to describe themselves. The contemporary concept of the closet as a metaphor for hiding one's homosexual identity from others or oneself did not emerge until the late 1960s and early 1970s, despite the claims of some scholars.[24] In all the letters examined for this study, the word "closet" appeared only once: "Perhaps if everyone would take sex out of the dark closet into which the word [*sic*] has flung it, we would all be better human beings," wrote Dwayne from Livermore, California, in 1960.[25] Dwayne referred to sex in general, not homosexuality in particular, suggesting that his usage of "closet" lacked the specific meaning and implications that the term later assumed. In contrast to the virtual absence of the word "closet," however, *ONE* correspondents used the phrase "coming out" dozens of times. Gay people in the 1950s did not "come out of the closet." Instead, they "came out to gay life."[26]

Instead of relying on the closet metaphor, the letters show that postwar gays and lesbians thought of themselves as wearing masks. Metaphorically the mask represented an adaptive negotiation with a hostile society. The mask was both liberating and tragic: liberating because it allowed many gay people to avoid job discrimination and police harassment, tragic because it was necessary at all. The difference between a mask and a closet is not merely semantic. To declare most homosexuals "closeted" in these years conforms to stereotypes that they were lonely, scared, invisible, helpless victims. The closet metaphor implies that gay people consciously denied their authentic selves, and it eliminates the historical agency of an entire generation of gay men and lesbians to define their own sexual identities. In contrast, the mask metaphor restores agency because gay people controlled when to put on or remove their masks depending on the context and situation. Situational passing as heterosexual—that is, wearing the mask—was not a denial of their authentic selves, but instead provided gay people with the necessary security that *allowed* them to consciously identify as homosexual and participate in a subaltern, camouflaged gay public sphere.[27] Passing, ironically, brought their homosexual identities into sharper focus. The mask metaphor emphasizes adaptation and resilience rather than capitulation to the whims of a hostile society.

Figure 2, Boston Area Mattachine Newsletter cover, May 1959, and Figure 3, *The Ladder* cover, October 1957, illustrate the use of the mask metaphor in homophile publications. In Figure 2, masks with vaguely creepy smiles hang on a hat rack outside a door with the Mattachine logo. (The word "Mattachine" in fact derived from the Arabic word for mask.[28]) Figure 3 depicts a woman holding a mask with a tear on it, hinting at the tragic dimension of the mask. Once the mask is removed, the woman's face gazes forward in a more upbeat manner. Lesbians and gay men wore heterosexual masks in the offices where they worked, on streets where they walked, and often in their homes with family members. They removed these masks in contexts they felt were safe to do so.

Most of *ONE's* correspondents were men. Women only constituted about 10 percent of the letter writers. This deeply frustrated *ONE's* creators because they wanted the magazine to represent men and women equally. ONE, Inc., like the Mattachine Society, was founded entirely by men, and consequentially *ONE* magazine focused on topics that impacted gay men disproportionately, such as police entrapment. Women played important roles in *ONE's* history, but *ONE's* female activists often felt marginalized by the men. Still, most installments of *ONE* featured lesbian poetry, fiction, and the monthly "Feminine Viewpoint" column. Though their letters were significantly fewer, the ones they wrote suggest that women suffered from many of the same anxieties regarding employment and family life as gay men. At the same time, though, lesbians had to grapple with postwar sexism and patriarchy, complicating their lives in unique ways compared to gay men.

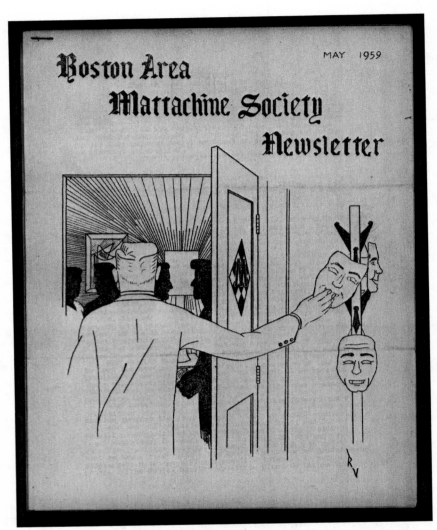

Figure 2. Boston Area Mattachine Newsletter cover, May 1959.

Figure 3. *The Ladder* cover, October 1957.

Occupationally, white-collar workers were twice as likely to correspond with *ONE* compared to blue-collar workers. Survey data suggests that nearly one-fifth of *ONE's* correspondents worked in education, such as teachers, librarians, or college students.[29] The magazine's educated, middle-class bias reflected a broader homophile movement strategy of portraying gay people as dignified, respectable, and successful citizens deserving of their equal rights. In this vein, *ONE* was a "serious" magazine. A self-identified member of the "laboring class" complained about the magazine's highbrow pretensions in 1956, "What the hell do I care about Plato, Socrates, Walt Whitman, etc. . . . . Remember that some of us are just plain ordinary guys and plainer fare is more to our taste. Highly literary efforts with too many dictionary words may be just what some of the big city, effeminate fags want, but simpler, more practical, down to earth articles fill the need of the country and small-town boys and those of us of the laboring class with limited educations who work like, who look like, hairy chested He Men."[30] The magazine's educated middle-class orientation also reflected the fact that substantially more Americans identified as middle class after World War II due to the strong economy and spikes in college attendance and home ownership caused by the G.I. Bill. The character of homosexual identity thus became more middle class after the war as well.[31] *ONE's* editors deliberately catered to this growing gay middle-class demographic in order to overcome what they perceived as negative stereotypes about all gay men being working-class effeminate "fairies" and "pansies" that had been fashionable in New York City and other large American cities during the 1920s.

Despite the male, middle-class biases, there is striking geographic diversity in the letters. The letters used in this study came from every state except Alaska and South Dakota. For most of the country, the percentage of letters *ONE* received from individual states roughly equaled those states' percentage of the total national population. For example, approximately 5.4 percent of *ONE's* letters came from Illinois, and according to the 1960 census, 5.6 percent of the total U.S. population lived in Illinois—a close equivalent. There were exceptions to this trend. Letters from Western states, California especially, were overrepresented compared to national population data. Southern states were underrepresented except for Texas and Florida. Overall though, the letters reflect proportionate state population data.

The letters' geographic diffusion shows how gay people were increasingly cohering into a national minority during these years. Before World War II, efforts to suppress gay communities occurred at local levels. Gay communities were more isolated from one another. After the war, gay people created multiple ways to communicate with one another that transcended regional or local subcultures. The homophile movement and its publications, especially *ONE*, were an important dimension of this growth of postwar national communication networks.[32] Similarly, for the first time, efforts to suppress gay people were being coordinated nationally by a federal government convinced that gay people represented a threat to *national* security.[33]

Approximately one-third (32 percent) of the letters came from cities of 500,000 people or more, twice the percentage (16 percent) of the general population living in cities of that size according to the 1960 census. The fact that *ONE* received so many letters from large cities should not be surprising considering that large cities had been focal points of U.S. gay life since the late nineteenth century. This data also reminds us, however, that even though gay people disproportionately resided in large cities, most gay people in terms of raw numbers did *not* live in large cities. More than one-half of the letters (54 percent) came from towns with fewer than 100,000 people.

Aside from this demographic data, there are limitations about the letters to consider. Compared to oral histories, which delve deeply and strategically into an individual's life history, the letters provide only a fragmentary glimpse into an individual's thoughts at the particular moment he or she wrote the letter. Everyone has an agenda when creating written documents, and some correspondents undoubtedly shaded the truth or omitted significant facts in order to elicit a sympathetic response. Ultimately, the letters represent only those who wrote them. But the sheer abundance of letters and their descriptive richness counterbalance many of these limitations. By analyzing the documented thoughts of more than 700 gay men and lesbians—thoughts directly from the 1950s and early 1960s, unfiltered through decades of memory and subsequent events—patterns can be discerned and cautious generalizations offered about the larger population of gay and lesbian Americans during the cold war's peak years.[34] These voices shed critical light on the social history of McCarthyism and other aspects of postwar American life.

A word on terminology: throughout this book, I interchangeably use the phrases "gay people," "gay men and lesbians," and "homosexuals" to refer to persons primarily attracted to their own sex. I use these terms rather than more fashionable academic terms, such as "same-sex sexuality" or "queer," in order to replicate the correspondents' own vocabulary in describing themselves. Historians must take care not to impose the present onto the past. People in the past had their own unique ways of viewing the world, and the historian's primary job is to understand and interpret those worldviews. My own experiences as a historian, teacher, and gay man figure into how I interpret the letters, but as much as possible I have let the letters dictate the structure of book, the issues raised in each chapter, and the vocabulary employed. I have tried to listen carefully to these letters without letting subsequent events or concepts distort the analysis. Gay people in 1955 would not have known about the 1969 Stonewall riots, 1970s-era gay liberation, or the AIDS epidemic, and therefore would not have thought about their lives in relation to these events. They had other things on their minds, such as the Kinsey Reports, McCarthyism, and the memories of World War II. In order to understand the postwar gay and lesbian zeitgeist, we must approach the *ONE* correspondents on their own terms, not ours.

1

ONE Magazine and Its Readers

The publication of *ONE* magazine's first issue in January 1953 was a watershed moment in the history of American sexuality. Though not the first American publication to cater to homosexual readers (male physique magazines had been coyly cultivating gay male readers for years), *ONE* was the first American publication openly and brazenly to declare itself a "homosexual magazine." Many of its early readers doubted the magazine would last long. A reader, Ned, explained to *ONE* in a 1961 letter, "When the fifties were young I bought my first copies of *ONE* at a bookstore a few blocks from my studio on Telegraph Hill in San Francisco. As I remember, those first copies were not very professional looking; and perhaps the contents were not impressive. But the mere fact that a bit of a magazine dared present *the* subject in writing by those who *were* [homosexual] was impressive. If anyone had predicted, however, that the mag. would live into the sixties, I'd have expressed doubts. One did look doubtful in those days."[1] *ONE*'s survival also seemed unlikely given the widespread antigay sentiment circulating throughout American society in the 1950s. Was *ONE* even legal? Could it be considered obscene for merely discussing homosexuality in affirmative tones? No one was sure in 1953. Yet *ONE* survived until 1967, by which time the country's political, social, and cultural mood had shifted so dramatically that *ONE* seemed quaint and old-fashioned compared to the dozens of other gay publications populating newsstands and bookstores.

ONE emerged from the Los Angeles–based "homophile movement," the term gay and lesbian activists used to describe their movement (and frequently themselves, as "homophiles,") in the 1950s and early 1960s. *ONE* tapped into the anger, outrage, and frustration gay people across the

17

country felt. Thousands of gay people regularly read the magazine. They appreciated the opportunity to be part of an unprecedented national dialogue about the status of gay people. A man from Williamsburg, Virginia, for example, wrote to *ONE* in 1956, "*ONE* is more than a magazine to me. It's a vehicle through which communion is made with thousands of brothers whose outlook, ideals, problems, etc. are my own. It is one of several important links with the world of our minority without which I would feel very parochial, not to say isolated."[2] Many readers who wrote letters to the magazine echoed this sentiment. For example:

> "I realize that 'One' is probably better informed about the bars and other conditions than any other group in the country—aside from the grapevine yours is almost the only news."[3]

> "I know of no other person near or far that I could speak frankly to or that I feel that I could promote a friendship with and have homosexuality as a common understanding."[4]

> "Thank you for your voice in the darkness."[5]

> "You have given me courage and strength over the years far more than you can ever know."[6]

This book focuses on this nationwide community of *ONE* magazine readers. Before analyzing their letters, however, examining the magazine that generated their letters is necessary. This chapter describes the magazine's character and contents, describes key individuals behind the magazine, and contextualizes *ONE* within the broader homophile movement of the 1950s and 1960s. Despite its somewhat amateurish quality and rancorous behind-the-scenes disputes, it was a remarkable magazine. Publishing an openly gay magazine in 1953 was no simple task, especially a magazine that so pointedly challenged society's hostile treatment of gay people. In an acutely repressive moment, when gay people were being entrapped by police, rooted out of jobs, and demonized as political subversives, *ONE* challenged its readers to believe that homosexuals had a fundamental right to exist in American society. They had the same rights to life, liberty, and the pursuit of happiness as anyone else—not to mention rights to associate with one another, to be gainfully employed, to be treated fairly in the justice system, and to engage in private sexual behavior between consenting adults. Despite the hostile society surrounding *ONE* in 1953, the magazine's survival testifies to the growing civil rights impulse of ordinary gays and lesbians throughout the country throughout the 1950s and 1960s.

Creating a Homosexual Magazine

The American homophile movement of the 1950s consisted of three primary organizations, each founded and based in California. The first group, formed in 1950, was the Mattachine Society. According to Mattachine founder Harry Hay, McCarthyism spurred the group's formation. Hay feared that McCarthy and his followers might precipitate an all-out, fascist-style purge against homosexuals:

> The anti-Communist witch-hunts were very much in operation [in 1950]; the House Un-American Activities Committee had investigated Communist "subversion" in Hollywood. The purge of homosexuals from the State Department took place. The country, it seemed to me, was beginning to move toward fascism and McCarthyism; the Jews wouldn't be used as a scapegoat this time—the painful example of Germany was still too clear to us. The Black organizations were already pretty successfully looking out for their interests. It was obvious McCarthy was setting up the pattern for a new scapegoat, and it was going to be us—Gays. We had to organize, we had to move, we had to get started.[7]

At first, the Mattachine Society was a secretive organization consisting of small discussion group "cells" scattered throughout Southern California. After gaining publicity because of its efforts fighting the entrapment arrest of one of its members, the Mattachine Society assumed national dimensions and new chapters emerged in New York, San Francisco, Denver, Chicago, and a handful of other major cities throughout the 1950s. Mattachine leaders hoped to build a coordinated, national coalition of homophile activist groups, but the Mattachine Society never performed as effectively at the national level as it did within local contexts. The national Mattachine movement thus never quite cohered, and in 1961 leader Hal Call severed ties with all regional chapters, effectively ending any ambitions of becoming an effective, national gay rights organization.[8]

In 1955 a lesbian homophile organization called the Daughters of Bilitis began conducting meetings in San Francisco. A year later, the Daughters started publishing a monthly magazine called *The Ladder*. Although considerably smaller than the Mattachine Society and its branches, the Daughters of Bilitis was an important source of lesbian political mobilization in the late 1950s. In the 1960s, *The Ladder* embraced viewpoints that would be labeled "lesbian-feminist" during the 1970s. The Daughters of Bilitis was the only major homophile organization devoted to lesbians. The Mattachine Society and ONE, Inc., welcomed lesbians, but men dominated both organizations.[9]

ONE, Inc. (the official corporate name of the organization that published *ONE* magazine), emerged in late 1952. The movement's "middle child," it has received the least scholarly attention. Yet because of the organization's national orientation, its stability, and its visibility (through the magazine), ONE, Inc., was arguably the most prominent homophile organization during the mid- to late 1950s and early 1960s.[10]

ONE, Inc., was founded in October 1952 by a small group of Mattachine activists in Los Angeles who were frustrated with the Mattachine Society's obsessive secrecy and explosive internal disputes. They quit Mattachine because they believed that a gay magazine could more effectively unite a national gay and lesbian minority than the Mattachine's secretive "cell" structure. *ONE*'s first editor, Martin Block, explained in an oral history, "We weren't going to go out and say you should be gay, but we said, 'You can be proud of being gay.' You could be proud of being yourself. You could look in the mirror and say, 'I'm me, and isn't that nice?' That in itself was radical."[11] At first *ONE* was only available by subscription, but by May 1953 newsstands in Los Angeles and New York were selling it openly. By the late 1950s newsstands in dozens of cities sold it.[12]

ONE's founders had no experience publishing a magazine, and they had modest goals for success. *ONE*'s circulation averaged 3,000 to 5,000 issues per month during the 1950s and early 1960s, but its impact on postwar gay consciousness was greater than these circulation figures suggest. Between 1953 and 1965, ONE, Inc., distributed more than 500,000 copies of the magazine, copies that were often shared among gay social networks and between friends. In 1955 the Mattachine Society began publishing its bimonthly *Mattachine Review*, modeled after *ONE*, but with less than half the readers. *The Ladder*'s circulation peaked at 1,000 per month.[13] For most of the 1950s, *ONE* was the most visible, widely read gay and lesbian publication in the United States. It provided the blueprint for *Mattachine Review*, *The Ladder*, and many other subsequent gay publications.

A civil rights impulse infused the essays, reviews, fiction, poetry, letters, and illustrations found in *ONE*'s densely filled pages each month. Condemnations of McCarthyism were common in the early years, evidenced in article titles such as, "To Be Accused Is to Be Guilty," "Are You Now or Have You Ever Been a Homosexual?" "You Are a Public Enemy," "And a Red Too," "Are Homosexuals Security Risks?" "Miami's New Type of Witch Hunt," and "Inquisition."[14] These explicit rebukes of antigay discrimination mingled with essays describing homosexuality in other parts of the world, scientific research on sexuality, famous gay people throughout history (such as Plato, Michelangelo, and Tchaikovsky), as well as reviews of books, plays, and movies with gay themes. Many of *ONE*'s contributors argued that homosexuals comprised a distinct minority with a rich history and culture. *ONE*'s editors believed that knowledge of this history and culture was an essential building block for creating a gay civil rights movement because it freed gay people from internalizing the negative characterizations of homosexuality routinely found in mainstream psychology, organized religion, popular culture, and the criminal justice system. Instilling gay pride was a key aspect of the magazine's civil rights impulse. Thus, an essay chronicling the male lovers of Alexander the Great was just as politically relevant as an article decrying antigay police raids or political persecution.

As a nonprofit organization, ONE, Inc., relied heavily on volunteers. While dozens of volunteers worked to create each issue, a small group of core activists performed the bulk of work and established the editorial tone of the magazine over the years. One of the most important individuals was Dorr Legg, who served as *ONE*'s business manager (under the name William Lambert) and a frequent editorialist. Born in 1904, Legg worked primarily as a landscape design architect until 1948 when he was arrested in an antigay police sweep in Detroit with an African-American boyfriend. In his words, "my life was wrecked."[15] Legg relocated to Los Angeles and joined the Mattachine Society in the early 1950s, but disliked the organization's secrecy. When a small group of activists discussed starting a magazine independently of Mattachine, Legg jumped aboard and devoted the rest of his life to ONE, Inc. Legg was the first gay activist in the United States to receive a regular salary for his efforts. During the magazine's heyday he spent most of his waking hours at the *ONE* office tending to *ONE*'s business affairs, writing stories and editorials, and replying to correspondence from readers. When curious subscribers visited *ONE*'s office, Legg usually greeted them. After *ONE* magazine folded in 1967 and ONE, Inc., reinvented itself as an educational institution, Legg remained the organization's undisputed leader until his death in 1994.[16]

Another important figure in ONE, Inc., was Jim Kepner, a major gay activist who reportedly wrote more than 2,000 articles on gay history and culture in dozens of publications until he died in 1997.[17] Born in 1923, Kepner was an abandoned baby raised by fundamentalist Christian parents in Galveston, Texas. After a stint in the military, he wandered around the country working at odd jobs. In 1942 he witnessed a brutal police raid on a gay bar in San Francisco, an incident that spurred him to begin collecting documents on homosexuality. Largely self-educated, with no formal academic degrees, Kepner was the first serious historian and archivist of gay culture in the United States. He wrote about gay history and culture long before the subject was academically acceptable, and his immense volume of published work in the gay press from the 1950s to the 1990s shaped all subsequent writing on American gay history. He also operated the first gay historical archives open to the public out of his apartment in the 1970s. More than anyone else involved with *ONE*, Kepner recognized the importance of homosexuals learning about their shared history as a vehicle for personal understanding and social liberation.[18]

Legg and Kepner largely shared a similar vision of gay rights and culture, but they had strikingly different personalities. Intellectually, Legg was thorough and methodical, while Kepner possessed a capricious and creative "grasshopper mind" that jumped quickly from idea to idea. Legg was known to be prickly, stubborn, and authoritarian—historian Martin Duberman noted he was "long rumored to have ice water in his veins."[19] Kepner, in contrast, is fondly remembered as warm, patient, and self-sacrificing. Legg came from a privileged background and voted Republican, whereas Kepner was working-class, left-wing, and active in labor unions and (briefly) the Communist Party. Like Mattachine founder Harry Hay, Kepner had been expelled from the Communist Party after party members discovered his homosexuality. Whereas Legg lived comfortably and was financially supported by his long-term partner John Nojima, Kepner struggled to balance his passion for writing about gay culture and history with trying to earn a living, working graveyard shifts in a Los Angeles milk carton factory and writing for *ONE* during the day.[20]

The third member of *ONE*'s inner circle was Don Slater. Slater edited the magazine for most of the 1960s and helped coordinate *ONE*'s distribution. Slater was born in 1923 in Pasadena, California, the son of a YMCA athletic director. He trained for eight months in Colorado as a ski patroller for the U.S. Army during World War II before receiving an honorable discharge due to illness. He then earned a B.A. in literature at the University of Southern California, working in the library and bookstores. He had a confrontational personality and was defiantly libertarian in his worldview. While attending USC, for example, he refused to pay dozens of parking tickets he accumulated on the grounds that "the state had no business telling him where he could park."[21] In 1964 *Life* magazine photographed Slater for a feature story called "Homosexuality in America." In his crisp white dress shirt and fashionable skinny tie, Slater personified the businesslike respectability that the homophile movement sought to convey. The photo (alongside one of Mattachine leader Hal Call) provided millions of Americans with their first glimpse of a "gay activist."[22] During the early 1960s, a rift emerged between Legg and Slater that exploded into a major conflict in 1965, splitting the organization in two.

In addition to Legg, Kepner, and Slater, a long-term lesbian couple, Joan Corbin and Irma "Corky" Wolf, better known by their pseudonyms Eve Elloree and Ann Carll Reid, shaped the character of *ONE* magazine in important ways. Elloree was the magazine's primary illustrator. Her striking line drawings gave the magazine visual appeal. Her cover art was the first visual contact that most people had with the magazine. Many of these covers, such as Figure 4, *ONE* Cover, December 1956, were abstract, consisting of a pattern of lines, squares, and other shapes. In other covers, such as in Figure 5, *ONE* cover, July 1955, her illustrations complemented an article or story in the magazine.[23] Inside the magazine, Elloree's drawings broke up the visual monotony of pages covered in text. Readers frequently praised her clean, minimalist artwork.

Figure 6, Eve Elloree illustration, *ONE* magazine, December 1953, is a typical Elloree illustration, depicting two men from behind carrying bags of groceries. The drawing accompanied a fictional story about a disturbed police officer who spied on a pair of homosexuals only to find they led mundane domestic lives. This story and the illustration have many typical homophile movement characteristics. The men are clean-cut and dressed conservatively. We do not see their faces, reflecting the masked anonymity pervading these years. The groceries symbolize domesticity and suggest that the men's relationship was serious, not merely a "trick" or one-night stand. The drawing is simple yet endearing. Figure 7, Eve Elloree illustration, *ONE* magazine, March 1955, offers a contrast by depicting the darker side of postwar gay life in the form of a gay arrest victim. The three bare trees and bench suggest the scene is a park. A young man sits on the bench looking toward a path, down which walk a police officer handcuffed to a young man. The young man on the bench has probably been cruising for sex; now he has perked up, attentively watching the cop and arrestee as they walk toward him.[24]

Corbin/Elloree's partner, Irma Wolf/Ann Carll Reid, was *ONE*'s chief editor from 1954 to 1957, and a frequent contributor to the recurring column "The Feminine Viewpoint." Wolf offered the following glimpse her life with Corbin in a letter to a *ONE* contributor:

> I live on one of the rare QUIET streets in L.A., in a little house with a little yard. Have two cats, Willow (part Siamese) and Inca (part Burmese). I share the house with One's art director [Joan Corbin] who keeps it full of books, music, and art—and the magazine which keeps it full of papers, letters, manuscripts, carbon paper and people! Still room for me because I'm quite

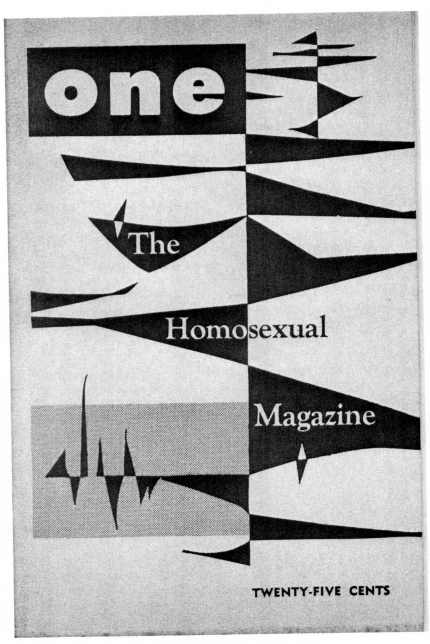

Figure 4. *ONE* cover, December 1956.

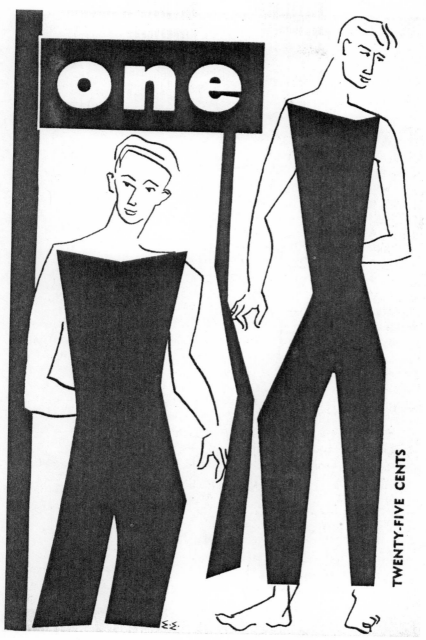

Figure 5. *ONE* cover, July 1955.

Figure 6. Eve Elloree illustration, *ONE* magazine, December 1953.

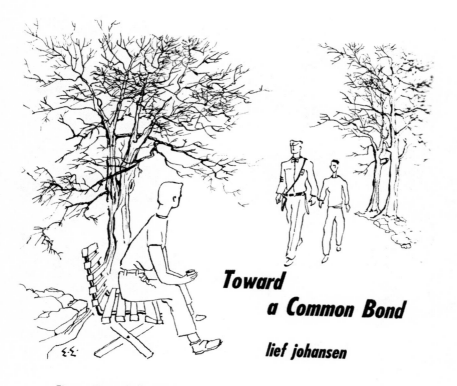

Toward a Common Bond

lief johansen

Figure 7. Eve Elloree illustration, *ONE* magazine, March 1955.

> small, but still spry at the age of 33. When I'm not typing,
> bar-b-quing or talking I'm reading—Rabelais, Millay, Charlotte
> Armstrong, Mathew Head, Francoise Mallet, Colette. . . .[25]

When Reid quit *ONE* in 1957, she expressed the common frustration that *ONE* was unable to attract more lesbian readers and contributors. After Reid's departure, Elloree continued to draw for *ONE*, although less frequently during the 1960s than during the 1950s.[26]

Each of these individuals, and dozens of other *ONE* volunteers, worked in cramped office space in the sweatshop district in downtown Los Angeles. The office was in a large building that stretched between two city streets. The bottom floor was occupied by a Goodwill store. The building was so dilapidated that horror movies had been filmed there. *ONE*'s first office was a mere ten-by-twelve-foot room, and *ONE* added adjacent rooms as they became available. By 1959, the office had grown to four rooms in addition to a six-by-ten-foot cubicle that served as a reception area and, later, a copy room. A narrow five-by-ten-foot room was later added for the library and storage space. A large fourteen-by-twenty-two-foot room served as meeting space, a classroom, and function room. The growth of ONE, Inc.'s office space reflects its steady growth as an organization, reflecting the homophile movement's incremental growth during these years.[27]

In addition to the volunteers working in *ONE*'s Los Angeles office, *ONE* had contributors across the country who sent in their own original essays and short stories. A notable contributor to *ONE* was gay novelist James Barr Fugaté. The success of Fugaté's 1950 novel *Quatrefoil* (written under the name James Barr) made him the best-known figure on *ONE*'s staff. *Quatrefoil* sold 50,000 copies and is considered a classic postwar gay novel.[28] In the mid-1950s, Fugaté corresponded extensively with *ONE*'s staff from his home in Holyrood, Kansas, and he contributed several short essays to the magazine. He also let ONE, Inc., publish his dark and depressing play *Game of Fools*, which centered on four college students who were arrested for homosexuality and faced a variety of reactions from their families.

Fugaté's most important contribution to *ONE* was allowing his photograph to be published in *ONE*'s April 1954 issue (Figure 8, James Barr photograph, *ONE* magazine, April 1954).[29] This marked the first time an openly gay man volunteered his photograph to appear in a nationally distributed publication—no photos of Legg, Kepner, or Slater ever appeared in *ONE* magazine during the 1950s. "We are fully cognizant of the social significance involved here," wrote a member of *ONE*'s staff to Fugaté after receiving the photo. "We admire your courage."[30] Such gay visibility in 1954 was unprecedented and remarkable considering Fugaté's personal anxiety about McCarthyism. He warned Dorr Legg in December 1954, "Do you honestly believe the FBI hasn't secured every name and address by the simple means of photographing one of your monthly mailings when you brought it into the Post Office? Or are you naif enough to suppose that there isn't a fat file on each of you (and me) and your activities in spite of your pseudonyms? Remember, we *do* live in a Police State. McCarthy's revelations did much to open our eyes about the methods and disregard for rules of the secret police."[31] Dorr Legg hoped that the publication of Fugaté's photo would allow the magazine "to have a regular department of photos with a little story, to break down this dreadful phobia we have all partaken of too deeply."[32] Volunteers did not rush to *ONE*'s office to be photographed, however, and over the years the magazine published only a handful of photographs of gay-identified individuals. The first photo of Fugaté to appear showed only his face and shoulders—he is well-dressed in his bow tie. His smile has a certain portrait-studio strain about it as he looks directly at the camera. The second version (Figure 9, James Barr photograph, *ONE* magazine, October 1954) of the photo is cropped wider, revealing a medium-large black dog sitting next to him. The dog appears friendly, yet the chain around his neck and Fugaté's glove give the photo a slightly menacing quality. The dog seems to guard Fugaté and protect him from the penalties of his unprecedented visibility.

Of note, all of these key *ONE* figures were white. Although many people of color played important roles in the magazine, they avoided leadership roles and served in a more low-key manner. An African-American member of *ONE*'s founding group, for example, suggested the name *ONE*, taken from a Thomas Carlyle poem that proclaimed "a mystic bond of brotherhood makes all men one." One of the original signers of incorporation and a frequent art contributor was a Latino dancer named Antonio Reyes (partner of Don Slater) who worked at Los Angeles's Mexican-themed Olvera Street during the 1940s and 1950s.[33] The essay "The Friday Night Quilting Party" noted the diversity of *ONE*'s rank-and-file volunteers: "The most startling thing about these men is their diversity," wrote the author, "One is short and forty, and looks like a Texas dirt farmer. One is early twenty [*sic*] and good looking, and might be off the campus of UCLA. One is white, one is Oriental, one is Mexican, and one is Negro. There are two young men who are obviously married, for they work together with that comfortable air of mutual bitchiness that is peculiar to men who know each other well."[34]

Unfortunately, this same sense of diversity is not reflected in the pages of *ONE* magazine. *ONE* writers occasionally compared

Figure 8. James Barr photograph, *ONE* magazine, April 1954.

Figure 9. James Barr photograph, *ONE* magazine, October 1954.

discrimination against homosexuals to racial, ethnic, and religious discrimination, but the magazine largely ignored the experiences of nonwhite gay men and lesbians. Occasionally there was an exception, such as a lengthy letter written by "Miss J" in 1957. She wrote that her experiences as an African-American lesbian did not seem too different than other letter writers:

> I faithfully read the issues quite like that hungry fox (or rather, vixen; the world cares about that distinction business so much). And the letters which you print make me feel that my feelings about all of you and the work you are doing is not terribly different from what others have said in their letters, one way or another. Your articles and stories cause me anger, confusion, inspiration, encouragement, and every other emotion I can think of. A thousand different points of criticism, praise, argument and pure discussion occur to me in the course of a single issue, but as I read the letter columns, sooner or later someone else writes about it, or you have an editorial about it, and I am spoken for.[35]

Only a few dozen letter writers identified themselves as African American, and even fewer self-identified Latinos or Latinas and Asian Americans wrote to *ONE*. Many nonwhite letter writers, however, would have left the issue unstated, so whiteness should not be presumed in every letter that does not mention a race or ethnic identity.

A Typical Issue of *ONE*

The cover of *ONE*'s April 1955 issue posed the provocative question "Are Homosexuals Neurotic? Albert Ellis Ph.D." Ellis was a major figure in developing cognitive behavioral therapies and the author of more than fifty books by the time of his death in 2007. His Ph.D. status is displayed prominently on *ONE*'s cover in order to bolster the magazine's appearance of professionalism and respectability.[36] Eve Elloree's cover art depicted neurosis in its nightmarish collection of hands and faces surrounded by jagged lines, white triangles, and a gold background resembling broken shards of glass (Figure 10: *ONE* cover, April 1954). The same white and yellow motif carries into the article along with two mask illustrations (Figure 11: First page of "Are Homosexuals Necessarily Neurotic?" by Albert Ellis). The message seems to be that wearing the mask of heterosexual conformity, despite its practical benefits, might drive a person crazy.

Figure 10. *ONE* cover, April 1955.

ARE HOMOSEXUALS

NECESSARILY

NEUROTIC?

n the January 1955 issue of ONE, The Homosexual Magazine, there are two articles whose writers contend that homosexuality is not necessarily neurotic, and who imply that homosexuals can be just as "normal" as, and in some ways perhaps more "normal" than, non- homosexuals. Thus, in "Literature and Homosexuality," David L. Freeman writes: "But there is a way out of the morass of degenerate mediocrity. Ideals of the original Mattachine, concepts eloquently set forth by Cory, and principles adopted by ONE magazine (all indirectly reinforced by Kinsey's researches) embrace an altogether new approach: Homosexuals are not necessarily neurotic and, when they are, their neuroses generally spring from their homosexuality in a heterosexual world. This approach provides an entirely new, optimistic rallying point for America's five to fifteen million homosexuals and should be a clarion call to all of them aspiring to do creative writing in the interest of their minority."

one

8

Figure 11. First page of "Are Homosexuals Necessarily Neurotic?" by Albert Ellis.

Opening the magazine, the reader first encounters a list of places where *ONE* could be purchased. This issue listed newsstands and bookstores in New York City; Buffalo; Paterson, N.J.; Atlanta; New Orleans; Cleveland; Minneapolis; Salt Lake City; Los Angeles; Berkeley; and San Francisco; as well as in Mexico City, Amsterdam, Copenhagen, and Hamburg. Opposite these listings is a donation solicitation. *ONE* operated as a nonprofit corporation, included little paid advertising, and was usually on the verge of financial ruin. To raise money, *ONE* offered its readers a basic annual membership for $10, entitling subscribers to receive the corporation's annual report in addition to a magazine subscription. A "sustaining" membership for $50 allowed members to attend corporation meetings. Following the solicitation was ONE, Inc.'s official mission statement, "A non-profit corporation formed to publish a magazine dealing primarily with homosexuality from the scientific, historical, and critical point of view . . . to sponsor educational programs, lectures and concerts for the aid and benefit of social variants, and to promote among the general public an interest, knowledge, and understanding of the problems of variation . . . to sponsor research and promote the integration into society of such persons whose behavior and inclinations vary from current moral and social standards."[37] While use of the terms "variants" and "variation" would be offensive today, their use in the mission statement reflected the Kinsey Report's influence on *ONE*'s writers and editors. Dr. Alfred Kinsey was a saint to the homophiles because of his radical view that homosexuality was merely a benign *variation* of human sexuality and not some horrible genetic mistake. The mission statement also conveyed the hope that heterosexuals might find *ONE* interesting and useful. Judging from the correspondence, however, few heterosexuals, aside from psychologists, sex researchers, and clergy, showed much interest in the magazine. In a few cases, heterosexual family members of homosexuals wrote letters asking for information, but it was generally a gay magazine reaching a gay audience.

Letters to the editor appear on pages 6 and 7, discussing a wide range of issues. In one letter, a reader from Syracuse, New York, praised *ONE*'s discussion of "morals and ethics," while a San Francisco reader complained about an article's "swishy" tone. A letter from Sacramento questioned the morality of heterosexual breeding in an overpopulated world. A Dallas correspondent shared an anecdote from a book he read claiming that all famous spies were homosexual. A reader from Boston was stung by *ONE*'s rejection of his short story for publication, "At what type of reader is *ONE* aimed? What social, economic and education level is this type of reader? Is *ONE* aimed at an heterosexual [*sic*] group mainly to neutralize present antagonisms towards the homosexual, or do your editors really believe they are compiling a magazine FOR homosexuals? If the first is true, much fictional work in *ONE* is vague; if the second is true, your stories are downright and naively insipid!"[38] Indeed, *ONE*'s audience was highly opinionated and not shy about severely critiquing the magazine's contents. Usually *ONE*'s fiction and poetry were singled out as especially amateurish. *ONE*'s editors struggled to find competent writers, and when submissions were low, the overworked editors wrote short stories themselves under pseudonyms. As a result, quality varied widely.

The last letter praised a column Norman Mailer had written for *ONE* several months earlier. Mailer was probably the highest profile writer to write for *ONE*. His article, "The Homosexual Villain," explained how he had routinely disparaged homosexuals in his books until receiving an unsolicited copy of *ONE* magazine in the mail; he then found himself "not unsympathetic" about gay people for the first time. Mailer stated that as a consequence of reading *ONE* and Donald Webster Cory's 1951 *The Homosexual in America*, he was rewriting portions of his current project, *The Deer Park*.[39] The letter writer explained that Mailer's "journey from bigotry to something approaching understanding" had caused him to rethink his own homosexuality. The Mailer piece "has given me courage to undertake the most important task of all. This is to approach a few of my best and truest heterosexual friends and explain, as gently and understandingly as possible, something of myself to them. For how else are those who labor with an imaginary homosexual stereotype to see through its illusion unless they see a contradiction in the flesh?"[40] As this letter demonstrates, *ONE* inspired this reader to rethink his own visibility in a manner that foresaw the "coming out" strategy of gay liberation organizations in the late 1960s and 1970s. By publishing the letter, *ONE* circulated the idea of gay visibility as a political strategy for thousands of other gay men and lesbians to ponder.

Pages 8 through 12 contain Albert Ellis's cover story, "Are Homosexuals Neurotic?" Dr. Ellis's essay argued that "exclusive homosexuals" *are* neurotic, but so are "exclusive heterosexuals" because human sexuality is inherently polymorphous and diverse (echoing the conclusions of the Kinsey Reports).[41] Many *ONE* readers strongly disagreed with Dr. Ellis on this point. "I have never in my life, read such a mixed up idea on neurosis," wrote a man from Indianapolis in a letter published in *ONE*'s July 1955 issue. A woman from Denver added, "Are we to assume that the major part of our society today is composed mainly of neurotic individuals because they are 'fetishistically attached to one particular mode of sex activity?' or, to put it another way, not promiscuous? Oh—come, come, my dear doctor, what of the societal golden wedding anniversaries?"[42]

Ellis was one of several heterosexual medical professionals to regularly contribute to the homophile movement, along with UCLA researcher Evelyn Hooker and *ONE*'s in-house psychologist and advice columnist, Blanche Baker. Despite his sincere engagement with the movement, however, Ellis's theories did not always sit well with *ONE*'s readers.

ONE's most popular recurring column, "Tangents," which appears on pages 15 through 17, was a potpourri of information mailed in from readers across the country concerning "gay news, censorship, conformity, civil rights, gender oddities, and other subjects that seemed to relate to our field of interest," according to its creator, Jim Kepner.[43] The April 1955 installment of "Tangents" reports, "Miami's year and a half homo-hunt may provide blueprint for nation. . . . Kinsey again calls sex laws useless." Police crackdowns were described in New York City (forty-two arrests one night in Times Square and the Village), Baltimore (leading to the arrest of two college professors and a teacher), London, and Buenos Aires. Gay bars in Los Angeles and San Francisco were suffering from legal harassment, and Minneapolis police were threatening to shut down a female impersonation show at the "Gay Nineties" bar.[44] Each month, "Tangents" offered *ONE*'s readers an invaluably broad social perspective by documenting gay and lesbian persecution across the country and even throughout the world. It was the first time gay people had access to such information in the United States.

Following "Tangents" was the short story "Passing Stranger" by Clarkson Crane. *ONE*'s fiction often described lonely figures shuffling through urban environments looking for signs of gay life, meeting danger, excitement, hesitation, and apprehension along the way. "Passing Stranger" reflects a general gloominess present in much of *ONE*'s fiction. In the story, spectators gather to watch a man paint a picture onto a bar window. A handsome young man joined the crowd, and the painter's concentration was shaken. The young man became enraptured with the man's painting, and the painter could not keep his eyes off his attractive observer. As the painter finishes his picture, the crowd begins to disperse but the handsome young man remained. Then it started to rain. The story concludes, "The painter watched him go—his red shirt and his blond hair. He saw him reach the corner and linger, again undecided. He watched him cross the street and drift on. Then he lost sight of him and did not see him again until he was so far away (just a red splotch in the rainy dullness) that seeing him was hardly worth the trouble. The melancholy of the rain filled the bar window."[45] Unconsummated affairs were common in *ONE*'s fiction. Any sexual contacts had to be implied because of censorship concerns.

Several short pieces follow "Passing Stranger." There were four book reviews, including *One Arm* by Tennessee Williams ("Williams' reputation must find basis elsewhere"), *Whisper His Sin* by Vin Packer ("compact, competently written, if somewhat over-dramatized"), and two books discussing the homosexuality of the Roman Emperor Hadrian. James Barr Fugaté described homoerotic themes in the work of Ernest Hemingway and André Gide in his short essay "Camping in the Bush," which was followed by a one-page essay about the Dutch homophile magazine *Vriendschap*. The next two pages contained excerpts from Plato's *Symposium*. *ONE*'s editors reprinted Plato on several occasions to remind readers that major architects of Western thought were homosexual.[46] This was part of the magazine's civil rights impulse to instill a sense of pride in its gay readers.

Between two short poems is the regular *ONE* feature "The Feminine Viewpoint." Most of *ONE*'s contents emphasize the gay male experience, as this installment of "The Feminine Viewpoint" explains. "Compared to the male homosexual," Marlin Prentiss wrote, "the lesbian has a very easy time of it indeed, at least as far as persecution by a hostile society is concerned. Unless she chooses to deliberately advertise her anomaly by adopting a pattern of behavior that would be no more acceptable in a heterosexual than a homosexual, she is allowed to live a reasonably normal life, without the constant fear of exposure and the ensuing ridicule, ostracism, and legal prosecution which makes the lives of so many male homosexuals such a horror."[47] Many lesbians disagreed with Prentiss's rosy depiction of lesbian life. They wrote letters describing the same "constant fear of exposure" gay men suffered. Her comments, however, suggest why the homophile movement catered more to gay men: lesbians were considerably less likely to be arrested or fired from their jobs due to homosexuality. The monthly "Feminine Viewpoint" represented *ONE*'s most significant effort to include lesbians in its national discussion, and lesbians appreciated the column, but they also yearned for more lesbian content.

The final pages of the issue contain advertisements. *ONE* advertised its own back issues as well as the *Mattachine Review* and various European homophile magazines, and page 44 features an advertisement for "Unwanted facial and body hair permanently removed" at an address in Sherman Oaks, California. Another advertisement offers flamboyant mail-order clothing for men, including a pair of shorts called "High Tide," described as "The shorty-short legs, trim fit, laced front for sun and fun."[48] These clothing ads became a source of controversy for *ONE* readers who complained that they compromised the serious tone of the magazine.[49]

ONE's general format and contents changed little over the years. In 1956 the editors experimented with a longer, bimonthly issue for a few issues, but they found this hurt reader loyalty so they shortened the magazine to thirty-two pages and resumed monthly production. In 1957 *ONE* magazine changed its slogan from "The Homosexual Magazine" to "The Homosexual Viewpoint." As Dorr Legg explained, this was meant to highlight that homosexuals, collectively, had a unique viewpoint on the society around them. "The words 'The Homosexual Viewpoint,' " he wrote, imply "that the things they see and hear and feel have a special hue and coloration. . . . [I]t is the viewpoint of the homosexual looking out upon a world from within himself at the mores and standards of men, so that he may pass judgment upon them and determine for himself which are good and which are bad."[50] Stories in the mass media about homosexuality usually ignored "homosexual viewpoints." The slogan change represented *ONE*'s editors' efforts to ensure that homosexuals had a voice in public debates about homosexuality.

Surveillance and Censorship

The country's first self-proclaimed homosexual magazine, unsurprisingly, drew attention from authorities that wanted to shut down *ONE* but lacked the formal power to do so. The FBI had agents spying on the homophile movement since at least 1952, part of the bureau's Sex Deviate Program launched in June 1951. Despite field reports stating that the homophiles were not engaged in communist activity, FBI Director J. Edgar Hoover instructed field agents in 1956 to confront *ONE* about an article insinuating that gay people worked for the FBI. Two agents visited *ONE*'s office demanding to speak to the article's author, David Freeman. Dorr Legg offered to forward a message to "David"—not mentioning that "David Freeman" was a pseudonym and did not really exist. The agents returned a couple of days later, insisting to see Freeman and warning Legg that the article about gay FBI agents was slanderous. Legg allegedly told them that in order for the article to be considered slanderous in court, the FBI would have to prove beyond doubt that no homosexual agents worked in the agency. The agents left in frustration. Despite Hoover's personal interest in *ONE*, his agents got no further than Dorr Legg's desk.[51]

Far more significant was the U.S. Postal Service's seizure of *ONE*'s October 1954 issue on grounds of obscenity. The Post Office had served as a major organ of censorship in the United States since the passage of the Comstock Law in 1873. The October issue was the second issue of *ONE* to be seized by the Post Office—*ONE*'s August 1953 issue, with the words

"Homosexual Marriage?" on the cover, had been held up for a couple of weeks, but released on further review. The October 1954 seizure was more serious, however, as the Post Office held to its position that the contents were obscene. *ONE* continued publishing in the wake of the seizure, but the incident sent a chill through the organization and its readers.

Los Angeles postal officials deemed a poem, a short story, and an advertisement in the issue obscene. The poem was called "Lord Samuel and Lord Montague;" and the offending verses included:

> Lord Samuel says that Sodom's sins
> Disgrace our young Queen's reign
> An age that in this plight begins
> May well end up in flame. . . .
> Would he idly waste his breath
> In sniffing round the drains
> Had he known "King Elizabeth"
> Or roistering "Queen James"?

The offensive advertisement was for the European homophile magazines *Der Kreis* and *Vennen*. The ad contained nothing obscene, but postal officials argued that *Der Kreis* and *Vennen* contained lewd material (nonpornographic nude photos) and therefore *ONE* was guilty of pandering. The short story, the lesbian romance "Sappho Remembered," was deemed "lustfully stimulating."[52] *ONE*'s lawyer Eric Julber, who vetted each issue carefully for obscene content, was convinced the seizure was an attempt to harass and intimidate *ONE* out of business, and working pro bono he fought the seizure in the courts. In 1956 a lower court agreed with the postal officials that the contents were obscene, and the Ninth Circuit Court of Appeals held up that decision the following year. Undaunted, Julber filed an appeal with the U.S. Supreme Court, and in January 1958 the U.S. Supreme Court ruled in *ONE*'s favor. Five years into its publication, *ONE*'s legality was officially confirmed. The case represented a major victory for the homophile movement.[53]

ONE, Inc.

In addition to publishing a monthly magazine, ONE, Inc., created other publications, operated a library and research center, held educational classes and seminars, hosted public talks by distinguished speakers on homosexual subjects, and even organized the first official "gay tour" of Europe for American tourists.[54]

Beginning in 1955, ONE, Inc., hosted an annual Midwinter Meeting every January. These meetings brought together homophile activists and *ONE* readers to hear lectures and conduct roundtable discussions regarding the status of homosexuals in the United States. The theme of ONE, Inc.'s 1960 Midwinter Meeting, for example, was "The Homosexual in the Community," and it was held in downtown Los Angeles. Jim Kepner delivered the welcoming address, which was followed by a panel including a priest, a psychologist, a teacher, and two homophile activists discussing the role of homosexuals in the community. After lunch, *ONE* attorney Eric Julber described the magazine's editorial policies. Dorr Legg delivered a paper eruditely entitled "Normative Factors and Cultural Determinants in the Dynamics of Homosexual Pairing," and UCLA psychologist Evelyn Hooker delivered a paper on her research. The rest of the afternoon and evening included roundtable discussions, a cocktail hour, banquet, poetry readings, and folk singing. The next day featured a special session, "Meet Dr. [Blanche] Baker," followed by a performance of James Barr Fugaté's play *Game of Fools*, which had been published by ONE, Inc. Attendance at most Midwinter Meetings was a few hundred people.[55]

Another major ONE, Inc., project was the One Institute, launched in 1956 and largely the brainchild of Dorr Legg, which offered college-level courses and seminars on homosexuality from a homophile perspective. Legg, Don Slater, Jim Kepner, retired University of Southern California Education Professor Merritt Thompson, and others developed and taught their own courses in subjects that explored homosexuality in science, literature, history, religion, drama, and philosophy. During the 1950s and early 1960s, several hundred gay men and lesbians in the Los Angeles area attended One Institute classes and earned credit toward a degree in homophile studies. The One Institute received accreditation in 1982 from the state of California and continued to operate as an educational organization until the early 1990s.[56]

As ONE, Inc.'s activities grew, so did its publication roster. The corporation had a book press that published a handful of books in the 1950s and 1960s. In 1956, ONE, Inc., began publishing *ONE Confidential,* a newsletter reporting on corporate events and other internal matters. "It is hoped that reports on the whys and wherefores will better knit [the Corporation's] friends into an effective working unit, dedicated to the goals for which ONE was founded," the first issue stated.[57] Circulation peaked around 400 a month. In 1958, ONE, Inc., began offering *ONE Institute Quarterly: Homophile Studies*, an academic journal intended to showcase research being conducted at the One Institute. Most issues contained three or four long essays on topics similar to those found in

ONE magazine, such as homosexuality and the law, famous homosexuals in history, anthropological studies of homosexuality, or the latest scientific research. The quality of writing and scholarship in the journal varied immensely—one reader criticized it as "argumentative, sarcastic, and polemical."[58] Nineteen issues of *Homophile Studies* were produced from 1958 to 1969.

During the rapid growth of the gay liberation movement in the late 1960s and 1970s, a younger generation of activists frequently dismissed the historical significance of *ONE* magazine and ONE, Inc.'s related activities. To the gay liberationists, *ONE* seemed apologetic, conformist, assimilationist—in essence, not sufficiently "radical" or "militant." Such a bias seeped into the first generation of academic scholarship on the homophile movement, which described the 1950s homophile movement as a "failure" due to its "conservative" nature.[59] The history of ONE, Inc., however, suggests that the homophile movement was neither conservative nor a failure, but instead dynamic, creative, and effective in instigating national public dialogue about gay rights and the broader cultural meanings of sexual identity.[60] Undoubtedly, the homophile movement was small compared to the gay activism of later decades, but *ONE's* mere survival was an unprecedented achievement in the United States. As chapter 2 describes, this achievement was the work not merely of gay activists in Los Angeles, but a nationwide network of volunteers who ensured that *ONE* would be available for purchase on newsstands every month, and readers who braved the risks of postwar gay identity by purchasing and reading the magazine.

2

Newsstand Encounters

ONE Magazine's Volunteer Agents and Public Visibility

ONE did not appear on newsstands throughout the country by seren-dipity or magic. The civil rights impulse that saturated *ONE*'s pages was also evident in the magazine's distribution. A grass-roots network of gay men and lesbians, persons who shared *ONE*'s desire to improve the collective status of gay people, brought about the magazine's national proliferation and visibility. As the first official "homosexual magazine," this process was not without challenges, complications, and anxieties.

A Washington, D.C., man, Brad, for example, made it his mission in 1954 to convince at least one newsstand owner to sell the magazine. He first went to a newsstand that sold male physique magazines—maga-zines that officially were devoted to exercise and health, but unofficially catered to gay male readers with photographs of nearly naked men. The newsstand owner, however, failed to make the connection between *ONE* and the physique magazines, and "was disgusted at the idea of [*ONE*] magazine and would be entirely uninterested," Brad reported back to ONE, Inc. "I pointed out to him that he had [physique] magazines there showing men in sexually arousing poses and lightly clad, as well as a nudist organ, but I could not convince him of the lack of a difference. Of course, he is ignorant of the motives behind these other magazines." Brad had better luck convincing the owner of Bill's Smoke Shop, located in a red-light district a half-mile north of Capitol Hill, that *ONE* was a sure seller.[1] Indeed, the first twenty-five copies sold out quickly, and the owner doubled his order to fifty copies. *ONE* continued selling briskly over the next few months, but then two FBI agents showed up at Bill's Smoke Shop and spooked the owner profoundly. All they did was ask if he sold *ONE* magazine. He said yes. The agents thanked him and disappeared without further comment. Then silence. Worry. Questions. Why did they need to know? Who would they tell? A business license commissioner? J. Edgar Hoover? Was his newsstand doomed? Anxiety hit the owner like a sledgehammer and he cancelled his order. *ONE* magazine disappeared (temporarily) from Washington, D.C.[2] Brad would have to find other newsstands to sell *ONE* or convince the owner of Bill's Smoke Shop to reconsider his decision.

As this example shows, *ONE*'s national proliferation occurred painstakingly, newsstand by newsstand, city by city. The process was complicated, involving hundreds of volunteers across the country. The existence of this national network of volunteers challenges the commonly held belief that the homophile movement was so "tiny" and West Coast–based that "everyone involved knew everyone else involved."[3] In fact, a significant grass-roots dimension to the homophile movement has been overlooked by scholars who have focused on the movement's leaders and internal conflicts. The ONE Archive's correspondence files shed important light on these grass-roots volunteers who operated discreetly and avoided publicity or recognition for their efforts. Dorr Legg, Don Slater, and Jim Kepner shaped *ONE*'s editorial tone, but its monthly distribution was a nationwide group effort.

ONE's arrival at newsstands represented more than just the first American gay magazine. It provided the first example in the public sphere of a stable, visible gay institution. *ONE*'s newsstand visibility existed among networks of veiled gay institutions, such as bars, bathhouses, cruising areas, and softball leagues, found in most American cities during these years. *ONE* proclaimed itself "The Homosexual Magazine" on its cover, rejecting the ambiguity, innuendo, and coding used by these other gay institutions. (Gay bars, for example, never put signs in their windows announcing "homosexuals welcome here.") *ONE*'s appearance on urban newsstands tagged certain intersections, streets, or neighborhoods as gay enough to justify the risks of selling the magazine. *ONE* magazine put gay culture visibly into public space, and it hinted at the masked gay institutions nearby.

Because of the unique way *ONE* proclaimed its homosexual identity in public space, spotting *ONE* on a newsstand for the first time was an earth-shaking experience for many lesbians and gay men. In letters to *ONE*, many readers described how seeing the magazine for the first time made them feel connected to a national gay and lesbian community larger than they had imagined. It was a profound revelation. Newsstands thus became important sites of representation and resiliency for the national gay minority during the 1950s and early 1960s. Countless thousands of individuals who never bought the magazine saw it openly displayed in busy places such as Times Square in New York City, Hollywood Boulevard in Los Angeles, or, eventually, in Washington, D.C.'s Lafayette Square. *ONE's* public display allowed individuals to browse through the magazine without necessarily buying a copy—a terrifying ordeal for some—therefore reaching far more people than its average monthly circulation of 3,000 to 5,000 suggests.

Distributing the First Gay Magazine

ONE's creators had no experience distributing a magazine. They improvised a lot. For the first several months of the magazine's publication, the goal was to generate enough interest in the magazine to justify continuing its publication. To achieve this, they mailed sample copies to members of Mattachine Society chapters, sex researchers such as Alfred Kinsey and George Henry, and anyone else they could think of who might appreciate the magazine. These mailings indeed generated an awareness of the magazine, but they quickly realized that *ONE* would never survive without conventional commercial distribution outlets.[4]

Gay bars seemed like a logical place to sell the magazine because they were the key social institution of gay life following World War II. "Locally we are selling many hundreds of copies monthly through arrangements with certain bars," *ONE* business manager Dorr Legg explained in May 1953. "Some of these are sold directly from the floor by our agents. . . . Others are sold by the bars themselves and the receipts turned over to us monthly."[5] Legg initially encouraged volunteers in other cities to look to gay bars as distribution points as well, but this enthusiasm for bars did not last long. Legg admitted in a 1994 oral history that the first time he entered a bar to sell *ONE* magazine, patrons "almost dropped dead."[6] By January 1954, he was telling volunteers that bars were "unsuitable outlets" because so many bar owners were afraid to handle the magazine.[7] Gay bars across the country underwent routine police surveillance and harassment, and many owners feared that the mere presence of "The Homosexual Magazine" in their bars could prove damaging in court if prosecutors tried to establish that a bar catered to gay or lesbian clients. Many bars were owned by organized crime syndicates and had no interest in advancing a homophile agenda. A small number of gay bar owners supported *ONE's* goals and agreed to sell the magazine on a short-term basis until *ONE* could establish better distribution outlets. Thus, this "bar phase" made many gay people aware that *ONE* existed (especially in Los Angeles), but bars failed as dependable distribution outlets.

As more gay people became aware of *ONE*, volunteers stepped forward to assist with the magazine's distribution.[8] Dorr Legg established a profit-sharing system with these volunteer distribution agents, though many of them expressed little interest in making money. Many of these early volunteers simply gave away handfuls of copies at their own expense to generate awareness of the magazine. A volunteer in New York City told Legg in December 1953, "Some friends and I strolled through the Village, our arms loaded with back issues. We went into all the gay bars and Café Espressos, etc., giving them to anyone who reached. A little more of this and *ONE* will be known the length and breadth of Manhattan."[9] As the magazine's business manager, Dorr Legg handled much of the communication with these volunteer agents, and he offered them encouragement but little specific advice for them. Be creative, he told them. Be persistent. Good luck.

By late 1953, *ONE*'s distribution efforts had shifted from gay bars to newsstands. Newsstand visibility was critical to *ONE*'s survival because so many people feared subscribing. The importance of newsstand visibility and the challenges facing volunteers are highlighted in the experiences of several volunteers in the San Francisco Bay Area. *ONE*'s first Bay Area volunteer agent was a "well-recommended and most enthusiastic young man" who secured several subscriptions, sold dozens of individual copies, and then vanished without a trace, pilfering money owed to *ONE*.[10] A woman named Eleanor took over distribution duties in the Bay Area from mid-1953 to early 1954. At first she gave away free issues to "some very good contacts among people who are teachers, recreational leaders and social workers." These contacts expressed "considerable enthusiasm" about the magazine but were afraid to subscribe. "I am wondering whether you have also come up against this particular problem of 'fear,' " she wrote.[11] Vowing to overcome her own fear, Eleanor pushed ahead and quickly found three places willing to sell *ONE*: City Lights Bookstore, a sandwich shop, and a newsstand near the University of California, Berkeley. The sandwich shop did not carry the magazine for long however—in Eleanor's words, "the 'feared' occurred": "One of the owners works in the Juvenile Detention Home and his juveniles came in one night and got a hold of the magazine. They live near by and dropped in frequently. For a civil servant this is taking too much of a risk."[12] Like the owner of Bill's Smoke Shop in Washington, D.C., the sandwich shop owner in San Francisco became overwhelmed with anxiety at the prospect of continuing to sell *ONE*. Such moments of panic were not unusual, forcing *ONE*'s volunteers to repeatedly seek new distribution sites to maintain existing circulation levels.

After seven months, Eleanor resigned from her duties, citing her lack of time as well as her frustration over infighting between ONE, Inc., and the Mattachine Society. "I do not feel this is the time for two organizations . . . to be cutting each other's throats," she wrote.[13] Despite her frustration with the homophile movement, Eleanor's brief stint as a volunteer made a significant contribution by establishing several dependable Bay Area distribution outlets, including City Lights Bookstore, which played a central role in the San Francisco beat scene and was where poet Allen Ginsberg regularly read copies of *ONE*.[14]

Conrad, an Oakland resident, lasted only a few weeks as a volunteer agent. During his first week in December 1953, he told Dorr Legg he was having difficulty describing the magazine to newsstand owners. Legg replied, "A large distributor here has assured us that so long as we carry 'The Homosexual Magazine' on the masthead it will sell. In time to come the word will tend to lose its first shock and the fact become established that this is indeed the 'official' voice of a minority."[15] Despite Legg's encouragement, Conrad resigned two weeks later. "It has been a *great* disappointment to me that I was successful in obtaining only three newsstands to handle *ONE*," he explained. "I even had a small sign painted and placed in one of the more patronized 'gay' bars in town, hoping to create a demand for *ONE* at newsstands—but all was for naught." Conrad was pessimistic about *ONE*'s chances for long-term success. "Let's face it! There are few 'gay' people who would be foolhardy enough to ask for *ONE* at a newsstand. Most of them, as I, are content enough to leave well enough alone without 'crusading' or trying to change laws so men could marry. I for one wouldn't write my Senator of any such changes."[16] Despite his general pessimism for *ONE*, he in fact had made a small yet lasting contribution to the homophile movement, adding three more newsstands to *ONE*'s steadily growing national distribution network.

Indeed, these minimal, incremental gains frustrated many volunteers, but for others, such small steps forward were well worth the anxiety and effort. In 1956, for example, a Kansas City couple named James and Doug spent a long afternoon trying to get their local newspaper to accept a classified advertisement publicizing *ONE*. Taking a cue from the magazine, they did not shy away from using the word "homosexual" in their proposed classified advertisement. When they went to the newspaper office to submit the ad, the employee behind the counter refused to accept it. James argued to the employee that the newspaper had no basis to reject the ad because the newspaper had just published a story about the play *Tea and Sympathy* and its homosexual themes.

After waiting hours to speak to a supervisor, they were told once again that the newspaper would not accept the ad because "they didn't solicit that type of business." After pointing to the newspaper's story on *Tea and Sympathy*, emphasizing the word "homosexuality" in "bold type at the heading of the article," James and Doug eventually wore down the reluctant classified supervisor who finally approved the advertisement. Their efforts required not only patience and persistence but also overcoming a significant degree of fear for what, in retrospect, seems like a trifling accomplishment. The civil rights impulse comes through clearly in their letter explaining why they refused to take "no" for an answer: "Oh yes, incidentally," James wrote:

> . . . before this man would approve the ad I had to give him my name and address, so I did. After all, I figured that if it did get in the hands of the police that they couldn't do any more than put my name on a "Suspect List" . . . (I Hope!!). After all, I well realize that you can't stand up for our cause and not be so named. [Doug] and I are both willing to "stick our necks out" in the interest of providing enlightenment, and only hope that we can get others to follow.
>
> I already know that when I tell some of my friends (gay ones) what we did in getting this ad in the paper that they will tell us that we both are just looking for trouble. Unfortunately, there are ever so many that are quite willing to reap the benefits that we are working to pave the way for, but in the meantime want to sit far out on the back fence to watch what is going on.[17]

ONE's creators back in Los Angeles of course were familiar with such anxieties. Shortly after the Post Office seized the October 1954 issue, *ONE*'s staff resorted to stuffing subscription copies in mailboxes in towns neighboring Los Angeles in order to avoid further problems from the Los Angeles Post Office.[18] Meanwhile, *ONE*'s reliance on volunteers was leading to mix-ups and late deliveries at newsstands. A *ONE* editor woefully wrote in early 1955, "It all boils down to this: we are finding ourselves pushed out into the main current—into the big-time, yet none of us are quite prepared for such a pace or yet capable of keeping up. The little 'groupy' over-the-coffee-cups days are past. We are growing up fast. And it is rough on all of us. . . . Finances, Finances. Structural problems. Literary problems. . . . Personalities. We yell loudly at each other and then keep right on. What else can we do?"[19] Despite these growing pains, during the next ten years, from 1953 to 1963, volunteer agents helped facilitate *ONE*'s distribution in most large U.S. cities, including San Diego; Long Beach; Los Angeles; San Jose; San Francisco; Berkeley; Portland, Oregon; Seattle; Salt Lake City; Denver; Detroit; Chicago; Toledo; Cleveland; Kansas City; Omaha; Tulsa; Oklahoma City; San Antonio; Dallas; Houston; New Orleans; Baton Rouge; Mobile; Fayetteville; Sarasota; Miami; Atlanta; Knoxville; Baltimore; Washington, D.C.; Philadelphia; Pittsburgh; New York City; Boston; and Portland, Maine.[20] Once *ONE* established itself in an area, new volunteers emerged, and other newsstands became more willing to sell the magazine.

Volunteers were critically important to *ONE*'s distribution because professional magazine distributors were unwilling to handle *ONE* magazine in its early years. Dorr Legg told a Milwaukee volunteer agent in 1955, "To put it briefly: the big ones won't touch *ONE*; the small ones are no good. We have tried both! So it boils down to our doing the job ourselves."[21] In 1953 a professional distributor in Los Angeles promised to put *ONE* onto 200 newsstands only to disappear with money owed to ONE, Inc., ruining several relationships with newsstands in the process. *ONE*'s creators learned to be wary of professional distributors.[22]

Eventually, several small distribution companies that specialized in "risky" magazines gained ONE, Inc.'s trust and handled *ONE*'s distribution in Southern California, New York, Detroit, and elsewhere. Central Magazine Sales Ltd. of Baltimore, Maryland, for example, distributed *ONE* magazine along the eastern seaboard in 1964 along with fifty nudist titles, dozens of physique magazines, and "hard to get pocket editions" of controversial books such as *Tropic of Cancer, Fanny Hill, Hindu Art of Love,* and the *Kama Sutra.*[23] Dealers with experience selling controversial publications were more familiar with obscenity laws and court rulings and knew which newsstands attracted gay clientele. Unfortunately, these companies had trouble paying their bills and were prone to police raids.

Newsstand operators and professional distributors who sold *ONE* were important allies to the homophile movement. Profit was the main incentive for them, but sometimes a deeper idealism figured into their handling of the magazine. A distributor based in Costa Mesa, California, for example, told *ONE* in 1961 that he carried the magazine more for principle than profit. "Even though not personally interested in homosexuality," he was impressed with *ONE*'s quality:

> I used to be a social scientist and was a lecturer at USC; in my own mind, at least, I am what might loosely be called an intellectual. . . . I find [in *ONE*] more real thought and coming-to-grips with THE problem of our time—the proper relationship between individual and society—than in almost

any other magazine with which I am acquainted. I know that you have read [Robert] Lindner's *Must You Conform?* Consciously or otherwise, you and the others who publish *ONE* are certainly doing a good job of following his prescription for constructive rebellion.[24]

Some of the professional distributors may have been gay; ONE sources offer little indication one way or another.

Newsstand Visibility

ONE's appearance on newsstands reflected several broader trends at play in post–World War II America. The rise of television, for example, compelled other media, especially magazines, to seek smaller, more specifically targeted audiences rather than a general mass audience. The idea of a "homosexual magazine" made sense in such a context, as *ONE* joined *Playboy, The National Review, Sports Illustrated,* and other magazines catering to specific audiences.[25] In addition, overall newsstand magazine sales declined precipitously throughout the country in the late 1940s and early 1950s, largely due to the rapid growth of suburbs, which caused more people to subscribe to magazines rather than to purchase them at newsstands.[26] This decline in newsstand sales motivated some newsstand operators and distributors to take chances selling riskier material, such as a "homosexual magazine."

Several years before *ONE*'s debut in 1953, male physique magazines had carved a gay male niche on newsstands.[27] *ONE*'s first editor, Martin Block, commented that many newsstands "carried the physique magazines that had photographs of men in a jock strap or posing strap. They knew they had customers for the physique magazines, so why not sell *ONE* magazine as well?"[28] For *ONE*'s volunteer agents, such as Brad from the beginning of the chapter, the first newsstands they usually visited were those already selling physique magazines. When newsstand proprietors agreed to sell *ONE*, they usually displayed it on their shelves directly adjacent to their physique magazine selections. This caused headaches for some physique magazine publishers, who, as *ONE* quipped in 1957, "try to give the impression their publishers would drop dead if they thought any homosexuals bought their mags to look at the pictures."[29] One way that physique magazines deflected suspicions that they catered to gay male audiences was by publishing vitriolic homophobic articles. *Bernarr MacFadden's Vitalized Physical Culture,* for example, published an April 1953 article outrageously titled, "Homosexuality Is Stalin's Atom Bomb to Destroy America." The author of the article, "Dr." Arthur Guy Mathews, accused homosexual literature such as *ONE* as having the "intent of corrupting the morals of our youth in order to render them useless on the war fronts and in home defense. It is a known fact that sex degenerates and homosexuals are cowards who shriek, scream, cry and break down into hysterical states of psychoses when they are called upon to defend our shores from the enemy."[30] Not all physique magazines resorted to this tactic, however; the popular *Physique Pictorial* (operated by a gay man) usually ignored the subject of homosexuality.

In 1956 a photograph in *Collier's* magazine unintentionally captured *ONE* on a newsstand in Times Square, demonstrating its proximity to physique magazines (Figure 12, *ONE* magazine on New York City newsstand). The photo features actress Kim Novak "scanning the morning papers"; just to the left of Novak's head is the March 1956 issue of *ONE*, surrounded by other magazines of interest to gay men. To *ONE*'s left is a physique magazine with a red background and next to that is a cover photo of a man posing on what looks like a beach. Just above Novak's shoulder we see *Man* magazine. Interestingly, *ONE* and its physique neighbors occupy prime territory on the newsstand, centered with their entire covers fully displayed. Most of the other magazines on this

Figure 12. *ONE* magazine on New York City newsstand.

newsstand are obscured except for their titles. This visibility is striking considering that a series of police raids the previous year had caused *ONE* to disappear from every Times Square newsstand for a brief period (it was still available "under the counter").[31]

ONE's visibility, combined with its ambiguous legal status until the 1958 Supreme Court ruling, made *ONE* a potential target for censorship. Newsstand operators had second thoughts about carrying the magazine when police began inspecting or raiding other newsstands or bookstores in town. Dorr Legg, utterly convinced of *ONE*'s legality, had little patience with newsstand operators who complained to him that local censors "forced" them to stop carrying *ONE*. Yet as a penny-pinching business manager and strong believer in free market capitalism, he was forgiving of economic justifications for discontinuing *ONE*. If nobody was buying *ONE* at a particular newsstand, then discontinuing it was simply a logical business decision. Legg chastised dealers as cowards, however, if they discontinued *ONE* when sales were brisk.[32]

From the seller's perspective, however, this could be a difficult distinction to make. Ted's Book Shop in Kansas City, Missouri, for example, stopped carrying *ONE* in 1955 after a rash of local newsstand raids. "I see nothing obscene in your magazine," the owner explained, "however for the few copies sold and small amount made it would not pay us to jeopardize our business by having to answer to the authorities and be thrown into court and have our name mentioned in the newspapers, radio and television as the other places have been mentioned."[33] Because this was Kansas City's only *ONE* outlet at the time, several local readers sorely missed the magazine. Jerry, a barber who was unemployed because of a gay arrest, visited Ted's Book Shop on ONE, Inc.'s behalf and urged the owner to reconsider his decision. The owner told Jerry that he needed assurances of safety beyond those of Dorr Legg. "Previous owners told him that police ban prevented further sales of the mag in K.C.," Jerry reported.[34] The sources do not indicate whether Jerry was successful or not in convincing the owner to resume carrying *ONE*, but distribution records indicate that Ted's Book Shop was once again selling *ONE* by 1961. In 1964, however, another reader complained that *ONE* was unavailable in Kansas City.[35] Such disappearances and reappearances of the magazine at certain newsstands were common in many cities, frustrating readers.

Police crackdowns against "obscene" published materials plagued newsstands throughout *ONE*'s existence, but *ONE* was usually not the specific target. Newsstands selling *ONE* usually sold other controversial publications such as nudist magazines, paperback novels with lurid covers, violent comic books, or risqué literature such as *Lady Chatterley's*

Lover or *The Well of Loneliness*. A series of liberal U.S. Supreme Court rulings on obscenity during the 1950s encouraged some newsstand operators to take chances selling more daring material. The most important of these rulings, *Roth v. United States* in 1957, overruled the 1873 Comstock Law by declaring that "sex and obscenity are not synonymous." The *Roth* decision suffered from vague wording, however, relegating subsequent obscenity rulings to a "constitutional twilight zone."[36] In response to the *Roth* decision, as well as the increasing availability of sexually oriented publications, federal, state, and local government agencies conducted a flurry of obscenity investigations during the late 1950s. In California, for example, a 1957 State Senate committee conducted public hearings on obscene magazines, but the hearings stalled on the first day when committee members could not agree on a definition of "obscene."[37]

In some cities, certain city officials had authoritarian control over newsstand standards, and occasionally *ONE* became the specific target of censorship crusades. This occurred in New York City in 1954, although city officials did not seek an outright ban of *ONE* being sold—just its public display, as we saw in Figure 12. A letter from *ONE*'s New York City volunteer agent describes the city's efforts to force *ONE* "under the counter":

> Mr. McCaffery, city license commissioner holds the power of life and death over these hundreds of small newsstands on streets through the city. He can arbitrarily cancel a license without any explanation whatsoever. Recently an inspector brought him a copy of *ONE* which he picked up at a stand. It was not long following that several "key" dealers were given summons to appear at his office. Individually he told them that while he did not have the authority to tell them not to [sell the magazine, they should not] display it openly on their stands. This is tantamount to telling them not to sell it because to do so would be impossible from a sales standpoint. This has affected well over half our stands in NY, and almost all the up-town area. The village has not yet been affected—this is downtown of course.[38]

During the next year, several readers reported newsstand crackdowns in Times Square and elsewhere in New York City.[39] Other widespread newsstand crackdowns were reported in Philadelphia, Atlanta, and Los Angeles. *ONE* was banned outright in Minneapolis in 1954 and New Orleans in 1960.[40] Sometimes, even the most valiant efforts of volunteers could not overcome a city's efforts to prevent *ONE*'s display.

Grass-roots censorship groups often pressured city officials to crack down on newsstands. The Citizens for Decent Literature, founded in 1959, was perhaps the most nationally prominent of these groups. The column "Dear Abby" mentioned the organization to a mother in 1960 who complained about the easy availability of "sex-mad magazines."[41] The Citizens for Decent Literature was the brainchild of Cincinnati lawyer Charles Keating, later of the "Keating Five" Savings and Loan Scandal. A reader named Neil described the group's efforts in Chicago in 1965, "[A] couple of years ago, Citizen's Committee for Decent Literature, or some such organization, made a big fuss, there was an arrest of a Loop newsstand operator, and fine or a jail sentence—and thereafter for a time the Loop newsstands looked like the local branch of Baptist Publishing House. Now things are back to normal—including, as I stated, the appearance of ONE and even the little Mattachine Newsletter in a couple of places."[42] In 1965 Citizens for Decent Literature produced a short educational film, *Perversion for Profit*, which warned against the "floodtide of filth . . . of newsstand obscenity" that was "threatening to pervert an entire generation of American children." The film devoted several minutes to male physique magazines, closing the segment with a close-up of *ONE* with "The Homosexual Viewpoint" prominently displayed. This editing trick implied that *ONE* was a physique magazine with an overt homosexual agenda. *ONE* was clearly on the organization's radar, although the way the film implies that *ONE* was an erotica magazine suggests that they never bothered opening a copy or deliberately misrepresented its contents.[43] Organizations such as the Citizens for Decent Literature contributed to a climate of fear against gay people, but by the late 1960s, such groups were outmatched by the decade's sexual revolution.

ONE and the Gay World

ONE's newsstand distribution was important because so many readers were afraid to subscribe. Two-thirds of *ONE* magazine's sales occurred at newsstands, compared to only one-third of total U.S. magazine sales during the 1950s.[44] A man from Daly City, California, explained that he had considered subscribing to *ONE*, but he "held back after discussing the matter with a European-born friend of mine, an ex–Nazi-refugee. He advised against it fearing that THEY might get a copy of the list. Fear, being the contagious thing that it is, I refrained, knowing the [*sic*] I could purchase it locally."[45] A man in Santa Monica, California, expressed a similar, common McCarthy-era anxiety in 1956: "I am not a joiner of organizations," he wrote, "having seen the dire consequences of acquaintances admitting membership in various organizations 10 to 15 years ago, almost all without the slightest inclination toward the now said subversive activities. . . ."[46] Another man added, "This is supposed to be the 'land of the free' but we are not free. If ever it is the 'land of the free' I will re-subscribe."[47] Readers often panicked and cancelled their subscriptions when their copy of *ONE* arrived in the mail with the brown envelope torn open.[48] In a climate of anxiety and censorship, purchasing *ONE* at a newsstand made sense because it shifted much of the risk from reader to newsstand operator.

ONE's display on public newsstands occurred among the networks of camouflaged gay institutions that comprised gay life in the 1950s and early 1960s. In most cities, newsstand agents tried to place *ONE* within a city's gay "circuit"; that is, on newsstands near gay bars, bathhouses, public restrooms (known as "tea-rooms"), and theaters where gay male cruising routinely occurred.[49] Newsstands near large public squares and central urban parks, usually reliable cruising grounds, were safe bets. A gay guide from the 1950s listed the following public squares and parks as some of the most popular cruising spots across the country:

> Boston: Botanical Gardens, Beacon Street side
> New York City: In addition to two sections of Central Park, also
>   Rockefeller Center, Bryant Park, and Riverside Park
> Philadelphia: Rittenhouse Square
> Washington, D.C.: Lafayette Park
> Miami: Bayfront Park
> Chicago: Grant Park and Lincoln Park
> New Orleans: Jackson Square
> San Francisco: Union Square
> Los Angeles: Pershing Square, eastern arm[50]

Gay cruising in densely traveled spaces was highly ritualized and generally imperceptible to nonparticipants. Men used eye contact, body language, or small talk, such as asking for a cigarette or the time, to connect with each other; one person would then follow the other to a more private place.

ONE's availability at a particular spot in a city signaled that the masked institutions of gay life were nearby. For lonely gay men, *ONE*'s presence on a newsstand hinted that gay individuals and even *crowds* might be found in nearby bars, theaters, parks, or gymnasia—a thrilling prospect that could elicit powerful feelings of group identification. A 1958 *ONE* story, "Gay Beach," elaborated on the joys of gay crowds:

> Doesn't the sight of that crowd thrill you? Right out in the open, hundreds of our people, peacefully enjoying themselves in public. No closed doors, no dim lights, no pretense.
>
> I often lie awake nights wondering how long it'll take our group to become aware of itself—its strength and its rights. But I hardly even appreciate just how many of us there really are except when I come here. Except for a few minutes on the Boulevard after the bars close, this is the only place where we ever form "a crowd," and there's something exciting about seeing homosexuals as a crowd. I can't explain how it stirs me, but I think beaches like this are a part of our liberation.[51]

A cover photo of a gay crowd at a beach accompanied this article (Figure 13, *ONE* cover, July 1958). In an era before gay pride festivals, when gay crowds were elusive and hard to find, photographing a gay crowd (especially for a magazine cover) was a major challenge. The photo is daring in clearly showing several individuals at a beach identified as "gay." On the other hand, of the five individuals positioned to face the camera, three have their heads turned away, hiding their faces, another man has turned his face to the side exposing just his profile, and another man wearing dark glasses with his face to the camera is so far away that his face is obscured. The other figures are too small to be identified.

While most of these camouflaged gay institutions catered to gay men, *ONE's* public visibility was also important to its lesbian readers. Many lesbians enjoyed rich social lives in bars, bowling alleys and softball leagues, but overall lesbians claimed less public urban space compared to gay men.[52] The 1950 publication of the classic lesbian novel *Women's Barracks* signaled the beginning of a major boom in paperback lesbian fiction, and by the early 1960s, hundreds of new paperback lesbian fiction titles appeared every year. Some of these books catered to a prurient heterosexual male audience, but others were written by lesbians and enjoyed a large lesbian readership. As disposable commodities, these mass-market paperbacks often used lurid, provocative covers to sell copies, and by today's standards might seem offensive in their tragic depictions of lesbian life. But for many lesbians in the 1950s and 1960s, these books provided essential information for understanding their sexual identities.[53]

As a result of this lesbian fiction boom, bookstores, libraries, and newsstands became important public spaces for many postwar lesbians. A woman from Texas wrote in 1960:

> Bookshops provide a fertile field for striking up conversation with broadminded people interested in a variety of subjects.

Figure 13. *ONE* cover, July 1958.

Talk to everyone you meet instead of standing around like a clam. Sooner or later, by the law of averages, you'll meet someone who will either open that subject or give you an overture to do so, and it is always *comme il faut* to offer the talker a cup of coffee in a nearby restaurant to continue the conversation.

There are so many novels of the gay world around that it's easy to bring the subject up naturally in the guise of literary discussion. The reaction you get will tell you if you are talking to a potential friend or a potential danger.[54]

Bookstores and newsstands that carried a wide selection of lesbian fiction were more likely to carry *ONE*. Despite *ONE*'s emphasis on gay male experiences, *ONE*'s appearance at a familiar newsstand or bookstore could have the same earth-shaking impact for women. One lesbian explained in an oral history how reading her first copy of *ONE* was a major turning point in her life: "God help us! I was home! So I proceeded from there. That was the beginning of my real life."[55] Lesbians faced fewer choices on the newsstands compared to gay men, so *ONE*'s effort to reach lesbians was important to them. By the mid-1960s, *The Ladder* was available in many large cities as well, but never at as many newsstands or bookstores as *ONE*.[56]

Newsstand Encounters

Buying a gay publication such as *ONE*, a physique magazine, or a lesbian novel at a public newsstand could be a daunting experience in the 1950s. "It took courage to purchase one of those little magazines in 1955," wrote a historian of physique magazines. "A man's heart beat faster just walking up to the newsstand."[57] Sweaty palms, an upset stomach, or other nervous symptoms might afflict gay readers as they bought *ONE* for the first (or even tenth) time. Readers reported feeling higher self-awareness, paranoia, and a sense of being watched at the moment they purchased *ONE*. Staring endlessly at the shelves, eyes darting furtively on the lookout for heterosexual friends, coworkers, or family members, was not unusual. Mr. P. from Union City, New Jersey, explained, "While passing a newsstand in Times Square I noticed your Magazine, but was too self-conscious to buy it. After passing the stand two more times and looking to left and to right to make sure there wasn't anyone watching me I quickly walked over to the stand, grabbed *ONE*, handed the man fifty cents and quickly walked away. This was my informal introduction to your magazine." Mr. P.

admitted that he suffered from shyness, spending many nights searching Greenwich Village for gay companions. "Over the years I have become very lonely and disheartened," he wrote.[58] Purchasing *ONE* at a public newsstand required readers to briefly remove the heterosexual masks they usually wore in public—a terrifying prospect for many gay people.

Mindful newsstand operators took steps to alleviate their nervous customers' anxieties in order to earn their loyalty. This was described in a letter from Mr. L. of New York City:

> This evening I glanced at the newsstand as I bought my evening paper and there, clipped among the physique magazines, was the current issue of *ONE*. I returned a few hours later when the homeward crowd had thinned. Without a word, the dealer gave me a folded issue of the late edition. I knew that when I unfolded the newspaper in my room I would find *ONE* inside.
>
> And so it has been ever since, a year ago, I first became aware of the Magazine and with a studied casualness scanned through many magazines. Finally in desperation I picked up two or three and snatched a copy of *ONE*, threw a dollar bill in the direction of the dealer and hurried away.[59]

Experienced newsstand operators could even assist those "coming out" to gay life by pointing out the locations of inconspicuous gay bars, hidden cruising areas, and secret tea-rooms nearby. A veteran Chicago "cornerman" wrote in his 1957 memoir, "A cornerman has to know the town in general pretty well, and his neighborhood in particular, especially when his corner is in a hotel neighborhood like mine. He has to know where this and that business place is; this and that amusement place; and this and that hotel." His memoir suggests that many newsstand operators were experts on neighborhood underworlds, including prostitution, gambling, narcotics, and gay life.[60]

Merely seeing *ONE* on a newsstand could deeply impact an individual's sense of their sexual identity. A Los Angeles "All-American boy" wrote in 1958, "Not too long ago, three years to be exact, I saw a copy of your magazine on a newstand [*sic*] in Times Square, N.Y. and scornfully laughed saying, 'Now they've got a paper for Homos too,' with another friend. Little did I realize at that moment that I'd become 'ONE' myself." A reader from New York City claimed that he had no idea he was homosexual until seeing the magazine on the newsstand.[61] A twenty-one-year-old man from Florida wrote that coming across his first issue of *ONE* "shook me up. I realize now that I am not alone really and that helps."[62] The existence of the magazine told gay people that there were people like them all over the country. For some this was obvious, but for others, deprived of accurate or useful information about homosexuality throughout their lives, it was a revelation.

After being purchased, *ONE* usually disappeared into a briefcase, purse, or newspaper for later reading in private. Some readers collected the magazine, others destroyed their copies immediately after reading in order to avoid accidental discovery by family members or nongay friends. Some readers used *ONE* to promote gay visibility, putting their civil rights impulse into action. Mr. D. from Evanston, Illinois, for example, explained how he read *ONE* while "riding Chicago's [el]. People see the title, but I've never been insulted, sneered at, propositioned, nor humiliated."[63] A Connecticut man confessed, "I've been a coward for years, but I've decided to help *ONE* to be more well known. As yet I can't leave the Magazine in view around the house, but I've started leaving it in view on the seat of my car, etc. It takes courage, but that's something *ONE*'s editors certainly have shown in their work."[64] It is hard to consider these individuals "activists" in any formal sense, but they consciously advanced gay visibility at great risk to their livelihoods. However limited these actions may appear by today's standards, these cumulative efforts established a more daring standard for gay visibility years before gay liberation and the Stonewall uprising of 1969.

ONE's availability was especially important to men and women with little gay life in their local areas, but even in large cities, gay men and lesbians often depended on the magazine to feel connected to other gay people. *ONE*'s unexplained disappearance from a newsstand disconnected them from the gay community they found within *ONE*'s pages. A lesbian from Philadelphia complained after *ONE* disappeared from her local newsstand, "I have been miserable these last few months because I have no one to discuss my problems with."[65] *ONE*'s disappearances also provoked questions about the status of the homophile movement and the safety of local gay life: Is *ONE* finished? Did it run out of money? Did postal authorities shut it down? Was it raided by police? Is the homophile movement finished? Is *ONE* available somewhere else in town? Another town? Should I ask the dealer what happened? Write to ONE, Inc.? Was the owner harassed? Arrested? Does possessing back issues put me at legal risk? Am I on a list? Should I risk subscribing? Is there a crackdown in town? Are the parks safe? The bars? The sidewalks? Is this *the big* crackdown? *ONE*'s disappearances were not merely inconvenient; they could also be signs of danger.

The impact of *ONE*'s disappearances varied by location. In New York City or Los Angeles, copies were always available, even during crackdowns, if one was willing to ask for it. The number and location of newsstands in these cities ensured its availability somewhere. In 1957 in New York City, for example, *ONE* sold briskly at twenty newsstands along the Broadway theatre district, 42nd Street (nine stands alone), in Times Square, and in Greenwich Village.[66] In Los Angeles, *ONE* was almost always available downtown on Broadway, around Pershing Square, and in Hollywood.[67] In other cities such as Cleveland, Denver, Kansas City, Phoenix, or Tulsa, there may have been but one newsstand that carried *ONE* at a particular moment. In these cases, *ONE*'s disappearance was a blow to readers who depended on the magazine for connecting them to a larger gay world.

In some cases, *ONE*'s disappearance was a call to put a civil rights impulse into concrete action. Asking a newsstand operator, "What happened to *ONE*?" led several readers into roles as volunteer agents who conducted personal crusades to ensure *ONE* remained available locally. Readers became outraged when city officials compelled newsstand owners to remove *ONE*. For example, Al wrote in 1960, "New Orleans has classed One as obscene, and is demanding that it be removed from the newsstands, by city ordinance."[68] A few months later, Al wrote back to *ONE* explaining he was "sick and tired of being pushed around" in New Orleans and would legally challenge any antigay police harassment that occurred in his presence.[69] Another reader, bitter that *ONE* was unavailable in Dallas, told *ONE* that he wanted to start a homophile organization in the area, "Instead of sitting around on our butts crying because we are lonely, let's do something about it," he wrote.[70] For many gay men and lesbians, *ONE*'s very existence suggested that gay activism was possible. No matter how quixotic homophile activism seemed in the 1950s, people *could* organize themselves and fight back. Even Frank Kameny, the man who organized the first White House picket lines in 1965 to protest the federal government's antigay policies, was inspired to escalate his activism shortly after *ONE* and the *Mattachine Review* temporarily disappeared from newsstands in Washington, D.C.[71]

When *ONE* disappeared from newsstands, it was usually due to production or distribution problems rather than harassment or censorship. *ONE*'s overworked staff considered the magazine's monthly production miraculous in light of their dearth of reliable writers, artists, and editors, to say nothing of the magazine's complicated distribution methods. The first two years were especially difficult. During 1954, for example, incremental delays forced *ONE*'s editors to skip the August and September issues.[72] Making matters worse, newsstands sometimes rotated their stock in confusing ways. Oscar from Chicago mentioned in his letter to *ONE* that local newsstands "may, one week, display 20 or more [physique magazines], plus other 'unusual' material—and the following week, [the stands] may be limited to a half-dozen magazines such as Life—and the daily papers."[73]

ONE's heavy reliance on volunteer agents during its early years also disrupted consistent delivery to newsstands. Professional distributors improved the magazine's availability, but unpaid debts and unsold copies were points of contention with newsstand owners throughout *ONE*'s existence. ONE, Inc., had a stingy return policy that required distributors to return an entire copy of the magazine for refund credit rather than just the magazine's cover, as was standard industry practice. *ONE* wanted to resell the unsold copies as back issues. This policy irritated many distributors. Some of them refused to comply, creating squabbles over amounts owed and straining distribution in Los Angeles, New York, Detroit, Cleveland, and Philadelphia. When these problems led to *ONE*'s disappearance from a newsstand, readers however often assumed the worst: that ONE, Inc., had been shut down or that local authorities were launching broader gay crackdowns. Roy in Atlanta, for example, sent an alarmed letter to *ONE* when the magazine disappeared from the shelves of his local newsstand, the Dixie News. The newsstand operator refused to tell Roy why he discontinued carrying *ONE*. Ray wondered, was this a crackdown? In fact, according to Dorr Legg, Dixie News had not paid its bills.[74]

Most months from 1953 to 1965, however, *ONE* magazine successfully found its way to thousands of gay and lesbian readers. Despite its frequent disappearances from specific newsstands over the years, *ONE*'s overall stability as an organization and its visible distribution were remarkable achievements that posed a significant challenge to the anti-homosexual sentiments circulating in American culture after World War II. The growing availability of homophile publications, physique magazines, and lesbian fiction during the 1950s encouraged further strides toward open visibility on the part of gay men and lesbians.

3

Imagining a Gay World
The American Homophile Movement in Global Perspective

*O*NE received letters from all over the world. Most of its non-U.S. correspondence came from Canada and Western Europe, but a small number of letters trickled in from Central and South America, Africa, the Middle East, India, Southeast Asia, Japan, and Australia.[1] Newsstands and bookstores in Amsterdam, Copenhagen, Hamburg, Vienna, Buenos Aires, and Mexico City sold *ONE*.[2]

ONE highlighted its international readership in February 1960 by publishing a sample of letters from several continents. A reader in Denmark recommended the "new Danish magazine *Eos* . . . one of the best in the field," and a French reader similarly recommended a "new French magazine *Juventus* . . . it is very superior." A reader in Australia complained that Australian customs officials had seized his August 1959 issue of *ONE*; he instructed *ONE*, however, to "keep sending my copies in the usual way." Mr. S. from Cali, Colombia, was relieved to tell *ONE* that he had at last received his order from ONE's book service—the book had been misplaced in his local Post Office for weeks while he worried that it had been seized by customs. A letter from Tokyo explained that homosexuality was not stigmatized in Japanese culture, and the correspondent recommended "the only exclusively gay magazine in Japan. It has the title of *Adonis*, is entirely in Japanese, on slick paper, and is a little thicker than ONE." A reader from Singapore stated he liked *ONE* better than European homophile magazines, but he wished *ONE* would offer pen-pal service "as I have been longing to contact your members and away from European type of gay bars [to] discuss our daily problems."[3]

The international context is critical for understanding the character of the U.S. homophile movement. American historians sometimes write about the rise of U.S. gay and lesbian politics as though the rest of the world did not exist.[4] These letters, however, demonstrate a desire among homosexuals around the world to communicate with each other and share experiences. Both gay oppression and gay civil rights had important international dimensions in the 1950s. Persecution of homosexuals occurred in many parts of the world, but *state-driven* persecution (as opposed to religious or family-driven persecution) was largely a phenomenon of English-speaking countries, with the exception of Germany. One might expect the homophile movement to develop accordingly; however, aside from the United States, the homophile movement was most visible and active in European countries where homosexuality was already legal, such as the Netherlands, France, Denmark, Sweden, and Belgium. The United States (and the United Kingdom to a lesser extent) occupied a point of overlap between two distinct global geographies: one of a particular style of government-driven antigay persecution, the other a particular style of collective, organized resistance represented by homophile organizations. In this way, the American movement was distinctive. But in other ways, gay persecution and activism in the United States were parts of larger global trends.

ONE's editors were deeply curious about homosexuality elsewhere in the world. Their access to information about homosexuality in non-European countries was limited, but they knew more than most Americans because of their library, subject files, and, importantly, letters from readers who lived or traveled in other countries. The editors frequently published these letters along with essays and short stories with international themes. Sometimes this material was flagrantly "Orientalist" in the way it portrayed non–Euro-Americans as exotic, mysterious, decadent, and primitive, but other homophile writers emphasized the possibility that national, political, religious, and racial divisions could be transcended through the universally shared experience of homosexual desire.

This chapter seeks to reconstruct how *ONE's* editors and readers comprehended the gay world outside of the United States. To *ONE's* editors, an awareness of homosexuality's global dimensions fueled the civil rights impulse by normalizing homosexuality, making it seem common and mundane rather than aberrant and threatening. They could point to other countries where homosexuality was legal and say, "if there, why not here?" Looking beyond U.S. borders, gay acceptance—or at least an end to prohibitions against homosexuality—seemed more possible. It was also reassuring to American homophiles to know that they were not the only people on the planet engaged in the controversial cause of gay rights. Knowing they had allies around the world bolstered their confidence in ways that American scholars have largely ignored.

English-Speaking Panic

When the U.S. government began removing gay people from government jobs in earnest in 1950, the government pressured at least two of its English-speaking allies, Canada and the United Kingdom, to follow its lead and conduct their own antigay purges. Within weeks, Canada commenced a U.S.-style government crackdown against homosexuals, and by the late 1960s, the Canadian Royal Mounted Police had compiled a list of more than 9,000 known homosexuals—a project similar to the FBI's Sex Deviate Program.[5] *ONE* subscribers in Canada frequently complained that Canadian postal authorities seized their copies of the magazine. Things got worse in 1958 when Canadian postal authorities cracked down on *ONE*'s entry into the country following a less-than-flattering story about *ONE* published in the sleazy Canadian tabloid *Justice Weekly*.[6] During this crackdown, for example, a Canadian bookseller told *ONE* that back issues he had planned to sell at his store had been blocked at the border, so he had to send the magazines to a friend in Seattle while he figured out a way to smuggle them into Canada.[7] Canadian homosexuals thus could easily relate to the situation in the United States, although no Canadian homophile organizations existed until the mid-1960s.

British correspondents frequently complained to *ONE* that the United Kingdom's official intolerance of gay people rivaled that of the United States.[8] As with Canada, U.S. officials pressured the U.K. to adopt a zero-tolerance attitude toward gay government employees.[9] The hysteria peaked in the mid-1950s when London police launched a massive crackdown against gay bars and cruising areas throughout the city. At the heart of the British homosexual panic was a well-publicized scandal known as the Lord Montagu affair, involving the wealthy Lord Edward Montagu, Montagu's cousin, two Royal Air Force men, and journalist Peter Wildeblood. According to the British press, the men had enjoyed a wild gay party together at Montagu's estate. During the investigation, the two Royal Air Force men escaped punishment by identifying the other three men involved, who were subsequently imprisoned for homosexual offenses. Wildeblood, incarcerated for eighteen months, emerged as Britain's first prominent gay activist in the wake of the scandal. He wrote two books in the 1950s about his experiences, one on the Montagu case (*Against the Law*, which sold in excess of 100,000 copies) and a more general book on homosexuality (*A Way of Life*).[10] Wildeblood noted his growing reputation as a gay activist in a 1956 letter to *ONE*. "One rather interesting thing is the way I've been invited to lecture by several organizations here—including an undergraduate society at Oxford which I addressed last week. The reception was extraordinarily cordial; prolonged applause and a very full account of my speech (attacking the present laws) in the local press."[11] In another letter he wrote, "I don't think anyone has appeared on a public platform as a homosexual before, and the attitude of the audience is remarkably sympathetic, with one or two exceptions, of course!"[12] The Montagu case—an embarrassment to the British government—led to reconsideration of the U.K.'s laws against homosexuality and in 1957, a Parliamentary committee known as the Wolfenden Committee recommended that homosexuality be decriminalized. The following year, the first British homophile organization formed: The Homosexual Law Reform Society. This group worked to carry out Wolfenden Committee recommendations and decriminalize homosexuality, which eventually occurred in 1967.[13] The Homosexual Law Reform Society had a narrow focus on legal reform and avoided many of the broader cultural approaches of the U.S. and other European homophile organizations.[14]

A negative tone pervaded *ONE* correspondence from other English-speaking countries as well. Australia underwent a gay panic in the 1950s as police authorities declared that "homosexuality was the greatest danger facing Australia."[15] Dorr Legg explained to a *ONE* reader in 1963, "The information we have regarding social attitudes in Australia is extremely negative. We know of persons there who have been arrested for having ONE magazine in their possession; others who have been prevented from receiving it or any other mail on the same topic. Travelers tell us it is a very rigid and conventional society in such regards although here and there in their bigger cities (there are but two or three) a certain amount of gay life does manage to keep going somehow—not an encouraging picture it would seem."[16] In the mid-1960s, Australian *ONE* subscribers explained that "there are no clubs and no magazines at all," and "Here in Australia the gay crowd is unorganized[,] there [are] no lawyers who are gay to defend when they are in trouble."[17] A Daughters of Bilitis chapter emerged in 1969 as the nation's first gay rights organization, but homosexuality remained criminal in all of Australia well into the 1980s, long after the United Kingdom and most of the United States had decriminalized it.[18] Things were bleak in New Zealand as well. A reader reported that the "personal position of an individual homosexual in New Zealand is extremely precarious. A small, almost a family, society keeps a far too watchful eye on any deviants from accepted positions."[19]

Homosexuality's criminal status also extended to South Africa; according to a *ONE* subscriber, "a Homosexual goes about as a fugitive" in South Africa.[20]

These downbeat letters from English-speaking countries were a stark contrast to letters from continental Western Europe. Homosexuality was legal throughout Western Europe, except in West Germany, the United Kingdom, and Norway. Many Western European countries base their laws on the Napoleonic Code, which has no prohibition against homosexuality among consenting adults. In Norway, antihomosexual laws were generally not enforced, but the existence of the laws had "the effect of intimidating many homosexuals . . . and of upholding people's prejudices against us," according to a homophile newsletter.[21] American and European homophiles agreed that continental Europe, even where homosexuality was illegal, was more tolerant toward gay people than the United Kingdom or the United States. A traveler from Dallas described Northern Europe in glowing terms to *ONE* in 1962: "In Holland, Sweden, Denmark, and Norway, there is freedom. Freedom like no where else in the world."[22] A British man was equally impressed by Southern Europe, "And all the time, in every place, I had no difficulty in contacting 'our' people and you know we feel alike, love as fervently wherever we meet and, seemingly have the same sorrows; that of family misunderstanding, awkwardness among friends and all the rest: but, be it said now among the Italian and the Greeks there is not the same hostility as is to be found in the English speaking world. It must have something to do with the 'terrible legacy' of the Cromwellian Puritanical Era, what think you?"[23] To Europeans, the American anticommunist scare was partly to explain for the difference in social climate; as a Dutch homophile activist commented in 1953, "in Holland there are no McCarthys, who see in every homophile a communist."[24]

The European perception of American intolerance is captured in a review of the popular Broadway play *Tea and Sympathy*, which appeared in the Swiss homophile magazine *Der Kreis*. In the play, a young prep school student named Tom Lee is harassed by his classmates because of his effeminate manner and suspicions that he is homosexual. The play is an indictment against McCarthyism by depicting Tom in a sympathetic manner; however, the play suggests that Tom deserves sympathy only because he is being *falsely* accused of homosexuality.[25] This premise outraged the European reviewer: "There is not one sentence which would speak in favour of the boy if he had really turned out to have homosexual tendencies . . . the audience is never for a moment left in doubt that eventually he will come through with a clean breast and be proved innocent of that 'unspeakable' vice." To the reviewer, *Tea and Sympathy* epitomized broader American intolerance, "The play represents a most severe judgment of homosexuality in general, and it is sad to realize how utterly ignorant people in the States are of this complicated problem. They don't seem to have an idea that to pass judgment in such a way is a sign of very low intelligence as well as of great intolerance. As long as such prejudices are predominant in the United States no change of the laws dealing with homosexuality can be expected."[26] To this writer, the United States was hopelessly retrograde in its repressive attitudes toward gay people. Clearly, however, the United States was not the only country struggling with intolerance, as the McCarthy-style political persecution of homosexuals was a fixture of English-speaking countries throughout the world. And even in European countries where homosexuality was legal, various forms of bigotry and discrimination still existed.

A Transatlantic Homophile Movement

European homophile organizations after World War II existed largely to combat ostracism and prejudice from families, churches, and communities. These organizations also frequently worked to equalize the age of consent for heterosexual and homosexual behavior. The origins of gay rights activism in Europe extend back to German Karl Ulrichs's influential mid-nineteenth century writings about "Urnings." By the early twentieth century, Magnus Hirschfeld, founder of the Scientific Humanitarian Committee and the Institute for Sexual Science, led a robust, highly visible movement to overturn Paragraph 175, the German law banning homosexuality. Hirschfeld was well-known throughout Europe and a minor celebrity, having appeared alongside German movie star Conrad Veidt (himself gay) in the 1919 feature film about homosexual blackmail, *Anders Als Die Anderen* [*Different from the Others*]. A lively gay press emerged in Europe in the early twentieth century, but in the 1930s, Nazism immediately stopped the European homophile movement. German Nazis burned Hirschfeld's Institute for Sexual Science, including its extensive library, to the ground in 1933, obliterating decades of sexuality research. Hirschfeld, who fled Germany in 1932, witnessed the destruction of his life's work while watching a newsreel in a Paris movie theater.[27]

The only European homophile organization to survive the Nazi purge was Switzerland-based Der Kreis [The Circle], founded in 1932. After World War II, at least a dozen European homophile organizations emerged throughout Northern Europe during the late 1940s and early 1950s. By 1956 homophile organizations existed in Belgium, Denmark, France, West Germany, the Netherlands, Norway, Sweden, Switzerland,

and Italy.[28] Clearly, American organizations such as the Mattachine Society and ONE, Inc., were not creating a new movement, but rather joining a movement already in progress. Paul, a Parisian, commented in 1953 that he was glad that Americans had *"at last"* formed gay organizations.[29]

In addition to battling against gay prejudice and discrimination, the European homophile organizations also served as social clubs—something the American homophiles avoided because of homosexuality's illegal status. Some American homophile leaders complained that the European organizations spent too much energy on social functions and parties, resulting in "a lack of philosophic analysis and vagueness in direction."[30] Whereas *ONE* and Mattachine operated in spartan, dingy offices, for example, Netherlands-based COC (Cultuur-en Ontspannings Centrum) offices included a bar and a dance floor large enough to accommodate hundreds of "club members" who attended regular events and parties.[31] Der Kreis also had a busy social calendar, including "Dancing every other Wednesday, discussions, lectures (both by club members and outsiders), musical evenings, lantern-slide entertainment, floor shows and plays at the big meetings."[32] Der Kreis organized a massive annual party called Herbstfest: "It always takes place on the first weekend in October," according to Der Kreis leader Karl Meier (who used the pseudonym Rolf). "It covers a Saturday night (until 5:00 A.M.) and . . . Sunday from 3:00 P.M. until midnight. There is usually a play . . . furthermore there is around midnight a big floor show, as you call it (though actually it takes place on a stage) and, naturally, as much dancing as you want to, with two bands on two floors of the house."[33] American homophiles, fearing police raids, avoided such lavish entertainment.

The publications of these organizations reflected the more pronounced social character of the European homophile movement. None of the American homophile magazines (*ONE*, *The Mattachine Review*, and *The Ladder*) offered pen-pal listings, travel guides, or physique style photography—editors feared backlash from police or postal authorities. European homophile magazines, in contrast, offered all of this material. For the traveler eager to find gay clubs, bars, hotels, or theaters around the world, there was the German magazine *Der Ring* [The Ring]. Its articles were in German, but its travel guides worked in any language. For pen-pal correspondence, the Danish magazine *Eos* [The Others] featured up to seventy-five (male only) pen-pal notices in each issue, nearly one-third in English, from most parts of the world. *Der Weg* [The Way], based in West Germany, also had about fifty or sixty pen-pal listings in each issue. For those seeking nonpornographic nude photos of men, the Danish magazine *Vennen* [The Friend] published full-frontal photographs along with the social commentary of its articles. The German *Der Freund*

[The Friend] also published photos of male nudity. *Der Kreis* [The Circle] with a circulation around 1,000, was multilingual (French, German, and English) and published travel listings, pen-pals requests, and nude photos.[34]

The ability to publish these features reflected the more tolerant legal climate in Europe toward homosexuals—even in West Germany, where homosexuality was illegal like in the United States. Importantly, however, these publications were not as readily available to the general public as the American publications, especially *ONE*. They were generally not available on public newsstands. To receive the magazines, a person had to join a club and pay fees in addition to the magazine subscription. Thus, the bolder content of these magazines was tempered by their more limited and less visible distribution compared to the American organizations, and, therefore, the circulation for most of these magazines was in the hundreds .rather than the thousands. As the European homophiles saw it, maintaining a low profile fostered good relations with the authorities that tolerated them.[35]

Indeed, most of these organizations enjoyed good relations with their respective national authorities. Denmark-based *Vennen* was the only major European homophile organization subjected to a large-scale government crackdown. As a letter from a Scottish homophile activist described it, the 1955 crackdown resulted from distributing nude photos of models younger than age eighteen:

> I warned them of the extreme danger of sending such photos to Britain in the present state of persecution in regard to everything homosexual. But, it seems, they ignored my warnings. [Jorgen] Tews wrote when I was in Hamburg last May to tell me that the premises had been raided in 29th March last and that everything had been seized. He seemed to think he, himself, was in no danger, but I am sorry to tell you he got seven months imprisonment last April for pornographic offences also for corrupting minors. And I gather a whole lot of other men have been sentenced to imprisonment for the same offences. I was told that over 800 men had been interviewed by the police in Copenhagen alone![36]

Other European homophile organizations condemned *Vennen*'s reckless behavior. An *Eos* editor told *ONE*, "Vennen is the 'enfant terrible' of the homophile press, and all the European magazines without exception have turned them their backs."[37] The crackdown against *Vennen* contrasted with the more respectable reputation of *Der Kreis*, as Rolf explained to *ONE*, "THE CIRCLE has excellent relations with the Zurich police. Every issue of the monthly as well as every print of the Picture Service is sent to the 'Sittenpolizei' (appro. The vice-squad of the U.S. police) and we have had no complaints from them in the whole course of our existence. The monthly is also listed at the Staatsbibliothek Bern [State Library, Berne]."[38] While groups such as Der Kreis enjoyed significant longevity, some European groups came and went quickly. A letter from a German homophile activist hinted at the chaos of the postwar homophile movement in West Germany, where homosexuality was still illegal: *Hellas* and *Die Gefährten* [The Fellows] had both folded in 1954, *Die Insel* had changed its name to *Der Weg*, and *Dein Freund* had changed its name to *Humanitas*. The latter, *Humanitas*, had emerged as the most important German magazine, and the group that published it, Gesellschaft für Menschenrechte was "the German homophile organization" according to the correspondent.[39] As in the United States, there was a shared sense of mission as well as a competitive rivalry among the European organizations that could sometimes lead to bickering, factional disputes, and messy internal politics.

Like the American homophile movement, the European movement was male dominated. Few women participated in these organizations. The most prominent was probably Anna Volk (known as Mammina), who edited Der Kreis's publications from 1932 to 1942.[40] The only European lesbian organization known to have existed during these years was the Copenhagen-based Alle for EEN Klubben (All for ONE Club), which operated from 1954 to 1957.[41] The Daughters of Bilitis was thus the first lesbian rights organization to sustain itself for longer than a few years, making them pioneers on a worldwide rather than merely national scale.

Perhaps the most ambitious European homophile organization was the Netherlands-based International Committee for Sexual Equality (ICSE), which sought to coordinate homophile organizations and activists worldwide by hosting annual homophile conferences in Europe and publishing a multilingual newsletter. Formed in May 1951, ICSE held its first international homophile conference the same year in Amsterdam. In subsequent years, conferences were held in Frankfurt, Paris, and Brussels. Attendance at each conference ranged from 100 to 500, comparable to a Mattachine convention or ONE Midwinter Meeting. Representatives from many countries participated at ICSE conferences in the early 1950s, including Australia, Austria, Belgium, Denmark, France, the Netherlands, Italy, New Zealand, Norway, Portugal, Spain, Sweden, Switzerland, Syria, the United Kingdom, the United States, and West Germany.[42] Coordinating an agenda among so many countries was a major challenge, according to the group's founder, "The distribution of members and affiliated organizations, over some 30 countries all over the world, often prevent the work from being run smoothly, and so does the constant lack of funds. Our main objectives: coordinating and stimulating studies in the phenomena of male and female homophily, as well as furthering the international exchange of the results of these studies, are constantly striven at, and up to the present date, with increasing success."[43] The ICSE was the only European gay rights organization with a truly international orientation. Ultimately, however, the challenges in coordinating such an organization proved too daunting for its founders and sparse resources, and it folded in the early 1960s.[44]

The homophile movement was thus a complicated interconnected network of organizations spread over two continents. American and European homophiles routinely wrote in each other's publications, attended homophile conferences together, and, when they could afford it (which was not often), visited each other. In 1958, Der Kreis leader Rolf, for example, spent eight days in Los Angeles. He guest lectured at the ONE Institute, attended parties hosted by ONE volunteers, lodged with a ONE staffer, and enjoyed "a private showing of the famous [Kenneth Anger avant-garde film] Fireworks at the home of another Corporation member."[45] After returning home he told ONE, "I cannot tell you how much I have enjoyed meeting you all and being able to stay with you. . . . My thoughts are still very much with you."[46] Several years later in 1964, ONE, Inc., organized the first official American "gay tour" of Europe, with stops at the headquarters of several major European homophile organizations. This time, Rolf hosted ONE volunteers, showing them a famous local church and driving them around the Swiss Alps.[47] Such instances of travel bolstered the sense of shared vision of the American and European homophiles, despite their differences.

Whereas the American homophiles felt connected to the European movement, they knew very little about the existence of gay organizations or publications elsewhere in the world. Japan had something similar to the homophile press—after World War II, there was a boom in Japan's "perverse press," which focused on a range of nonprocreative sexualities such as transvestitism, S/M, and homosexuality. Like ONE, this perverse press offered an affirmative perspective on same-sex behavior and frequently "associated male homosexuality . . . with periods of high cultural attainment, such as classical Greece, the medieval Arab world, Renaissance Italy, and Genroku Japan."[48] In the mid-1950s, the gay rights organization Fuzoku Kagaku Kenkyukai (FKK) emerged with a motto very similar to ONE: "Homosexuals have confidence! You are not perverts!"[49] The most visible gay publication in Japan was the aforementioned Adonis, published from 1952 to 1962. Like European homophile magazines,

Adonis offered erotic male photography as well as listings for pen pals and gay bars. Unlike the European and American magazines, however, there was little civil rights impulse in *Adonis*. Not only was homosexuality legal in Japan, but Japan's Buddhist and Shinto religious traditions were considerably less hostile to homosexuality compared to the Catholic and Protestant churches in the United States and Europe. Homosexuality was only a problem in Japan if it disrupted marriage plans. Instead of appealing to Japanese gay men's sense of justice and self-esteem, *Adonis* offered a style of erotic writing that would not become legally permissible in the United States until the late 1960s and 1970s.[50]

Outside of Japan, American homophiles knew very little about the status of homosexuality in the rest of Asia except for occasional travel reports or letters. Some Asian correspondents complained about homosexual repression in their countries, some described conspiracies of silence, and others stated that homosexuality was widely accepted. A letter from Ceylon (Sri Lanka), for example, claimed, "To our knowledge almost 70% of Ceylonese are homosexuals."[51] This incredibly high number suggests that the Ceylonese probably had a looser interpretation of what constituted a "homosexual," but such claims of mass acceptance astonished and encouraged the American homophiles in their quest for American acceptance of homosexuality.

In 1956 *ONE* received a letter from an Italian homophile activist who claimed to have been involved with an Indonesian-based gay rights organization called the Han Temple Organization, also known as the Homosexual World Organization (HWO). The letter is somewhat cryptic, but suggests that a widespread alliance of Asian gay rights organizations existed to promote worldwide acceptance of homosexuality.[52] This same correspondent (a count and New Age guru named Bernardino del Boca) seems to have sent a similar letter, years earlier, to Robert Lindner, author of best-selling books *Rebel without a Cause* and *Must You Conform?* Lindner became fascinated by HWO, and wrote about it in *Must You Conform?*, but after Lindner's death in 1956, nothing further has been written about it in the English language. According to del Boca, HWO was a secret organization organized on "an island in Indonesia," which had "created a Centre on the island, for all homosexuals that do not like to live among heterosexual people." The HWO leadership included Europeans and Asians, suggesting that this may have been the first gay rights organization in history (predating the Netherlands' ICSE) with a genuinely global orientation. "The President of this Movement is a Chinese doctor (now a Buddhist Priest). He is helped by 15 people," including two European medical doctors, two English engineers, "Indonesian Princes," and "a well-known Dutch writer." The HWO was "in touch with all the Asiatic (and centuries-old) organizations of homosexuals like the Buddha-Shakti Sect of Siam, the High Rooms of Macao, the Moon Flower Rooms of China, the Sons of Mauna Loa of Hawaii, etc."[53] In 1954 Lindner explained in a public lecture that the Han Temple Organization had been created in the 1930s, broke up during World War II, and was then revived after the war under the name Homosexual World Organization.[54] Lindner seemed convinced the organization was real, and del Boca's stationary used the letterhead "Han Temple Organisation," suggesting this organization actually existed. Assuming del Boca's descriptions were accurate, the existence of this organization points to much larger global gay civil rights movement in the mid-twentieth century (and perhaps earlier) than Western scholars have ever imagined.

The Keval

ONE, Inc.'s interest in the international status of homosexuality was demonstrated throughout its history. In 1954, for example, several activists (including Jim Kepner) spent two weeks trying to establish a chapter of ONE, Inc., in Mexico City. Despite a vibrant yet secretive gay subculture in the city, they got "an embarrassed, negative reaction" and abandoned their efforts.[55] Their curiosity about the rest of the world was best demonstrated in the few books published by the fledgling ONE Press over the years. For example, the book *Homosexuals Today 1956* devotes nearly one-third of its pages to international homophile activism. To this day, it remains the most complete English-language record of the post–World War II European homophile movement. An even broader assessment of the global dimensions of homosexual behavior, however, was offered in ONE Press's *The Keval and Other Gay Adventures*, written by frequent *ONE* contributor Harry Otis.[56] *The Keval* was a book of short stories based on Otis's research and travels around the world. It blended fact and fiction, and ultimately was just one man's—an American's—concept of how homosexuality was conceptualized and practiced around the world. Yet *The Keval* is an important source for understanding how American homophiles imagined homosexuality to exist outside of the so-called First World of the United States and Western Europe during the 1950s. Harry Otis's stories on homosexuality in faraway places, compiled in *The Keval* and published regularly in *ONE* magazine, were rare glimpses of gay life outside of North America and Europe for *ONE*'s readers who were unable to travel so extensively themselves. Otis's writings thus influenced thousands of gay American's attitudes about the global dimensions of homosexuality.

Harry Otis, *The Keval's* author, was born in the Ozarks and raised in Colorado. He lived an adventurous life. As a young man, he worked as a dancer in Vaudeville, nightclubs, and Broadway musicals, and later as a choreographer. While living in Los Angeles in the 1920s, Otis worked as a dancer in a speakeasy window, sometimes in Asian drag. Later in life he directed plays for the blind and plays for prisoners. He worked extensively with developmentally disabled children and according to the back cover of *The Keval* he "developed a theurapeutic [*sic*] system of rhythms which is used in many institutes today." His extensive world travel inspired and informed *The Keval*.[57]

As a book written by a "Westerner" dealing primarily with "Eastern" peoples, *The Keval* falls within the sphere of "Orientalist" literature as described by Edward Said and postcolonial scholars. According to Said, Orientalist literature stereotypes all "Eastern" peoples as mysterious, exotic, irrational, superstitious, and sexually uninhibited—in short, inferior and in dire need of superior Western guidance through colonial occupation.[58] Much homophile writing on non-Western peoples emphasizes their primitive simplicity, and indeed, *The Keval* exhibits some Orientalist tendencies.[59] For example, Otis occasionally portrayed non-Western environments as homosexual paradises, places of uninhibited sexual decadence where mysterious and bizarre homoerotic rituals built to explosive climaxes to the amazement of American tourists and other outsiders. In a story set in Singapore, for example, a firewalking ceremony builds to a pulsating climax after young men dance in the nude. A similar ritual occurs in a story set in Bali. Otis conveyed sexual decadence through detailed descriptions of lavish homoerotic royal courts, such as a story set in Ottoman Turkey in which two young men visit the royal court and are surprised to see eunuchs with "more jewels than any concubine in the harem," "expensive clothes," and hair dyed scarlet, sitting on "ivory inlay teakwood thrones."[60] A story set in Moghal India, around 1500 also describes a lavish homoerotic court, in which the emperor's "handsome personal slaves wore only jeweled loin cloths. . . ."[61] Such scenes give the impression of the non-Western world as an alluring sexual paradise, a common fantasy in Orientalist writing.

While Otis replicates some of the Orientalist tendencies common during these years, ultimately, however, *The Keval* subverts them by emphasizing the universality of homosexual desire and diversity of global sexual practices. Despite the occasional Orientalist "homosexual paradise" motif, most of the book emphasizes the common travails facing people who are attracted to the same sex throughout the world. Many of Otis's non-Western characters worry about their family discovering their true sexual desires, and some face punishment and ostracism when the discovery is made. In a story set in Ancient India, for example, a handsome young member of a prominent family takes up an ascetic lifestyle after his father discovers that the son is having an affair with a local elephant trainer. The father murders the elephant trainer, and the son takes up asceticism to "free himself from wanting another friend like the trainer."[62] In other stories, characters must use deceptions and wear heterosexual masks. For Otis, the social bond of same-sex desire transcended racial stereotypes, national borders, and deeply entrenched notions of East and West. Homosexuality put non-Western characters into the realm of the known, even the familiar, not the mysterious, unknown, or "other." Otis's emphasis on the worldwide camaraderie of homosexuals implicitly challenged the notion that the globe could be casually divided into simple divisions of First World or Third World, East or West.

Otis occasionally used language and descriptions invoking stereotypes, but overall his non-Western characters were not reduced to stereotypes. Otis avoided portraying them as one dimensional or "simple;" they are complex human beings living complex lives. The most recurring stereotype in the book, in fact, is that of the Ugly American: usually tourists, complaining loudly about local customs to the annoyance of locals and more enlightened tourists. In a story set in post–World War II Tokyo, for example, a blond American woman lights a cigarette on Japanese palace grounds. She responds rudely when a palace guard asks her to not smoke. "The blond stiffened. 'What nonsense!' she sneered. 'On our White House lawn we do as we wish. Kids even roll eggs.' "[63] In the story set in Bali, a sexually repressed American male tourist lashes out at a hotel desk clerk for what he considers to be inappropriate displays of public affection in the hotel lobby between two men. " 'If they did such disgusting things in the States, they'd be ridiculed,' he fumed. . . . 'You'd know right away what they were. Decent people wouldn't have anything to do with them.' "[64] The frequent inclusion of these overbearing, buffoonish characters serves to question Western superiority and the legitimacy of colonization. The non–Ugly American tourists, in contrast, exhibit an appreciation for the complex diversity of the world and are genuinely curious about other cultures.

Orientalist writing typically reinforced the broader European mission of conquest, imperialism, and colonialism. As scholars have noted, homosexuality loomed large in the colonial experience. Foreign Service workers had reputations for loose sexuality in general and homosexuality in particular. Government workers who were discovered to be gay were routinely shuffled off to colonies to avoid scandals. Many gay employees seeking tolerance requested transfers to colonial settings.[65] The disproportionately male colonial work environment facilitated situational homosexuality, as described in a 1964 letter to *ONE* from Mombasa, Kenya. Albert, a young man, wrote that "most all the young European men who come here to work are single, and after being here for several years find themselves caught in a net, as there are hardly any white women here to go with. Therefore they resort to homosexual activity."[66] Ironically, many European colonizers (especially the British) sought to eradicate homosexual behaviors from the people they were colonizing. In such situations, homosexuality usually went underground and became invisible to colonial administrators. Orientalist writing usually ignored the homosexuality of the European colonizers, whereas homosexuality among colonized persons was evidence of their inferiority.

In contrast to Orientalism's sympathy for colonialism, Otis's stories have a decidedly anticolonial bent. A story set in British India, "Druga's Solution," for example, portrays British viceroys as sexually repressed hypocrites, while the colonized subjects appear adaptive, resilient, and dignified. The story dramatized the ways that colonized subjects kept alive indigenous traditions by removing them from the sight of colonial authorities. In the story, a Raja's many wives had to be hidden because "their Excellencies" disapproved of polygamy. A single wife is chosen to entertain the viceroys; she carefully explains to the Vicerene that wives in polygamous relationships often "prefer to be with women."[67] The Vicerene fails to grasp the lesbian implications of the statement before herself becoming smitten with another of the Raja's wives. Otis's critique of colonialism is shown by portraying the Vicerene as a self-righteous fool deluded by her own sense of self-importance. A story set in Jerusalem, "Stars over Jordan," criticized colonialism more directly. An American traveler meets a young Palestinian man whose family has been recently displaced by British policies relating to the creation of Israel. The family lives in a small, spare dwelling, and the father lacks employment after being forced to abandon a profitable fabric business. "They were allowed to take only what they could carry on their backs and, because the British forbad the men to carry arms to protect themselves, thousands of Arabs died, his father and brother included."[68] Homosexuality barely figures into the story; its sole purpose is to sympathize with an Arab family that has been displaced by colonial forces.

Sexual tourism is a recurring theme in *The Keval*. Many colonies gained independence in the years following World War II, yet the rise of sexual tourism ensured that many Europeans and Americans would continue to imagine former colonies as places of uninhibited sexuality.[69] In one story, for example, a married couple, Horace and Bertha Dobbs, visit Bangkok, Thailand. Bertha was a classic Ugly American, loudly complaining, " 'It's outrageous the way those boys run around naked,' Bertha snapped between her loose dentures. 'But what can you expect when their fathers go around in those sleazy outfits that don't hide anything. Believe me, in Kansas they wouldn't get away with it.' "[70] Horace, in contrast, has no complaints about the nudity—in fact, we learn that Horace enjoys long business trips with his male secretary, Nick. When checking into the hotel in Bangkok, the desk clerk told him, " 'Should Mr. Dobbs ever desire a boy or a girl, a room will be available.' Horace thanked him and wondered how long it would be before Bertha got her usual dysentery."[71] Indeed, Bertha's dysentery soon arrives and Horace ventures downstairs to talk to the desk clerk. While Otis depicts sexual tourism in many de-colonized parts of the world, he ignores the concurrent trend of newly emergent anticolonial and nationalist leaders condemning homosexuality as something evil brought into their cultures by European colonists. Such "reverse Orientalism" (or "Occidentalism")—the idea that *Western* cultures are sexually decadent, unrestrained, and pose a threat to formerly colonized peoples—has led to some of the world's most homophobic regimes in recent history.[72]

The Keval forms an interesting dialogue with letters to *ONE* about homosexuality around the world. Both the letters and book provide context for one another. For example, if we pool all the letters about Japan, two dimensions of postwar Japanese gay life come to light. The first dimension was a gay world deeply connected with the American occupation, a world dominated by American military servicemen and American style gay bars. The second dimension was a more traditional Japanese attitude that viewed homosexuality as a benign curiosity rather than a major source of personal or political identity. A man who had just returned from Tokyo, for example, told *ONE* that he "met with intelligent Japanese homosexuals who told me that the percentage is quite large, that the Japanese take a sensible attitude, and, for the most part, . . . stay away from European type of gay bars, having their own quiet gathering places everywhere, including Tokyo, where there are perhaps close to 70 or 80 tea-houses (not to be confused) where they meet, discuss and/or make arrangements in their own quiet way."[73] Collectively, these letters reflect both the proliferation of the distinct Western concept of homosexual identity around the globe (a proliferation that largely followed the paths of colonialism), as well as the persistence of traditional indigenous models of sexuality in the face of Western hegemony.

Otis's story set in Tokyo highlights tension between these two dimensions of Japanese gay life. In the story, a jaded gay American traveler, Craig, who had lost a lover in a car accident six years earlier, meets a young Japanese man, Masarus, at a religious shrine during a New Year's Eve celebration. Masarus explains that he fell in love with Chester, an

American soldier, but Chester had returned to the United States and married a woman, ending their relationship. Craig and Masarus, grieving over their losses, fall in love at the shrine. Craig soon learns that, despite the greater tolerance of homosexuals in Japanese society, Masarus's family has rejected him. "Craig bit his lip. Listening to the youth was like looking at himself in the mirror and he wondered if their families were similar in other respects."[74] Homosexuality was not a problem as long as gay Japanese men fulfilled their family obligations and married women.[75] The Western model—which Masarus would have been exposed to through his previous lover—allowed the possibility of same-sex couples forming long-term partnerships with each other. This caused many gay men to question whether they could actually marry a woman and raise a family in good faith. Masarus is thus caught between competing notions of homosexuality at play in postwar Japan—by adopting a Western view of homosexuality and by desiring a long-term lover, he no longer fit into the more traditional Japanese model.

A 1958 letter to *ONE* from a young man in Bombay, Rajiv, captures the same tension. Rajiv adopted a Western concept of homosexual identity while being educated in London; back home in India, however, he felt isolated, lonely, and unable to connect with the Indian homosexual practices that had gone underground during British occupation. He wrote:

> Quite apart from the law, which is as harsh in this country as it exists in yours or the United Kingdom, the tragedy here is not only the appallingly strong social and religious prejudice, but an almost complete lack of awareness of the very existence of the problem. In modern, large and cosmopolitan cities like Bombay, and amongst families and social groups of Indo-Western and Western educational standards, the mere reference to homosexuality—let alone an academic discussion of it—is strictly taboo. There is no reasonably decent place where one can remove this stifling mask; though I'm quite certain that thousands of unknowns like me, in this very city, must be labouring for breath as I do—some too zealous in guarding their "abominable" secret; others still making desperate attempts towards self-acceptance and the conflicts within.[76]

Clearly India was no homosexual paradise for this young man. Expecting a Western version of gay life in India, he complained that "there are no gay coffee bars or clubs or meeting places where one could shed the veneer" in India.[77] Homosexuality had been practiced discretely among Indian elites for centuries but British rule instilled an "aggressive

Puritanism" among modern Indians.[78] Despite the end of colonial rule in India a decade earlier, Rajiv could not connect with the older patterns of homosexuality. The colonized patterns lingered.

The Keval has three stories about India. None of them address Rajiv's specific frustrations, but they do reflect how dramatically the status of homosexuality changed over the centuries in India. One story, based on an actual memoir written by the first Moghal emperor around 1500, describes homosexual love in the Moghal court as common and unproblematic. The emperor, his son, and other members of the court fall in love with other men. A second story, set in Kashmir about a kidnapped young man, also suggests that homosexuality was a routine fixture of Indian society. The third story, "Druga's Solution" mentioned earlier, described how sexual practices such as polygamy and homosexuality went underground after colonization. By the 1950s, older patterns of homosexual behavior had been underground for so long, or so warped by the inequities of colonialism, that they could be unrecognizable to a person like Rajiv who understood his sexual identity through a Western lens.

Rajiv's frustrations were shared by Pablo, a man from Buenos Aires, Argentina. Pablo complained he was lonely and could not connect with local gay life. "I have no friends 'like us' here," he wrote, "except those foreigners coming from Europe and that I know through friendship's message in Der Kreis, Vriendshap, Eos, etc. . . . We have nothing here. No associations, no clubs, no bars, nothing."[79] One would expect cities as large as Buenos Aires and Bombay to have had some sort of organized gay life in the 1950s. Indeed, American homophile activist Bob Basker explained in an oral history that he had no problem finding an extensive yet discreet gay social world during the 1950s near Buenos Aires on islands accessible by ferry.[80] Pablo blamed his inability to find gay life on "the almighty influence of the church and the family," which "makes things very difficult to us and 'our way of living.' "[81] No doubt the strong influence of the Catholic Church in Latin America compelled high levels of discretion among Argentinean gays and lesbians. Yet, like Rajiv, Pablo seemed to be looking for more specifically European–North American manifestations of homosexuality than perhaps existed in South America at the time.

Like Pablo's letter, *The Keval*'s stories about Latin America also emphasize discretion and silence. A story set in Rio de Janeiro, Brazil, for example, describes a boarding house that serves as a sanctuary for gay men ("viados") away from the prying eyes of church and family. In the story, several of the tenants prepare for Carnival, dressing as Mae West, Marie Antoinette, and the Statue of Liberty (by a U.S. visitor). Only during Carnival, during this temporary inversion of all social rules, the story suggests, could these men publicly express their homosexuality. During the rest of the year, they must carefully guard their privacy and keep to themselves. Otis makes a similar point about discretion in a story set in Peru. A tourist falls for an attractive train operator on the way to Machu Picchu. They lean against each other during the ride, unnoticeable to others. They do not speak or make a specific acknowledgement of each other. Their silence is a metaphor for the broader patterns of silence expected of gay people throughout Latin America in these years.

The silence of South American homosexuals, however, pales in comparison to the silence of gay men and lesbians in the Second World communist countries. In the correspondence examined for this study, not a single letter came from the Soviet Union, Eastern Europe, or China, which is ironic considering how the U.S. government associated American homosexuals with communist subversion. Scholars have argued that after a brief moment of tolerance for homosexuals in the Soviet Union during the New Economic Policy of the 1920s, homosexuals experienced brutal repression under Stalin. Approximately 1,000 people were prosecuted each year for homosexuality from the early 1930s through the 1950s in the Soviet Union. Many of these individuals were sent to labor camps. There were pockets of gay life in some tourist areas of Eastern Europe and Cuba, but Stalin's antihomosexual policies proliferated throughout most of the communist Second World.[82] China's repression of homosexuals in these years was partly due to Mao's communist revolution, which drew from Stalinist interpretations of Marxism, as well as deeper Chinese anxieties about Westernization and industrialization. Like many colonized countries, the British instilled a deep homophobia into many Chinese institutions that lingered into its communist era.[83] Reflecting the silence of the letters, *The Keval* had nothing to say about any communist countries.

Stepping back and looking at this body of international correspondence to *ONE*, a few tentative conclusions about American homophile perceptions of the rest of the world can be offered. First, whereas mainstream European and American Orientalist writers posited homosexuality as an indicator of cultural inferiority and source of division between the West and East, the homophiles considered the global presence of homosexuality as a major source of unity and evidence that the very labels "West" and "East" were suspect. Indeed, they viewed the global presence of homosexual identity in almost utopian terms. Second, although homosexuality was legally accepted in much of the world, family life proved the most universal obstacle to full social acceptance. Even more than organized religion, the basis of objections to homosexuality throughout the world most often centered on a perceived need to perpetuate a particular family structure. Finally, while the homophiles were aware that much of the non-Western world was more accepting of homosexual practices, they seemed only vaguely aware of the ways that Western colonialism had spread a virulent homophobia to many parts of the world that for centuries had accepted homosexual behaviors. Indeed, the global proliferation of a singular Western concept of homosexual identity was a double-edged sword. On the one hand, it had the power to unite masses of persons attracted to the same sex under a shared concept that made unified political action possible. On the other hand, the Western concept of homosexual identity was loaded with negative associations, such as the stigmas of medical pathology and Christian abomination. The Western concept of homosexuality thus also gave rise to the distinctly Western concept of homophobia throughout much of the world.

Gay rights activism based on this Western model and geared toward eradicating the homophobic dimensions of this model was limited to Western Europe and the United States in the 1950s and early 1960s, but assumed truly global dimensions in the late 1960s and 1970s as gay liberation-style organizations appeared in most parts of the world. In the 1950s, American gay men and lesbians did not invent gay activism but rather adapted an existing international movement to the particular social and political climate of the McCarthy era. This uniquely American model of gay rights activism, with its emphasis on political justice and equal rights, proved highly influential around the world in subsequent decades.[84]

4

ONE Magazine Letter Archetypes

Most of *ONE*'s correspondents wrote to the magazine to begin, renew, or cancel a subscription. They usually used the preprinted subscription form found in each issue, but some individuals penned subscription requests on their own stationary. These requests often said little more than "Please renew my subscription." Many readers were reluctant to disclose personal information about their homosexuality in written correspondence handled, delivered, and possibly inspected by the U.S. Postal Service, which was, after all, part of the federal government.

Other readers felt no such reluctance. They filled the blank spaces of their stationary with information about themselves, their local gay subcultures, and their viewpoints on a wide range of topics. Some readers were eager to have their letters published. They wanted to express themselves to *ONE*'s community of readers and see their words printed (although usually not their names—most letters were published anonymously) in a national publication. Other correspondents instructed *ONE* not to publish their letters because of personal details they revealed about themselves, their families, or their employers. Some correspondents planned their letters meticulously and chose their words carefully; others composed their letters spontaneously as an afterthought to their subscription renewal.

We might expect letters to *ONE* to be gloomy and depressing considering the widespread persecution against gay people as well as the contemporary perception that gay people spent the 1950s hiding "in the closet." Certainly, some letters conform to these expectations. Overall, however, the letters reveal a group of people creatively asserting their right to live their lives as gay people. They were not necessarily proclaiming this right to heterosexuals, but they were increasingly proclaiming this right to themselves and one another.

But what exactly would a mass American gay rights movement look like? What should its goals be, and how should gay people pursue these goals? These letters, written from 1953 to 1965, addressed such questions by participating in the first published, ongoing, national brainstorm session devoted to improving gay people's collective status. The letters reveal which issues occupied their everyday thoughts: their jobs, families, marriages, harassment from police, and loneliness, to name a few of the more popular topics (see the appendix for a list of the most popular topics).

The chapters thus far have focused on letters describing specific aspects of *ONE* magazine—its contents, its distribution, and its international reach. From this point forward, however, we turn to letters that discuss common themes of everyday life beyond the homophile movement. This chapter overviews the most common recurring themes in the letters, such as police harassment, descriptions of local gay subcultures, calls for collective action, and laments about misery and loneliness. The chapter highlights the civil rights impulse in these letters as well as provides an overview of several major letter "archetypes" before delving into subsequent chapter-length analyses of other popular themes such as family life, marriage, gender behavior, and antigay discrimination in the military and teaching profession.

Legal Letters

The most frequently discussed topic in the letters was employment. Chapters 5 and 6 analyze employment anxieties in detail, but such employment anxieties did not exist in isolation of other anxieties. In particular, job anxieties closely intertwined with the second most frequently discussed topic in the letters: the legal or criminal justice system. When people were arrested for homosexual offenses, a reasonable chance existed that their employers would find out. If the person were a teacher or government worker, her or his chances of getting fired were especially high.

Approximately 10 percent of the letters discussed legal issues, usually describing gay arrests, requesting lawyer referrals, or asking general questions about the law. Getting arrested represented the direst threat to one's right to live a gay life. Not only could an arrest ruin a career and poison family relations, but it could also imprison a person for years and take away his or her most basic rights. Anxiety about getting arrested suffused participation in gay life. When arrested, gay people surrendered all freedom if they could not make bail. If they made bail, the arrest would consume their lives for some time. Navigating the legal system was difficult because most lawyers refused to defend homosexuals. Most gay arrest victims paid fines and were paroled, but many were imprisoned. Newspapers often printed the names and addresses of gay arrest victims, fueling the disapproval and ostracism gay people suffered from their employers, their families, their churches, and other social networks.[1] Dorr Legg described the trauma of such an experience in a ONE Institute lecture: "The publicity, however limited and perhaps confined to but the circle of family and intimate friends, is always sufficient to work profound changes in the individual. That which he strove so long to conceal from the world is now revealed for all to see by the blinding spotlight of exposure to the eyes of the state. The individual's entire personality pattern built up so long and with such great pains and with such care has with one blow been entirely shattered."[2]

A sense of unfairness pervaded the process. Arrests were often made through entrapment, secret surveillance, and other questionable police tactics. Gay people were routinely denied basic legal protections because of antigay bias in the criminal justice system. For example, evidence of previous crimes—normally inadmissible in trials—was routinely used as evidence of criminal predisposition in trials involving homosexuality. Facing such challenges, gay people rarely fought the charges against them, even when police had fabricated the charges. Gay people usually entered a plea bargain to make the situation go away as quickly and quietly as possible.[3]

Police harassment of gay people dates back at least to the late nineteenth century in the United States. The practice grew along with the Progressive Era impulse to bring civic and moral order to the chaos of urban life. Gay crackdowns most often occurred during election seasons. In Los Angeles in the late 1930s, for example, an effort to recall a corrupt mayor led by an eccentric local restaurateur provoked widespread vice crackdowns in the city, including bars that served gay and lesbian clientele. In San Francisco, similarly, police raids of gay bars routinely occurred before elections so city officials could produce statistics demonstrating how well they were "protecting" the public. The letters frequently connected antigay police raids with local political campaigns.[4]

Antigay police harassment increased after World War II. According to legal scholar William Eskridge, "The period after World War II . . . did not innovate aggressive police tactics [against gay people] but did much to regularize, popularize, and modernize them." Two trends sparked these more coordinated, aggressive police efforts. The first was the rapid growth of gay urban subcultures across the country after World War II. Gay bars suddenly appeared across the American urban landscape in cities such as Albuquerque, Hartford, and Richmond for the first time.[5] More antigay crackdowns occurred after the war because there was substantially more gay social life on which to crack down. The second trend was McCarthyism. Regardless of local politics, McCarthyism justified police crackdowns against homosexuals in the name of national security. The FBI, which spied on thousands of gay people through its Sex Deviate Program, routinely exchanged information with local police agencies throughout the country.[6] During the lavender scare in Washington, D.C., government officials explicitly connected the communist threat with the need to arrest homosexuals. This was done most effectively by Washington, D.C., police chief Roy Blick, the star witness of the U.S. Senate's 1950 investigation into "Homosexuals and Other Sex Perverts" working for the government. Blick bragged before a Senate subcommittee about his ability to entrap homosexuals and used the hearings as an excuse to launch massive police raids against gay bars, public restrooms, and parks throughout the city. Police chiefs throughout the country emulated his tactics; *ONE* readers reported large-scale police crackdowns in Boston, New York City, Pittsburgh, Philadelphia, Miami, New Orleans, Omaha, Detroit, Dallas, Denver, Boise, Portland (Oregon), San Francisco, San Jose, and Los Angeles.[7] No doubt other cities, suburbs, and smaller towns experienced similar crackdowns as well.

The letters described four stages to the arrest process: worrying about getting arrested, the arrest itself, navigating the legal system, and serving time. A letter from John, a Los Angeles resident, nicely captured the "worry" stage: "There seems to be an unusual amount of harassment going on these days around the Hollywood area, by both uniformed policeman and plainclothesman," he told *ONE* in his 1961 letter. John's worries had been aroused after a disturbing incident involving a friend. "A good friend of mine, who lives close to the heart of Hollywood, was recently stopped by a uniformed policeman while engaged in no more detrimental act than walking down the street towards his home. He had just gotten off duty from a very respectable hotel desk clerk job that he holds, and was dressed very neatly in suit, white shirt and tie." John described his friend's appearance to emphasize that he was "respectable" and undeserving of the policeman's attention. "After identifying himself, he was further delayed by a barrage of personal questions regarding where he had been, where he was going, why was he taking this route, etc.?" To John, the nature of these questions hinted at a crackdown on gay men cruising along that street. His friend had not been cruising, but the interrogation deeply bothered John. "Refusal to answer [the officer's questions], I suppose, would have resulted in his having been taken down to the police station and held on suspicion. As it was, he supplied answers and finally allowed to go on his way. Now I know it is city election season . . ."—here John connected his friend's interrogation with a local election, although he did not elaborate on this point. To John, his friend's interrogation seemed like something that might occur in the Soviet Union. "I . . . grant that law authorities are within their rights to ask citizens to identify themselves. But what about these personal questions? Does the citizen have any rights in this matter? If not, we indeed live in a police state."[8]

What really troubled John was that police could detain him for several days if he refused to answer their questions. "This 72 hour period that a citizen can be held on mere suspicion is a very vicious thing itself," he wrote, "as I am sure you would agree. It can, besides the embarrassment and mental anguish, cause a loss of prestige and even a loss of livelihood." John realized that a person's life could be ruined merely for *suspicion* of being gay, and that such suspicion could arise simply by walking down a particular street. His friend's incident was not an isolated case. "It seems very apparent," he added, "from many different cases I have known and heard about in recent years here in Los Angeles, that the policeman has no responsibility whatever to his superiors, or to the citizen he has taken in on *suspicion*, to establish any reasonable foundation for the suspicion, or even to inform the citizen of what crime he is suspected."[9] John understood that being gay in the 1950s and early 1960s required paying attention to police surveillance patterns. By carefully reading local newspapers or staying informed through friends, gay people could assess their relative safety at any given moment. This could lessen the danger of getting arrested, but never eliminate it entirely.

The most common subgroup of legal letters concerned the second stage: actually getting arrested. Firsthand or secondhand descriptions of arrests comprised approximately 40 percent of the legal letters. A 1964 letter from Carl was typical. He wrote from Louisville, Kentucky, and like the previous letter writer, Carl believed that a local election influenced his arrest. "I was at the Lindsay Turkish Bath in Indianapolis, Indiana, when it was raided the day before Election Day. Everyone says it was a political move since the bath hadn't been raided for 20 years." Carl's letter protested that the bathhouse raid was unwarranted and bogus. "The horrifying thing is that the detectives in charge of the raid are saying that they *saw* things going on—which IS NOTHING BUT *LIES*! 36 patrons of the Bath were arrested." Like John's letter, the whole incident reeked of totalitarianism. "Among the [arrested] was a professional writer. He has contacted his agent in New York, and is planning to write an article based on the raid, the unConstitutional treatment given by the police, and so on, and his tentative title is 'I WAS ARRESTED IN INDIANAPOLIS,

INDIANA (U.S.S.R.—?)' "[10] Carl's claim that the officers could not have witnessed sexual contact between male patrons of the bathhouse was plausible given the politicized nature of gay arrests. At the same time, some gay sex most likely was occurring in the bathhouse. Antigay police raids usually targeted the right places, and police frequently used surreptitious surveillance techniques patrons did not notice, such as undercover officers, peepholes, or trick mirrors. In the 1960s, bathhouses in major urban areas served a largely gay clientele, although a dwindling number still served primarily heterosexual (usually immigrant) communities. Even in these, however, discreet gay sex often occurred at certain times, usually at night.[11]

Regardless of what the police had or had not seen, Carl was suffering consequences from the raid. His family was upset, and he not only faced a fine of between $100 and $1,000, but also a possible two-year prison term. *ONE* replied to Carl with a lawyer recommendation—about 30 percent of the legal letters asked for lawyer referrals.[12] Initially, providing any referrals was difficult for *ONE*, but over the years its contacts grew, especially in major cities such as Miami, Chicago, Los Angeles, and Philadelphia, and Dorr Legg and other staffers recommended lawyers who accepted gay arrest cases and sometimes even won in court. Eventually, ONE, Inc., was able to provide lawyer referrals to approximately one-third of the individuals requesting them.

Carl wrote back a few weeks later with an update. The lawyer was excellent, he reported, but the situation had become "more complicated and serious." Carl had entered the third stage: dealing with the criminal justice system. His lawyer argued that the charges should be dropped because the detectives had no warrant, and Carl remained determined to prove his innocence. According to Carl, "two detectives lied . . . grossly at the preliminary hearing that they saw another person and myself in a 69 position." Carl took a polygraph test to disprove these allegations and passed it with "flying colors."[13] There were no more letters from Carl, and *ONE* learned nothing further of the Indianapolis bathhouse raid. Similar incidents point to two probable outcomes. If Carl's attorney could demonstrate egregious misconduct on the part of law enforcement, such as a lack of warrants for certain types of surveillance, then there was a reasonable chance a judge would drop the charges. Carl's polygraph test was probably inadmissible as evidence, however, so he may have been convicted if a judge or jury chose to believe the testimony of the police officers rather than Carl and the other defendants. In such a situation, his attorney probably would have worked out a deal involving a fine (usually a few hundred dollars, but sometimes much more) and parole. Gay people who could not afford their own attorneys and who had to rely on public defenders were more likely to go to jail or mental hospitals and face higher fines as a result of their arrests.[14] Yet even if Carl were absolved of all charges, the stigma of the arrest would have complicated his family relations and possibly caused him to lose his job.

Another letter detailing the complications of the legal justice system came from Christopher, who lived in a Dallas suburb. "I was recently arrested for sodomy, a felony. In such a small town as this is, a charge of this nature normally wouldn't be brought to court. Homosexuality is turned away from and ignored completely."[15] This last statement may seem surprising, given the homophobic reputation of smaller towns compared to large cities, but many small towns and suburbs were in a state of denial about homosexuality that could result in significant degrees of freedom.[16] Christopher certainly thought the attention he was getting was unusual. The cause of his misery was an ambitious prosecuting attorney, but with a twist: "The county's prosecuting attorney, *himself a homosexual*, has tried to cite me as an example for motives other than sodomy."[17] The letter did not elaborate on these motives. The prosecuting attorney brings to mind Senator Joseph McCarthy's chief assistant, Roy Cohn: a gay person unashamedly persecuting other gay people in order to cultivate political favors, build a career, and deflect suspicions about his own homosexuality.[18] Christopher saw his arrest as part of a broader pattern of political corruption in his town. "Other lawyers here have agreed that his stand in this case is quite unjust. . . . The police department is more corrupt here that you can imagine and is the laughing stock of all Texas." Unfortunately, he could not find a lawyer to represent him. He explained, "During this matter, I have found that the average attorney either knows little about the laws regarding homosexuality and homosexuals themselves or is hesitant to take the case due to a number of personal reasons."[19] These difficulties were common, and exacerbated an already stressful ordeal.

Approximately 10 percent of the legal letters were written by persons in the final stage of the arrest process: incarceration. A slight majority of these came from prisons, the rest from mental hospitals. A young man named Warren wrote a letter to *ONE* in 1964 as "a 'patient' at the Norman Beatty State Hospital (State of Indiana). I am here as a homosexual, and legally classified as a Criminal Sexual Psychopath (C.S.P.)." He had worked at a bus station in a midsize town in Indiana, and "while employed there, I met a young man with whom I became very attached. Unfortunately, the relationship was very one-sided, unknown at first to me. Because of various circumstances, . . . the young man (a minor by the way) revealed our relationship to his parents who in turn notified the police."[20] Warren himself was nineteen or twenty years old when the affair occurred, and he referred to his lover as a "young man," suggesting they were not far apart in years. Still, the fact that a legal minor was involved undoubtedly contributed to his being incarcerated. The designation "criminal sexual psychopath" was meant to apply to violent sexual criminals such as rapists and child molesters, but police agencies often cast a broader net when responding to hysteria about sex crimes, especially if they involved children.[21] Clearly, a distinction can be drawn between a consensual affair between a twenty-year-old with someone a few years younger and the sorts of grisly rapes, abductions, and murders that spurred the passage of enhanced sex crime laws in the 1930s through 1950s. Imagining a comparable penalty if Warren's affair had been heterosexual is difficult.

Warren had been incarcerated in a county jail while awaiting his trial. "Is it necessary to relate my experiences at the county jail?" he wrote. "I have never in my life been a prostitute, either by force or by choice. At jail I was subjected to all sorts of humiliating and in some cases terrifying experiences."[22] After his trial, he was given a two-year minimum commitment at the hospital with the possibility of life if his homosexuality was not cured. In cases such as Warren's, patients were usually released after two years whether they were "cured" or not—medical professionals could better distinguish common homosexuals from genuine threats to society than could the criminal justice system.[23] But rules were rules, and for at least two years he would have to pass his time in the hospital. "I have been assigned to work in the laundry. In my spare time, I go to a psycho-therapist 3 hours per week. I also play the organ for the Catholic Mass on Sunday, and occasionally for the Protestant Services. My religion is Unitarian."[24]

Warren's case represented the most severe violation of his rights for participating in gay life and having an intimate same-sex affair. Yet despite his traumatic ordeal with the criminal justice system, his understanding of himself as a gay man remained intact. "The fact that I am a homosexual does not embarrass me, nor am I particularly proud of my alleged 'pathological' condition," he wrote. "This factor has existed in my life since a very young age; I am not aware of living in any other manner, nor do I feel that I care to live otherwise, however, regardless of my personal opinions, I am obligated by state law to remain here 'until such time that the psychosis has been permanently removed.'"[25] Despite his loss of freedom, despite his imprisonment and psychotherapy, he retained the power to define his own sexual identity. Whatever he might tell his doctors to get released from the mental hospital, he still thought of himself as a gay man.

In sum, letters concerning the legal system revealed four clear arrest stages, and each stage posed unique limitations to gay people's rights, agency, and ability to live one's life as a homosexual. The anxiety of getting arrested injected fear into all gay interactions and social life. Gay arrests were often sudden, unexpected, and traumatic, but once the dust settled, decisions had to be made about how to negotiate the criminal justice system. Getting a fair trial was difficult, time-consuming, and expensive, but not impossible. In the worst-case scenarios, gay people went to jail or mental institutions and surrendered most of their freedoms, but even in these cases they did not lose the power to define themselves as gay people, despite the powerful social and political forces working to undermine that sense of self-definition. Such power represented a significant, albeit limited, defiance against efforts to eradicate homosexuality from society.

Rights Letters

The same number of people who wrote letters to *ONE* describing their experiences with the legal system also wrote letters to *ONE* with clear calls for collective action. *ONE* magazine instilled and reinforced this ethic in its readers, but it is notable that *ONE* received more of these "rights letters" (about 10 percent of the total letters) compared to letters depicting the more stereotypical view of postwar gay people as lonely, isolated, and conflicted about their sexual identity (about 7 percent). Rights letters unambiguously captured the civil rights impulse of postwar gay men and lesbians. Gay people struggled to put this impulse into concrete political action, but just because gay people were not marching in the streets or "coming out" to everyone they knew does not mean this impulse should be discounted. Having a civil rights impulse required having an affirmative or neutral view of oneself and one's sexuality, which required a significant effort of individual assertion rejecting the ubiquitous, disparaging theories about homosexuality (sickness, sin, perversion) and homosexual people (criminals, child molesters, threats to national security) in order to come to an understanding of one's homosexuality that was unproblematic, accepting, and frequently prideful. In other words, for gay people to accept their sexuality required a flagrant rejection of the predominant negative social and political baggage attached to homosexuality in these years.

Both the civil rights impulse and the difficulties putting this impulse into concrete action were expressed in a 1955 letter from Lawrence in

Cleveland. Lawrence wanted to start a homophile group in his area, but was unsure how to go about it. "It seems a shame we haven't been able to organize, for mutual benefit and discussion, here in Ohio as you have in California," he wrote. "Cleveland ought to be ripe for such an enterprise among us. Isn't there something we can do—those of us who want to?" His use of the words "we" and "us" implied that he was not the only person in Cleveland thinking about these things. "It simply doesn't seem fair for us to live our lives undercover, never knowing when the vice squad (and their companions) will catch up to us with their usual tactics of guilty before judged. In a land of freedom, we should be able to see a little more of that freedom. Some day??"[26] This letter shows that even in places where no homophile organizations existed (Cleveland would not have its first group until the 1960s), there were people thinking about collective action. In spite of his frustrations with the repressive atmosphere—and perhaps because of these frustrations—Lawrence imagined a day when things might be different, when he, as a gay man, could enjoy the same freedoms of association, freedom to work, and fairness in the criminal justice system as heterosexuals. His hypothetical "some day??" would come, but before such a day could come, Lawrence and thousands of other gay people spent years thinking about it, imagining it.

Police crackdowns against gay communities often stirred up this rights ethic and brought it to the surface. Al in New Orleans (mentioned in chapter 2) wrote an archetypal rights letter in 1960 in response to police harassment. "We, here in New Orleans, are getting sick and tired of being pushed around, and harassed." Like Lawrence, his use of "we" points to collective outrage in his community, not merely his own individual outrage. "There are several of us who have decided to get out and go to the bars," he continued, "and should we be a part of some raid, then we will pursue counter legal action to the hilt. We've decided that we can't whip the whole city as individuals, but we are willing to try like hell. We can't whip the whole police force and the D.A., but we will give it a whirl and give them a run for their money." Despite the noticeable increase in police harassment, Al and his friends were willing to make legal martyrs of themselves for the greater good of their community. "Harassment is going to end here, or else. We live here, and we are determined not to move away to other places where the situation is no better, if not worse."[27] Rather than hide, or seek gay life elsewhere, Al made the conscious choice to defend his American right of free association. New Orleans was his home, and he was not going to be driven out by police harassment. He was not going to change his mind, and his letter made it clear he was not alone in doing so.

About a year and half later, Al wrote another letter to *ONE*, explaining that his lover had been arrested and charged with a "crime against nature." His civil rights impulse was intact. They were going to "fight it all the way. Nothing is going to be gained if we don't."[28]

"Rights letters" came from all age groups (including a letter writer in his eighties), but a disproportionate number of them came from letter writers in their teens and twenties. They seemed to have a greater expectation of personal freedom compared to letter writers in their thirties and forties. Their outspoken calls for gay rights foreshadowed the youthful gay liberation movement of the late 1960s and early 1970s and reflected the broader generational split at the heart of 1960s political activism.

An eighteen-year-old lesbian, Lori, for example, wrote a lengthy letter in 1960 after reading *They Walk in Shadow* by J. D. Mercer. This strange, rambling book argued that homosexuality represented stunted evolutionary development rather than a psychological condition. It had given Lori a lot to think about.[29] Despite the book's rather negative view of homosexuality, it reminded her that "there's hope for the freedom everyone was given according to the Constitution. That's America's biggest fault, it's shown in our laws and foreign policy, we just can't mind our own business! Consequently, we go blundering in where we don't belong and make enemies, at home as well as abroad." She was clearly thinking about her sexuality in political terms. "This is a great country and as soon as we get rid of the big noses and frightened hypocritical moralists who write our laws only to go home, pull down the curtain, and do just what they've condemned, when we rid ourselves of morons like this, we'll not only be great, but we'll be the Greatest country in the world."[30] It was possible that the election of John F. Kennedy a few weeks earlier had influenced the letter's buoyant tone. Lori's letter also exhibited a defiant sarcasm and humor common to many rights letters. She wrote:

> What an idiot I am, telling you people all this when you know more about these things than I ever will. But you know, that's probably because I'm "sick," or I am a "commie," or "perverted," maybe I'm all of these. Good lord, what a mess! What shall I do, what shall I do? Go to a head shrinker, "no, no that never works." Remove my glands, "now you're just being silly." Shoot me quick with them there female hormone shots. "Tsk, tsk, not proven." I know—lock me up. "Yes, yes, that's the answer lock her up." I realize this now because after all if I was allowed my freedom, I'd cause the population to decrease or something like that.[31]

Rather than dwelling on the miseries of gay oppression, Lori's letter demonstrated a confidence about the future. For an eighteen-year-old, she had clearly given her sexual identity a great deal of study and thought. Most striking was how she scornfully mocked the conventional wisdom that homosexuality was a sickness or threat to national security. Her attitude became increasingly common for gay people, especially younger gay people, throughout the 1960s.

A 1963 letter written by sixteen-year-old Daniel expressed a similar youthful defiance. Daniel's letter avoided the sarcasm of Lori's letter, but his assertion of his right to live his life as a gay man was particularly strong. "I want to be a homosexual and know that I am destined to surely be one. I don't need psychiatrists [sic] help or any kind of help from anyone, and I don't want it. I probably will never get married and I never want any children if I do. Don't try to recommend a doctor of any kind because I will fight it and won't accept it. I don't want my parents to find out! I want to live the life of a homosexual, and have all of the joys, if I can have the wonderful chance."[32] It is tempting to conclude that *ONE* magazine simply instilled this pride ethic into young impressionable gay people such as Daniel, but his comments indicated that he had barely read the magazine—*ONE* never recommended psychiatrists to cure readers of their homosexuality. Daniel's letter suggested that he held his prideful attitudes about his sexuality before encountering *ONE*. His only hesitancy involved his parents finding out.

Caution must be exercised in drawing broader conclusions from these letters—we would expect *ONE*'s readers to be more assertive than the general gay and lesbian population because of the magazine's contents. At the same time, it is surprising that amidst the anxieties and tragedies involving jobs and arrests, such a broad cross-section of gay men and lesbians in the 1950s and early 1960s asserted defiance more often than despair in their letters. Certainly the magazine influenced this, but more often it seems that *ONE* gave its readers an opportunity to work through preexisting feelings of outrage and defiance. *ONE*'s civil rights impulse was not simply inoculated into its readers, but part of a dialogue in which readers shaped the tone and spirit of the magazine as much as the editors did.

Lonely Letters

ONE received substantially more rights letters compared to "lonely letters," which constituted approximately 7 percent of the letters. Whereas the rights letters were resilient, defiant, and unapologetic, the lonely letters had a sense of despair, gloom, depression, and defeat. Lonely letters fit the stereotype of gay people in the 1950s as isolated and tragic. Despite the dramatic growth of gay life after World War II, some gay people were unable to make meaningful contacts with other gay people because of job anxieties, family pressures, geographic isolation, personality issues, or bad experiences.

Yet even in these gloomy letters, there was a silver lining. They shared with the rights letters the belief that things *should* be better by imagining a brighter future in which they were not so lonely. They conveyed an awareness of gay life and, usually, a desire to join it. Ironically, their loneliness typically resulted from a conscious decision on their part. An individual might decide that his or her career was more important than participating in gay life, for example, and choose to cut himself or herself off from other gay people. Such a choice might ultimately lead to despair, frustration, and loneliness, and it was an unfortunate choice to feel compelled to make, but a choice nonetheless.

Such self-imposed loneliness was described in a 1958 letter written by Theodore, who lived on Long Island, New York. Like many letter writers, he had avoided gay life because of his career: "My life has been one of frustration and anxiety. My vocation has made it necessary that my life conduct be restricted. As I grow older I feel extremely lonely and want companionship with others who would understand my feelings. I am now in my middle thirties."[33] There was a clear tone of regret in the letter. Theodore had imposed a false dichotomy upon himself, imagining as mutually exclusive his ability to participate in gay life and have a career. Other letters showed that the two could be balanced, despite the risk involved.

Other letter writers avoided gay life because they held negative attitudes toward gay institutions and other gay people. No doubt internalized prejudice, self-loathing, or elitism figured into these attitudes. Bad experiences or a dislike of gay bars could also influence a person to isolate him or herself from other gay people. Joey, a college student living with his parents in Baldwin, New York, wrote in 1962 that he had gone to gay bars for several years but "they still disgust me. I shun the occupants of these places and intimate relationship fosters guilt feelings because of the character of the person involved." He knew a few gay people outside of the bars, but complained that "intellectual stimulation with them is very limited. My closest friends are 'strait' [*sic*] but long standing relationships prevent their knowledge of my condition." Despite these frustrations, Joey was capable of imagining himself in a long-term gay relationship. "So far I have not found anyone with whom I can have a relationship of dignity, pride, and true understanding, therefore a terribly lonely life."[34] Joey's cry of loneliness thus contained a vision of something better: the possibility of a serious long-term same-sex relationship involving "dignity" and "pride."

Only about 12 percent of the lonely letters stated they were completely cut off from other gay people, aside from reading *ONE*. This represented less than 1 percent of the total letters in this sample, a surprisingly small number considering the postwar stereotype of 1950s gay people as lonely and "closeted." An anonymous individual in Sioux City, Iowa, wrote such a letter on Christmas day in 1961. "I ordered a copy of your magazine about October 1960 and enjoyed it very much, but I also found it extremely frustrating not to be able to share it with absolutely anyone. The name really fits the way I feel, but I think 'Al-one' would be a better title."[35] About 15 percent of the lonely letter writers (also less than 1 percent of the total letters) stated they had never had gay sex before. Such was the case with Randolph, a New Jersey college student who lived with his parents. He wrote woefully in 1963, "My eyes are worn from the useless tears of loneliness, and my body torn from holding back my heart for all too long a time." Most letters avoided such melodramatic soliloquies. "My heart is dying from lack of love, and I cannot let myself live in death anymore. Please, if nothing else, pity me! Try to help. I know I am only one of many who are 'one,' but before I die, I want to meet them!!"[36] In contrast to letters describing self-imposed loneliness, Randolph seemed completely unaware of how to find gay bars or connect with gay life. From his point of view, this exclusion was beyond his control. Living with his parents probably did not help the situation. Still, even in such a despairing lonely letter, there was the optimistic hope that someday he would find gay social life and true love. Furthermore, he seemed to have no problem accepting his homosexuality.

In sum, although these lonely correspondents struggled to connect meaningfully with other gay people, they still exercised important degrees of control over how they conceptualized and practiced their sexual identities. Their ability to live their lives as gay people was compromised but not eliminated. Usually, the correspondents' isolation derived from conscious decisions in the context of life factors such as work, family, and the risks of arrest. McCarthyism and other antigay persecutions did not *force* gay people to limit their interactions with one another. Unless they were imprisoned, they were free to live as gay persons if they accepted the risks that came with that decision. Most *ONE* correspondents were willing to take these risks to varying degrees. They significantly outnumbered the lonely people who chose not to accept these risks.

News Report Letters

Approximately 8 percent of the letters shared information about local gay life from around the country. Much of this information made its way into

ONE's popular column "Tangents." Some readers sent in newspaper clippings of police raids, gay arrests, or gay scandals; other readers reported openings and closings of gay bars. Correspondents sometimes described vibrant gay social life in surprising places. One man, Clark, had recently moved to Sacramento, California, for example, and described the city as a gay paradise in a 1961 letter. "What a weird place this is! I was here during the war, but there's nothing left of the town I knew. There is a great deal of sex activity—and it is more open than in most places. Seems to be very little fear of the police, and propositions come at you from every direction and you can take your pick—from a neat clean young man to a skid-row wino-bum. One young wino offered to do anything I wanted for only 5 cents. Times are bad and competition is keen."[37] Of California cities with gay reputations, Sacramento has never registered very high. The letter reminds us that a person need not live in the expected hubs of gay life, such as Los Angeles or San Francisco, to have enjoyed an active gay life in the 1950s. Things were not always so tolerant in Sacramento, though. Three years earlier, in 1958, "Tangents" reported a wave of highly publicized arrests in Sacramento.[38] In such situations, gay life went underground and became less visible for a while, but it never went away. Gay life could be found in all parts of a city such as Sacramento: "Today I wandered into a section of the town that is largely Mexican," Clark added, "and you know what? They are just as queer as the rest of us. And language is no barrier."[39]

Approximately 30 percent of the news report letters focused on local police activity, either reporting crackdowns or stating that police activity was quiet. Al from New Orleans—the same Al mentioned earlier—gave details of local police harassment in a letter from 1960. "We had a nice place here where the gays could dance with other gays, and the police closed it on the grounds of obscenity. The others were just forced out of business one by one and two by two. Now we have only four [gay bars] left." Al was worried that gay life might not recover from the current crackdown, the worst in memory. He saw the gay bar crackdown as part of a broader police strategy to rid New Orleans of all homosexuals. "The idea, I understand is to force the gay people out on the streets so they can be picked up for loitering, vagrancy, public display of homosexuality, etc. . . . The rest of the kids here are back out on the street which hasn't been going on in nearly six years. We had places to go, and we went. We gladly abandoned the streets. We gladly abandoned the parks. We gladly abandoned the museums and such. We had places we could go."[40] Al feared that pushing gay people out of the bars made them more vulnerable to police harassment. It was a valid concern, but Al might have underestimated gay people's ability to wear heterosexual masks in such a situation. When bars became unsafe for gay people due to police harassment, gay people did not hide in their homes but went other places—in this case, certain streets, parks, and museums. Gay people exercised more caution in such public settings, but ultimately, in a city as large as New Orleans, they figured out ways to find one another regardless of the police.

News report letters reflected that gay rights were not merely conceptualized as an individual matter, but increasingly imagined as a collective matter. Just as gay individuals struggled to put their civil rights impulses into practice, communities struggled to assert their presence, character, and identity in a hostile social and political landscape. Patterns of police harassment and the openings or closings of gay bars became important barometers measuring a gay community's ability to assert its right to exist (however surreptitiously) at a particular moment in time. These letters also demonstrated the limited impact of police crackdowns on gay communities' assertions to exist. Many individuals suffered devastating losses of freedom during such crackdowns, but communities usually adapted and survived. The McCarthyite goal of eradicating gay social life proved impossible to achieve because too many gay people were asserting a gay identity to themselves and one another. Ultimately, the police were significantly outnumbered.

Moving and Traveling Letters

Approximately 6 percent of the letters described gay people traveling, moving to new places, or at least pondering one of these options. About half of these moving and traveling letters discussed gay life outside the United States as described in chapter 3. Gay people were just as curious about gay life in other parts of the United States. They traveled for many of the same reasons as heterosexuals: to see monuments or historic places, to visit friends and relatives, or experience nature. They also moved or traveled to find environments that might be more hospitable to their gay identities compared to where they currently lived. Stereotypically, this meant going to large cities, but the letters demonstrated the opposite trend as well—gay people leaving the big city and settling into smaller towns, suburbs, or rural areas.[41]

Gay travelers had to wear their heterosexual masks carefully, especially when traveling in couples or groups. Gay couples needed alibis to explain their relationships when booking hotels or tours, eating in restaurants, and other common traveling situations. When probing questions were asked, gay couples became "army buddies," "business partners," "siblings," or the old standby "roommates." Such alibis had to be coordinated in advance because any discrepancy between the two partners might have dangerous consequences. For interracial gay couples, traveling was even more complicated, as suggested in a 1959 letter written by E. A. from Chicago. E. A.'s short letter asked *ONE* about safe lodging for a trip he was planning from Chicago to Los Angeles with his partner. They wanted to avoid the penalties of gay visibility, but also find some sanctuary from the anxieties of such duplicity. "Is there any night clubs where we may spend an enjoyable, reserved, evening (nothing obvious) with our own kind?"[42] E. A. asked. The words "nothing obvious" revealed his expectation that they would keep their sexual identities low-key, even in gay-friendly environments. Such interracial couples not only had to contend with antigay bigotry, but also the hundreds of "sundowner towns" in which law enforcement warned black travelers to be gone by sundown or face mob violence. Such racial complications were compounded by the games they would have to play to obfuscate the intimate nature of their relationship. But just as significant, the letter reflected a willingness to accept these risks and anxieties in order to connect with gay life outside of their local city. The letter asserts their right to travel and move freely around the country in spite of the multiple dangers involved.

Several letter writers dreamed of moving to Los Angeles, which they imagined as a paradise of sunshine, beautiful people, and movie stars, with a large, vibrant gay social life. Reality was more complicated, but, like New York and San Francisco, Los Angeles was an important focal point of the burgeoning national gay minority. Simon, from a small town in Missouri, wrote a letter in 1956 asking about job prospects in Los Angeles.[43] Dorr Legg gave an encouraging reply: "Since about 1950, L.A. has been in a chronic state of boom. I can't imagine anyone coming here who truly wants a job and not being able to find one. But I do say a person should have a little to tide him over for a few weeks because it is a peculiar place in many ways and it takes some time before you can tread your way through all of the intricacies of this vast and scattered area. So, do not worry about work if you really wish to come. I am sure you would find something suitable."[44] Over the years, however, Legg's tone shifted dramatically when readers expressed a desire to move to Los Angeles. He warned them that Los Angeles was not the gay paradise they imagined. Aside from the aggressive police tactics used against homosexuals in the city, finding a job could be a major challenge for new arrivals. Compare Legg's optimistic 1956 reply to Simon to his grumpy 1965 reply to an eighteen-year-old also hoping to come to L.A. and find a job: "We would suggest that you stay right where you are unless you can come to Los Angeles with enough money to live for at least 6 months."[45] More generally, Legg was suggesting that gay people must plan their moves carefully and avoid simply hopping on a bus to the nearest big city. They might find themselves in a worse situation than the one they were leaving.

Letters to *ONE* were written voluntarily with no specific guidance from the magazine. Collectively, they offer a general sense of the issues on gay people's minds in the 1950s and early 1960s. In each of the categories described above, the letters revealed the complexities, intricacies, and difficulties in living one's life as a homosexual in these years. Gay fears of job loss and arrest, their lonely sufferings and defiant resiliency reflected the repressive political climate of the time. The letters reflected the myriad ways that the lavender scare in Washington, D.C., rippled throughout American society. But the letters also show that gay people did not hide in metaphorical closets in these years; instead, they found creative ways to assert their right to live their lives as gay people. Even in the most tragic, repressive situations, gay people made conscious choices that would determine their ability to survive. No matter how limited these choices, they were still choices. In spite of legal prohibitions, they exercised their rights to participate in gay culture and think of themselves as members of the gay minority. They retained significant degrees of control over their lives in the face of McCarthyite terror.

Ultimately, the issue that most preoccupied this group of correspondents was employment. Gay people working within the military-industrial complex of the growing cold war security state, whether as military draftees or as employees for government-contracted private companies, worried most acutely about their jobs because of federal government investigative machinery designed to sift out and banish gay workers. Their anxieties and their civil rights impulses are the focus of chapter 5.

5

"Branded Like a Horse"
Homosexuality, the Military, and Work

The anxieties unleashed by the federal government's lavender scare were captured poignantly in the character of Brigham Anderson from Allen Drury's Pulitzer Prize–winning novel *Advise and Consent*, which was published in 1959. Anderson was a handsome, confident U.S. Senator from Utah, married with a young child. During contentious hearings over a Secretary of State appointment, Anderson's political enemies conspired to use evidence of homosexuality to destroy him. They sent him a letter stating that if he did not drop his opposition to their favored appointee, they would reveal to the world that Anderson (a Mormon) had had a monthlong sexual affair with a man while serving in the military in World War II. Anderson's personality dramatically changed after getting the blackmail note: he became moody and impulsive, prone to rash decisions and snapping at people. Eventually his wife found one of the notes and confronted him about the affair. Unable to cope with the prospect of the press finding out the truth about his past, Anderson fatally shot himself (in the 1962 movie version he slit his throat).[1]

Gay people often committed suicide in mainstream novels and films in the 1960s, perpetuating the postwar stereotype of gay people as tragic figures with a frightening secret. Reality was more complicated. Most gay people did not kill themselves over the possibility their homosexuality would be discovered. But they did worry about this possibility, and like Brigham Anderson, persons who had served in the military worried the most. Ironically, gay people who risked their lives for their country by serving in the military suffered worse treatment than gay people who had not served in the military.

The letters reveal three main ways that the military worked against gay people. First, gay and lesbian people serving in the military feared being dishonorably discharged. Similar to federal government agencies, the military routinely cracked down on homosexuality in its ranks and investigated gay people in a McCarthyite manner involving secret files, naming names, and blacklisting. Second, thousands of people discharged from the military due to homosexuality discovered that getting a job in civilian life because of their homosexual discharges was exceedingly difficult. A record of a homosexual discharge marked a person and acted as a blacklisting mechanism for a range of professions. Third, gay people who worked for private companies in the defense industry discovered that their employers were often required to follow the same procedures as the federal government for exposing and removing gay people from their payrolls. Intensive background checks and even Rorschach tests indicating homosexuality could end a promising career.[2]

As stated previously, employment was the most frequently mentioned topic in the letters to *ONE* magazine. Similar to persons suspected of communist loyalties, many gay workers knew they would be blacklisted from their professions if their homosexuality were discovered. For some of these workers, the solution was to rigidly separate their professional and social lives. However, the creeping presence of the military in American life due to cold war anxieties complicated this effort. From the late 1940s to the 1960s, the most intensive investigations into homosexual employment occurred within the cluster of institutions that Dwight Eisenhower famously referred to as the "military-industrial complex." As the institutional bonds grew between the federal government, the military, and the private defense industry, antigay regulatory mechanisms swept across the country like a poisonous cloud.

Homophile activists and *ONE* readers were outraged that the military would treat its veterans so poorly. That American citizens who happened to be homosexual were being denied the right to earn a living after risking their lives to defend American freedom seemed unconscionable. In 1961, a *ONE* subscriber suggested that military service should be "one of our strongest bargaining points. Most kids I know 'came out' in the service. Having fought for our country, I think we have every right to make demands for our rights and protection. I feel there is something seriously wrong with the minds of those who call us undesirables, when many of us gave our time, blood, and lives to defend the rights we don't have."[3] Homosexual military discharges not only compromised gay people's work lives, but also denied them the generous benefits of the G.I. Bill in education, housing, and health care. Similar to the post–World War II African-American civil rights struggle, the potent combination of military service and subordinate civilian status instigated deep anger and collective activism, fueling the postwar civil rights impulse among American lesbians and gay men.[4]

Undesirable Employees

Approximately 13 percent of the letters used in this study touched on employment, more than any other issue.[5] This is not surprising considering the ways that McCarthyism targeted the work lives of its victims through blacklisting. Approximately one-quarter of these "job letters" described an actual job termination and one-third of them expressed worry about job termination. Losing a job or career represented a devastating loss of financial security, personal identity, status, and the ability to live an independent life. It meant depending on friends and family, maybe even moving in with them. This could significantly restrict an individual's ability to have a gay social life. Losing one's job due to homosexuality meant making difficult choices. After such an experience, people could choose to cut themselves off from gay life completely, or they could choose to assert their right to be gay more boldly. They had to choose whether to stay in the same line of work or start over in a new job or profession. Sometimes relocating made sense—but where? A big city with lots of gay social life, or somewhere isolated where a gay person might be left alone? Being fired due to homosexuality did not necessarily ruin a person's life, but picking up the pieces required hard thought and putting difficult decisions into practice.

Most homophile organizations considered job discrimination the most pressing issue facing the gay minority. Based on letters and phone calls received, ONE, Inc.'s Social Service Committee in 1958 ranked job anxieties over police harassment, family anxieties, or loneliness as the most significant issue confronting its readers.[6] Similarly, the Chicago-based Mattachine Midwest asked sixty of its members in the mid-1960s to rank a list of problems on a three-point scale, with "three" counting as the most significant problem. These Mattachine members gave the most points to "fear of being exposed as a homosexual and what this may do to my work life" (100 points), winning out over "inadequate sexual and personal life" (sixty-six points), "lack of community acceptance" (forty-one points), "emotional difficulties" (thirty-nine points), and "police trouble" (twenty points).[7] In 1955 Mattachine Midwest hosted a series of discussions devoted to the topic of employment. According to the organization's newsletter, "All agreed it was wise to keep one's sex interest as deeply submerged as possible on the job. . . . Some business organizations pass up top-notch talent because of an insistence that employees conform in every way."[8] Most gay people did not lose their jobs, but the data suggests that news of firings traveled along gay social networks and instilled a deep anxiety throughout the country. Worst-case scenarios loomed in the postwar gay and lesbian imagination.

Approximately one-fourth of the job letters expressed fear of losing jobs specifically in the government or military. Lonnie, a federal government worker, for example, instructed *ONE* not to print his name if the magazine published his letter because he happened "to depend for my living on a government job, and have no doubt that should a letter such as these just once appear in print over my signature, I would be fired immediately."[9] Clearly, he had given this matter a lot of thought and worried about the possibility (despite the fact that *ONE* never published correspondents' names unless they specifically gave permission to do so). His choice of words underscored his anxiety: he had "no doubt" he would be fired "immediately." Such comments reflected the specific anxieties of purchasing, contacting, or subscribing to *ONE*, as well as more general anxieties about gay visibility in everyday life.

Plenty of gay or lesbian people outside of government employment also worried about their jobs. Ray, from Chicago, described how an unfortunate incident wrecked his business career. He wrote in 1957, "Several years ago I was the victim of an entrapment, and because I was at that time on the way up in the business world, with a very fine job, the blocks were thrown at me. Cost—$8,000.00 to quiet things up. Also the loss of my job. It has taken two years for me to begin to recover my former prestige—in a different line of business, where no one knows of the past."[10] Ray paid a major price for his participation in gay life: $8,000 (the equivalent of approximately $65,000 in 2012), a lost job, and two years of turmoil. He chose to embark on a new career in response to his crisis. Yet he did not stop participating in gay life. His tragic experience did not deter him from thinking of himself as gay and living his life as a gay man.

A letter from Omaha, Nebraska, described the intense psychic toll a gay job firing could have on an individual. "I was first persecuted about 4 years ago," Greg wrote, "when I worked for a large insurance co. in Los Angeles. I became too friendly with another young man that worked in the office, although we never had sexual intercourse. I didn't realize until then I was homosexual." Awakening to his sexual identity caused distress in his professional life. "I became very neurotic, couldn't sleep nights, and my health deteriorated greatly. Finally after finishing the project I was working on I was fired and told they would give me good technical references but that I couldn't get along with other people. I've never been the same after that experience. It took over a year to find another job, and I've had my present job almost three years." To deal with his anxieties, he "found the best defense was to load myself up with tranquilizers" prescribed by his psychiatrist, and he recommended this option to gay people facing similar emotional distress.[11] The drugs helped Greg cope with a terrible situation and get through each day.

Whether or not an individual had served in the military, most gay men and lesbians hid their homosexuality in their professional lives. But saying that all gay people always passed as heterosexual on their jobs is inaccurate. The Daughters of Bilitis conducted a survey of 100 gay men and 100 lesbians in the late 1950s, and the findings suggest that only a minority of homosexuals passed as heterosexual to *everyone* in their work environment (see Table 1, Homosexual Visibility on the Job). Passing as heterosexual was rarely an all-or-nothing process, but rather, selective and situational. Gay and lesbian workers exercised important degrees of control over when, where, and to whom they revealed their homosexual identity.

This data suggests that lesbians concealed their homosexuality more carefully at work compared to gay men, reflecting gender discrimination and glass ceilings in postwar American workplaces. Lesbians faced discrimination based on their sexuality as well as their gender, yet had to be considerably more financially independent than most married heterosexual women. Lesbians worried immensely about their ability to maintain such independence.[12] "It was a very scary time," explained Del Martin, a founder of the Daughters of Bilitis, "and in some ways more scary because women always had more problems economically, so that if you worked your way up the academic ladder, for instance, you're not going to jeopardize that because you had to be so much better than men would have been."[13]

Blue-collar workers often escaped the intense background scrutiny facing many white-collar and professional workers. Membership in

Table 1. Homosexual Visibility on the Job

Homosexual Identification at Work	Men	Women
No Fellow Workers Know	12	39
Some Fellow Workers Know	37	50
Most Fellow Workers Know	18	4
No Reply or Doubtful	33	7
Total	100	100

a labor union, however, created additional layers of background scrutiny that could expose a worker's homosexuality. One man described such an experience to *ONE* in 1960. His brother was helping him find a job through an electrician's union, but when the union asked to see a copy of his military discharge and learned it was for homosexuality, he immediately became disqualified for all work as an electrician in the area. Furthermore, the man's brother refused to speak to him anymore. "I will end up in a mental institution if I don't find a job and stop sitting around the house brooding over my discharge," he wrote.[14] *ONE*'s in-house psychologist, Blanche Baker, responded to the man's letter, "Surely there must be small business concerns like privately owned gas filling stations, lunch counters, handy man and errand services, etc. where there is not such a detailed investigation of your past experience as there is in union and government controlled organizations," she wrote. In other words, lower your standards and avoid unionized jobs.[15]

Some gay men and lesbians believed that changing their sexual orientation (or at least *pretending* to change their orientation) was the best strategy for maintaining or resuming a professional career. Judges occasionally offered conversion therapy in lieu of jail time for homosexual arrests, allowing some homosexuals to keep their jobs.[16] Several choices of conversion therapy were available in the 1950s and 1960s. Psychoanalysis was popular, but also costly and time-consuming. Behaviorist aversive-conditioning techniques, usually involving drugs or electrical shocks, became more common in the 1960s. There was a nausea-based therapy where a person sat in a darkened room for hours listening to vomiting noises while looking at naked images of the same sex.[17] For some gay people this effort at conversion was sincere; for others, it was just a farcical ritual to stay employed. *ONE* railed against all such conversion efforts as torturous, ineffective, and barbaric.

Military Discharge Blues

If a person had received a "blue discharge"—a dishonorable, undesirable, or general military discharge due to homosexuality (printed on blue paper, hence a blue discharge)—then he or she was less likely to find and maintain a job. According to one blue discharge victim, "I had applied for a job at G.E. and I told them about my discharge. He said he could have hired me if I had served my time in prison for murder but not with that discharge. The Emporium (a department store) told me, we're sorry, we don't employ homosexuals. I tried to get a job with a trucking firm but they asked about the discharge. Wherever you go that discharge hangs over your head. Eventually it forced me into an occupation I hate."[18] The blue discharge was the primary blacklisting mechanism used by the U.S. military against gay people. During World War II, the military discharged approximately 10,000 servicemen and women because of homosexuality or suspected homosexuality. The expulsions declined by 50 percent after the war, but returned to their wartime levels (despite a significantly smaller military force) during the early 1950s as a result of the lavender scare. Overall, the U.S. military issued approximately 30,000 blue discharges from 1952 to 1965, an average of 2,150 each year. The Navy expelled the most homosexuals, approximately half of the total number.[19]

Throughout most of the 1940s, the military made no distinction between consensual sex and homosexual rape, nor did it distinguish homosexual behavior from a mere confession of homosexual desire. In October 1949, the military revised its policies and began categorizing homosexuals into three classes. A Class I homosexual was an individual accused of homosexual rape, seduction of a minor, intimidation, or blackmail. These cases usually resulted in a dishonorable discharge or imprisonment. Class II, the most commonly applied category, applied to individuals who had engaged in consensual homosexual acts or had propositioned others for sex. These cases typically resulted in an undesirable discharge, a less severe penalty than a dishonorable discharge. Class III homosexuals were those with homosexual desires who claimed they had not committed an actual homosexual act. These cases could result in general or honorable discharges, depending on the individual's record.[20]

Small adjustments were made to these classifications over the years. In 1955 several U.S. Congressman introduced clauses to consider good character, military record, and mitigating circumstances to temper the severity of these policies.[21] In 1958 additional provisions allowed honorable discharges for Class II homosexuals and discouraged less-than-honorable discharges for Class III homosexuals.[22] Many military leaders, however, disliked these changes and demanded bolder action in expelling homosexuals from the military. In 1955, for example, an Army general demanded an investigation because he was "disturbed about the number of homosexuals being discovered among the officers in the U.S. Army," according to an Army report. Investigators concluded that current methods of homosexual detection were sufficient, but expressed concern that "some military personnel are interested in *ONE* and may possibly subscribe to the publication. It is not possible to ascertain the number of military personnel subscribing to the publication without the publication's mailing list. It is doubtful if all newsstand purchasers could ever be identified." The report concluded that no homosexual organizations such as the Mattachine Society or the Daughters of

Bilitis existed within the military, despite the interest in *ONE* magazine by some of its personnel.[23]

Certain military officials argued that homosexuals (like communists) blended unnoticed into the military population and threatened to infect other soldiers with homosexuality. A 1953 Navy edict declared that homosexuality must be eradicated from the Navy in order "to prevent young persons in the naval service from falling victim to this vicious and degenerate practice. . . . It is a prime characteristic of homosexuals to zealously attempt to enlarge the group of social outcasts to which they belong."[24] Gay people were "security and reliability risks who discredit themselves and the Navy by their homosexual conduct." The Army declared in 1966 that homosexuals impaired "the morale and discipline of the army" and that "homosexuality is a manifestation of a severe personality defect which appreciably limits the ability of such individuals to function effectively in society."[25]

Such policies baffled and infuriated gay people who wanted to join the military. Elson from Virginia commented to *ONE* in 1961, "the Government agencies and the Armed Forces continue from month to month and year to year to discharge or force out homosexuals without realizing how much manpower they are losing. . . . Instead of giving the Communists additional weapons against us as a nation, we should be depriving them of as many weapons as possible."[26] In Elson's view, the fear of homosexuality was hampering the struggle against communism.

Enforcement of antihomosexual policies varied throughout the military. Some officers zealously enforced them. A 1961 letter from Jesse, for example, described how a friend in Air Force basic training had encountered a homophobic officer prone to raving diatribes against gay people in the form of "educational lectures":

> One particular lecture was a great shock to me, as also to my friend. It was a hate and smear, witch-burning tirade against homosexuals, a real hell-fire-and-damnation "pep" rally designed to whip up the most savage of emotions and cause "barracks buddies" to report on one another. The homosexual was branded as an animal to be hated, tortured, persecuted ("The Air Force is a high class organization," he ranted while proceeding to prove just the opposite). Worst, and most shocking of all, this officer branded all homosexuals as would-be traitors to their country, who would and will defect to the communists and sell out America. I am very accustomed to the usual type of attack on homosexuals, but this is pretty

below-the-belt. . . . I was in the Air Force myself during [the] World War II years and never encountered anything like this.[27]

Jesse's final sentence suggests his own experiences were far different from his friends, and other letters reported a more lackadaisical attitude toward homosexuality among the high-ranking members of the military. "The official policy is completely antihomosexual, but judging from my own experience practice varies greatly from service to service, post to post, and time to time," wrote Wayne, a professor at Vassar College in 1959. In his experience, many military officers left gay people alone. "Probably no commanding officer would admit to sheltering homosexuals, but I believe that sometimes they find it convenient not to examine their men's private lives too closely."[28] Another example of military tolerance came from Sean, who described a friend who had freely admitted to his draft board that he was homosexual only to be told, "this no longer made any difference, and that all he had to do to conform to the Army regulations was not to have sex on the base. . . . The young man in question has been in the Army for about three months, and has been rapidly advanced because of . . . ROTC experience."[29] Sean asked ONE if the military had changed its antigay policies. Dorr Legg replied, "in different areas under different jurisdictions there may be a loosening or a tightening, according to who is boss."[30]

Many trademark tactics of McCarthyism characterized gay military discharges, such as requiring victims to identify other gay people, humiliating public exposure, and professional blacklisting. A soldier's homosexuality usually came to light because of other gay people already under investigation. By naming names, a person increased his or her chances of receiving a general or honorable discharge, and future employers were less likely to look into the details of such a discharge compared to an undesirable or dishonorable discharge. Once identified, military authorities used interrogations and psychiatric evaluations to determine whether the suspected homosexual belonged to Class I, Class II, or Class III. Individuals who refused to sign confessions appeared before administrative boards consisting of officers with the power to call witnesses and present evidence against the accused. In most cases the person was found guilty. On their way out, gay discharge victims were told to expect no back pay, no military benefits, and, according to an Air Force document, "substantial prejudice in civilian life."[31]

Like civilian police arrest victims, military blue discharge victims usually signed whatever piece of paper was put in front of them to end their ordeal as quickly as possible. Out of 165 Army officers expelled for homosexuality from 1953 to 1955, for example, only 11 officers challenged their accusations, and all 11 of these resulted in courts-martial and discharges.[32] The Air Force's Application for Discharge (Class II), issued in 1956, was a typical confession to homosexuality in the military. The application consisted of six statements:

1. I have been informed by my commander that he proposes to initiate action against me under AFR [Air Force Regulations] 35–66 (Class II).

2. I have read AFR 35–66 and understand that under regulation I am entitled to an impartial hearing by a board of officers and that at that hearing I am entitled to counsel and to present evidence and call witnesses on my behalf. I hereby waive my entitlement to counsel and to present evidence and call witnesses on my behalf. I hereby waive my entitlement to appear before the board and I *request* discharge without the benefit of board proceedings. I understand that, if this application is approved, I may be discharged under other than honorable conditions.

3. I also hereby tender my resignation for the good of the service from all appointments held by me in the United States Air Force. . . .

4. I *understand* that, if I am discharged under other than honorable conditions, I may be deprived of many rights as a veteran both under Federal and State legislation and that I may expect to encounter substantial prejudice in civilian life in situations where the character of service rendered in the Armed Forces or the type of discharge received may have a bearing.

5. Legal counsel has been made available to me. (I did not avail myself of legal counsel) (name of counsel) on (date or dates).

6. I voluntarily sign this application of my own free will. A copy of this application has been retained by me.[33]

Tens of thousands of men and women, in a panicky haste, signed military confessions such as this in order to minimize whatever damage their blue discharges would create in their lives. In signing such a document, soldiers and officers consigned themselves to a future of impending, systematic personal and professional discrimination. Most felt they had no choice but to sign it, despite all of the document's language intended to give the appearance of a voluntary confession.

Many persons who signed such discharge confessions had distinguished careers and extensive combat experience. Dan from Pennsylvania, for example, was a sixteen-year Army veteran when two lovers "got scared" and named him during an investigation. Dan pled guilty to homosexual charges to avoid publicity. He received a dishonorable discharge and nine months detention at Fort Leavenworth—an unusually harsh penalty for a Class II discharge. "The ironic thing," Dan wrote in 1960, "is that several other men were guilty of similar behavior in another outfit but they were just transferred to other units." He blamed an overzealous enforcer for his severe punishment, "My colonel got excited and threw the book at me but when the other fellows were accused saner heads convinced him to use less drastic measures. Everyone was amazed at the deal I got inasmuch as I had an outstanding military record. I have the Silver Star, Purple Heart, eleven battle stars, served in World War II and twice in Korea during combat and had outstanding units as a first sergeant." An Army psychiatrist testified during Dan's hearing, and Dan believed that "the Court Martial Board was influenced by the psychiatrist's report. . . . Of course the idiot knew that I had entered a plea of guilty so his statement seemed silly." Military branches during the 1950s relied increasingly on testimony from psychiatrists and other scientific experts. Dan wrote this letter to *ONE* shortly after his release from prison. Lacking a job, Dan had moved back home with his parents, who lived in a small Pennsylvania town with a population of 1,800. Dan knew no other gay people in the area. "I am now out of the Army; out of a job; out of circulation."[34]

Prison sentences were usually reserved for those who fought their charges, such as Edward who had been named as homosexual during an investigation. "At my trial," he wrote, "I proved by the sworn testimony of a full colonel that at the time I was alleged to have been having an illicit affair, I was actually working in the Colonel's office with him and several other officers, and that we did not leave our office until 2:30 A.M. I was still convicted, dishonorably discharged, and sentenced to five years' hard labor." Had Edward just signed a confession, he probably would have been spared prison. This was why people confessed so readily even when the specific charges against them were untrue. There was no further correspondence to indicate whether he served the full five years or was released early. He noted in his letter that the prison chaplain was also gay, and that the prison psychiatrist had been genuinely helpful to him during this stressful ordeal.[35]

Lesbians were subject to the same unjust proceedings as gay men. A self-described "career-driven" woman who was "gung-ho" about the Air Force explained in *America's Working Women: A Documentary History* that she was "like a lamb to slaughter" during the proceedings against her. During her interrogation sessions, "they [her investigators] would produce a whole list of names. They must have had a whole goddamn squadron of names," she explained. After refusing to name any names, she became the focus of a court-martial. "Once the court-martial was in session, nobody read me any rights, told me I could have a defense counsel, or that it was my right to have somebody on that board representing me." They asked her questions such as "Did I realize that I was a security risk being homosexual? . . . The entire process took about fifteen minutes." Given the opportunity to defend herself, she said, "I don't think I deserve this, . . . to be discharged from the service, because I feel that my record speaks for itself, that I have never done anything injurious or harmful to anyone else." After a few minutes of conferring, the board told her she was to receive a "general discharge." The discharge derailed her career plans to become "a thirty-year WAF [Women in the Air Force]."[36]

Even when a person cooperated with military authorities, the impact of a military discharge could be devastating. A man named Geoff told *ONE* that military authorities had discovered his "discrete" affair with another man while stationed in France during the 1950s. Geoff lived a "double life"; he was married to a woman and had children. "I immediately tendered my resignation. All the higher brass were so frightened that I would tell all I knew about homosexual activities in the European Command and create a big scandal that they hustled me out of France and discharged me at Fort Hamilton, N.Y., on 12 Feb. 1957." Because of his discharge, the military hastily expelled his family from France as well. They lost all of their furniture and most of their other possessions because the military allowed them to take only what they could carry on the plane. Geoff received no pension despite nineteen years of military service; all told, a devastating attack on his family's financial stability.[37]

Other letters similarly described family anxieties caused by military expulsions. A man named Jack told *ONE* he had become the subject of an Army investigation after getting caught masturbating in a shower. After Jack admitted he was gay under intense interrogation, his superiors "offered me two choices: accept a general discharge NOW or face a court-martial and get booted out later. Naturally I accepted the general discharge." He was going home for Christmas, but after that, "I don't want to be near my folks and I'm not at all sure how they'll react[;] I guess I'll head for California and settle near Los Angeles."[38] Timothy, an

African-American machinist living in South Carolina, also reported significant family anxieties as a result of his blue discharge. He told *ONE* in
1958 that he had moved back in with family. "I am having to live off my
parents right now and the situation is not so good as I cannot answer certain questions that eventually will come up," such as why he was having
so much trouble finding a job. He had not yet told his parents the truth
about his discharge. He wrote, "My type of discharge prevents me from
obtaining and holding a decent job. I received a Class II Homosexual
discharge for being associated with friends of that nature. Of course I
am of that nature myself but still feel I was done an injustice by being
labeled or branded like a horse."[39]

These blue discharges deprived gay and lesbian veterans of the
generous G.I. Bill benefits that hoisted many World War II vets into the
middle class. They also disqualified homosexuals from a broad range of
jobs and occupations in civilian life. Blue discharges, according to historian Leisa Meyer, branded homosexuals as "social misfits, and most
employers were unwilling to hire individuals whom the military had
deemed unacceptable."[40] Ronald, a former Navy medic, for example,
described how his blue discharge hampered his ability to keep a job.
Ronald decided not to tell his first employer (a meat packing company)
about the discharge, but a polygraph test exposed this fact and cost him
the job. He lost another job as a retail clerk because of the discharge as
well. "I know that your magazine does not run an employment agency,
but let us say I didn't know who else to turn to," he wrote. He asked if
ONE magazine would pay his bus fare to Los Angeles and help him find
a new job. "I am 29 years old and I know that I have a lot left in me to
prove that I can still be a useful citizen to this country if just given the
chance."[41] Ronald was not the only person to request bus fare from *ONE*,
but the magazine's resources were too meager to fulfill these requests.

Most employers asked about military discharges as a matter of routine, and some asked for documentation as a condition of employment.[42]
Lesbian and gay job candidates faced a choice: tell the truth or lie. If
they told the truth, their chances of getting the job usually plummeted.
If they lied about the nature of their discharge or claimed to have accidentally "lost" their documents, they were more likely to get hired, but
would worry about their employer discovering the truth in the future. At
a certain point, most gays and lesbians adapted by finding an employer
who did not ask about their discharge or who did not care that they were
homosexual. Some individuals learned to conceal their homosexuality,
and some switched careers, jobs, and professions. Like a homosexual
arrest, a gay military discharge posed daunting challenges but was not
necessarily the end of the world. Mr. S. of Los Angeles told *ONE* in 1960:

I was discharged from the services because of being a homosexual, and of course thought my life was ruined. Well, I
got hold of myself and found by using the excuse of being
in school I could explain away the years in the service. To
explain away the 4-F draft card was easy—a bad back, which
no one can prove differently.

I have met quite a number of men who have "gay discharge" records from the services. Most have stopped worrying
about it and done something for themselves. But there are
still some who are afraid to try to get away from the past and
look to the future.

There are plenty of jobs which don't ask for service records. As long as you have filled your time in the service they
hire you. I was one of three hundred and fifty discharged at
the same time, so there must be a lot of men with UD [unde-
sirable] discharges running around.[43]

The letter suggested that a little deception could go a long way in overcoming the obstacles of a gay discharge. Different careers, positions, and
bosses elicited different levels of background scrutiny, so there was a
level of chance involved whenever a person with a gay military discharge
looked for a job. Eventually, something would work out, but getting there
might involve suffering. Daughters of Bilitis activist Helen Sanders con-
curred in 1957 that she knew many people who had figured out ways to
get around their discharges. Sanders admitted, however, that gay people
should avoid civil service or government jobs.[44]

Beyond the Military

As a result of the growth of the military-industrial complex, which insti-
tutionally linked government security policies with private defense companies, military homosexual investigations sometimes spilled over into
civilian workplaces. A pair of letters from a Florida doctor, Tim, provides
a detailed narrative describing how a civilian's life could be turned
upside-down because of the military's paranoia over homosexuality.
While serving as chief anesthesiologist at a Key West, Florida, general
hospital during the late 1950s and early 1960s, Tim enjoyed numerous
love affairs with male military personnel stationed at a nearby naval
base. He did little to conceal these relationships. In the case of one boyfriend, he wrote, "I was introduced to his ship mates, his officers, and
to his brother who was serving aboard the same ship. To the best of my

knowledge there was no talk about us even though he moved into my home and drove my car daily. We frequently entertained members of his crew for dinner or for general gatherings in my home."[45] The boyfriend shipped out after a year and a half, ending the affair, but Tim soon fell for another sailor, "a member of the weight-lifting Body Beautiful Club. This one, too, I made no secret of and even became so bold that I took him (upon invitation) to visit ranking naval officers with whom I worked. He was known as 'Tim's boy' and frequently invitations would arrive which said, 'and bring along your Boy.'" Over the years, Tim's house became a popular gathering place for local gay servicemen. He had several more affairs, including one with a member of the elite flying squadron the Blue Angels.[46]

Eventually Tim's lack of discretion caught up with him. In February 1961, Tim returned home late at night and learned from a friend that "the police were looking for me and that I should leave the country at once." The next day at Tim's hospital, two sheriff's detectives asked to speak with him on the lawn outside the hospital "so we could not be 'overheard.'" They explained he was being charged with having committed a "crime against nature" with three sailors. One of these sailors had been a steady boyfriend; another, a one-time encounter. Tim was certain he had never met the third sailor before.[47]

Tim was arrested, jailed, and his bail was set at the exorbitant amount of $6,000 (the equivalent of approximately $44,000 in 2012). He learned from friends that he had been named during a large-scale homosexual crackdown in Miami, which was notorious for antigay crackdowns in the 1950s. "Seems a fabulous faggot in Miami had been giving a party which was raided and 'there were more than thirty members of the armed forces present in various stages of undress.' [Tim was quoting a newspaper clipping.] Included were several from Key West. These men were told that they would not be prosecuted if they would inform on homosexuals in Key West and appear against them in court!" Three of the sailors questioned had mentioned Tim's name.[48]

Because of his prestigious position at the hospital, Tim was a big catch for the local prosecutor. His arrest became front-page news. A newspaper article portrayed him as "a combination of Bluebeard and Elmer Gantry," he wrote sarcastically. "It seemed that I stood on a corner with a tambourine and lured poor innocent sailors into my den where they were forced into a life of sin!" Tim was banished from his hospital, and the staff "was warned to have no contact with me upon pain of dismissal." Clearly he would not work as an anesthesiologist in Key West anymore.[49]

Tim suffered his greatest humiliation when the charges against him were read aloud in open court during his arraignment: "that you did take into your mouth the sexual organ of said witness and perform the detestable and abominable act of crime against nature. . . . And this was repeated three times!" Tim wrote. "Never has anything been so upsetting to me." Tim's regular lawyer refused to handle the case; five more lawyers he contacted refused as well. Tim eventually found, in his words, a "fix expert" who accepted his case but charged high fees—$300 initially plus a $500 retainer and, shortly after the trial got underway, another $1,000 without explanation. On the day of the trial, the courtroom was packed with reporters. Navy lawyers wanted to "make an example of this man (me) and show that conduct of this type could not be allowed in the Key West area." The prosecutor demanded Tim serve sixty *years* in prison. The fix lawyer told Tim if he paid him another $1,200, Tim's plea could be changed to guilty and Tim would only serve three years. "By this time I would have admitted anything to escape the threat of 60 years!" The deal was made, and Tim was sentenced to three years in prison. However, if Tim ever returned to Monroe County, he would still face the full sixty-year sentence.[50]

All of this happened very quickly and unexpectedly. Within a few days, his career was ruined. Tim's anesthesiologist license was revoked. He served a few months in prison before being relocated to a "halfway house." He told *ONE* he could only find a low-level office job through a temporary employment agency.[51] Tim's case demonstrated the heightened vulnerability of gay people working in jobs with any institutional or geographical proximity to the military. It was not Tim's open homosexual socializing that caught the attention of law enforcement, but the fact that this socializing involved military personnel.

Throughout the 1950s, a growing number of American workers found their jobs connected in some manner with the military or institutions related to national security. The cold war escalated contractual alliances and interdependencies between federal government agencies (especially the military) and private industries such as aerospace, computing, communications, and electronics. President Eisenhower gave an ominous warning about the growth of a military-industrial complex in his 1961 presidential farewell speech, and later in the 1960s these alliances between government and defense companies became a source of widespread social protest.[52] As more private companies performed government-contracted work related to national security, the antihomosexual policies of the federal government and military spread into private employment. Companies required more stringent security clearances for their employees, disqualifying thousands of gay people from working in this growing field. One historian estimated that "by 1953, approximately one in five Americans in the workforce—13.5 million people in all—had

gone through some form of loyalty-security check for possible government or defense industry employment, and millions of secret dossiers
for individuals had been created."[53] Detecting homosexuality was a major
goal of these background checks.

Homophile activists were well aware of this trend. Harry Hay, the
founder of the Mattachine Society, for example, remarked that many of
the earliest Mattachine members had been Southern California defense
industry workers worried about losing their jobs due to security clearances.[54] A disproportionate number were in Southern California because
of the massive growth of defense industries in the region during and after
World War II. An American Civil Liberties Union lawyer told a homophile convention in 1962 that the Defense Department "has the greatest
employment impact on the nation. . . . Ever since the Joseph McCarthy
era the Defense Department has held tenaciously to the witch-hunt on
homosexuals."[55] In other words, private companies involved in national
defense usually adopted the employment policies of the defense department, and antigay policies were just as widespread in the early 1960s
as the early 1950s when Joe McCarthy wandered the halls of Congress.

A series of letters from John, an engineer, captured the anxieties
many gay people suffered who worked in the defense industry. John
worked for a Dallas aircraft company and had just learned that he was
about to undergo a security clearance upgrade. Using the pseudonym
"Lloyd," he wrote in February 1959:

> I work in a defense plant and am in what is called a sensitive
> position, i.e.: I handle classified documents and other gov-
> ernment material. The highest classification of any material I
> have ever handled, or needed to handle, since I've been with
> the company is *confidential*. Now, when I started to work with
> the company several years ago, I was cleared for confidential
> *by the company* without difficulty in about one or two weeks.
>
> Three weeks ago I was notified that everyone in my
> group (including myself, of course) was expected to submit
> an application for *secret* clearance. *Secret* is a much higher
> classification than *confidential* and is done by the government,
> not the company, and requires three months of intensive in-
> vestigation, not one or two weeks. I've even been told that it
> costs the government $6,000 for investigation of one person.

John explained that a past admission of homosexuality was haunting
him. It involved the military, but not a blue discharge. "When I was called
up for my examination by the draft board many years ago, I submitted

to the examining doctor a psychiatrists' affidavit to the effect that I am homosexual. After he read the affidavit, the doctor made one statement which until recently did not worry me: 'This will go down on your record, you know.'" John volunteered the information because he had no desire to serve in the military. "I'm now wondering if I'm going to have to pay the piper for having so obtained my 1V-F rating." Unsure whether the background check for his enhanced security clearance would include a report from the draft board or not, he asked *ONE* what he should do. "Would I be better off to quit my job and go to work for some other company which does not require a secret clearance? If so, do you know of any aircraft companies which do not require secret clearances in the engineering department?"[56] John seemed to sense his homosexuality would be discovered.

The day after writing his letter to *ONE*, John was fired from his job. His secret had been discovered. After a week passed with no reply from *ONE*, John wrote another letter to the magazine, repeating his story and adding a $5 contribution with a self-addressed envelope. He wanted to avoid becoming "washed up in my line of work in the aircraft industry. So please, oh please, hurry!"[57] As more time passed with no reply from *ONE*, John became convinced that the U.S. Postal Service had seized his letters. He explained in his third letter:

> I am led to the belief that you never received either of my two letters. This implies that the post office opened them and read them—information which was never intended for their eyes— and then refused to deliver them to you. There was absolutely nothing in either letter . . . which was the least bit obscene or in any way unmailable. I know the trouble you've had and that bunch at the Los Angeles post office ought to be ousted from their jobs and whole rotten lot of them thrown in prison and the keys thrown away. But there's nothing I can do about it except tell you about it. That is, if this letter ever gets to you. Now, on those first two letters I did not put my return address on the outside. On this one I am. This may make a difference. If you receive this letter, I trust you will make a prompt reply via the enclosed envelope. . . .[58]

Not only was he out of a job, but now he had to worry about an entirely separate issue. Postal censorship was not an unreasonable hypothesis, but in reality Dorr Legg was behind in his correspondence.[59] Usually Legg responded to letters in a timely matter—the next day, or within a week— but when ONE, Inc.'s projects piled up, correspondence could sit on his desk for over a month. This is what happened to John's letters. John sent one more panicked telegram, and then his correspondence ends. Like Tim, John's career was finished because of his professional proximity to national defense. Without the need for the enhanced security upgrade, his homosexuality most likely would have continued to be hidden from his employers.

Gay people were not automatically second-class citizens in postwar America. They *became* second-class citizens through ritualized humiliations such as gay military discharges and job discrimination. Such experiences tested gay people's skills in adapting to difficult situations. One man explained how his military discharge had given him "a certain fox and hounds shrewdness." It had enhanced his ability to "take social disguises, alertness for danger in social situations. . . . You become more alert and more aware because it's necessary, it's like the fox being able to hear the hounds baying even though they're not in earshot . . . it's sort of a super sensitiveness, to danger . . . it's self preservation."[60]

Such experiences also made many gay people more aware of the broader political and social forces working against them, fueling a civil rights impulse and a desire to fight back. Andy, from Highland Park, Michigan, described the awakening of his political consciousness in a 1954 letter. Andy wrote to President Eisenhower and forwarded a copy to *ONE*. He wrote his letter in the same year that the landmark U.S. Supreme Court decision *Brown vs. Board of Education* outlawed racial segregation. Andy's letter echoes the spirit of the civil rights movement, and like so many activists for racial integration in the 1950s, military service was at the heart of the matter:

> My father and grandfather were both naval officers during [World War I]. They fought to help keep this nation free from the enemys [*sic*] of freedom. When I got out of high school, I joined the United States Army to help defend my country against all our enemys. I was a proud proud person wearing the Army uniform. I was proud to go anywhere my country sent me. . . . After 9 months I was relieved from serving my country for the rest of my life. They told me that my kind of people was not good enough for this country's service, now or ever.
>
> It was then I began to take a second look at my country. I began to see we don't have the freedoms our forefathers fought for. We were supposedly given the right to be heard, but we have been silenced. . . . When we try to stand up for our rights, we are shoved down deeper into the barrels of slavery. . . .

My people have fought and died for this country. They wanted to have the freedoms promised us. We all want peace and understanding, but we haven't received either one.

I am a homosexual: a person who loves his own sex. People say it's wrong for me to be this way, I have been this since I was a child. I believe that God has the right to give the greatest gift of life and that is the love of life for his fellow man. It is a God granted gift that no man or woman has the right to take it from another person.

I was worried at one time for being what I was, but then I decided to pray for help and the answer was given to me. Live your life clean and decent and give your Love to the one you think deserves it. Live your life together and be joyful and happy with life.[61]

This letter captured the growing social consciousness, group identification, and resilient spirit of gay men and lesbians in the 1950s. In the first paragraph, Andy referred to "my kind of people"; later in the letter he wrote simply "my people." The collective experiences of military humiliations and job anxieties highlighted the depths that McCarthyism bore into the postwar gay and lesbian experience. The experiences spurred such an outrage that homosexuals ultimately emerged as a more cohesive national minority.

The military was not the only sphere of employment that posed enhanced dangers for gay and lesbian workers. At least as anxiety-ridden was the field of education. From elementary schools to prestigious universities, gay people working as teachers, professors, librarians, and administrators (as well as students) worried intensely about losing their jobs. The next chapter examines the plight of gay and lesbian educators.

6

Classroom Anxieties
Educators and Homosexuality

In the popular 1953 Broadway play *Tea and Sympathy*, a teacher named Harris befriends a sulky, naive, and effeminate teenage student named Tom Lee. Both Harris and Tom Lee are rumored to be gay at their elite prep school, and rumors fly wildly after other students witness the two swimming in the nude at a local beach. Eventually the rumors make their way to the dean's office, and Harris learns his job is in jeopardy as a result. Unaware that other students had witnessed them, Harris assumes that Tom had told the dean about their outing and perhaps lied that something sexual had occurred between them. Harris confronts Tom:

> HARRIS: [The dean] didn't call you in and ask you about last Saturday afternoon?
>
> TOM: Why should he? I didn't do anything wrong.
>
> HARRIS: About being with me?
>
> TOM: I'm allowed to leave town for the day in the company of a master.
>
> HARRIS: I don't believe you. You must have said something.
>
> TOM: About what?
>
> HARRIS: About you and me going down to the dunes and swimming.

TOM: Why should I tell him about that?

HARRIS: (*Threatening*) Why didn't you keep your mouth shut?

TOM: About what, for God's sake?

HARRIS: I never touched you, did I?

TOM: What do you mean, touch me?

HARRIS: Did you say to the Dean I touched you?

TOM: (*Turning away from Harris*) I don't know what you're talking about.

HARRIS: Here's what I'm talking about. The Dean's had me on the carpet all afternoon. I probably won't be reappointed next year . . . all because I took you swimming down off the dunes on Saturday.[1]

Harris's paranoia captured the anxiety thousands of gay and lesbian educators suffered in these years. Persons suspected of being gay or lesbian were watched more carefully by their bosses and colleagues, and rumors or accusations could end a career. Harris's paranoia also reflected patterns of McCarthyism because he assumed Tom had informed on him. Tom, completely unaware anything might have been inappropriate about their swimming together and that others might read sexual meanings into it, truthfully denied informing on his teacher. Ultimately, Harris lost his job, and Tom suffered taunts and harassment from his classmates for the remainder of the play. (Interestingly, the character of Harris was cut from 1956 movie version of *Tea and Sympathy* because filmmakers wanted to tone down the story's gay themes.)[2]

Teachers have long been held to higher standards of public morality than other professionals because they serve as role models. In years past, teachers were prohibited from "smoking, drinking, dancing, cursing, theatre-going, divorce, breaking the Sabbath, or (for women) staying out after dark," according to one scholar.[3] Homosexuality had always been considered unacceptable for teachers in the United States, but before World War II it was less talked about in the field of education and there were significant degrees of freedom within that silence. After World War II, however, after the Kinsey Reports and the lavender scare, there was more of an urgency to discover and dismiss lesbian and gay teachers. Not only were gay people national security threats in an era of cold war peril (hence, untrustworthy in a classroom), but many experts feared that gay teachers might "infect" students with their homosexuality. Many psychologists, the socially recognized experts on homosexuality in the 1950s, believed that homosexuality was a socially acquired trait, that it was "learned behavior." Homosexuality resulted when something "went wrong" during a child or adolescent's psychosexual development, according to their theories. Experts usually blamed overbearing mothers, but they also warned of the grave dangers posed by gay or lesbian educators at all levels of education.[4]

Before World War II, gay and especially lesbian teachers blended into their professions easier because unmarried people dominated the profession. In 1920, for example, 78 percent of teachers were single women (including those divorced or widowed). By 1960, however, that number had dropped to 29 percent. Schools aggressively pushed to hire teachers who were married, which drew more attention to the bachelor and "spinster" teachers who might be gay or lesbian.[5] Gay people in heterosexual marriages also had to be extra cautious in their behavior.

The letters show that gay and lesbian educators dealt with the anxieties of their profession in several ways. Most commonly, they had discrete gay social relations completely separate from their work lives. This meant no trysts with other faculty, employees, or, in the case of college campuses, students, and it usually meant traveling to distant cities or gay bars to participate in gay life. A smaller number were willing to take the risk, going to local gay bars and cruising areas, but this was asking for trouble, especially at public institutions compared to private schools or colleges. Caution and desire commingled uneasily. The more active a faculty member's gay life, the more likely her or his name might surface to a dean, such as what happened with Harris in *Tea and Sympathy*. The letters show that some teachers avoided local gay social scenes and preferred to connect with other gay people through the mail by having gay pen pals or subscribing to physique or homophile magazines. This seemed like a safer alternative, but many gay teachers learned the hard way that mere investigation into obscene mail by the U.S. Postal Service could end their careers. The safest option was celibacy, but because rumors alone could kill a career, even celibacy was no guarantee of security. For gay and lesbian teachers, there were no ideal choices for maintaining a career and living a gay life. All choices contained risks with serious consequences.

Teaching Anxieties

Public schools, including institutions of higher education, were expected to have zero tolerance toward gay teachers and faculty because of their influence over impressionable American youth. The goal, which was to rid *all* of them from the profession, was reflected in a 1954 newspaper article describing the arrest and subsequent dismissal of a school principal in Burbank, California. District officials boasted that the dismissal meant that the district was now completely free of "sex deviates."[6] In addition to arrests, school districts conducted their own investigations to determine who was gay and lesbian. A man in Yuma, Arizona, wrote that his partner "was involved in the 'perge' [*sic*] to rid the teaching profession of supposedly undesirables—assistance given by a very sick member. Never any legal action taken, just mountains of mental pressure." In true McCarthyite form, the partner's name came up during an investigation, and he became the focus of a separate investigation solely on that basis. The partner quit teaching because of the pressure.[7]

Given such a zero tolerance attitude, many gay and lesbian educators separated their professional and sexual lives as much as possible. They avoided local gay and lesbian gatherings, bars, and cruising areas, instead going to neighboring towns, cities, or regions to meet other gay people. "My sexual conquests are never in my home community—hence I cannot be regarded as a bad influence in the institution it is my privilege to serve," one teacher wrote.[8] Distance between home and school also dampened anxieties over discovery. A high school teacher in West Hollywood, Florida, explained in an oral history that he lived nineteen miles away from his school (which he considered a long commute) because he knew "that I couldn't be a teacher, a homosexual, and also live" near the school where he worked. He added that local police officers wrote down license plate numbers of cars parked at gay bars and threatened patrons with publicizing this information. "I always parked my car far away," he stated.[9] Aliases were common when gay teachers went socializing. At school social functions, such as Christmas parties, a cautious gay or lesbian teacher might bring a member of the opposite sex (often gay or lesbian themselves) as a date to give the appearance of heterosexuality and quell gay rumors.

The zero tolerance attitude did not necessarily deter gay people from becoming teachers, but striking a balance between professional life and social life required considerable thought. Too much caution meant isolation from gay life, which could cause despair and loneliness. Too much boldness, however, could result in excruciating anxiety over the fear of discovery or possibly a wrecked career. A letter from Sarah, who lived in Bay Shore, New York, demonstrated the types of questions that ran through many teachers' minds during the McCarthy years:

> How frequently do teachers lose jobs because of suspicion in this area? I have read in recent issues of *ONE* about teachers in Florida who have been having trouble.

Would a school give a reference to someone whom they had
  let go under these conditions (assuming that the individual
  had not carried out any debatable activities in school)?
Would this person be blacklisted by other schools?
Would such an event be reported in local newspapers?
The envelope that *ONE* is mailed in has a return address. Does
  the post office keep track of who received mail from such
  addresses? (This sounds ridiculous, but I read something
  in a local paper recently indicating that this is so.)
Can any kind of legal action be taken against a person if it
  is known that the person receives ONE publications or
  engages in work for the organization?
Might the information be given to the person's employer?[10]

There was little way for a person like Sarah to know the answers to these questions. Being in the dark about the scope of gay teacher purges itself provoked significant anxiety. Aside from occasional media reports of specific arrests and firings, such data was not available. If she asked anyone in her school district these questions, she would immediately raise suspicions about herself.

Sarah's questions also revealed her mistrust of the U.S. Postal Service. One of her major concerns was whether subscribing to *ONE* might get her fired. The answer was yes, it could, but probably would not because postal officials tended to be more concerned about visually stimulating homosexual materials circulating through the mails, such as physique, nude, or pornographic photographs. Postal officials were also more concerned with gay pen-pal networks than with letters to *ONE*. Thus corresponding with *ONE* was relatively safe, but many teachers and educators learned to exercise caution whenever using the U.S. Postal Service. Nothing that was sent through the mail was really private, as a letter from a woman in Long Island revealed: "[W]hen I drove to the Post Office I saw the bastard handling the mail holding the letters up to the light!"[11] Certain postal inspectors kept a close watch for homosexual material sent through the mail and passed evidence along to the FBI.

Approximately 5 percent of the total letters examined for this study mentioned anxieties or incidents involving the Post Office. Of these "postal letters," slightly under half of them expressed worry about their mail being investigated, and approximately 60 percent of them described actual incidents involving postal officials. Many of these postal letters involved seizure of material crossing international borders. Americans receiving gay material from European countries wrote approximately one-third of the letters describing postal incidents, and one-fourth were from Canadian subscribers who complained that Canadian officials had seized their copies of *ONE* at the border.[12] Such scrutiny was less likely for domestic mail, but in theory and in practice, anything sent through the mail could be seized and investigated at any stage in the postal system.

Teachers wrote a disproportionate share of these letters about postal harassment, suggesting that many gay teachers relied heavily on the mail as a means of connecting to gay life. Compared to going to a gay bar, meeting other gay people through pen-pal services or exploring gay culture by receiving books and publications in the mail felt safer. It was, in fact, not safer because of postal officials' broad authority in seizing mail. Several letters described the career damage that could occur when postal officials merely investigated suspicious mail. Ed from Pittsburgh, Pennsylvania, for example, described how Post Office inspectors unexpectedly showed up at his friend Mr. M.'s school administration offices one day. "They were investigating some friend of his in California for sending through the mail obscene stuff. It seems they found some letters of Mr. M. in his desk in California. So they had to check out all such people." Ed believed no sexual affair had occurred between Mr. M. and the correspondent, and he doubted that the letters contained any incriminating content. No charges were ultimately filed against Mr. M. But because postal inspectors had visited his school, the principal asked him to resign or face a school investigation into his personal life. Mr. M. feared the publicity such an investigation might generate, but he did not want to quit teaching either. Mr. M. complained to the principal's superiors, but he received (in Ed's words) "a kick in the pants." In other words, they dismissed him and ignored the fact that no charges had been filed against him. He contacted several lawyers, but all refused to take his case. "It seems an utter shame to let a good teacher like him go," Ed wrote. "I had the worst time getting down to work this week of exams with all this emotion charged atmosphere."[13] Suspicion alone ended Mr. M.'s teaching career.

Another letter, from Franklin, described a teacher friend named Leon who was fired from a school near Dallas, Texas, after he joined The Adonis Club, a pen-pal group. Leon "was an excellent teacher—by far better than average," wrote Franklin. "He was highly regarded by both teachers and pupils." Leon was heterosexually married and led a quiet life. Leon had homosexual desires, according to Franklin, but he was not active in gay life and did not have gay affairs. The letter explained, "Being timid and afraid, he had few friends. So I guess this is why he joined the 'Adonis' club. I understand he received a letter from his pen-pal (a wrestler) saying, among other things, '. . . and I would like to get you in a wrestler's lock until something hard develops.' Thus encouraged, [Leon] wrote back in a similar manner." A postal inspector opened and read

Leon's mail, and Leon was charged with sending obscene mail across state lines. "Regardless of whether he is convicted or acquitted, his name is ruined," Franklin continued. "He will never again be able to teach in Dallas, and very probably not anywhere else. . . . Leon was always so very careful (except for that one mistake), and yet his life is now ruined. Can the rest of us feel free? Which one of us will be next?"[14] The example demonstrates why ONE's editors so steadfastly refused to publish pen-pal ads in the magazine.

Horror stories of arrest victims and postal investigations fueled anxiety for gay and lesbian teachers. Yet for every victim, there were far more gay teachers who were not fired. Similar to the military, which also had a zero tolerance policy toward gay people, school administrators might be aware of a teacher's homosexuality but chose to look the other way. According to a speaker at ONE's 1960 Midwinter Meeting, "it worked out that since there were so few good teachers, a homosexual who was a good teacher, who led a discreet life, and who conformed outwardly in conduct and appearance, was in very little danger of losing his career."[15] A teacher interviewed in ONE emphasized the same point, "The swishy type of homosexual couldn't get a job, or couldn't last if he did, not in a public system," he explained. Most homosexual teachers were undetectable because they went out of their way to be a "model citizen." Some male teachers overcompensated by exaggerating their masculinity, or perhaps became heavily involved in coaching sports.[16] The gay purges in education ruined many individual lives, but ultimately failed to eradicate gay men and lesbians from the teaching profession. In spite of the repressions against them, gay people continued to assert their right to work in their chosen field, and usually did so successfully if a bit nervously.

Gay Educators and the Legal System

As with so many other gay professionals, the worst fear for most teachers was getting arrested for a homosexual offense. The indignities of a gay arrest—the entrapment, the unfairness of the legal system, the consequences of exposure—were amplified for gay and lesbian teachers compared to most other workers. When teachers were caught in police raids, entrapment, or other types of gay arrests, police chiefs and judges usually went out of their way to inform schools about the arrest. In California, state law required law enforcement authorities to notify school superintendents whenever a teacher was arrested for any type of sex offense, even when the charges were dropped or proven false. Termination was the usual outcome.[17] Dorr Legg told a fired teacher in Michigan not to seek work in California, at least not as a teacher, "As to the teaching possibilities in California, they are absolutely nil in the state of California for a person having had an arrest (not even a conviction); this applies to public schools. Private schools of course have their own rulings and would doubtless vary a good deal. The public situation is legally mandated under state law and apparently the follow-up and checking of information is pretty thorough. It is better to report these facts than to build up false hopes."[18]

Some gay teachers fought their firings in court, but until the late 1960s they always lost. Thomas Sarac, an elementary school teacher, for example, appealed his firing and loss of his teaching license after being arrested by an undercover police officer in a Long Beach, California, restroom in 1962. Sarac argued that his private life had no bearing on his teaching, but he lost all of his appeals. In 1967 an Ohio man became the first gay teacher to challenge his firing and be reinstated. This initiated a wave of favorable legal rulings for gay teachers in subsequent years. Until this case, the legal system treated gay teachers as a legitimate threat to society.[19]

Once a gay teacher was arrested and fired, it was unlikely that person would ever work again in the field of education. A letter from 1962 described how a teacher fired for a gay arrest had spent three years searching for another teaching job, but to no avail. He was considering moving to Canada, but the immigration process required he reveal any criminal charges, and he feared the consequences of revealing his arrest to immigration authorities.[20] Lesbians had an advantage in this area because they were considerably less likely to be arrested compared to gay men. A woman explained in an oral history: "It was totally different for men and women. There was one publicized case in which six women were arrested, but they were quickly let go. In none of the newspaper articles back then [1950s] did they talk about lesbians."[21] Even though lesbians suffered less police harassment than men in general, many lesbian teachers still avoided bars.[22] If a woman's homosexuality came to light and she lost her job, she had fewer choices compared to men in pursuing a new career because of widespread workplace discrimination against women.

Anxieties over gay arrests extended into higher education as well. In 1955 newspapers across the country reported the disastrous downfall of Clark Kuebler, a rising academic star. Kuebler never wrote a letter to *ONE*, but press clippings of his scandal provide an exceptional degree of detail describing his arrest and its consequences on his career. The clippings highlight many common themes in letters to *ONE*: the unfair use of police entrapment, the devastating professional consequences of gay arrests, the humiliation of media publicity, and the physical distance educators tried to use to insulate their work lives from whatever gay social life they dared to experience. Kuebler, in fact, was 3,000 miles from home when his arrest occurred, but even that distance proved insufficient to protect his career. Perhaps most importantly, Kuebler's case highlights the common refrain in the letters that an accusation alone could destroy a career in education regardless of the veracity or outcome of that accusation. In Kuebler's case, all criminal charges were ultimately dropped against him, but the homosexual nature of the accusations alone nonetheless ended his career in a flash. Because Kuebler's case represents a nationally publicized worst-case scenario for any gay person working in education, a brief detour from the letters is necessary to reconstruct his "tragic experience."

At the time of his arrest, Kuebler had just been appointed provost at the University of California, Santa Barbara.[23] The campus, formerly Santa Barbara State College, had joined the prestigious University of California system several years earlier and was in the process of moving from downtown Santa Barbara to its new location in nearby Goleta. Kuebler's job was to oversee the campus's rapid expansion that was planned for the next several years. He had previously been a classics professor at Northwestern University in Evanston, Illinois, and, at age thirty-five, had assumed the presidency of Ripon University in Wisconsin, where he quadrupled the school's endowment in twelve years. His arrival at Santa Barbara in February 1955 was greeted with considerable local fanfare.[24] By November 1955, his career in education was over.

According to the clippings, Kuebler visited New York City in November 1955 to recruit faculty for the English Department. Late one evening, he was strolling along 56th Street near Lexington Avenue, an area known for gay male cruising. Kuebler engaged in conversation with a younger man, and the two men returned to Kuebler's room at the Biltmore Hotel. In the room, a fight broke out when the younger man revealed that he was a vice squad officer. Kuebler was arrested for assault and "loitering in a public place for the purpose of soliciting men to commit a crime against nature."[25] Newspapers throughout California and across the country, including the *New York Times*, reported the arrest.[26] Professors at the Santa Barbara campus were warned "not to discuss with students, townspeople, etc., the matter reported from New York. [University of California] President Sproul will issue whatever information is appropriate," according to an internal memo.[27] Clearly this was embarrassing publicity for the University of California system and for its bourgeoning Santa Barbara campus in particular. Sproul gave a public statement a couple days after the arrest:

The information from New York concerning Provost Clark Kuebler which has come by wire and the newspapers is difficult to believe in view of his long and distinguished career at Ripon College and the fine reputation he has earned in his short stay at Santa Barbara College. No judgment should be passed upon him by anyone until all of the facts are known. *At the same time it is necessary to add that administrative officers of a major educational institution as holders of a high public trust must live fully in accord with the moral and ethical standards set by the society they serve.*[28]

Kuebler, meanwhile, maintained his innocence. He told reporters after posting bail, "This was all a gross mistake. The situation was misunderstood. I am at a disadvantage at this moment, . . . and the finger of suspicion puts me in the blackest position. The charge is not true."[29] The comment indicates that Kuebler was acutely aware of what the accusation alone could do to his career, regardless of his arrest's outcome.

Whereas most arrested gay men simply signed confessions in order to minimize publicity, Kuebler's professional prominence ensured press coverage regardless of his plea. Striking a plea deal in his situation would have been widely interpreted as admitting guilt and almost surely would have ended his career. So he chose to fight the charges, which was also risky because of the embarrassing details that might surface in court. Indeed, the arresting officer, David Kelley, a former Marine who had been a police officer for three years, spared no detail trying to prove that Kuebler had aggressively initiated their encounter and had been eager for sexual relations. Kelley stated, "I was rounding up undesirables on the East Side. This man (Kuebler) stopped me in front of a tavern at 139 East 56th Street, near Lexington Avenue, and asked me the time."[30] Kelley claimed that Kuebler had introduced himself as a shoe manufacturer representative named Carl Kress. Kress bragged about knowing Albert Einstein, then, "he suggested, finally, that we have a couple of drinks at his hotel, the Biltmore. I agreed to. He asked me a lot about myself and I said I was a student at NYU—which is the truth." (Kelley was enrolled part-time in NYU's law program.) In the hotel room, the two men had a couple of drinks, and then, without warning or explanation according to Kelley, Kuebler "stripped to his underclothes, invited me to stay for the night and made his proposal. Then I made my identity known." Kuebler supposedly panicked and offered Kelley a $30 bribe, and then the professor physically attacked Kelley, forcing the officer to subdue and handcuff him. Kelley then learned Kuebler's true identity.[31]

Kuebler gave a very different account of what happened that evening. Kuebler testified that he was the victim of a "shakedown" and that Kelley had initiated everything. Officer Kelley had approached him—not the other way around—and asked for directions to Grand Central Station. After a brief conversation, Kelley followed Kuebler back to his room and barged in uninvited. Kuebler testified he thought Kelley was trying to rob him. "Inside the room," Kuebler explained, "the detective told me I was in a compromising position and asked me what it was worth to me. When I said I was going to call the police, he said he was going to charge me with being a God-damn homosexual. I hit him before I knew he was a police officer." One source quoted Kuebler that he hit the officer "as any man would."[32] Kuebler's version thus portrayed corrupt officer Kelley entrapping and blackmailing Kuebler, and Kuebler reacting as any red-blooded heterosexual American male should react. Although we ultimately cannot know who was telling the truth, it must be noted that Kuebler's behavior on the street had clearly tipped off officer Kelley in some way that Kuebler was looking for a sex partner, or else Kelley would not have followed Kuebler back to his hotel and arrested him—regardless of the details of what happened in the hotel room. Having observed and participated in the cruising rituals of gay men, undercover vice officers like Kelley usually targeted the right people—that is, people who were gay.

During Kuebler's trial, several prominent witnesses (including two bishops) testified about his high moral character and his involvement in the Episcopal Church. After three days of testimony to a packed courthouse, the judge dismissed the charges declaring, "There is not a jury in the world that would convict this man today."[33] Kuebler was exonerated; the charges were dropped. But there was still the matter of his job back in Santa Barbara. As Kuebler himself recognized, the "finger of suspicion" was pointed at him, and it would not go away just because he had won his trial. University of California regents at first were unsure how to handle the situation. A special regents committee met shortly after the charges were dropped to discuss Kuebler's status with the university, but nothing was decided. Kuebler disappeared for a week after his hearing, then returned to Santa Barbara to attend church, but by mid-December he had not yet returned to campus. A full regents meeting was conducted at this time, and shortly after the meeting, the regents announced they had accepted Kuebler's resignation.[34] Kuebler gave a "bitter" statement to the press explaining that the media coverage had damaged his career beyond repair. "During the past six weeks I have tried to evaluate objectively the results of my tragic experience in New York. Clearly exonerated in a court of law, I am innocent of the charge and its ugly implications, and yet the publicity given to the false accusation has done me irreparable damage." His statement employs the language of a McCarthyism victim: "There are always those who consider an accusation a conviction of guilt. Either they habitually believe the worst of others or they are jealous of the success the accused may have had or dislike him for what he is or stands for and use the accusation as a weapon for character assassination. . . ." He further stated that his "first interest is in the university," and he was "determined that my personal tragedy will not stand in the way of Santa Barbara college's future."[35] Publicly, then, Kuebler maintained his innocence on the specific charge as well as "its ugly implications" that he was homosexual. We cannot say for sure that he was gay based on the evidence here, but gay entrapment victims usually did not publicly confirm their homosexuality in the 1950s. Denials were the norm. To me it seems more than likely that Kuebler was gay and looking for an evening tryst while far away from home, but consistent with the patterns of McCarthyism in the end it made no difference. His academic career was destroyed either way. He quit education entirely and entered private business.[36]

The extensive press coverage that ruined Kuebler's career ensured that thousands of gay men and lesbians in Los Angeles, New York, Chicago, San Francisco, and elsewhere read about him over their morning coffee. They would have recognized the patterns and coded words. Whether or not Kuebler was gay, they would have identified with his ordeal. For gay educators in particular, such news would have been a grim reminder of the dangers of involvement in gay life, even when one is 3,000 miles from home.

Anxieties in Higher Education

If gay educators escaped postal investigations or police arrests, they could still become the victim of a campus's own internal investigation. *ONE* magazine readers reported widespread purges of gay faculty, staff, and students, for example, at colleges and universities in Florida, North Carolina, Pennsylvania, Delaware, Michigan, Texas, and California.

The largest antihomosexual purge in higher education occurred in Florida. The Florida situation reflects how politics (in this case, state politics) was often the motivating fact behind gay purges in higher education. In 1956 the Florida State Legislature created the Florida Legislative Investigation Committee, better known as the Johns Committee after its creator, Florida State Senator Charley Johns. The Johns Committee intended to investigate the Ku Klux Klan (KKK) and the National Association for the Advancement of Colored People (NAACP) in Florida. Initially, segregationists used the committee to attack the NAACP in Florida, but after a rash of bad publicity, the Johns Committee shifted its focus in 1958 to homosexuality in Florida's colleges and universities.[37] In addition to the usual national security arguments against gay people, committee members claimed that homosexuals in colleges posed an imminent threat to Florida's youth because they were mentally unstable and therefore likely to seduce students and, following the military's logic, turn students homosexual.[38]

From 1959 to 1963, investigators working for the Johns Committee combed college campuses in Florida using undercover surveillance and aggressive interrogations to identify homosexual faculty and students. At the University of Florida in Gainesville, the investigations resulted in sixteen firings of mostly tenured faculty from a variety of academic departments. "Tenure didn't mean a goddamned thing," explained one victim of the investigation. "If they wanted to get rid of you they would find a way."[39] Following the patterns of McCarthyism, the committee offered leniency to persons who named other homosexuals after they had responded affirmatively to the question "Do you know now, or have you known in the past any teacher in the public school system of this state who is a homosexual?"[40] Another victim of the purge, a literature professor, explained, "It was a fearful time. Every waking moment—fear. Fear of disgrace. Fear of losing my job. Fear of no money. It was awful. It was a horrible experience. It was all conspiratorial; at times, I felt like I was in a chapter of a Dostoevsky novel."[41] Lesbian and gay students were dragged into the investigations and warned to change their sexual orientation through psychiatric treatment or face expulsion.[42] In the first year of the investigation alone, the committee pressured the university to expel approximately fifty students because of homosexuality. The investigation spread to other colleges in Florida, and then to high schools. By 1961 the committee's investigations had stripped approximately fifty high school teachers of their teaching licenses.[43]

Sixty-five of the 320 persons the Johns Committee formally investigated were lesbians. Most of the lesbian investigations occurred at the Florida Industrial School for Girls in Ocala. Investigators threatened to publicize the names of any women who refused to cooperate with the investigation. Most lesbians, along with most gay men brought before the committee, cooperated in a limited manner, offering a few names of other homosexuals while trying to protect close friends. Some deflected the committee's questions using strategic "memory loss."[44] Many of the committee's targets, however, caved in under the pressure and named every homosexual they could think of in order to save their careers.[45]

Several gay Floridians alerted *ONE* magazine about the Johns Committee's investigations. Paul wrote from Fort Lauderdale in 1959, "I guess you heard that 14 persons were fired for Homo activities at Florida U. It made first page headlines in the local paper. I got so mad I forgot to clip it."[46] Paul's comments reflected how the wave of fear extended beyond the campuses to anyone who read about the firings in their newspapers. Harold, who wrote from Miami in 1960, also captured the climate of fear generated by the purges: "The University of Florida (within the last year) has recently hired a former FBI agent to run the campus security department at their Gainesville Florida school. According to the varied sources (and stories I hear from acquaintances and friends), the agent is running a 'purge' of homosexuals at the school and is kicking homosexuals out of the school right and left. I know personally of several who have been kicked out and many more who've had the wits scared out of them."[47] Fred, writing from Riviera Beach two years later in 1962, told *ONE* "Governor Bryant's committee has finally reached this area. Local police have been given lectures on the menace of homosexuals and how to recognize them."[48] *ONE* magazine's quip about the purges reflected the underlying political dynamics of these investigations: "As always, it seems the myopic witch-hunter can't tell the difference between communists, integrationists and homosexuals."[49]

By 1963 the Johns Committee was losing steam. Critics increasingly questioned the committee's mission and its information-gathering tactics. Jonathan, writing from Gainesville, informed *ONE* in August 1963 that the committee was "looking for a new whipping boy among the Castro sympathizers here in Florida. If this proves to be the case, we here in Florida can expect some relief from the series of 'witch-hunts' we have experienced in the past."[50] In a misguided effort to restore its credibility, the committee published the 1964 report, "Homosexuality and Citizenship in Florida," also known as "the purple pamphlet," which ludicrously claimed, among other things, that homosexuals posed a greater threat to children than child molesters. Critics ridiculed the report, and the Florida legislature disbanded the Johns Committee in 1965.[51] A man from Sarasota told *ONE* that, "Richard Gerstein, the state attorney[,] has banned the report from being distributed in Dade County. The gay people here may have the last laugh after all."[52] Educators in Florida breathed easier, but they still had to be careful. Similar efforts to fire gay teachers in Florida could reemerge at any time (as they did with a vengeance in the 1970s).

The Florida investigations demonstrate the heightened danger facing homosexual faculty and students at public colleges and universities as opposed to private ones. Public institutions relied on tax dollars and were more likely to become entangled in political controversies. A former Indiana State College student told *ONE* that he had been expelled "in regard to my being homosexual. The dean informed me that since homosexuality was illegal in the state of Indiana and since Indiana State College was a state supported school, I would have to be excused."[53] Some colleges suggested conversion therapy as a way to stay in school.

Private colleges were more lenient in such cases. Dorr Legg lectured at the ONE Institute that gays and lesbians found more freedom at private schools, colleges, and universities. "The private boys' school is able to employ teachers who cannot find a place in public schools; the private college may employ those ineligible for a state university," he explained.[54] Private schools often avoided the degrees of institutional transparency found at public institutions. Private universities could handle a homosexual scandal quietly, and they often succeeded in avoiding the controversial publicity gay scandals usually engendered.

The fact that these crackdowns were occurring shows that there was a significant amount of gay activity happening on campuses, in Florida and elsewhere. A few letters to *ONE* reported gay social worlds or lively cruising areas at colleges and universities.[55] A graduate of the University of Southern California, for example, wrote, "the swish crowd from the studios . . . haunt[s] the campus."[56] Historian John Howard has described vibrant gay social lives at colleges and universities in Mississippi consisting of "a complex web of friendship ties, queer residential quarters, campus cruising areas, and off-campus networks of house parties and nightclubs."[57] Gay sex occurred routinely but discretely on most campuses in the late 1940s and early 1950s, as described by a man named Ralph who attended college in these years, "What I would do was to sneak around and do things. I would sneak in the bathroom and play around under the stalls, you know. In the library, those big study tables. We'd sit and put our feet in the other person's crotch, under the table. I had several different guys that we would sit across from each other, so we could play footsie under the table. They were guys in my classes. Some of them were in the religious groups I was in. But we never talked about it."[58]

Amidst the surreptitious sex and lesbian crushes, there may have been more formal, organized gay and lesbian organizations on college campuses under the guise of campus literary clubs, culture clubs, drama clubs, or secret societies. In 1954 *ONE* received a brief letter hinting at this possibility from an organization called "Bib 'N Tucker" at San Francisco State University. A member of this group wrote to *ONE* complimenting the magazine. "We have read [*ONE*] with avid interest and find it has much to offer the 'gay' college set. . . . Our organization has been formed along these lines. Do you have any information about groups of similar character? Some of our members have shown a desire to further your crusade and wish particulars on your career opportunities. . . . P.S. Since we are a campus group please withhold our name from publication."[59] According to San Francisco State archivist Meredith Eliassen, Bib 'N Tucker was a "popular social sorority . . . established in 1931 to create interest in campus fashions." They held a fashion show for charity every year and also hosted dances, parties, and other social functions. It lasted until the late 1960s.[60] Was it a lesbian organization? Certainly not publicly. A photograph shows the women of Bib 'N Tucker having a toga party with a male fraternity, and former members have reminisced on the Internet about a "candle ritual" when their sorority sisters became engaged to be married.[61] Of course, this letter to *ONE* could have been a college prank by a rival sorority, fraternity, or disgruntled member. But the letter's tone is sincere, especially the demand that *ONE* not print the organization's name. Perhaps a core group of lesbians had founded the organization, as the letter suggests, and perhaps lesbians remained active in the group over the years as heterosexual women joined. If the purpose of Bib 'N Tucker was primarily a lesbian organization and secondarily a fashion club, it would have had to pass as heterosexual just like individual gay and lesbian college students. Such an organization would have had to manage its public image very carefully, especially after World War II. Only further research can determine whether Bib 'N Tucker was in fact a lesbian organization founded decades before the first openly gay student organization.

Whereas scholars have described lively gay social scenes on college campuses in these years, the letters *ONE* received from individual college students tended to emphasize loneliness and isolation. Some gay and lesbian college students simply had no idea how to connect with other gay people, either on or off campus.[62] Living arrangements for students coming to terms with their sexuality could be complicated, as indicated by a New York University fraternity member who told *ONE* that he had "to control [his] emotions and fears at all times because of the fact that someone might find out what I really feel for a few of the [fraternity] members."[63] Gay college students—especially those in fraternities—could expect harassment and intimidation if their homosexuality was revealed. Passing as heterosexual to other students was just as important as passing as heterosexual to school authorities. Harry Hay described gay harassment at UCLA in a 1958 letter to Dorr Legg: "Saturday A.M., 5–3–58," he wrote, "there was a most interesting banner (large block letters in blue on white background) reading 'DEVIATE—GO HOME,' strung clear across the front of the Delta Tau Delta House on 649 Gayley Ave. just west of the UCLA playing fields."[64] Before open gay student organizations emerged in the late 1960s and 1970s to offer safety and community on college campuses (the first such organization appeared at Columbia University in 1965), gay students had to deal with such harassment alone.[65] If they complained to college authorities, their sexuality would be questioned and they might be expelled.

Because of the antigay pressures on both students and faculty, academic discussions of homosexuality tended to be clinical and condemnatory in both the sciences and humanities. Homosexual viewpoints were marginalized, pathologized, or ignored altogether in academic discourse. Scholars appearing sympathetic to homosexuals in their classrooms or research might look suspicious to a department chair, dean, or provost, especially if he or she were unmarried. On some campuses, discussion of homosexuality was simply taboo. "Colleges are afraid of the subject," commented a professor from San Jose.[66] "There just isn't any information here," added Robert, who was attending college in Iowa.[67] Another man wrote that the books on homosexuality at the University of Tennessee at Knoxville "are in the Special Collections room under lock and key. The public library has none."[68] Dorr Legg, himself a former academic, speculated that some gay academics made antihomosexual statements in public to deflect suspicion about themselves, contributing to the broader antihomosexual climate of postwar academic life.[69] Gay and lesbian undergraduates, despite being at institutions of higher learning, had very little information available to them to understand their sexuality.

Graduate students, like undergraduates, also suffered from loneliness; like faculty, they worried about the consequences of discovery on their budding academic careers. A graduate student at Brown University in Providence, Rhode Island, for example, reported that his school was "replete with snooping busybodies," and because his oral exams were approaching, it would be best if *ONE* did not publish his letter stating that he read the magazine in the school library.[70] Richard, a history graduate student at the University of Michigan, had a particularly disastrous experience after getting caught in a campus police raid of a men's restroom. He explained to *ONE* in 1962, "Recent difficulties in Ann Arbor, Michigan, have caused me to lose my teaching position in the East and have caused the chairman of my doctoral committee to fail me in my dissertation work, which was very near completion." Richard, a decorated World War II veteran, was writing a dissertation on Union Army efforts to educate black Americans during the Civil War.[71] He was naturally upset about being expelled after so many years of work, and he asked *ONE* for religious counsel. ONE, Inc., arranged for a minister in Michigan to visit Richard, and the minister reported to Dorr Legg, "The PhD applicant in question got caught up in one of the recurring witch-hunts at Ann Arbor and was ridden out of the grad school. I think some 27 were picked up at the same time: all by the usual police trap. The gentle man had one previous scrap, in Detroit, but the judge threw the case out on proof that the Detroit vice-cop resorted to 'propositioning!' " According to the minister, Richard was in some degree of denial about his homosexuality, and he only indulged in homosexual acts when he felt particularly lonely. "As to employment in teaching I have suggested his acceptance of bids to small colleges or private secondary schools, and that if questions are asked to answer them with forthrightness himself rather than getting tarred by reputation through his references. He would do better in this far from U. of Mich. area. He has some contacts in the West and I hope he exploits them."[72] These words suggested that there was still a glimmer of hope for Robert's teaching career, but he would require luck and would probably have to relocate. Despite the minister's advice to be honest with future employers about his arrest, Robert might have found inventing a story about why he did not finish graduate school (health crisis, financial concerns) easier, hoping that no one looked into his records too deeply.

Another Michigan graduate student, Brandon, shared his experiences with *ONE* about the police raids on campus. "The situation was hilarious," he wrote in 1963, "The administration brought in twenty five pink cheeked vice squad men who posed as students and what a revelation! It seems the purge revealed an amazing number of men eager to participate—yes, even instructors. All the doors of the johns had to be removed because they had shielded dating arrangements."[73]

For gay and lesbian college faculty, students (graduate or undergraduate) posed a special danger. Students were supposed to be off limits to all faculty, but heterosexual affairs between faculty and graduate students—and sometimes undergraduates—were tolerated in a way that gay and lesbian affairs were not. Homoeroticism between teachers and their students has been around since ancient Greece. In the late nineteenth century, the German-based "Uranian poetry movement" emphasized the erotic bonds of professors and students while providing an early gay rights discourse.[74] This tradition, never as strong in the United States as in Europe, dissipated in the postwar lavender scare. Like Harris from *Tea and Sympathy*, gay faculty knew they had to be very careful in their interactions with students, and even innocuous socializing could raise suspicions. A sexual advance from a mature, attractive student could send a sexually repressed professor into a maelstrom of confusion, anxiety, and ecstasy. A lesbian, J. M., working at a women's college in the United Kingdom, described her anxiety in a 1960 letter to *The Ladder*, "Visualize, if you can, 18 pairs of female eyes watching every move you make and listening to your every word. Eyes that criticize—condemn—envy—approve—speculate, or adore. Undisguised eyes that sweep over you from head to toe with unmistakable significance. By far the most difficult to handle is the attractive girl who has a 'crush' on you and goes out of her way to make her presence heaven—and unknowingly—hell."[75] J. M. stated that she had never had a sexual experience with a woman. She relied on celibacy for professional security.

Another letter described the negative consequences of sexual involvement with students. A music professor explained that while he was in his thirties, he occasionally had sexual contacts with students. One day, however, he rejected a student's advance, and the student complained to school authorities that the professor had made sexual advances toward him. His resignation was "suggested," so he quit; luckily he found a job at another school. "Thanks to that one experience," he told *ONE*, "I have ceased all pleasure-seeking [with students]. And I feel that it is the wisest thing to do." In fact, he abstained from sex entirely while school was in session. He told *ONE* he only had sex with his partner of five years during the summer when "my work . . . is more conducive to this type of activity."[76] Like J. M., he chose celibacy to deal with the sexual tensions inherent in his job.

"The Force," a fiction story in *ONE*, explores the temptation of college students by describing a professor visited in his home by an attractive male student seeking help on a literature paper. The story dramatizes the anxieties gay educators often suffered, "Professor Knight had never let himself fall into any trap because [he was] fully cognizant that exposure in the academic world, even rumor, meant the end of a career, no matter how brilliant. . . . He had accepted this limitation when he squarely faced joining the profession five years ago, and since, in spite of attractions, had preserved a glacial coolness toward temptations. The more obvious a student was, the more the professor became withdrawn and frigidly controlled." Temptation overwhelms the professor's caution, however, and the affair is consummated at the end of the story. " 'Come with me, Dan.' He took the student's hand in his own and without releasing him drew him over to a seat by the blazing fire."[77] The story ends abruptly—the reader is left to guess whether the professor suffered any consequences for the affair. Either way, the letters suggest that anxieties of discovery would have severely compromised the affair's pleasure. Even if he got away with it, he would have perpetually worried that someone, sometime, might find out—especially considering how careful he had been about such matters in the past. Such worry might serve as a deterrent against future affairs.

As is evident from the experiences described in this chapter, gay people underwent great sacrifices to work as educators. Gay teachers sacrificed considerable personal security. They had to be more careful about what they put in the mail. They routinely sacrificed participation in gay social life and suffered loneliness as a consequence. Some sacrificed sex altogether by choosing to be celibate. Such sacrifices underscore the idealism of these individuals who were dedicated to serving their communities and who believed that their teaching could make the world a better place. Such idealism made their firings and persecutions all the more tragic. Yet, the fact that so many gay people endured the anxieties of the McCarthy era in order to work as educators shows that gay people continued to exercise significant degrees of agency over their daily lives. Despite the firings and persistent anxiety, gay people continued to work in the field of their choosing in the pursuit of personal and professional fulfillment.

7

Family Anxieties

Parent and Family Responses
to Homosexual Disclosures

Tom Lee, the harassed protagonist of *Tea and Sympathy*, has a strained relationship with his father, Herb. Herb cannot bear the idea that his son might be homosexual. Herb searches for clues to disprove the rumors, but he is repeatedly disappointed. Herb cringes at the effeminate way Tom plays tennis. He begs Tom to get a butch crew cut. Worst of all, Tom is slated to play Lady Teazle—in full drag—in the school's production of *School for Scandal*. (Herb forces Tom to quit the play.) Herb acknowledges the gulf between them and makes a gesture toward trying to understand Tom better. "I want to be your friend, Tom," he says with great seriousness. "I know there's something between fathers and sons that makes it hard for them to be friends, but I'd like to try."[1] Herb is delighted to learn that Tom has visited the town prostitute, but becomes despondent on learning that Tom failed to perform sexually with the woman. By the end of the play, Herb's efforts to understand Tom have utterly failed. As Tom faces expulsion for visiting the prostitute, Herb is so overcome with anxiety and shame that he cannot bring himself to enter Tom's room and say goodbye. As the curtain falls, Tom's family has abandoned him.

For many gay people in the McCarthy era, Tom's fate represented their worst fear. Family issues weighed heavily on the minds of people who wrote letters to *ONE*. Approximately 8 percent of the letters used in this study discussed family life. This chapter examines the letters discussing family acceptance or rejection, usually between heterosexual parents and their lesbian or gay offspring. These letters show that historians have exaggerated the hostility of families toward their gay members during these years. Arlene Skolnick, for example, wrote in *Embattled Paradise: The American Family in an Age of Uncertainty*, "Just as communism was the ultimate political evil, homosexuality was the ultimate crime against the family. In that hostile climate, most homosexuals remained in the closet."[2] In fact, when family members learned that one of their own was gay or lesbian, reactions were varied, nuanced, and sometimes surprisingly accepting. There were outright rejections, and bad *initial* reactions were common (as they still often are today), but the letters show that compromise and accommodation were the most common reactions to a homosexual disclosure. Once the secret was out, *ONE* correspondents took careful steps to foster accommodation within their families while asserting their right to be lesbian or gay. The postwar civil rights impulse had a significant impact in the intimate sphere of home and family. Once gay people had successfully convinced their families to accept them, convincing the rest of society to do so became easier to imagine.

There was no expectation to "come out" to family members in these years—indeed, the phrase "coming out" referred only to other gay people, not heterosexuals such as family members. Passing as heterosexual within the family was not a simple matter. It often required duplicity that could strain family relations. Many suffered anxiety over the prospect of being discovered, which often occurred in less than ideal circumstances, such as the result of a gay arrest or from being fired from a job. Such discoveries could seem earth-shattering in light of the intense idealization of the middle-class nuclear family occurring within American culture after World War II. Politicians and psychologists argued that healthy, strong, heterosexual nuclear families were an essential home-front strategy in the cold war against the Soviet Union. Deviations from this idealized family structure made the country more susceptible to communist takeover by weakening its moral fiber.[3] In this context, homosexuals (once again) were outcasts and security risks. Yet within the intimate bonds of family life, it was not "the ultimate crime" to be lesbian or gay. It was a crisis, perhaps, but a crisis that could be handled numerous ways with various outcomes.

Discovery Anxiety

In the twenty-first century, dozens of books are available to help guide gay people through the daunting experience of "coming out" to their families. In the 1950s and early 1960s, no such books were to be found at the local bookstore or library. Little affirmative discourse was heard about homosexuality outside the homophile movement and the male and female Kinsey Reports. Information about homosexuality in the mass media tended to be negative and alarmist. Mainstream psychology labeled homosexuality a mental illness. With these factors working against them, one can hardly be surprised that gay people—even those who unproblematically accepted their sexual identities—worried how their parents, siblings, and relatives would react to the news they were homosexual. This was especially true if the news emerged because of a gay arrest, firing, or other tragic circumstance. Lacking ritualized coming out strategies for their families, lesbians and gay men had to be creative and thoughtful in explaining their circumstances when this necessity arose.

Most letter writers assumed that parental reactions to their homosexuality would be catastrophic. "My parents don't know that I am gay, and thank goodness too," explained a nineteen-year-old male in Oklahoma City. "My father would do everything short of killing me."[4] Such comments were routinely expressed in the letters. Ron wrote from Connecticut, "If anyone in my family, especially my parents, ever knew about my nature, I would be dis-owned and rejected."[5] The Indiana State College student facing expulsion in chapter 6 similarly explained that his father "dislikes deviates very much and I am sure that shock of the fact that his son was 'queer' and his paralleling action to that fact could possibly ruin his and my futures."[6] Bill, from Woodland Hills, California, described his family anxieties in religious terms: "I am a Christian and so are my parents and family. They must never find out because they would worry about my life after death," he explained.[7]

As these comments suggest, gay people felt no obligation to reveal their homosexuality to their parents in these years. Parents were similarly afraid to broach the subject and often kept suspicions about their child's homosexuality to themselves. With neither side forcing the issue, many gay people did not know whether their parents knew (or even suspected) they were gay or not. Lesbian fiction author Marijane Meaker captured this uneasy silence in a conversation with author Patricia Highsmith in the late 1950s. Meaker complained to Highsmith about the deceptions involved in being a lesbian:

> "And how about all the lies we tell our parents?" I finished one of my speeches once. "We tell lies, and we write lies home. How about all of that?"
>
> "I never do and I never did," Pat said flatly.
>
> "You never lied to your mother and father?"
>
> "My mother and my *stepfather*. I never brought it up. I *tried* to like men. I like most men better than I like women, but not in bed."
>
> "Do your mother and stepfather know you're gay?"
>
> "I think they assume I am," Pat said.[8]

Variations of this ambiguous phrase, "I think they assume I am," are found in several letters. "My parents have never discussed homosexuality with me, but I'm sure they must know about me," wrote Simon from Bronson, Mississippi, in 1956. "They are kind, loving people, but somehow I never thought that I could tell them." He felt comfortable telling other members of his family, though. "My great-aunt and my sister know, and accept me."[9] Avoiding the issue may have prevented explosive confrontations, but it also perpetuated the nagging anxiety of discovery in the future. Like fibbing about a military discharge in order to get a job, the truth could catch up to them at any moment.

A man from Phoenix, Arizona, powerfully captured the strains of family anxiety in his letter to *ONE*. He had just been fired from his job for being gay, and he worried about his father's reaction. His downward spiral represented something of a worst-case scenario, "I was frantic and did not want to return home because I knew I would have to tell my Dad why I was fired. I drank on the street so I would be put in jail away from society and I would not have to face my own father. I had the nervous breakdown from these pressures. I was scared to death and wanted to commit suicide so I knew in jail, I would be saved from myself."[10] The young man's fears were not unfounded. Although he was not expelled from his family after telling his father about the firing, his home life became so stressful that he spent time in a mental hospital. Family anxieties had contributed significantly to his alcohol binges, suicidal desires, and incarcerations in prison and a mental hospital. Getting fired was bad enough, but the extra layer of family anxiety made the experience profoundly worse. The same was true for gay arrests. Marvin, an African-American man living in New York City, described his family anxieties after a gay arrest in Central Park in 1958. Unlike the man from Phoenix, Marvin was less worried about his family's reaction to his homosexuality than the ridicule his family was suffering because of his arrest. He wrote, "[T]he entire neighborhood is against me and I can not [*sic*] find any sort of work. I fear most for my family's jobs. . . . All these neighbors once pretended friendship [but] now use this pretense to strike at my family." Marvin was even too afraid to subscribe to *ONE* because of the risk it posed to his family. "There seems no way out," he wrote.[11]

In 1960 the Denver Mattachine Society published a letter in its newsletter from a young man explaining his gay arrest to his parents. He had been arrested for cruising in a public park, and he faced fourteen years in prison for committing, according to Colorado law, "the abominable crime against nature." The letter provides a detailed glimpse at the strategies of homosexual disclosure in the 1950s, and it captures the postwar civil rights impulse operating within the private sphere of family life.

The young man offered no apologies for being gay. Echoing the Kinsey Reports, he explained that his homosexuality was a common variation of human sexual behavior and not a personality defect or illness. "Simply, my eyes are not blue, they are brown; I am not left-handed, I am right-handed; I am not heterosexual, I am homosexual." Throughout the letter, he used affirmative tones and phrases to describe his homosexuality. For example, he described his adolescent sexual awakening with "the boy next door" as "natural and beautiful. A fulfillment of sorts. Could anything so lovely be wrong?" Yet he had learned about the harsh penalties facing, in his words, "the queer people." His letter employed the mask metaphor, "As I grew older I learned to mask my feelings and reactions and to present a false face to the world. I began to lead the double life of the invert—desperately wanting one thing, yet accepting another. Rather than cry out my feelings for a 'friend' to the world, I must suppress them. I could not share my joy with those dear to me. Even these 'friends' were not aware."[12] Despite the social hostility, he had discovered ways to have a positive attitude about his homosexuality. He learned in high school, for example, that Plato, Michelangelo, and Tchaikovsky were known to have had homosexual experiences. He also found comfort in a gay novel, "just a fiction story, no great contribution to literature." He explained in his letter how the book had given him hope: "That a modern author could write of love between two men was, to me, a release, a promise of what was to come. Can I explain how I felt? The tears which often came to accompany the night hours turned to tears of joy with my knowing that what I actually wanted *was*." As he grew older, he continued to conceal his homosexuality from his parents, but eventually told his younger sister. She cried, listened, and then accepted—"I leaned upon her and she gave me strength." He explained his frustration with the government's antigay policies, "Every invert walks with danger in his hip pocket. The constant threat of being exposed, blackmailed, arrested, or just hated by someone who doesn't take to our inversion. Even the government has classified us as 'security risks.' Why? Because in a key position we could be blackmailed, exposed. Yet how simple if we could be honest and forthright about it all. Our families would know, our employers would know, and accept. Then to whom would we be exposed?"[13] His observation gets to the heart of the absurdity and circular logic of the government's antihomosexual policies. Clearly his goal was to convince his parents that the only thing wrong with being gay was the irrational social prejudice one encountered. His parents had probably never given the matter much thought.

He stated he was wrong cruising for sex in a public park, but explained that social intolerance had driven him there in the first place. "It is difficult to find someone to love," he explained. "I think it is because everything we feel must be hidden from the world." He imagined a society in which gay people could experience the same visibility in their relationships as heterosexuals:

> How wonderful it must be to walk down the street hand in hand, proud of the one beside you. How wonderful to touch the cheek of the one you love in a crowded place. To live openly and with freedom with one you choose. Instead it must all be kept inside. We are burdened by guilt heaped upon us by a hostile world. We must be careful to wear a mask when away from our own kind. It is not an easy way to live. I hope you don't find it too alien that we experience the grandest emotion, love.[14]

Throughout the letter, the young man emphasized the common ground of gay and straight people. No matter how incomprehensible homosexuality might seem to his parents, love offered a bridge of understanding. His ultimate goal, he explained, was a stable relationship—a gay marriage. "I do feel that there is a need for a permanent relationship. I want that. Most others I know want that. . . . I believe in it and I hold it up as sacred as any other love. Is this so very different from the dreams of other people? From yours?"[15] The letter challenged his parents to imagine homosexuality as not so different from heterosexuality, despite the hysteria surrounding the issue.

We can only guess how his parents responded to his plea for acceptance. Clearly, the young man had crafted his message carefully. He emphasized points his parents could relate to and readily understand, such as love and stable relationships. His letter rejected the disparaging contemporary psychological theories of homosexuality by refusing to acknowledge them. Instead, he used his own perspective and experiences to describe the life of a homosexual. The letter demonstrated his own acceptance of his sexuality and his wish that society would take the perspectives of gay people like him more seriously. Ultimately, the letter was a stirring plea for acceptance and civil rights, yet written for an audience of two people: his mother and father. By publishing the letter, the Denver Mattachine chapter hoped to provide a strategic model that other gay people could use in telling their own families about their homosexuality.

One Big, Happy Family

Whatever the circumstances of a particular homosexual disclosure, the letters reveal a wide spectrum of family reactions. A best-case scenario came from a mother in Kansas City, Missouri, who had just learned that her twenty-year-old son was gay. She owned a large three-story house and had rented rooms to "gay boys" in the past. This exposure to the "gay world" facilitated unconditional acceptance of her son's homosexuality. "The people I have known so far of the gay world, are wonderful, talented fascinating people. I love them all," she wrote. "Since they come to our home, they are much more settled down, much happier, and much more secure—in our home they know they can be themselves and are protected, what a pity there can't be more straight people who understand and accept gay people." She threw parties hosting 25 or 30 "gay boys." She realized that many of her son's friends did not have understanding parents, so she compensated by creating a domestic surrogate-family environment where they could "be themselves and are protected."[16]

 ONE received a similar letter in 1959 from a grandmother in La Crescenta, California, who called herself "Bubbles" because she was "short and fat." Like the Kansas City woman, she also opened her home to her gay grandson and his friends to provide a safe and stable domestic environment. "For many years I have been interested and fascinated by 'the gay world,'" she wrote—both women used the phrase "gay world." "I have found that these misunderstood, unaccepted people are wonderful. They have a great deal more kindness than is ever spoken of. I have opened my home to them, where they can come and bring their friends. An evening is spent listening to hi-fi music, singing, dancing, or putting on a little theatrical show. Refreshments are always served. It is wonderful to see and hear their laughter. They surely 'have a ball.' It is just like one big happy family. Some come to discuss their problems, and everyone offers suggestions."[17] Both letters suggested that private homes could serve as important spaces for gay adolescents too young to attend gay bars or find gay life elsewhere. They also demonstrated how these two women used their socially expected roles as domestic homemakers to create safe havens for their gay offspring, havens that fostered self-acceptance and community.

Neither woman mentioned husbands, reinforcing a widely held perception that opposite-gender parents (mothers to sons, fathers to daughters) were more understanding and supportive of gay offspring than same-gender parents (mothers to daughters, fathers to sons). Social scientists have disagreed on whether this perception is accurate;

nonetheless, it has been a routine fixture of gay and lesbian literature throughout the twentieth century.[18] In gay fiction, mothers protected their gay sons from the condemnatory, violent reaction of fathers; in cases of lesbian daughters, fathers often remained calm while mothers become agitated and angry. In the short story "Night for Decision" published in *The Ladder*, for example, a young woman announced to her parents that she had broken off her engagement with a well-to-do man in order to be with another woman. The young woman's mother was shocked and speechless, but the father calmly reassured his daughter that he accepted her and would help her be accepted by other family members. His chief concern was her happiness.[19] Such fictional cross-gender alliances suggest that many gay people worried more about one parent finding out about their homosexuality than the other parent. Gay men in letters to *ONE* consistently worried more about their father's reaction than their mother's reaction.

Some parents accepted their son's or daughter's homosexuality on the basis that it was a temporary phase and they would grow out of it. Many psychiatrists reassured parents with Freudian theories that sexual development occurred in stages and teenage homosexual phases were not unusual. Data from the male Kinsey Report reinforced these theories by showing a significantly higher percentage of men temporarily engaged in homosexual behavior (37 percent) compared to "permanent" homosexuals (4 percent).[20] *ONE* magazine's consulting psychologist, Ray Evans, explained to a college sophomore in 1963, "People make a great many more allowances for young people, simply assuming they are not yet ready for marriage. Older men living together are much more likely to be subjected to derision than two fellows in their teens doing the same thing."[21] The sophomore had told Evans that his parents were fully supportive of his relationship with another young man. His parents had been "very understanding and willing to aid us provided we keep our relationship on the same moral level as their marriages."[22] Evans warned him that his parent's tolerance might dissipate as the young couple's "phase" persisted into adulthood.

On the other hand, companionship later in life provided an incentive for parents to accept their son's or daughter's homosexuality as a permanent part of their personality. As adults, gay sons and daughters were often in better positions to take care of elderly parents than heterosexual sons or daughters preoccupied with raising their own families. Such arrangements could alleviate loneliness for elderly parents as well as older gay men and lesbians. Gordon Westwood argued in 1960 that the social perception of gay men as "mama's boys" largely resulted from this tendency for homosexuals to assume a heavy burden of care for aging parents.[23] Gay pianist Liberace built a successful entertainment career around the idea, presenting himself on his popular 1950s television show as a lifelong bachelor eternally devoted to his mother.[24] Novelist James Barr Fugaté explained to *ONE* in 1954 his reasons for moving back with his parents in Kansas:

> My father is dying of leukemia; my mother is arthritic. I cannot abandon them again (I've done so twice), for I know that by remaining here, as quietly as possible, I prolong their lives and happiness. I couldn't live with myself if I failed to do everything in my power to make them love and understand me. My inversion is the one thing I cannot help, so I live with it here as unobtrusively as possible. I cannot have my friends here; I must go to KC or Wichita to find release, but this life has its compensations too.[25]

Such arrangements may or may not involve admissions of homosexual identity. If a family had never broached the subject before, it might never come up in later phases of life either. Fugaté's letter implied that his parents were aware of his homosexuality (Fugaté had a public reputation as a gay novelist under the name James Barr), but his statement, "I live with it here as unobtrusively as possible," indicates a compromise. His comments suggest that the issue of parental disclosure persisted throughout the lives of families with gay or lesbian members.

Shifting Attitudes

Despite the positive family reactions found in some letters, anxiety over family rejection was hardly unfounded. Daughters of Bilitis activist Billie Tallmij, for example, described an especially brutal parental reaction in an oral history. "We had one young woman from New Orleans who tried to tell her parents. They set up a gravestone with her name on it. They declared her dead and announced her death in the newspaper in an obituary. She lived with that for the rest of her life."[26] The incident represents a worst-case scenario, and the letters contain similar negative reactions. Lance from Colorado wrote to *ONE* that an angry lover had revealed his homosexuality to his parents. "My parents were dismayed and shocked beyond belief!" he wrote. "I had always been a good student, and above all a responsible person much respected by family and friends. Being the only son of a prominent family . . . my father was a hard driving 'self-made success . . .' the tragedy was irreconcilable. My parents have cut me off from all support, moral and financial."[27] Yet even when an initial homosexual disclosure was confrontational or explosive, attitudes often changed over time. The reaction Lance faced was not unusual, but the letters demonstrate that, in most cases, mutual efforts toward understanding and reconciliation followed such explosive reactions. Twenty-three-year-old Mr. C., for example, explained that after a bad initial reaction from his Puerto Rican–born parents after he broke off a marriage engagement, his parents "were able to try to understand my way of life. . . . They still love me as their son and I respect them as parents."[28] Rocky disclosures could even strengthen family bonds over the long term by instilling more honesty within a family. Arthur, a wheelchair-bound man from a New York City suburb, was initially kicked out of his parents' home, for example, but his parents later calmed down and invited him back home and allowed him the opportunity to educate them about homosexuality. "I'd like to write a booklet about it myself, but I just wouldn't know where to start such a thing."[29] His efforts to educate his parents were successful.

A letter from a mother in Pasadena, California, offered a nuanced perspective on her son's recently declared homosexuality. The disclosure troubled her, but she was learning there was more to being gay than the tragic mass media depictions. Her shy, introverted teenage son William was seriously involved with their landlord, a well-to-do man in his early twenties. The affair had been going on for slightly over a year. The mother had been hospitalized for nine months, during which William had lived with the landlord and his family. Despite her misgivings about homosexuality, she admitted that the landlord had been a positive influence on William. "The boy managed to get William in the most wonderful school and with his help William earned all A's except one B. During those nine months William became a completely new person. He made many new friends and his whole world expanded a thousand times." After the mother returned from the hospital, the landlord briefly served in the military until he was discharged for a minor health problem. During these weeks of military service, the mother wrote, "I came to realize how much the boy was doing for William and also how close their relationship had become. William cried himself to sleep every night. He worried all the time that something would happen to 'his fellow.'" After the boyfriend returned from the military, William told his mother everything:

> The manner in which he explained his relationship with the boy made me realize my boy was no longer a child and that the landlord was not a boy but rather a young man with a life in the building and that life included and centered around

William. William explained that he was in love with the boy. That he had been for over a year and that he also realized that their relationship was homosexual and that he hoped that didn't hurt me too much, but that he wouldn't give up his love for the boy. He also explained that he would continue to live with the boy unless I absolutely refused. He said that if I did refuse the boy had talked him into meeting my requests.[30]

Like the letter published in the Denver Mattachine newsletter, William explained his homosexuality to his mother strategically in terms she could readily understand. He emphasized love and a steady relationship, rather than sex or the dangers of gay life. Aware of false myths that older gay men seduced teenagers into gay life, William carefully explained to his mother that the landlord "had never made sexual demands or requests but rather the shared sexual relations had spontaneously developed on a mutually consenting and fulfilling basis." William further explained to his mother that the landlord had discouraged him from going to homosexual hangouts.[31] In other words, the landlord was protecting him from the more dangerous aspects of gay life. She need not worry about finding his name in a newspaper report of a gay bar raid. She was being forced to confront something she had never thought about before, and William was strategically explaining to her that being gay was not a bad thing. Slowly, she was accepting the situation.

Compromises could fail, however, despite good intentions. Nineteen-year-old Steve from West Virginia described his father's explosive initial reaction to his homosexuality. "Recently my father found a copy of 'One,' and he threw a fit, he called me every name in the book, he tried to get me to admit I was a homosexual but I wouldn't." Steve lived in a small town where "everyone knows everyone and everyone's business." The father "threatened to tell everyone about me and ruin me." It was probably an idle threat because "telling everyone" would have embarrassed the father also. Nonetheless, Steve "packed [his] clothes and left. I stayed that night at my friends [sic] house and was hitch-hiking the next day when he caught me." His father apologized to Steve for his explosive reaction, and they returned home together. In subsequent days, however, the goodwill deteriorated as his father demanded (in McCarthyite fashion) that Steve tell him the names of his gay friends. "[H]e has been making my life miserable. Every time I go someplace he insists on knowing with whom I went. He thinks I am having an affair with every boy I know. The honest truth is I don't know of another homosexual around here."[32] In response to Steve's letter, ONE arranged for a gay-friendly minister in Las Vegas to offer Steve a stable environment. "Come to Las Vegas where employment can be found, giving you a feeling of security and where we may counsel you," the minister wrote to Steve. The minister's letter, however, was returned to *ONE's* office "unclaimed," indicating that Steve might have fled home shortly after writing his letter to *ONE*.[33] The father may have returned the unopened letter as well. Despite the breakdown in father-son relations in this case, their brief reconciliation signified a gesture toward accommodation, albeit probably an unsuccessful one.

Gaining acceptance from siblings was also important for many homosexuals. Sibling reactions covered the same spectrum as parental reactions, and often shifted over time as well. John from Brooklyn wrote in 1962, "I've had a rough time wuth [*sic*] my family of six sisters but now they are sort of adjusted," indicating an initial rejection followed by a reevaluation from his sisters. "The sister that I am living with now, she sure is like the weather, one day I can tell her my escapades, the next day she would give me a rough time, but deep down she has a warms [*sic*] heart, and a deep feeling for the lonely ones, my sisters and I don't have much, but we do have strong bond of love between us, that is worth more than anything else in the world."[34] In such cases, family bonds proved stronger than hostile attitudes toward homosexuality. Homosexuality was transformed from a frightening abstraction into a human face, a face that family members continued to love once they overcame their initial shock. Still, siblings could pose problems. "My worst problem came into view when my three sisters began heckling me about getting married and raising a family," wrote twenty-year-old Daryl from a small town in Ohio. "I shrugged them off for as long as possible. I finally broke down and told them everything. My one brother-in-law was very understanding to a certain extent, but insisted on Psychiatric treatment. It proved useless. Eventually I was bluntly kicked out." Afterward, he reconciled with his family, but he was "still not trusted with my teenage nephews."[35]

In explaining themselves to their families, gay men and lesbians sometimes found allies in psychologists and psychiatrists. Contrary to the conventional wisdom that all psychologists were determined to convert gay people into heterosexuals in the 1950s, many psychologists in fact calmed anxious parents and urged unconditional acceptance.[36] An article in *The Ladder*, "One Parent's Reaction," for example, described a mother's acceptance of her daughter's lesbianism only after the mother visited several psychologists who explained the range of professional perspectives on homosexuality.[37] *Physique Pictorial* printed a letter in 1957 of a mother who was talked out of therapy for her gay son by a psychiatrist. The psychiatrist explained that psychotherapy could help her son cope with the everyday pressures of being gay, but it could not change his sexual desires. The mother wrote, "At first I was heartbroken but am now reconciled. James lives with another young man [Gene] who shares his interests, both are highly successful in films, are 'accepted' everywhere and I am now as proud of Gene as any of my other children."[38] Psychiatrists who rejected the idea that homosexuality could be cured through psychotherapy or other techniques were drowned out in the mass media by more sensationalistic, cure-oriented psychiatrists such as Edmund Bergler.[39]

Blame Mom

Many parents, especially mothers, would have blamed themselves for their son's or daughter's homosexuality. During the 1950s and early 1960s, middle-class mothers felt enormous pressure from psychologists and social critics to raise flawless children.[40] Fathers shared some of these anxieties, but rigid social expectations that fathers must be family breadwinners reinforced a "cult of motherhood" that left mothers feeling responsible for their children's development.[41] According to Stephen Mintz and Susan Kellogg, "Child care manuals of the 1950s were characterized by an undercurrent of anxiety. No previous generation of child care books had ever expressed so much anxiety and fear about children's health, safety, and happiness."[42] Many psychologists and psychiatrists in the 1950s and early 1960s believed that a child's sexual identity could not be taken for granted: it had to be steered, encouraged, and guided toward heterosexuality through proper parenting techniques. The 1950 pamphlet "Sex Questions and Answers," for example, explained that avoiding homosexuality "lay largely in early detection and prevention through the education of parents in the proper way to rear children for sexual and social effectiveness."[43] In other words, if the child turned out gay, it was probably the parents' fault. Judd Marmor, a heterosexual psychologist in the 1950s who later became involved in gay rights causes, commented that parents were also blamed for their children's autism and schizophrenia in these years. "I weep when I think of what we did to mothers, when I think of the thousands of mothers who were forced to live with guilt feelings about their autistic, schizophrenic, and homosexual children!"[44]

The postwar trend of blaming mothers for their children's homosexuality was heavily influenced by the theory of "Momism" popularized in the 1942 book *Generation of Vipers* by Philip Wylie. Wylie argued that the shortage of men on the American home front during World War II had given rise to overbearing mothers who spoiled children with affection and made them homosexual.[45] He, along with other parenting experts, urged fathers to assume a greater role in household duties and childrearing.[46] Psychiatrists routinely legitimized Momist theories in the popular press. A Columbia University clinical psychiatrist told *Picture Week* magazine in 1956, for example, that domineering mothers were the chief cause of male homosexuality: "Men are no longer the dominant sex in America. One need only look at television or movies—it's always the woman who is intelligent, who saves the day. Dagwood Bumstead is no longer a caricature, he's become the typical American male and under such circumstances his children might very well grow up to be homosexuals."[47] A June 1960 article in the *San Francisco Examiner* explained, "The chief instrument of conversion [to homosexuality] is the doting mother who overwhelms her son (usually an only child) with so much love, attention and devotion that he fails to develop the necessary masculine drive to strike out on his own."[48] Maurice Linden, a prominent Philadelphia-area psychologist, organized a "Campaign for Patriarchy" in 1960 to battle Momism in the American home. Linden explained in a *Los Angeles Times* article, "In too many families, the wife holds the role as chief decision maker. The children ask Daddy about something and he says—'Go ask Mother.' The child grows up with a muddled idea about a man and a woman's role in life. They think males are supposed to be passive and females aggressive in a masculine way—a role nature never intended for women." The return of patriarchy in the home would solve most family problems, Linden assured the public. Women should accept their subordinate role "without feeling that they're being stepped on."[49] Anxieties over female dominance and homosexual children intermingled in articles about Momism.

Armed with Momist theories from credentialed experts, the mass media placed impossible expectations on mothers. A 1955 article in *Coronet* magazine, "The Third Sex—Guilt or Sickness?" by Ted Berkman, for example, offered bewildering and contradictory advice on preventing homosexuality in adolescents. He attributed homosexuality to everything from faulty glands to "the haunting insecurities of the atomic era." Berkman offered the following advice to mothers:

> Avoid surrounding sex with mysterious taboos. . . . But don't go to the other extreme. . . .
>
> See that they have warmth and love from their mothers so that they will turn to women in later life for the same qualities. But beware of fostering overdependence. . . .
>
> If you were disappointed in the sex of your child, never let the child know it. Many homosexual drives are attributed to a frantic, though unconscious, desire to please the parents.

Be alert to overt signs of psychological difficulties, such as violent aversion to little girls on the part of a boy, or an insistence on playing exclusively with them.

Give your son particularly sympathetic attention during adolescence, when his glandular system is going through enormous readjustment. This is the time when the latent female component has most opportunity to come to the surface, because the dominant male element has not yet developed full power to repress it.[50]

According to Berkman, almost anything a mother did—or did not do—could result in a homosexual child. This discourse of Momism shaped how many mothers conceptualized homosexuality at the time and undoubtedly influenced their reactions when they learned their male offspring were gay. Momism did not necessarily influence whether a mother accepted or rejected her gay offspring, but the sense of guilt and responsibility many mothers would have felt contributed to the emotional impact of postwar homosexual disclosures in the family.

Theories that overbearing mothers cause homosexuality have declined significantly since the 1960s, and many people at the time believed such theories were nonsense—*ONE* contributors and readers especially. Most gay men who speculated about the origins of their homosexuality in *ONE* letters did not blame their mothers, but stated their homosexuality simply had always been there.

While Momist theories have declined, it is surprising how little else has changed in the ways gay people relate to their families. The patterns from the letters closely resemble patterns in contemporary research on gay people and their families. Despite all the coming out manuals available today, gay people still fear telling their parents and families more than anyone else.[51] When they do tell them, a bad reaction followed by a period of accommodation and reconciliation has remained the standard pattern. According to Charlotte Patterson, "Although interactions between lesbian and gay young people and their parents often suffer difficulties immediately after disclosure, they most often improve again over time as families assimilate this new information into existing images of the lesbian or gay child."[52] The major difference between the 1950s and today, aside from the voluntary nature of many disclosures, is the vast amount of information available to guide gay people and their families through the process—not just the coming out manuals at the local bookstore, but also organizations such as Parents, Families, and Friends of Lesbians and Gays (PFLAG) as well as movies, television shows, and Internet sites focused on the issue. In the 1950s and 1960s, there was *ONE* magazine or another homophile publication, the Kinsey Reports and a handful of other books, and not much else. Gay people were largely on their own, requiring them to be creative and thoughtful in how they explained their sexuality to their families. Gay people who never had such conversations with their families undoubtedly would have thought about the issue, thought about what they might say, and probably discussed the topic with other gay people. Even if they did not choose the circumstances of their disclosure, at least they could choose how to explain it to their families.

Families, in turn, responded in more complex ways than simply rejecting their gay and lesbian members. The letters show that family life often provided important spaces for tolerance and acceptance in the repressive McCarthy-era environment. Dismissing a homosexual from a job was one matter, but rejecting one's own flesh and blood was quite another. Even in the 1950s, in the era of the perfect family, in the era when homosexuality was officially labeled a disease, gay men and lesbians usually remained part of their families after their homosexuality was revealed. Homosexuality was a component of family values, not a threat to them.

8

Homosexuals and Marriage under the Shadow of McCarthy

In *Tea and Sympathy*, a housemaster's wife, Laura, takes pity on poor Tom Lee. She disbelieves that Tom's effeminacy, sensitivity, and fondness for classical music means he must be gay. But Laura is not so sure about her macho husband, Bill. During their brief marriage, their sex life has dwindled to nothing. He is cold and distant. Bill clearly prefers the company of his male students to her. Laura's suspicions are further aroused by Bill's explosive reaction to the rumors about Tom's homosexuality. Bill insists Tom be expelled from school. "I think you've got to let people know the school doesn't stand for even a hint of this sort of thing," he tells Laura. "He should be booted."[1] Laura suspects that Bill's unresolved sexuality might explain his harsh reaction to Tom. In a climactic moment toward the end of the play, Laura confronts Bill with her suspicion: "Did it ever occur to you that you persecute in Tom, that boy up there, you persecute in him the thing you fear in yourself?" The stage instructions make it clear that Laura has correctly identified Bill's latent homosexuality: "*BILL looks at her for a long moment of hatred. She has hit close to the truth he has never let himself be conscious of.*"[2] Laura realizes at that moment her marriage to Bill is hopeless. In the play's final scene, she seduces Tom (thus, as the *Der Kreis* reviewer complained in chapter 3, implying Tom was heterosexual).

In 1953, the same year *Tea and Sympathy* became a smash hit on Broadway, *ONE* magazine's August issue featured the words "Homosexual Marriage?" on the cover, representing the first serious discussion of same-sex marriage in a national publication (see Figure 14, *ONE* cover,

August 1953). The featured article, "Reformer's Choice: Marriage License or Just License?" by E. B. Saunders, criticized homophile organizations for avoiding the issue of marriage. Saunders feared the homophile movement was doomed to fail if its primary goal was to fight for gay men's legal right to be sexually promiscuous with one another. Mainstream heterosexual society would never endorse such a goal. The issue of marriage, on the other hand, would challenge gay stereotypes and elicit heterosexual sympathy. "[O]ne would think that in a movement demanding acceptance for this group, legalized marriage would be one of the primary issues," Saunders wrote. "What a logical and convincing means of assuring society that they are sincere in wanting respect and dignity! But nowhere do we see this idea prominently displayed in either [Mattachine] Society publications or in the magazine *ONE*."[3] Marriage could provide a bridge of understanding between gay and straight worlds and foster broader acceptance in American society. Long-term relationships were a common fact of lesbian and gay life, and Saunders believed these relationships should be highlighted by homophile organizations.

Approximately half of the family letters analyzed in this study discussed marriage. Some *ONE* correspondents endorsed opposite-sex marriages in order to pass as heterosexual, maintain a professional career, or raise a family. Unlike sexually repressed Bill in *Tea and Sympathy*, the letters show that some gay people in opposite-sex marriages enjoyed fulfilling gay relationships outside of their marriages. Living such a double life, however, could be stressful. Other letter writers echoed the "Homosexual Marriage?" article by describing long-term partnerships with persons of the same gender conceptualized as marriages, despite the absence of legal recognition. These relationships avoided many of the duplicitous anxieties of the opposite-sex marriages, but they had their own unique stresses, especially regarding a couple's visibility as "a couple." Maintaining a heterosexual front to society was more difficult while participating in a lesbian or gay marriage.

In both cases, the letters suggest that gay people in the 1950s and early 1960s went to great lengths to participate in the institution of marriage despite the social and legal prohibitions against homosexuality. Like heterosexuals, many gay people believed that marriage provided an important source of personal fulfillment. They participated in the idealization of marriage found in so much postwar American culture, such as television sitcoms, magazines, and family-centered suburban developments. Gay people routinely defied the stereotyped assumption that they were destined to be lonely spinsters or bachelors by participating in the institution of marriage in a variety of ways.

Figure 14. *ONE* cover, August 1953.

Opposite-Sex Marriage

Reader surveys conducted in *ONE* and *The Ladder* in the late 1950s and early 1960s demonstrate that opposite-sex marriages involving one homosexual member were fairly common. Out of 388 men in the *ONE* survey, 40 of them, slightly more than 10 percent, were in an opposite-sex marriage when they filled out their questionnaires in 1961. Another 36, slightly less than 10 percent, were divorced. Thus, about 20 percent of these gay men had been in an opposite-sex marriage at some point in their lives.[4] The 1959 *Ladder* Survey conducted by the Daughters of Bilitis found that 27 percent of its 157 lesbian respondents had been in an opposite-sex marriage at some point in their lives. Approximately 6 percent of these respondents were married when they filled out their questionnaires and approximately 16 percent were divorced. Slightly in excess of 3 percent were separated but not yet divorced, and a few women (2 percent) were widowed.[5] Taking the two surveys together, somewhere between one-fifth and one-fourth of surveyed homosexuals had been married to someone of the opposite sex.

Gay people felt the same intense pressures to get married as heterosexuals in these years when marriage was idealized as the ultimate source of fulfillment.[6] Dorr Legg described the postwar pressures to marry in a ONE Institute lecture: "The pressures of his society bear down upon him with all the subtlety of a ten-ton truck arguing night and day from every billboard, from the magazine ads, from the plots of every movie, from novels and short stories, from the tacit arrangements of business life, of credit practices, of career advancement, that there is but one worthy goal in life—marriage, MARRIAGE, M A R R I A G E."[7] For gay people, such pressure to marry a person of the opposite sex could be unwelcome and irritating, although hardly unexpected. Several *ONE* correspondents complained that family members and friends badgered them to get married. "My family is forever questioning my future plans concerning marriage," wrote one man.[8] Another man grumbled at a 1957 Denver Mattachine meeting, "well-meaning friends thrust prospective mates before us trying to make a match."[9] Such pressures contributed to gay people's family anxieties described in the previous chapter.

In the face of pressure to marry from family members and society, opposite-sex marriages served a variety of purposes for gay people. Some gay men explained that marriage helped them advance their careers and achieve professional success. A lawyer from Cleveland, Mr. T., explained in a published letter in 1962, "Recently an attorney of 35 with excellent qualifications was not accepted for employment by my firm in favor of another man, precisely because he was not a 'family man.' This is not an isolated case," he warned. "An acquaintance who is employed by an employment agency told me that many personnel managers tell agencies that regardless of qualifications to send them no applicant who is not married; the reason—instability." Mr. T. explained that he found sexual gratification with other married men. "I feel that we are making a better adjustment to life than most of the homosexuals you write about. We have the security of a home and a family. We do not hate our wives, on the contrary, we are fond of them. But we are not about to fight the world and jeopardize our jobs."[10] In his view, maintaining a "proper" family life significantly mitigated job anxieties.

Mr. T.'s position was controversial among *ONE* readers. Dr. E. from Michigan wrote a sarcastic reply to Mr. T.'s letter. "Well, well, well. Ducky for Mr. T. of Cleveland," he wrote. "Now all that the homosexuals need to do is marry and have children. Then, as pappas, they can have all the affairs they wish with other pappas, and approach (or should I have said 'make application to'?) personnel managers with the greatest assurance."[11] Despite the relief to his professional life, Mr. T.'s opposite-sex marriage could easily lead to emotional strain. The effort to keep such an important secret from his wife might wear him down over time.

Some lesbians and gay men participated in opposite-sex marriages because they believed that married life might cure their same-sex desires and awaken their "latent heterosexuality." Religious counselors, especially Catholic clergy, routinely recommended marriage as a way to overcome homosexuality in these years.[12] *ONE* letters warned that these marriages were doomed to fail. Over time, the lack of heterosexual desire became evident to the straight partner, as occurred with Laura and Bill in *Tea and Sympathy*.[13] When the homosexuality surfaced, the couple usually faced three choices: acceptance of the partner's homosexuality, psychiatric treatment aimed at curing the homosexuality, or divorce.

A woman from Long Beach, California, described her difficulty negotiating these choices in a 1956 newspaper advice column called "Most Sincerely, Jane Palmer." She had discovered her husband's homosexuality shortly after they married. "He was horribly miserable about his problem. My love for him did not alter—I only felt that somehow we would solve this problem, and we sought help right away." Eight *years* of professional therapy, however, had brought "only slight improvement." After viewing the first television broadcast dedicated to the subject of homosexuality (an episode of the Los Angeles–based *Paul Coates' Confidential File* in 1954), the husband "agreed to commit himself to the State Hospital" to cure his homosexuality. "No one knows of all this except my family." But after ten frustrating years trying to change her husband's sexuality, the woman was ready to give up on the marriage. She worried about the social disgrace her husband might suffer after his release from the hospital. "He will always be under suspicion for sex offenses," she wrote. But she still loved him, which complicated her decision: "His doctors have hinted that the best course would be to start a new life for myself and the children. But it tears my heart out to ask him never to see us again. It may sound as if I have no faith, which really isn't true. I could have faith in him if only he had indicated that he could control this terrible thing. But if his love for his children hasn't done it, what will?"[14] "What will?"—these words reveal her deep faith in the power of marriage, family, and domesticity to solve the crisis of her husband's homosexuality. No doubt the husband, by enduring years of useless conversion therapy, shared this faith in marriage and family as well.

The case is a reminder that the pressures to get married were accompanied by strong pressures to *stay* married. Some couples stayed together for years in a state of denial or unawareness about one partner's homosexuality. Other couples worked out compromises once the truth came out. In contrast to the woman from Long Beach, for example, a father of two told a Denver Mattachine discussion group how his wife preferred "his diversions to the failings of a woman-chasing husband, an alcoholic, or a non-provider."[15] He had disclosed his homosexuality to her before their marriage, and she said she could live with it. Sociologist H. Laurence Ross has commented, "The enjoyment of a common home, the advantages of the division of labor between man and wife, the companionship of the couple on a platonic level, the fear of inability to have an independent life, and . . . social respectability" often compelled spouses of differing sexual orientations to stay together rather than divorce.[16]

Overall, writers in homophile publications advised against getting into opposite-sex marriages because they so often required stressful, continuing acts of duplicity. But some homophile activists were open to the idea. A Mattachine Society representative, for example, argued on a 1959 panel discussion broadcast over New York City radio "if the heterosexual partner was not too demanding, a satisfactory relationship could be built upon companionship."[17] The two other members of the panel, a Daughters of Bilitis representative and a psychoanalyst, disagreed with the Mattachine representative and argued that these marriages were a recipe for disaster. *ONE* opposed the practice of opposite-sex marriage more consistently than the Mattachine Society, but all three 1950s homophile organizations expressed a range of viewpoints on this topic.

In the Daughters of Bilitis survey, a slight majority of the lesbian respondents knew they were lesbian before marrying. They married for a variety of reasons. Family pressure was common ("Wished to please parents and family," and "Family satisfaction," they wrote). Some married to pass as heterosexual, writing such comments as "Concealment—hunger for social acceptance." Others married in an effort to cure their lesbian desires: "To straighten out," in their words, "To see if I could lead a normal or heterosexual life," "To prove to myself as well as to others that I was not homosexual."[18] Miriam Gardner (whose real identity was science fiction author Marion Zimmer Bradley) explained in a 1960 *Ladder* article that social pressures toward youthful marriage for women had influenced her decision to marry an older man even though she suspected she was a lesbian.[19] "Naturally I married," she explained. "In the part of Texas where I now live, teen-age marriages are common: marriages of girls fourteen and fifteen are not at all unusual, and the girl who delays marriage until her twenties is the exception rather than the rule."[20] Sex with her husband was tolerable, she explained. But after giving birth to two children ("a joy"), her lesbian desires grew stronger, and she found herself increasingly frustrated in her marriage. Gardner sunk into a deep depression and began to take tranquilizers as she struggled to balance her devotion to her family with her sexual identity:

> My truest emotional level lies in the need I have—or seem to have—for other women. Yet I sometimes tell myself that if my present frustrating marriage ties were severed, if I were to marry a man nearer my own age who could fill my life with routine needs and children, I might still be able to put homosexuality behind me forever. . . . Our society will either force an irrevocable choice on me, or it will destroy me. Right now I neither know nor care which. I stand squarely at the crossroads, and the traffic is hell.[21]

Many lesbians found themselves torn between the competing loyalties of family and sexual desire.

The heterosexual spouse's attitude toward homosexuality influenced whether a marriage lasted. "Perhaps the deviate partner has broached the subject time and again in order to test the reactions of her husband, only to find a completely rejecting, narrow attitude and no spark of interest," wrote Nancy Osborne in *The Ladder* in 1957. "If there is no crack or chink in her husband's armor she is doomed to keep her secret rather than risk shocking and upsetting his faith in her and the harmony of her home." Osborne concluded that many women preferred to continue their marriages and "keep their fears within themselves, trusting to luck that the tightrope of their lives will remain intact and unthreatened."[22] A sympathetic husband, in contrast, might be willing to negotiate a marriage arrangement based on companionship with no sexual expectations. Even Marion Zimmer Bradley, struggling in her own opposite-sex marriage, agreed theoretically that "if the personality adjustment is suitable, there is no reason why a woman who is, or suspects herself to be, inherently Lesbian cannot make a happy marriage without in anyway denying her nature."[23] Bradley wrote that women who knew they were lesbian should avoid opposite-sex marriages, but if a woman discovered this fact too late, it did not necessarily mean the marriage must be terminated. Her own tortured experience, however, demonstrates the emotional pitfalls involved in such a situation.

Children also figured into why many lesbians married heterosexual men. Slightly fewer than 15 percent of the Daughters of Bilitis survey respondents had children.[24] Bradley wrote, "I am convinced that most Lesbian women who marry do so out of a conscious or unconscious desire to bear children and thus redeem to herself the real or fancied deficiencies in the maternal relationship."[25] Daughters of Bilitis activist Helen Sanders wrote in 1958, "Most Lesbians adore children. Many of them are mothers and have given up a great deal to retain their children."[26] The Daughters of Bilitis' first-ever monthly discussion group was dedicated to raising children in a "deviant relationship," and they later formed an ongoing childrearing discussion group.[27] Lesbians struggled to maintain custody of their children if their marriages failed. A mother's lesbianism provided legal grounds for removing children from her custody, resulting in painful, heartbreaking separations.[28] The prospect of custody battles in divorce courts provided a powerful incentive for lesbians to hide their sexual desires within an opposite-sex marriage. Worries over child custody exacerbated the routine worries of homosexual discovery within a family.

Several gay men also expressed a desire to raise children in letters to *ONE*. James from Chicago wrote that his boyfriend of nearly four months "thinks he wants to get married and have a family. He says that a man should have children and that this is one of the things that the homosexual relationship cannot overcome." James worried about his boyfriend's attitude. "We both know [of] too many marriages 'of convenience' which are worse than none at all."[29] Lacking sophisticated means of artificial insemination, the desire to bear children compelled many homosexuals to marry a person of the opposite sex and join in the baby boom of the 1950s.

One option for gay men and lesbians to negotiate the complexities of opposite-sex marriage was to completely abstain from homosexual behavior. Vince, writing from a small town in Utah, for example, admitted to *ONE* in 1955, "For fifteen years now I have been suppressing a desire for sexual relationship with another man. . . . I am married and have two children. My wife and I get along fine, but I know she desires more physical union than I care to supply. All I can think of is being in the arms of another man and consummating a love affair with him." His wife did not know "how I feel" about men, he wrote, and he feared becoming "a social outcast for ever. They are extremely strict here in this little Mormon community."[30] Similarly, a sixty-three-year-old finance executive from the Boston area told *ONE* he had avoided homosexual contacts throughout his thirty-three-year marriage, but found relief masturbating to male physique photos. "Would like homosexual experience: keep myself fit physically," he wrote.[31] Repressed married homosexuals in the 1950s could use physique magazines or lesbian novels to provide fantasies that might partially compensate for their lack of a fulfilling sex life.

Popular magazines occasionally advised women how to avoid marrying a gay husband. The advice was usually riddled with misinformation and stereotypes about homosexuality. A 1954 article in *Pageant*, for example, described several varieties of "unmarriable men," including a variety called "frigid men." Frigid men were "sensitive, often well-educated and talented," but "they literally flee from woman to woman, often leaving the girl in considerable confusion. Usually they hang around for only three to six dates. Then the possibility of intimacy frightens them off. . . ." The frigid man described in this article undoubtedly resembles the misadventures of a gay man pursuing heterosexual relations, although interestingly the article did not believe "frigid men" were homosexual. Genuine homosexuals, the article ridiculously claimed, despised women and wanted nothing to do with them. The frigid man, in contrast, "likes and appreciates women, often blindly adores them, and is capable of falling deeply in love." Indeed, gay men often *did* love their wives and had deep respect for women. Yet according to the logic of the article, the only possible explanation for a frigid husband was impotency, "What actually frightens him is a fear of sexual impotence with a girl he loves. Generally his history shows that in a series of fumbling adolescent sex experiences, often with prostitutes, he was impotent—and he felt so humiliated that he dare not risk it again. Sometimes men of this type fall in love and get married, thinking marriage will cure their impotence. However, it does not—and in many cases they have mistakenly and tragically committed suicide afterwards."[32] The article fails to mention that impotence could result from a lack of heterosexual desire; clearly the description of "frigid men" must include both gay and impotent men.

If a frigid man were discovered to be homosexual by his wife, the most common outcomes were denial, divorce, or accommodation. Some gay men worried about blackmail in such a situation. Marlon from New York City, for example, wrote in 1961, "My wife of 6½ years learned this past week that I am bisexual. She had been reading some mail of mine without [me] knowing it and I have one or two gay friends who keep in touch. So now I'm taking a post office box to preserve the privacy of my friendships and will wait to see whether dear wifey decides to divorce me or just blackmail me into continuing with marriage."[33]

In 1953 a sordid attempt at marital blackmail was described in press coverage of a tragic scandal involving pin-up girl and B-movie actress Rebel Randall, whose real name was Alaine Brandes. Randall married a wealthy Texas playboy named Glenn Burgess during a whirlwind Las Vegas affair. A drunken wedding was followed by a "kissless honeymoon." Later at Burgess's home in Texas, Burgess's mother bluntly told Randall that her son was gay. He had been married twice before with tragic results, she explained, including a suicide attempt by one of his former wives. In response to this news, Randall rented a car and drove twenty-six hours to Hollywood to meet with her attorney. Together, they drafted a letter demanding $500,000 from Burgess in exchange for not publicly disclosing his homosexuality. After receiving Randall's blackmail note, Burgess slashed his wrists at his father's Sunset Strip art studio. He survived the suicide attempt and explained from his hospital bed, "I couldn't stand the public disgrace of being called a homosexual by Rebel Randall and the press. You know that isn't true, and that it was only an attempt to get money out of me through blackmail."[34] In subsequent weeks, Randall denied ever writing the blackmail note, and then Burgess denied writing the suicide note accusing her of blackmail. Eventually, a court annulled the marriage.[35]

In some cases, an imminent opposite-sex marriage could jolt a frigid man or woman into realizing or admitting they were homosexual. Twenty-five-year-old Robert, for example, told *ONE* he was waking up to his homosexuality at the very moment he was due to marry a "wonderful woman." "Lately just once in awhile I have gotten a sort of feeling as if maybe I would least like to try, maybe just once and maybe from now on, homosexual experiences," he wrote.[36] A letter from Flint, Michigan, in 1955 described how a man abandoned marriage plans on the eve of his wedding after telling his girlfriend of sixteen months that he was in love with another man. Her response was sympathetic. "She knew of my feelings for this boy, as he was one of her best friends, and she understands why I love him. I am fortunate that I have her support and deep respect—a victory for *ONE* and its beliefs. Your magazine helped a great deal in gaining her understanding."[37] Both letters suggest that delaying marriage gave men and women more of an opportunity to come to terms with their homosexuality. In the rush for youthful marriages during the 1950s, however, many men and women found themselves married before realizing they were homosexual.

Gay people who neither suppressed their homosexual desires nor disclosed their homosexuality to their spouses lived double lives. This was quite common among correspondents in opposite-sex marriages—even some dedicated homophile activists passed as heterosexual to their spouses in opposite-sex marriages.[38] No doubt being married to a person of the opposite sex limited an individual's participation in gay life, but the camouflaged nature of gay social life in the 1950s accommodated the secrecy required for maintaining a double life within a marriage. Married men found anonymous sexual partners in certain public restrooms, public parks, and movie theaters, although these outlets carried the risk of arrest.[39]

Many married homosexuals preferred more substantial relationships instead of anonymous sexual encounters. An alibi could be helpful in deceiving the spouse. A Sacramento man, for example, told ONE that he enjoyed a long-term relationship with a man in another town on the pretext of "business trips." He explained that his marriage had been a failed attempt to cure his homosexuality.[40] Under similar pretenses of "business trips," a police officer with three children admitted having several long-term male lovers during the course of his fourteen-year marriage. He told ONE that these relationships were just as fulfilling to him as his opposite-sex marriage and family.[41] Despite the anxiety and peril of discovery, many gay men and women successfully maintained double lives for decades.

A small minority of marriages that did not require duplicity, secrecy, or double lives were opposite-sex marriages in which both partners were homosexual. In the Daughters of Bilitis survey, nine women (5.7 percent) reported marrying gay men in "marriages of convenience."[42] In these marriages, each member helped the other pass as heterosexual in a kind of marital conspiracy. Sexual fulfillment was found outside the marriage. These marriages might be "arrangements" largely intended to help one or both partners pass as heterosexual, but in many cases deep emotional and intimate bonds characterized the relationship, especially if the couple raised children together. Marijane Meaker, for example, described gay author Paul Bowles's marriage to Jane Bowles as "not just a front for a gay man and a lesbian, but a peculiar, involved dyad."[43] Many common heterosexual varieties of "marriages of convenience" exist as well—marriages for money, immigration status, military benefits, or marriages arranged by families. Ultimately, all marriages are complex and unique, regardless of the genders and sexualities of the participants.

Some scholars have referred to marriages in which one partner has same-sex affairs as "bisexual marriages."[44] Indeed, a man who occasionally has sex with his wife while he more frequently has sex with a man is, technically speaking, bisexual. Yet the word "bisexual" appears in only a handful of letters, and ONE magazine rarely used the word. The 1950s and early 1960s seem to have been a low point for bisexual identity, at least compared to the 1920s or 1970s when bisexual identity assumed a certain fashionable status. Alfred Kinsey avoided the word "bisexual" in his studies, preferring to describe sexual behavior as either "homosexual" or "heterosexual," which is ironic because so many of Kinsey's interview subjects had sexual experiences with both genders.[45] Therefore, Kinsey may have influenced this generation of gay people to avoid the term as well, and fewer people may have thought of themselves as "bisexual" in these years.

Also possible is that bisexual-identified persons were less interested in a *homosexual* magazine." Persons using the word "bisexual" to describe themselves have historically been marginalized in gay communities.[46] According to Harvard University English Professor Marjorie Garber, who authored a major study about bisexuality, gay people "stereotype bisexuals as self-indulgent, undecided, 'fence-sitters' who dally with the affections of same-sex partners, breaking their hearts when they move on to heterosexual relationships."[47] Self-identified bisexuals may have felt alienated by *ONE* and the homophile movement. That so many letter writers described recurrent sexual behavior with both genders yet consistently used the words "homosexual," "gay," or "lesbian" to describe themselves is, however, striking nonetheless. The use of such language suggests that these individuals considered their homosexuality their dominant sexual identity.

Thus, however functional some of these opposite-sex marriages may have been, they clearly represented a compromise with a hostile society. To be sure, opposite-sex marriages mitigated some of the anxieties of being lesbian or gay in American society by projecting a persuasive heterosexual front to friends, employers, and family members. But these marriages created unique and intimate strains for both partners.

'For God's Sake, the Queers Want to Marry Each Other'

The Daughters of Bilitis survey reported that 72 percent of its respondents were "presently engaged in a homosexual relationship" and 59 percent "have had homosexual relationships of 'some permanency' prior to this one."[48] We cannot assume that these women necessarily considered themselves "married." They may not, as Jess Stearn described in *The Grapevine*, have been in relationships with "jointly owned property, maintained joint bank accounts, and thought of their debts as joint obligations. Some had even drawn up dissolution papers governing the dispersal of effects in the event of a split-up."[49] But 59 percent of these women believed that the word "permanency" described at least one relationship in their lives, and "permanency" is certainly central to the meaning of marriage.

In contrast to the Daughters of Bilitis survey, the ONE survey explicitly used the word "marriage" in its questionnaire, thus allowing a clearer sense of the word's appropriation by gay male couples. In the ONE survey, 42 percent of the 388 respondents had been in a same-sex "marriage" for at least one year, while another 9 percent had been in a same-sex marriage for less than one year. Forty-three percent had never been in a same-sex marriage. These correspondents, mostly young adults in their twenties and thirties, reported average marriage lengths between three and six years.[50] In total, approximately one-half of the ONE survey respondents agreed that the word "marriage" described at least one of their long-term same-sex relationships.

These surveys demonstrate that long-term same-sex couples were a substantial portion of the lesbian and gay community in the 1950s and early 1960s, regardless of whether the word "marriage" was used. To be sure, the rates were lower than heterosexual marriage rates, but that so many lesbian and gay couples maintained marriage-like relationships is surprising because these relationships exacerbated homosexual visibility for both partners.[51] Not only did the individual members have to pass as heterosexual in many contexts, but the partnership itself had to pass as heterosexual. These couples learned to avoid public displays of affection that heterosexual couples blithely take for granted, such as public hand-holding or pecks on the cheek. Gay couples invented elaborate alibis to their families, friends, and coworkers in order to spend time together. Some of these gay women and men were simultaneously in opposite-sex marriages whereas others presented themselves as "bachelors" or "old maids" to their straight friends and family. But they were not old maids or bachelors to themselves, each other, or their broader circle of gay friends. They were just as married as Ozzie and Harriet.

Generally, these couples neither desired nor sought legal recognition of their relationships as "marriages." To seek such recognition was akin to confessing a crime and would bring unwanted visibility. As long as homosexuality was illegal, legal recognition of same-sex marriage was an impractical goal.

Some homophile writers were uncomfortable applying the word "marriage" to same-sex relationships at all, disagreeing with Saunders's 1953 "Homosexual Marriage?" article that legal recognition of same-sex marriage should be a homophile movement priority. They feared that throwing the word "marriage" around too loosely might provoke a backlash. Herman Lynn Womack, a defendant in a landmark obscenity

Supreme Court case in 1960, for example, wrote to *ONE* in 1962, "Have you any idea what the mere thought that these things are discussed, much less seriously advocated, does to middle class America? This is completely apart from the considerations of whether homosexuals really want such things, etc. etc."[52] *ONE* contributor Marcel Martin (a pseudonym often used by Dorr Legg) similarly worried that heterosexuals would never accept the concept of gay marriage. In his view, "the fact of the matter is that 'marriage' means to everyone in his right mind the union of a man and woman in matrimony, and Webster's *Unabridged Dictionary* forthrightly defines it as such. Furthermore, the word has legal status, religious significance and social acceptance only as it applies to a man and woman united in wedlock to become a husband and wife." Martin feared that nothing would persuade people otherwise.[53]

Martin's pessimistic outlook on gay marriage contrasted however with other homophile writers who encouraged gay people to think of their partnerships as "marriages," even if legal recognition did not seem practical at that moment. In a 1963 essay, "Let's Push Homophile Marriage," for example, writer Randy Lloyd suggested that marriage was a basic human experience that transcended legal status, "Marriage is no more a strictly heterosexual social custom than are the social customs of birthday celebrations, funerals, house-warming, or, for that matter, sleeping, eating, and the like. I participate in those, not because they are heterosexual or homosexual things, but because I am a human being. Being homosexual does not put one out of the human race."[54] For Lloyd, marriage was a subjective understanding between two partners regardless of legal sanction. Lloyd believed that homosexual marriage was "a new modern concept" occurring on a larger scale than ever before in the United States, which suggested that more gay couples were establishing long-term relationships in these years. Yet visibility was a problem. "Marriage, it has been said, is a private affair. A homophile marriage is a *very* private affair. . . . It would be a very rare homophile marriage that did not have on one side or the other some good reason for shunning publicity."[55] Lloyd eloquently described how the need for privacy hampered the creation of these partnerships in the first place, "Heterosexual society screams against the promiscuity of homosexuals, but by their laws and anathema regarding homosexuals they drive us underground and force us to live 95 percent of our lives 'passing' as heteros with so little time left to socialize with other homosexuals that an eat-and-run sexual fling is about all that can be managed. To find a marriage partner, one must meet many prospects, and on a social basis, not on a furtive and desperate wham-bam-thank-you-ma'am basis."[56]

ONE readers gave Lloyd's column a mixed reaction. One correspondent questioned why gay people would want to impose the limitations of marriage on their relationships. A Southern California homophile activist named Tony Foster explained he "did not find fault with the article itself," but he worried that heterosexuals might ridicule the idea. ONE should not push the issue. "Can't you hear our enemies saying, as they read it, 'For God's sake, the queers want to marry each other'?"[57] In his view, gay marriages were fine as long as they were contained within the gay world. The idea of same-sex relationships as "marriages" had to be presented to the heterosexual public very carefully. Fear of backlash permeates most discussions of gay marriage in homophile publications.

The fear of backlash helps explain why none of the letters in this study described gay wedding ceremonies. Indeed, the dangers of visibility prevented most lesbian or gay couples from having a "wedding" comparable to heterosexual marriage ceremonies. Any wedding ceremony had to be carefully contained within gay social circles. In a *Ladder* article, homophile writer Jody Shotwell described with skeptical indifference a lesbian wedding at a "private home on a quiet street." "We had, of course, heard of gay weddings, but in most cases the couples were men." At this wedding, most of the guests were lesbians, although the male "manager-bartender of a local gay bar" performed the ceremony. Shotwell questioned the motives of the ceremony. She thought it might reflect insecurity within the relationship. Why show off? Why put on such a public display and jeopardize everyone's safety and security? Shotwell agreed with Randy Lloyd that gay marriage was a subjective understanding between two individuals. "Having no status in the law of the land, the homosexual marriage must be maintained only through the mutual love and devotion of those involved—and this love and devotion must be dependent upon their feelings and behavior, not upon any public exchange of vows."[58]

Despite the lack of wedding ceremonies in the letters, many long-term same-sex partners viewed themselves as conventional boring married couples. A domestic impulse is evident in the sources. In some cases, marriage and home life replaced other forms of socializing such as going to lesbian or gay bars. A Bakersfield, California, man wrote to ONE in 1959 after moving into his partner's home (with the partner's mother), "We must realize that single and married homosexuals have few things in common. The single queens talk on and on about tricks they've had, or nearly had. The married team is more interested in the chair they've just had reupholstered, the new set of silver that their savings have enabled them to buy, or other terribly boring household or common experiences with which the single queen has no patience."[59]

A 1959 letter from a male couple in Sheridan, Wyoming, similarly emphasized the domestic life. One worked as a horse breeder, the other as an accountant. Both men had previously been in opposite-sex marriages.[60] "We have been friends for about eight years. We have been married for a little over six years now," wrote Curtis. He described their social life with other couples, gay and straight. "Until recently we lived in a little country house, but have just moved into an exclusive apartment house in town. We know many homosexuals, some single and some married for convenience, but are very particular which ones we choose for close friends. We also know many 'straight' couples and are accepted by most. We entertain both heterosexuals and homosexuals, and sometimes mixed crowds of both, but with everything always very circumspect."[61] Whether the straight couples knew the two men were a gay couple is unclear from the letter—they were "accepted" by straight couples, yet "everything" remained "circumspect." This ambiguity implies that Curtis and his partner probably offered alibis about their relationship to some friends, but not necessarily to everyone. Still, they maintained a surprisingly busy social life for a gay male couple—in Wyoming of all places. A subsequent letter from Curtis had a different tone, emphasizing that not everyone in their community accepted them. "We are looked down on for living together and establishing a home together," Curtis stated, "even by persons who are 'straight' and living alone [and who] are very lonely." Their visibility as a same-sex couple clearly annoyed some while others were ignorant of the relationship's sexual basis or simply were not bothered by it. Regardless, they remained committed to a quiet domestic life: "Can't we have a normal home life and live as a family?" Curtis wrote.[62]

Domesticity even crept into the erotically charged world of male physique photography. The mainstay of the postwar physique movement, gay-owned and operated *Physique Pictorial*, for example, offered several domestic-themed photo spreads in contrast to its usual framing of male models in scenes of cowboy and Indian bondage, motorcycle gangs, or ancient Roman gladiators.[63] In 1961 *Physique Pictorial* published a sequence of photographs, "Joe and Don" (see Figure 15), depicting a male couple having a quiet evening at home. In the photographs, a man wearing blue jeans greets his friend in a Navy uniform at the door, inviting him inside. After stripping down to physique pouches, they cook a meal together, serve food to each other, wash the dishes, relax on the couch, and then flex their muscles in front of a living room Christmas tree.[64] The photographs have an undeniable intimacy: peeking in the oven together, feeding each other, handing over a dish to dry. They look happy and content in their cozy domesticity.

One of *Physique Pictorial's* main illustrators, the mysterious Art-Bob, occasionally drew homoerotically-charged scenes depicting home and family as well.[65] According to Bob Mizer, the owner and operator of the magazine (who, according to one scholar, was probably Art-Bob himself), *Physique Pictorial* readers flooded him with letters praising these domestic scenes of "good-natured boyish comradeship," to use his coy phrase.[66] These popular illustrations celebrated the mundane joys of two men sharing household duties with one another, hinting at long-term gay relationships. Some even celebrated the joys of childrearing, such as "2 A.M. Daddy" (see Figure 16).[67] The illustration alludes to gay men in opposite-sex marriages, although no woman is present in the illustration. The man's feminine pose, dainty slippers, and perfect hair enhance the homoerotic aesthetic of the drawing. His facial expression seems both confused and seductive. The illustration captures how gay people imagined themselves as a part of, not apart from, the powerful domestic impulses of the 1950s and early 1960s.

Most gay married couples used passing strategies in certain contexts to offset the suspicions their partnerships created. This was especially true for men. Lesbians could better conceal their long-term relationships by referring to their partner as a "roommate." This was generally effective because, historically, heterosexual unmarried adult women routinely lived together to share expenses. Men who lived together, especially older men, were more suspect.[68] But even long-term partners who did not share a residence needed alibis to pass as heterosexual. For physique culture enthusiasts, for example, the term "training partner" could mask a more intimate partnership. As the 2005 film *Brokeback Mountain* suggested, fishing or camping buddies might be lovers. A long-term male sexual partner might also be a "business partner." There were advantages for gay men owning businesses together. These individuals avoided the common anxiety of worrying about their boss firing them for homosexuality because they were the boss. But there still were clients, employees, and other business associates, so some degree of concealment was necessary to run most successful businesses. Bill from New Orleans, for example, told *ONE* that he and his partner of ten years ran a "reputable business" together, but they avoided "notoriously gay bars as so much controversial publicity has been cropping up, off and on, in the papers. We never did go to these bars, maybe four in ten years. We always feared for our reputations and jobs etc."[69] Owning a business did not eliminate all of the job anxieties, but it could allow two men to share their lives together in a camouflaged, socially accepted manner.

Similar to the "business partner" alibi were arrangements in which a wealthy, usually older, man or woman "kept" a lover under the pretense of employment, such as a personal secretary, assistant, or chauffeur. Liberace, for example, kept a lover as a chauffeur for many years.[70] Although it may be tempting to dismiss these relationships as merely enhanced prostitution, these were often complex relationships no less serious than

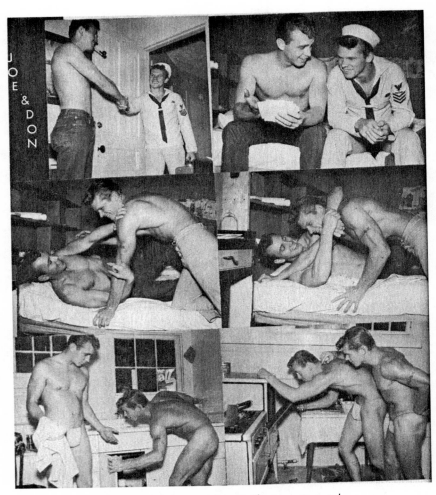

Figure 15. "Joe and Don," *Physique Pictorial.*

Figure 15 (continued). "Joe and Don," *Physique Pictorial.*

Art-Bob drawings
available at $1.50
each or 3 for $3.
from Art-Bob,
1611 N Avenue 56
Los Angeles 42,
California.
Art-Bob also offers
photographs of his
models.
Catalog and sam-
ples $1.

"2: A.M. DADDY"

Figure 16. "2 A.M. Daddy," *Physique Pictorial.*

any other marriage. As Dorr Legg explained in a ONE Institute lecture, "What may have started out as merely a cover-up . . . as an employer, employee relationship sometimes moves on over into a genuine business and emotional partnership."[71] We find these arrangements routinely among wealthy gay circles, and they often lasted (as in Liberace's case) until the death of the older partner.

The Gay Marriage of J. Edgar Hoover

At the same time that FBI Director J. Edgar Hoover was spying on gay people through the bureau's Sex Deviate Program, Hoover seems to have been involved in perhaps the most enduring same-sex marriage of a high-profile twentieth-century American. Most Hoover biographers remain unconvinced that Hoover and his chief assistant Clyde Tolson were sexually intimate with one another, but they all agree that Hoover and Tolson shared a deep and intimate friendship. Rumors of Hoover's homosexuality have been unreliable because critics and enemies usually spread them in order to make him seem perverted and monstrous.[72] I agree with eminent FBI scholar Athan Theoharis that secondhand tales of cross-dressing and fellatio photos should not be trusted.[73] Still, I think a strong case can be made that Hoover and Tolson should be considered a gay married couple, especially considering the broader patterns of gay marriage in these years. For more than four decades the two men were "nearly inseparable" in their professional and personal lives.[74] They worked side-by-side, vacationed together, and, for more than twenty-five years, ate lunch together everyday at the same table at Harvey's Restaurant in the Mayflower Hotel—a popular Washington, D.C., gay hangout at the time.[75] In photos and documents, their images and signatures routinely appear together. When Hoover died in 1972, he left nearly all of his assets, some $551,000, to Tolson as an inheritance.[76] The two men are buried a few yards from one another. Throughout their adult lives, they remained completely devoted to one another. Obviously they loved each other.

Lacking concrete proof of sexual intimacy between the two men, Hoover biographers (including Theoharis) are too quick to give heterosexuality the benefit of the doubt. If evidence of their homosexuality is weak, evidence of their heterosexuality is nonexistent.[77] Neither man ever showed any sexual interest in women. Cartha DeLoach, FBI assistant director from 1959 to 1970, commented that Hoover and Tolson led "monastic lives."[78] Given their prominent jobs, one can easily understand why they might have suppressed sexual feelings for one another. But if they were heterosexual, why would *both* men have suppressed all sexual desire toward women? Hoover's life makes no sense as a heterosexual.

Biographers' descriptions of the emotional intimacy between Hoover and Tolson bring to mind a specific variety of gay male marriage described in a 1959 *ONE* article entitled "Homosexual Marriage: Fact or Fancy?" by James Egan. Egan observed farmers in his native Ontario who "in no case . . . show the slightest signs of conventional 'gayness,' " yet spent their lives utterly devoted to one another.[79] They usually had no interaction with any sort of gay life and might have had no conscious awareness of their sexual identity. Like Hoover and Tolson, these men lacked heterosexual desires:

> Any attempt to explain to a normal man (or a psychiatrist) how these two differ from the other would meet with a scornful laugh and an accusation of "swishful thinking." But another homosexual would readily see the small "differences": the somewhat shy glances, the small gestures of affection, their obvious sincere pleasure in each other and their lack of interest in the others. When they come in [to a bar or restaurant] they will call greetings to their friends, but unlike the majority who will join a group at one of the tables, these two will invariably sit by themselves [as did Hoover and Tolson at the Mayflower every day]. . . . Their conversation will be quiet—not something to be shared with the others—not, of course, that it would be romantic. . . .

Egan argues that sexuality was beside the point in these "marriages." Sex might only occur after drinking alcohol, or possibly never at all. But the desire was there, trapped beneath layers of denial or ignorance. Such gay marriages were becoming less common since the end of World War II, Egan explained. They reflected an older model of male comradeship and masculine intimacy, one that would have been familiar to Hoover with his Victorian worldview. In Egan's words, "For these are the 'comrades' so beloved by Walt Whitman and theirs the 'manly love' of which he sang so beautifully in the Calamus section of *Leaves of Grass*. This is the purest form of homosexuality—unadulterated by the refinements of effeminacy or civilization. . . . Their friendship is noted (without complete understanding) and accepted by the community as something both natural and desirable."[80] Hoover and Tolson were undoubtedly aware that their highly visible and extremely close friendship raised suspicions they might be a homosexual couple. Hoover's mania for gathering information on persons critical of the FBI may have been part of conscious or unconscious effort to pass as heterosexual and quell such suspicions. With vast files of secrets and gossip capable of ruining anyone's reputation, who would dare publicly express the suspicion that Hoover and Tolson were anything more than "friends"? Hoover's persecution of gay people seems to have paralleled the way Bill persecuted Tom Lee in *Tea and Sympathy* as a twisted way of dealing with his own unresolved and unconsummated sexual desires.

Conceptualizing Hoover and Tolson as a gay married couple only makes sense when we recognize the diversity of marriage patterns by lesbians and gay men in these years. Gay people faced a broad array of choices in their personal relationships. Some preferred not to get too attached to intimate partners, but the homophile sources suggest that at least half of the postwar lesbian and gay minority chose to participate in marriage one way or another. Some chose to legally marry a person of the opposite sex, others chose to unofficially marry a person of the same sex. Both choices had advantages and disadvantages. Opposite-sex marriages allowed gay people to negotiate a hostile society more easily. They could blend in better and their professional lives were easier. They could raise children. But these marriages often caused personal strain, suffering, and turmoil. Fear of discovery fueled personal anxiety for those leading double lives. Other gay people chose to marry a person of the same sex and deal with anxieties of visibility as best they could. The pressures would have repeatedly tested the strength and durability of the relationship. Only strong relationships would have survived. To imagine oneself in a gay marriage in the 1950s required a certain audacity and further demonstrates the civil rights impulse at play in the intimate sphere of family life.

9

"I shall always cherish Sunday"

In 1964 Donny, a young African-American man who lived in Atlantic City, New Jersey, wrote an extraordinary letter to *ONE* magazine.[1] Over the course of nine typed pages, Donny described a gut-wrenching saga of sexual awakening, crushing heartbreak, and emotional breakdown. The first half of the letter was upbeat as Donny described coming out to gay life. He fell in love with his church pastor, and they had a brief, blissful affair. But then Donny's life became a nightmare. The pastor reunited with his wife, breaking Donny's heart. In deep despair, Donny told his mother about the affair, unleashing a chain of events that included suicide attempts, three months in a mental institution, and electro-convulsive therapy (ECT).

Donny's letter described events that occurred in the early 1960s. These were transitional years regarding African-American perceptions toward homosexuality. Scholars have argued that the black community was generally less hostile toward homosexuality for most of the early twentieth century compared to white society. Black newspapers, for example, reported on drag balls and other gay events with an enthusiasm unseen in the white press. Ironically, black tolerance of homosexuality dissipated as the postwar black civil rights movement gained momentum in the 1950s and early 1960s. The movement's middle-class leaders were determined to overcome centuries of degrading stereotypes about black people, especially stereotypes about black male hypersexuality. Civil rights leaders feared that white supremacists might cite gay tolerance in the black community as evidence of moral degradation or communist infiltration. The Black Power movement of the late 1960s was more blatantly homophobic and often characterized homosexuality as a means of white colonial domination. These trends, combined with the prominence of Christian churches in the black community, bolster the contemporary perception that black heterosexuals are more hostile toward homosexuality than white heterosexuals.[2] The accuracy of this perception, however, is debatable. Media pundits, for example, largely blamed black homophobia for the passage of Proposition 8 (which banned gay marriage) in California in 2008, but several scholars have noted that this perception was based on flawed exit polls. Religion, not race, was the primary variable determining whether an individual voted for or against Proposition 8.[3] Thus, claiming that the black community is inherently more homophobic than other social groups is an oversimplification.

Donny's letter contains both the older patterns of acceptance as well as the newer pressures the civil rights movement spawned. On the one hand, Donny suffered no guilt or shame over his sexual behavior. The affair with his pastor seemed as natural as any other love affair. In addition, Donny's pastor lived a surprisingly busy gay life. On the other hand, by the end of the letter, the pastor had reunited with his wife. Donny's mother reacted poorly to the affair. Also, Donny consistently refused to label himself "gay" or "homosexual" despite his clear sexual preference for men. In short, the affair itself echoed older patterns of tolerance, but the affair's tragic consequences pointed to the black community's new sensibility to downplay homosexuality.

Donny's letter was the only one used in this study that described in detail an affair between a clergyman and church congregant. Religion, however, was a common topic in the letters. Approximately 6 percent of the letters touched on religion in some manner. Some letters described anxiety about getting kicked out of churches whereas other correspondents focused on the theological or spiritual implications of same-sex desire and intimacy. Similar to family life, some gay people struggled to maintain their religious affiliations whereas others found creative methods of adaptation. Interestingly, Donny expressed no such struggle with his church or faith. At no point in the letter did he worry that his church might expel him or worry about his spiritual salvation. Donny's religious life and sexual life were unproblematically compatible.

The mere existence of Donny's letter is as remarkable as the story it tells. We must imagine Donny encountering *ONE* magazine on a newsstand or coming across it some other way, then spending the better part of an afternoon or evening typing intimate details of his life for strangers thousands of miles away. Donny gave no opinion of *ONE* magazine or the homophile movement, and *ONE* received no prior or subsequent correspondence from him. Yet *ONE* clearly inspired him to engage in the cathartic and therapeutic process of constructing a narrative about himself and sharing that narrative with sympathetic gay and lesbian activists. Donny's encounter with *ONE* allows us to step into his shoes and imagine his worldview as a young black gay man in the early 1960s. Donny's letter is an extraordinary life history of an ordinary individual grappling with many layers of postwar anxiety.

Donny Comes Out

ONE received Donny's letter on January 29, 1964. Actually, there were two letters—a short handwritten letter accompanied the longer typed letter. The short letter began in a jarring manner: "I have been male born. I was raped at the age of 7. I didn't know what the act was call." Donny considered himself a serious individual who didn't "twist and make a fool of myself," referring to the twist dance craze of the early 1960s. He also considered himself smart, "an honored graduate of 61." He stated he was not exclusively homosexual and had "many girl friends." He did not consider himself gay or even bisexual, but described himself as "the type of person who loves homosexuals." He had sex with men but would "only play the male role." He did not get along with his mother. She "humiliate[d]" him and they had "terrible arguments." He feared his mother would "call the law" on him because of their arguments. Donny struggled with suicidal tendencies and worried that he might "try and kill" himself "again." He was lonely. He asked *ONE* for help without specifying what type of help he needed. Just help.

Donny wrote both letters in an unusual colloquial style, unlike other letters the magazine had received. On paper, the writing appears disorganized and rambling, but read aloud it becomes clear, direct, and lively. The sentences are short and choppy while the paragraphs go on for pages. Donny's main letter opens with a short stanza about his suicide attempt that foreshadows the haphazardly poetic quality of the rest of the letter: "Love Died in My Heart The Night I Died / No' No Let Me Die. Why I wanted to die?" Donny's narrative attempts to answer why he "wanted to die;" this question forebodes the tragedy and "heart broke" about to unfold.

The first half of the letter, however, is upbeat. Donny confessed he was "nice looking" and could "charm the birds out of the trees." After graduating from high school in Richmond, Virginia, he and his mother moved to Atlantic City where he found work at a department store. His letter expressed none of the job anxiety characteristic of other letters to *ONE*. This might be because department store workers fit into a small pantheon of jobs stereotypically ascribed to gay men, such as hairdressing and interior design.[4] His refusal to consider himself "gay" or a "homosexual" probably also contributed to his nonchalance about losing his job. Class status is important here, more so than race. Several African-American *ONE* correspondents expressed job anxiety, suggesting that gay middle-class professionals of any race tended to worry more about losing their jobs due to homosexuality than blue-collar or retail workers such as Donny.[5] Donny barely mentioned his work life throughout the letter.

Donny's coming out to gay life began when Robert, a fellow department store employee, noticed Donny and spoke with him briefly. They met again shortly thereafter and Robert flirted openly with Donny, telling him, "When I saw you I said to myself their goes . . . a nice intelligent young man. I think maybe I could be friends with." At first Donny was unsure what to make of Robert's interest. Donny warned Robert that he was the "type who loves to Live fast, Love fast and die fast." Donny said he enjoyed New York City because he could get "losted in the crowd." Robert replied boldly, asking Donny to "come up to the house sometimes," adding, "because I am gay are you[?]"

Donny's reply suggests that this may have been his first encounter with the word "gay": He wrote, "I wasnt hip to this talk so I said I suppose so." This was the closest he came in the letter to identifying as gay—and only on the premise that he "wasnt hip" to the word's meaning. Donny expressed ambiguity about labels of sexual identity throughout the letter. At one point he stated, "I am not a homosexual," but he "just happen[ed] to be young and loved to find out everything was to be known." His sexual desires for men were a mystery to him. "I am a natural male and I dont know what on earth came over me," he wrote regarding a sexual encounter with another man. "How can you explain something like this." Despite his gay affairs, his immersion in a gay social circle, and his desire to spend the rest of his life with another man, Donny refused to refer to himself as a homosexual.

Donny's reluctance to identify as gay because he played the "male role" was consistent with early twentieth-century working-class gay culture as George Chauncey and other historians describe.[6] For much of the early twentieth century, sexologists and psychologists explained homosexuality as a consequence of "gender inversion," a man trapped in a woman's body or vice versa. According to this view, to be a male "homosexual" assumed both effeminate body mannerisms as well as passive sexual roles. This conceptualization excluded large numbers of men practicing same-sex sexuality from the category "homosexual." Gender inversion theories waned after World War II, but still continued to influence social patterns and individual conceptualizations of sexual identity, especially within working-class gay social circles.[7]

The rise of the black civil rights movement may also figure into Donny's reluctance to identify as gay. According to scholar Thaddeus Russell, "One of the best kept secrets of modern African-American history is that many black gays and lesbians were not only accepted, but also celebrated" during the first half of the twentieth century. However, "[a]t the height of the movement for integration, black queerness was replaced in public discourse and popular culture by black heteronormativity."[8] Scholars such as Tim Retzloff have cited the downfall of the flamboyant black minister Prophet Jones as evidence of this shift. Jones skillfully used radio and television to build a massive congregation of working-class and poor African Americans in Detroit. He never publicly admitted he was gay, but he did little to conceal the fact. His homosexuality was an open secret among his congregation. Other black ministers in Detroit (including singer Aretha Franklin's father) condemned Jones as a "degenerate" and a charlatan. In 1956 an undercover police officer arrested Jones for soliciting oral sex, and his career declined abruptly. Civil rights leaders believed that Jones and others like him must be kept out of the public spotlight; to win white sympathy for integration, they argued, black people must project an image of sexual normality.[9] This attitude crept into a 1957 Denver Mattachine Society meeting in which "Someone mentioned what seemed to be an unusual degree of abhorrence by Negroes toward Negro homosexuals, and this was corroborated by our Negro friends."[10] Donny expressed no specific identification with the civil rights movement, but many young black men coming of age in the late 1950s and early 1960s most likely would have internalized some of this newfound shame and embarrassment over homosexual behavior within the black community.

But only some. Despite Donny's reluctance to refer to himself as "gay," he expressed no shame or embarrassment about immersing himself into a gay social network. Robert first introduced Donny to his partner Freddie, "the husband," suggesting that Robert and Freddie considered themselves a married couple and presented themselves as such to other gay people. Robert volunteered to help Donny "find a nice friend" and "meet some more of the sassies."[11] Robert then introduced Donny to a hairdresser named Johnny (a "creep"), Bart, and a church pianist named Ralph. Bart and Ralph, like Robert and Freddie, were a married couple. Ralph was the "husband," Donny carefully noted in his letter. Whether Donny's assignation of "husband" was based on masculine gender mannerisms or some other variable, such as occupation or wealth creating an unequal power dynamic in the relationship, is unclear. At any rate, he perceived such marriages in opposite-sex gendered terms, using the labels "husband" and "wife" rather than "husband" and "husband." Donny clearly considered these legitimate relationships, even though he relied on a heterosexual framework to make sense of them.

After meeting these couples, Donny's social circle grew. He became friends with Richard, Brent, Chuck, Michael, Desmond, Alberto (the "Spanish guy,") Tucker, Emmanuel, and Gustavo (another "Spanish" man). Donny's frequent use of the words "light" and "dark" suggests that most of the men in this social circle were African American, except for the "Spanish" men whose ancestry may likely have been Puerto Rican, Mexican, or Cuban. These dozen or so men interacted with gay men from other gay social circles at gatherings in private homes. Through them Donny navigated a discrete gay social world of single gay men, gay married couples, and gay men in opposite-sex marriages. Eventually, Donny gravitated toward a prior acquaintance named Trey who quickly became the object of his deepest desire.

Trey

Donny was still in high school when he first heard Trey preach, and he was immediately smitten. "I watched wow every move he made in the sermon, it was pure lure sex," he wrote. Considering the central role of churches in black communities, it is not surprising that a young black man might discover love in his local pulpit. "The black church has always been a site of contradictions where sexuality is concerned," according to one scholar. "The entire church service may be likened to a sexual encounter: There is flirting, petting, foreplay, orgasm, and post-coital bliss. . . . Every aspect of the black church service is centered around the preacher's message; and at its height, a preacher's sermon may galvanize a congregation into a state of spiritual ecstasy that coalesces with feelings one experiences during orgasm."[12] Certainly Donny was not the only young man, white or black, to fall in love with a minister or pastor. And certainly Trey and Prophet Jones were not the only gay clergymen in American churches during these years.[13]

One year after hearing Trey preach for the first time, Donny came across Trey in his gay social circle. Donny complained he was tiring of his other gay friends ("these gays aint worth a dime a dozen," he wrote), and he turned his attention entirely to Trey. "I will never know what promp me but I went to Treys house" one night, during which "I went and laid beside him. . . . I begain to cress him and kiss him madly. Then some one walked in. It was the spanish guy Alberto. No Donny please dont some time when Alberto and no one is around. I see you stop playing round and means business." Trey was clearly receptive to Donny's advances. Donny returned when Trey was alone and "made loved to him with a passion that I never knew I possed." Donny then started seeing Trey regularly, telling his mother instead that he "was going out of town." Donny's letter suggests that his mother was unaware of their sexual affair, but she did express concern that Donny and Trey were spending too much time together: "she fussed I had to be carefully about Trey because although he was a minister, and was married but [his] wife left him." Fear of a gay affair was not explicitly stated, but something bothered Donny's mother about Trey. Perhaps she knew of Trey's homosexual proclivities through church gossip, or perhaps his homosexuality was an open secret similar to that of Prophet Jones.

Donny's uncle, on the other hand, probably knew that Donny's new friends were part of a gay social network. Early in the letter, Donny described Robert flirting rather openly his uncle. "He said to my unckle you sure have some dreamy eyes. My unckle only smiled. You will take us to Treys house? My Unckle said maybe sometimes." Robert replied, "Well I am available at all times." Donny panicked hearing this conversation. "Let's be going I replied before he gave his self away. Look I said when I got him out in the streets you are starting something now." Robert was unfazed. "Child I will always keep a spare cause I dont never know what might happen." Donny replied, "Well I said he dont like no dam gays." Robert said, "Well I was only teasing I didn't mean no harm." Notably, the uncle's response to Robert's subtly provocative advances was not hostility, but a smile. Perhaps the uncle was gay himself, despite Donny's claim that he "dont like no dam gays"—the letter never mentioned an aunt. Regardless, Donny was clearly terrified at the idea that Robert might give "his self away" to his uncle. Although Donny did not identify as gay, he nonetheless shared the common anxiety of discovery within his family.

Over time, Donny and Trey's affair intensified. Donny explained that after a party one night, "something happened to me." When they got home "that night I practically loved him all night long. How can you explain something like this." The relationship became more serious when Trey's other male lover, Gustavo, left Trey. "So one day Gustavo left took all his clothes and went. Trey liked him for only looks but when it came to the bed and talking while dressed he didn't stand a chance." To Donny, Gustavo's departure meant that a serious, monogamous relationship was possible. Donny was encouraged when "Trey promised me he would love me always no matter what." At this point in the letter, Donny made the remarkable statement that he loved Trey so much that he "gave up my girl friend and the daughter she bore me for him." This is the only reference in the letter to this girlfriend and their daughter. Other individuals in the letter, such as Gustavo and Trey, had girlfriends as well as boyfriends, leading double lives characteristic of many *ONE* correspondents. But Donny had no interest in such a double life. All he wanted was Trey. Perhaps inspired by the gay couples Donny had accepted as married, Donny proposed to Trey. He declared in the letter, "I made my vows no one will stop me." He told Trey, "This is for you darling. An engagement wedding band." Trey reacted ambiguously to Donny's proposal. "Donny I love you Donny pleas," he said, adding however, "I am going back to my wife you know that." Nonetheless, Donny and Trey spent a blissful Easter Sunday together—the high point of their relationship. "I shall never forget Easter Sunday," Donny wrote. "We went to the park. Seem as if the sun said to us its here, so devine and beautifully. So when we returned home I said promise me you will never leave me. And that their will be no one els. I promise he replied in his soft voice." Trey's promise was the culmination of Donny's coming out. The promise signified their future together as a gay married couple that deeply loved each other.

Betrayal

But Trey did not keep his promise, and Donny's life unraveled quickly in the days after that blissful Easter Sunday. He explained, "Finally church was over and at last I would be with Trey. I waited and waited he did not come out. I became very angry so I played smart and went to his house. I knocked politely on the door, but got no answancer. Then I saw all kinds of devils. . . ." Donny spotted Trey's car, indicating that Trey was indeed home. "I then called 'Trey' 'Trey' open this dam door. Because I know that you are in their. Then he cracked the door then said yes I am home. Then he slapped me in my face. My hand was in the door. Now will you please go home Donny. I shoved the door open and flew into him like a mad man. Although he was larger and older, but in my state of panic I was like insane. 'Why you dirty rotten son of a bitch. I spent money on you Ill kill you.' " A scuffle ensued; Donny gave Trey a black eye and bloody lip. Trey calmed Donny down and offered to drive him home. "I didnt know that blood was on his clothes and mine until I got to the street light." Trey said "Fix up your coat Donny the cops might arrest us." They walked together to Trey's car, and while getting in the car, Donny pulled a knife on Trey. Trey fled in terror. Donny stumbled home in emotional shambles. "I started to walking home. I cried I dont know what or how I got home. Maybe if I told my mother I loved him she would let me have him and be free." He returned home and "marched up stairs then I hollowed Look' at me see me mother. Yes all of those times I said I was away I lied. I love him mother dont harm him if you do I will kill myself." This was the first mention of suicide in the letter. His mother's reaction was not encouraging. "Mother looked like she had just seen the ghost of [Dracula]."[14]

The following morning, Donny felt too depressed to go to work. His mother woke him up. "Mother please don't make me go to work. Yes you must go to work," she replied. His mother's control over him made him suicidal again. "I got up and look at the gray cloudy sky. It hit me all of a sudden. All the things you wanted in life and the fun and all you[r] mother will never let you have them. I must die I said in a wisper." In preparation for his suicide, he wrote farewell notes and funereal arrangements. "Good-by I said to everything." He wrote a poetic farewell note to Trey, which he included in his letter to *ONE*.

Dear Trey,

I will be dead by the time you recive this letter. I never ever thought that you were such a no good person. But as a man was to a woman. I was true to you And you told me that you would never ever leave me. Like a fool I believed every word that you told me. But we made a bargain that if I died before you you would have a seacret moment with you. So please let me rest with that promise you made me before fill. I will love you to my grave. Life is no good without the ones that well we love so well. So I shall always cherish Sunday. I have swim the ocean blue just to prove my love to you. You will find no [one] loved you like I did, Care for you as much. What more could any man do. I hope your family back together. Never to know the days that pass, sweet will be the flowers and grass. Think not of me if someone ask, when you work at your task. Only the futre and not the pass as you go a long the greener path. In my sleep of death good by.

Sincerely Yours
Donny

After writing this note Donny went to work, where he remained depressed. When coworkers asked him what was the matter, he said, "Nothing I lied to be left alone." After work, he swallowed a handful of aspirin, which gave him a loud, rapid heartbeat.

That evening, Donny and his mother met with Trey and Trey's wife to discuss the situation. Trey did not deny the affair to Donny's mother, although he downplayed his interest in it. "[Y]ou may as well know. I didnt know what Donny was after when he came to my house. He is to finer boy to get messed up like this." The mother agreed adding, "do you know that he is my only dam son." She was angry at Trey for his breach of trust, for apparently taking sexual advantage of her son. "Let me tell you this dam much you keep away from my son and I will see he never bothers you again." Trey explained he had no ill feelings toward Donny and "will always speake to him." Donny squirmed in his chair listening to this painful conversation, "How I wished I could died." Now a relationship with Trey seemed impossible. After the meeting, a heartbroken Donny attempted suicide:

> Goodbye forever I said. I[n] my minde I said you will never see me again. I went to the store on the corner and bought me a bottle of sleeping pills. I looked in the mirrow he never said he loved me like I did him. I took 10 sleeping pills. I fixed my room extra special. I put my smile on like I knew a secret after I had written mother a note. Soon sleep came like sweet dream. . . . I was in my dream of everlasting beauty.

Donny was certainly not the only suicidal gay person in these years—in popular novels and films, it was almost obligatory that gay-identified characters committed suicide.[15] Joseph Hansen wrote in *ONE* that gay people were more prone to suicide compared to heterosexuals because of loneliness, fleeting relationships, and stressful family and professional lives.[16] Researchers have demonstrated that gay men and lesbians attempt suicide in greater numbers than nongays (although their success rate remains a source of debate) and that young African-American gays are significantly more vulnerable to suicide than white gays or heterosexual African Americans.[17]

Just because a gay or lesbian person has attempted suicide, however, does not automatically mean homosexuality was the primary reason even if it was a contributing factor. In some cases the connection is obvious, such as a suicide attempt while awaiting trial for a homosexual arrest.[18] More often, however, homosexuality is one factor among a larger nexus of suicidal variables. Due to its social stigma, homosexuality easily commingles with depression, anxiety, substance abuse, and other factors that contribute to suicidality. In Donny's mind, the problem was not his homosexuality, but his mother. She had "taken" Trey away from him. Donny was suicidal primarily because he was going through a traumatic break up with the first person he truly loved and with whom he wanted to spend the rest of life. Gay people hardly monopolize suicides of this nature—Emile Durkheim, for example, noted in his classic study of suicide that divorcees had higher suicide rates than married people.[19] Yet the alienation gay couples suffered in postwar social life undoubtedly exacerbated the impact of such breakups. A letter to *The Ladder* in 1958 noted that "Each of us has heard of, or been close to, attempted suicides among homosexuals and in addition, our divorces are not as efficiently handled as we would like to believe."[20] In Donny's case, homosexuality played a significant yet ultimately secondary role in his suicide attempt. In his own mind, the problem was not his sexual desires, but his mother's refusal to let him be with the person he loved, compounded by his lover's betrayal. If others could be in gay marriages, why not him?

After taking the sleeping pills, Donny's mother rescued him. "In my sleep sometime later I herd mother say 'My god' and ran out. . . . In a haze I saw the doctor the policeman. I was sleep. 'Donny whats the matter wake up.' No no. I want to die let me die. Then I saw light." Donny woke up in a hospital. He "cried but no tears came." After a series of convulsion fits subsided, Donny's mother and uncle picked him up from the hospital. Instead of going home, however, "they drove and drove. I look out then I saw Lions the VA hospital. I said to myself this is a mental institution." Upon arrival, Donny told a doctor that he had attempted suicide and "I failed . . . but the next time I wont, I wont." During his three-month stay at the hospital, his mother visited him regularly but "I hate the site of her. This physologist asked me why. I said cant you see she took everything away from me. What have I to live for only sweet death."

Imagining Donny's mother's perspective, her decisions indicate she wanted to protect her "only dam son." In one breath, Donny revealed to her that he had lied to her for months about his whereabouts, that he was gay, and that he was having an affair with a church pastor. All of this came at her very quickly, despite whatever suspicions she may have already held about Trey. She believed that an older man in a position of authority had taken advantage of Donny. Significantly, however, her decision to institutionalize Donny came immediately after his suicide attempt, not the revelation of his affair with Trey. She handled news of the affair reasonably by bringing everyone together to discuss the situation. But she could not handle the suicide attempt; that was her breaking point. Again, homosexuality was an important component of the situation, but violence and suicide were the main reasons Donny spent three months at the mental hospital.

Mental hospitals, like suicides, routinely figure into popular imaginings of gay life in the 1950s and 1960s.[21] Amidst the nationwide passage of tough sex crime laws from the 1930s to the 1950s, many psychologists and criminologists believed that mental hospitals offered better rehabilitative possibilities for sex offenders compared to jail and that a medical approach was more humane than a punitive criminal approach. The unfortunate consequence, however, was that anyone caught committing a minor homosexual crime might end up in a mental hospital until he or she was "cured."[22] Sometimes no crime was required. During a search for a child murderer in Iowa in the mid-1950s, for example, nearly twenty men were rounded up and put in a nearby mental hospital for no other reason than their homosexuality. A court demanded they be cured of their homosexuality before release, but their doctors did not believe homosexuality was curable and released them after serving minimum sentences.[23]

Iowa-style mass incarcerations were rare compared to individual incarcerations, however. Homosexual arrestees sometimes accepted mental hospital incarceration as part of a criminal plea bargain.[24] For example, a *ONE* magazine contributing artist named Sidney Bronstein found himself serving ninety days "observation" in the Atascadero prison/hospital in central California following an arrest for a misdemeanor homosexual offense in 1955. The judge in this case did not expect the hospital to cure Bronstein of his homosexuality, but he believed that psychotherapy would curb Bronstein's promiscuity and help him "adjust to society." He offered Bronstein a choice between ninety days in a mental institution or one year in prison. Bronstein chose the mental hospital after he learned that his destination would be the Norwalk hospital near Los Angeles. The staff at Norwalk, Bronstein explained in letters to *ONE*, had been influenced by Kinsey Institute researchers who advocated humane treatment of homosexuals and rejected the idea that homosexuality was a mental illness or could be cured. Bronstein believed three months here would be much more tolerable than a year in prison.[25]

At the last minute, however, he was sent to Atascadero instead of Norwalk. In the 1950s and 1960s, the Atascadero prison/hospital was considered a state-of-the-art integration institution for criminal justice and mental health. Atascadero specialized in reforming sex offenders, usually rapists and pedophiles, but sometimes an ordinary homosexual such as Bronstein arrived there as part of a plea bargain.[26] Bronstein wrote, "Physically, it's all very expensive: new buildings, 'modern architecture,' all the 'conveniences.' To me it's too close to '1984' however." Foreshadowing Ken Kesey's *One Flew over the Cuckoo's Nest*, he noted that the staff at Atascadero quickly labeled patients "uncooperative" whenever they questioned any procedure. After several days, Bronstein regretted his decision: ". . . plain jail in this situation is tolerable, even honorable, in a way; but 'commitment,' even for observation! . . . Tomorrow will be one week here. 11 weeks to go! If I am not psycho now, I may be by then."[27]

Bronstein's institutionalization differed from Donny's in two important ways. First, Donny's family, not a criminal court, committed him to the hospital. Second, many more variables than homosexuality were involved in Donny's case. Donny not only tried to kill himself, but he vowed to keep trying until he succeeded. While an untold number of gay people, such as Bronstein, were committed to mental institutions primarily because of their homosexuality, the same cannot be said for Donny and gay people like him who simultaneously suffered from severe depression, anxiety, violent behavior, psychosis, borderline personality disorder, or schizophrenia. These conditions were undoubtedly exacerbated by a homophobic society, but also existed independently of an individual's sexual identity. Thus, even though Donny's saga involved a stay at a mental institution, his circumstances must be distinguished from arrest victims and other victims of involuntary incarcerations such as Bronstein.

It is also unlikely that the ECT Donny received was intended to eradicate his homosexuality. "The agony black outs," Donny wrote about the procedure. ECT has been commonly confused with a different type of "shock treatment" called aversive electric shock therapy. Donny's ECT involved strapping him down and putting electrodes on his head that shot between 105 and 125 volts of electricity through his brain in order to provoke a grand mal epileptic seizure. The procedure included black outs, amnesia, and loss of muscle control.[28] This was done three times a week. Postwar medical literature suggests that ECT was overwhelmingly used on suicidal, severely depressed, schizophrenic, and psychotic patients. A few ECT experiments were conducted on homosexual patients in the 1940s, and researchers concluded from these experiments that ECT did not affect a person's sexual orientation. During the 1950s, the consensus of the mental health profession was that ECT was much too severe for homosexuality and unlikely to produce any results.[29] Psychoanalysis, not ECT, dominated the misguided postwar quest to "cure" homosexuals.

In the 1960s, however, behaviorist aversive electric shock therapy emerged as the newest fad to cure homosexuality. In this procedure, a person typically was hooked up to electrodes, shown pornographic gay images, and zapped with enough volts to cause minor discomfort and pain. Heterosexual images were then shown with no shock in order to readjust a person's sexual desires. Aside from the troubling scientific and moral implications of such a procedure, and the fact that scientific research overwhelmingly shows that the procedure does not work, it was considerably milder than ECT. It involved no seizures, unconsciousness, or amnesia. In fact, self-administered home kits were manufactured and sold in the 1970s.[30] (The technique is still used today by many Mormons as well as persons in the so-called ex-gay movement.) These two procedures, ECT and aversive electric shock therapy, have been confused with one another since the 1970s through the casual use of the phrase "shock treatment," and this confusion led to the myth that gay people in the 1950s routinely underwent ECT as a cure for their homosexuality. Donny's letter offers no evidence linking his ECT with his homosexuality, reflecting the consensus of the medical professionals.

Donny wrote his letter to *ONE* three months after leaving the hospital. Things were not going well with his mother at that moment. He was working as a male prostitute in Atlantic City. He was too angry to see Trey. "I want to hurt like I have been hurt. I know Trey loves me but I could never like him. One day he will need me and I want to come back. I will be able to see him like a begging dog." The letter concluded in a final swirl of poetic phrases, bitterness toward his mother, and, surprisingly, warnings about the dangers of homosexuality: "If you were born a homosexual please stay away from innocent boys. Now I cant love or pity nothing. . . . The birds of the air have nests. The fox of the ground have holes. But the sole of man has nothing, to shelter his sole. Boys stay away from Gaeys. I will never forgive my mother for doing this wrong to me. By locking me in an institution. And love well I sold my heart to the junk man."

The day after *ONE* received Donny's letter, Dorr Legg wrote a reply under the pseudonym Marvin Cutler—he used the pseudonym here because he feared Donny might not have been twenty-one yet. *ONE*'s staff was extra cautious whenever dealing with minors. As Legg saw it, Donny had three main problems, "(1) Your family relationship (2) your view on homosexuality (3) your human relationships." To deal with his family problem, Legg recommended that Donny move to New York City in order to get away from his mother. Legg then told Donny, "You feel that you have been seduced by homosexuals. When you were a child this was possible. But adults do not repeat such acts unless they choose to." Finally, Legg advised Donny to choose his friends carefully and maintain high standards. The reply concluded, "Over the years *ONE* magazine has printed many informative articles and stories. A subscription to *ONE* should prove helpful in the future but in addition a back order of one or two years could immediately give you much information."[31] Legg's advice can be interpreted cynically as an inappropriate effort to profit from Donny's misery, but *ONE*'s activists believed that their magazine could transform people's lives. It could help Donny understand his sexual identity and accept it more honestly.

Legg perceptively noted the importance of family bonds in the letter. Ultimately, Donny's story centered on three people: himself, his mother, and Trey. Their interweaving destinies demonstrate the many ways that family bonds remained a central dimension of life for many gay people. Donny's resentment toward his mother, and her protectiveness over him, fuel key events in his narrative, including the suicide attempt and the mental hospital incarceration. Yet in spite of it all, in spite of Donny's revelation about the affair with Trey, in spite of his work as a male prostitute, they remained a family unit—at the margins of functionality, perhaps, but still sharing the same roof and eating the same food. Donny remained her "only dam son." Furthermore, Donny's main wish was to have a relationship with Trey that can only be described as a marriage. A ring symbolized their love. Yet Trey's double life in an opposite-sex marriage ultimately trumped Donny's wish. At the heart of Donny's story was a complex web of family bonds.

Religion

In addition to the bonds of family, the bonds of church also underlay Donny's story. One is tempted to assume, based on current-day religious condemnations of homosexuality as well as broader currents of homophobia in the 1950s and early 1960s, that most churches in the postwar years preached vehemently against homosexuality and expelled any congregants discovered to be gay or lesbian. The postwar relationship between homosexuality and American Christian religious life, however, was considerably more complex. John Howard, for example, has described how Mississippi churches in the 1960s routinely facilitated gay relationships at church picnics, "style shows" featuring drag performers, and between members of the choir. According to Howard: "Although Protestant doctrine would more explicitly condemn homosexuality along with a rising gay activism after the 1960s, houses of worship nonetheless proved useful meeting grounds throughout the period. At church events, men met; in church space, they got to know each other better. Though congregations rarely extended clear-cut support to male-male couples, they were often aware of the men in their midst who might act on male-male desire. Within the complicated interstices of theologically inflected thought and within the opportune spaces of local church life, queer men could effectively maneuver."[32] Biblical passages condemning homosexuality were usually not emphasized, and silence rather than condemnation characterizes how many churches treated homosexuality in these years. Even in black churches steeped in the civil rights movement, homosexuality was not so much condemned as silenced.[33] Black ministers in the 1950s and 1960s did not want to draw unnecessary attention to the issue and preferred to project a positive image of sexual normality rather than loudly condemn the open tolerance of homosexuality within black churches that had prevailed in previous decades.

Donny's affair with Trey seemed to operate within such a silence. He expressed no anxiety over the prospect that church leaders or congregants would discover the affair—a stark contrast to his anxiety about his uncle discovering his relations with "the gays." He expressed no anxiety about being kicked out of his church or that Trey might suffer consequences should the affair become public. Nor did he express any theological or spiritual angst about his sexual behavior. Donny's nonchalance, however, was a striking contrast to many other *ONE* letters that discussed religion. Marvin in New York City, for example, previously mentioned in chapter 7, described significant church anxieties after his homosexual arrest in Central Park. "I fear reprisals to my family's jobs. Even the church is part of it. The church my family attends. Being a Negro, it's almost unbearable."[34] Marvin's reference to his racial identity suggests that because he was black, he believed church gossip had a particular power to destroy his—and his family's—reputations and professional status. Donny expressed no comparable concerns.

Homophile activists expressed a range of viewpoints about church tolerance. James Barr Fugaté wrote, "Most churches will reject you." A *ONE* survey respondent similarly noted, "Religious circles are the least tolerant of homosexuality of any group."[35] Jim Kepner, in contrast, believed that churches were becoming more tolerant of homosexuality in these years. He argued that Anglican, Roman Catholic, British Methodist, and Quaker churches in the late 1950s had reevaluated homosexuality and determined it was no worse than other forms of nonprocreative sex and might carry less social harm. Kepner added that many churches were abandoning the idea that homosexuality could be cured through prayer or science.[36] Catholic Bishop Fulton Sheen, for example, declared in 1960 that the Catholic Church should no longer try to "eradicate" homosexuality, but instead "transform" this impulse into a deeper love for God to make the "fires burn upward rather than downward."[37] Some religious leaders argued in the 1950s that celibate gay men made ideal ministers.[38] William Zion, a gay minister, noted in a speech delivered at the 1962 Mattachine convention that "during the past ten years something of a revolution has taken place in the attitude of the Christian Church toward homosexuality. Formerly a taboo subject, treated as a technicality and dealt with in Latin, the subject is now increasingly openly discussed with somewhat more understanding and somewhat more sympathy."[39] Similarly, a gay minister from Philadelphia wrote on his *ONE* questionnaire, "General religious feeling especially among Clergy is improving and more tolerant and understand[ing]," but "there is still a narrow sense of intolerance among the people in general."[40] In other words, in his opinion, clergy and church officials were likely to be *more*, not less, tolerant of homosexuality compared to the general public. Several *ONE* correspondents reported tolerance or silence regarding homosexuality in their churches, for example, "I find that ministers are not usually too critical—some ministers are not equipped to talk to or help homosexuals. Most just choose to ignore homosexuals."[41]

Donny's letter offered little insight into how Trey rationalized his sexual behavior as a pastor. One thing is clear: for a man of the cloth, Trey had a very busy gay social and sexual life. Donny's letter mentioned five boyfriends beside himself: Brent, Michael, Gustavo, an "old flame" named Emmanuel, and Richard. Richard in fact was still living with Trey during Trey's affair with Donny. He was awakened one night by Trey and Donny's loud sex. "I have to get my durn rest, because I have to work in the morning. Look here dam punk," Donny replied, "Trey had gone to the bathroom. You are just jealous of Trey because you used to go with him and now I do." Richard responded, "I havent touched him since you all started." We can only guess how Trey's multiple intimate same-sex relationships appeared to his heterosexual congregants.

A few clergymen who wrote letters to *ONE* admitted they were gay. One minister wrote, "I have had many men come to me with the problem of being in love with one of their own kind and have also indulged in this practice myself."[42] More often, ministers carefully (if a bit overenthusiastically) explained that their interest in *ONE* was solely for counseling purposes. One minister declared, "I wish I could afford to put ONE in the library of every clergy man and seminary in the United States."[43] Another thanked *ONE* "for increasing my understanding of an aspect of life which often has difficult Pastoral implications. While I disagree with many of the conclusions reached and judgments made in One, I have found it stimulating and helpful in a difficult area of my work."[44]

A few clergymen were directly involved with ONE, Inc., whose Social Service Department coordinated a small network of ministers around the country to counsel *ONE* readers facing religious or other crises concerning their homosexuality.[45] By 1964, all three major homophile organizations had formal ministerial allies. Both ONE, Inc., and the Daughters of Bilitis helped create the Council on Religion and the Homosexual to facilitate dialogue between religious figures and homophile activists.[46] The Mattachine Society went furthest in building religious alliances. Mattachine leader Hal Call excitedly told Dorr Legg in 1964 that his organization had established a program "just getting under way to train pastoral level ministers in six Protestant denominations for counseling adults and especially teenagers about sex problems and here again, especially about homosexual problems. We have sat in the offices of the San Francisco Council of Churches to work out this education program with the aid of some officials of that body." Call also told Legg that recent Mattachine meetings in San Francisco were held at an Anglican church.[47]

These alliances did not, however, negate the widespread intolerance for homosexuality within many Christian institutions. This intolerance was based on the belief that sexuality was a sacred gift from God and must only be used for procreation. A *ONE* subscriber in Eureka, California, learned this after mentioning to his fundamentalist bible study group that he was gay. Concerned about his soul, several members of the group wrote a letter to the man:

> Since we believe the Bible to be the only safe and sure guide-book we will tell you what it has to say. . . .
>
> The Apostle Paul has clearly stated who shall not enter the kingdom of heaven in I Cor. 6:9. Notice particularly the last line of this text. Then put with this Romans 1:26, 27 and you have the clear picture of how God feels about those who have given themselves over to the unnatural. Notice the 32nd verse also, regarding the fate of those who continue doing such things. It is a terrible thing to reap eternal death rather than eternal life. We are hoping that you will make your decision for Christ and leave the wickedness of this world.[48]

This position was representative of many Christian denominations, though the intensity varied dramatically from church to church, minister to minister.

Such religious condemnations of homosexuality created a crisis for many lesbian and gay Christians. Some turned away from organized religion as a consequence. When Jim Kepner was eighteen, for example, he abandoned plans to become a religious missionary in the Belgian Congo after realizing he was gay.[49] Others chose religion over homosexuality. A man from a small town in Ohio cancelled his *ONE* subscription in 1954 explaining, "Those who have homosexuality in their system must fight it because God has given them a cross to bear and he expects them to overcome it. Then and only then shall the individual achieve the Kingdom of Heaven."[50] In 1964 another man similarly declared he was making a clean break from homosexuality, "Please do not send any further correspondence or literature of any kind. I deeply regret all association with this type of thing. I am trusting in the Lord Jesus Christ as my personal Saviour and pray that he will help me to make a complete change in my life."[51]

Catholics in particular struggled to reconcile their sexual and religious identities.[52] Daniel, a Catholic in San Francisco, told *ONE* in 1961 that his religious beliefs had provoked a nervous breakdown following a gay arrest. To maintain his faith, he voluntarily checked into a local mental hospital, the Langley Porter Clinic, to change his sexual orientation. "I suppose I can see you sit back in your chair and give out a big laugh," he wrote to *ONE*: "I don't know if it is possible to change. At first I thought only of pleasing others, but now, I only think of the major issue in my life, and for the first time, I want to start facing facts. That is my RELIGION. I am Catholic, and I have repeatedly sent letters to you, begging you for some information on my religious acceptance, but to no avail. . . . I've tried going to different Priests, but I am forever being condemned to hell."[53] Two months later, *ONE* received another letter from Daniel. His stay at the mental hospital had caused him to abandon the idea of changing his sexuality. "I have been, am, and will be homosexual, and there are no ifs or buts about it," he declared. He was still unsure how to reconcile his faith with his sexuality, but he felt considerably more comfortable with the fact that he was gay.[54]

Some *ONE* correspondents figured out ways to embrace both their religion and their sexuality. Some stated that God had simply made them that way, so there must be nothing wrong with it regardless of what any earthly minister said. Other correspondents emphasized the compatibility of homosexuality and Christian love. One man wrote, "If Christ were upon the earth today I am sure he would not consider the homosexual different from those of other sexual desires. He would be, as we say, Christ-like and love and respect all of his flock. . . . These holier-than-thou clergymen should look around their own backyards before voicing their (usually wrong) opinions on homosexuality."[55] Some *ONE* correspondents interpreted bible passages in their own queer ways. A seventeen-year-old devout Christian male, for example, explained to *ONE* that biblical condemnations of sodomy actually referred to male effeminacy and female masculinity and had nothing to do with sexual behavior.[56]

The letters mentioned at least six gay churches in surreptitious operation during the 1950s and early 1960s. No doubt there were other gay churches *ONE* never heard about. These churches reflected the gay civil rights impulse in their bold rejection of the idea that homosexuality indicated spiritual defectiveness. Their existences challenged the stigmas against homosexuality within organized Christianity as well as broader social and political stigmas in American society. A young Miami minister, for example, eagerly told *ONE* in 1955 he was going to conduct his first gay service the following week. "I have invited a lot of gay people, as their salvation is important too, as many gay people have left their respective faiths because of the tension of others (heterosexual) persons when it is suspected that their morals may differ from the majority." The civil rights impulse is unambiguous: "I'm gay, and PROUD of it! God doesn't condemn me, as long as I accept Him and trust in Him."[57] Another gay church, the Los Angeles–based Church of the Cosmic Christ (Androgyne), also known as the Church of the Androgyne, focused on "the synthesis of the masculine and feminine dualities." Homosexuality and heterosexuality represented different paths to "Androgyne Awareness," according to one of the church's leaders.[58] A Washington, D.C.–based church published ads in *ONE* magazine reaching out to gay Catholics estranged from their faith. "LOOKING FOR SOMETHING?" the ad stated. "We like to think we have that 'something' here within the scope of our church. A church truly one and catholic, embracing any and all; A liberal church offering freedom to the inquiring mind, we do not attempt to judge, but only to serve." This gay-centric church went by several names, such as the Basilian Friars and the American Catholic Church, Diocese of Virginia-Maryland.[59] These experimental gay churches represented important precursors to the founding of the Metropolitan Community Church in 1968, the first openly gay-oriented church. The fact that these churches even existed not only demonstrates that many mainstream churches frequently rejected and alienated their gay congregants, but also that significant numbers of gay people in the 1950s and 1960s were devising creative solutions to reconcile their religion and their sexuality. These reconciliations reflected broader patterns of gay resilience and adaptation in a society bent on excluding them from a broad range of institutions.

Did Donny have a gay civil rights impulse? Not in any conscious way. But Donny exhibited undeniable boldness in his right to have a sexual and emotional same-sex relationship with Trey. In addition, like the founders of these gay churches, Donny suffered no conflict between his religious and sexual sensibilities. There was mystery, but no shame or hesitation. He simply hopped into bed with Trey because it felt natural, even though he could not "explain such a thing." Like Kinsey, he simply accepted it for what it was. Donny cannot be called an activist in any practical sense, but his stridency and lack of conflict over his homosexuality embodied the gay pride ethic already beginning to emerge across the country, an ethic that became increasingly more visible in subsequent decades.

Donny's nonchalance regarding his homosexual behavior not only foreshadowed the gay visibility of the future, but also echoed patterns from the pre-civil rights era when gay people were more visible and accepted in African-American communities. Donny's refusal to apply the terms "gay" or "homosexual" to himself was consistent with early twentieth-century working-class conceptualizations of homosexuality in which a "natural male" such as himself could not possibly be "homosexual." Yet he clearly was aware of the idea of gay identity, and—contradicting himself—included the "husbands" of the same-sex couples he encountered within the group of people he labeled "the gays." Donny selectively drew from past and present conceptualizations of sexual identity in order to construct his own sexual identity.

In a way, Donny was attempting to *pass* in his letter—not so much pass as a heterosexual, but pass as a nonhomosexual. Deep in his mind, however, Donny knew that the word "homosexual" applied to him. This was demonstrated by the fact that when Donny came across *ONE* magazine, he identified with its contents enough to spend hours typing his story to *ONE*'s staff. The letter's mere existence and extraordinary detail hinted at a significantly greater investment in his identity as a gay man than he, at that moment, consciously admitted to himself. Indeed, passing was a complicated phenomenon in the postwar United States, and the next chapter examines this issue in detail.

10

Unacceptable Mannerisms

Gender, Sexuality, and Swish in Postwar America

In the mid-1950s, playwright Robert Anderson and Metro-Goldwyn-Mayer (MGM) executive Dore Schary faced a dilemma. They wanted to turn Anderson's stage hit *Tea and Sympathy* into an MGM film, but the motion picture censorship code forbade movies with homosexual themes. Although Tom Lee was being falsely accused of homosexuality and was not actually gay (according to Anderson), the censorship code forbid even hints of homosexuality.[1] But Schary was determined to make the film because he believed *Tea and Sympathy* made an important statement against the way rumors could destroy reputations—a not-so-subtle critique of the Hollywood blacklist that had ruined hundreds of movie careers in the 1950s. To get around the censorship issue, Schary and Anderson decided to change the story so that Tom's harassment was not due to gay rumors, but instead solely provoked by his effeminate mannerisms. Schary believed that moviegoers on their own would make the connection between male effeminacy and homosexual suspicions, and the script revisions would placate censors. Censorship code enforcer Guy Shurlock was open to the idea, but he warned that the changes must "be so definitized that there should be no spot where it could be inferred that anybody is afraid he is a homo-sexual [sic]."[2] As a result, Tom's teacher Harris was deleted from the story and their scandalous skinny dipping scene was replaced with one depicting Tom sewing with faculty wives. Tom was thus transformed from a suspected homosexual into a neutered "sissy."[3]

Tom's harassment because of his effeminacy reflected a broader "masculinity crisis" preoccupying many politicians, journalists, and psychologists who argued that "the decline of the American male" undermined the nation's efforts to win the cold war. Domineering women and male homosexuals, these critics argued, were emasculating and "sissifying" the country.[4]

Anxieties about masculinity seeped into many letters to *ONE*, usually in the form of a pernicious hostility that many gender-conformist gay men directed toward visibly effeminate male homosexuals. Such hostility was hardly new in gay culture, but it became significantly more pronounced in the 1950s compared to previous decades. Before World War II, the concept of "gender inversion" shaped how sexologists and much of the public understood homosexuality. The proliferation of working-class fairies, queens, and pansies in turn-of-the-century New York City, for example, reflected the rise of gender inversion as a gay cultural signifier in the late nineteenth century.[5] Daniel Harris has noted that lesbians and gay men, unlike racial and ethnic minorities, have had to "invent from scratch those missing physical features that enable us to spot our imperceptible compatriots, who would remain unseen and anonymous if they did not prominently display on their own bodies" signifiers for recognition, such as gender inverted mannerisms.[6]

After World War II, however, the nature of gay identity assumed a more middle-class character, as did the rest of American society. Generous G.I. Bill benefits allowed millions of returning soldiers to buy homes and attend college—each important markers of middle-class status. The working-class gender inversion model faded as the dominant conceptualization of gay and lesbian identity, and in its place emerged a middle-class model that emphasized assimilation, respectability, and careerism.[7] Passing as heterosexual became more central to the American gay experience in these years, and tensions grew between those who passed as heterosexual and those who continued to appropriate gender inverted mannerisms. James Barr Fugaté noted these tensions in 1955 when he commented, "A growing malady among American homosexuals today, as we are forced into a more closely united group, seems to be a particularly irrational snobbery directed against our more effeminate members."[8] His use of the word "snobbery" hints at the class tension underlying the growing hostility toward effeminate gay men, commonly referred to as "swishes" in these years. Swishes thus suffered harassment from fellow homosexuals as well as mainstream American society. They were a stigmatized minority within a stigmatized minority.

This gendered fissure among gay people was regrettable and seemed to fly in the face of the civil rights impulse. We might expect *ONE* and its correspondents to have defended the right to be unapologetically swishy as a defiant protest against McCarthyite intolerance. Some *ONE* writers and correspondents defended swishes, but overall this was not the case. This loathing toward swishes, however, was strikingly consistent with broader patterns of U.S. history. Whenever an ostracized group (be it racial, gendered, or religious) has sought mainstream political or social acceptance, elites within that ostracized group have usually downplayed, criticized, or suppressed the more "extreme" members of the group—a process scholars refer to as "secondary marginalization."[9] Prominent black civil rights organizations in the 1950s and early 1960s, for example, sought to downplay more militant factions, while mainstream feminist organizations in the 1960s and 1970s, such as the National Organization for Women, marginalized lesbians. In the late nineteenth century, Mormons turned away from their tradition of polygamy as they sought statehood for Utah and ostracized polygamous practitioners. Shane Phelan has noted how bisexuals and transgender persons have been secondarily marginalized with contemporary gay rights organizations.[10] This pattern of sacrificing certain subgroups in order to gain mainstream acceptance, ironically, reflected the broader politicization of each group because its members were thinking more carefully and strategically about their collective image and status. During the McCarthy era, many gender conformist gay men feared that swishes' blatant defiance of masculine hegemony incited backlash and ridicule, thus dashing hopes of mainstream acceptance for gay people as a whole. Although often prejudicial and mean-spirited, the hostility toward swishes ironically represented the growing politicization of gay people as a minority.

Swish as Stereotype

Among *ONE* correspondents, "swish" was the most commonly used word referring to male effeminacy. Its meaning was broad, and the word encompassed other words associated with gay male effeminacy, such as "queen," "fairy," "faggot," and "nelly." The 1964 *Lavender Lexicon*, for example, defined "swish" as "A fairy, a faggot. Also, effeminate actions in public."[11] The words "queen," "faggot," "fairy," and "nelly" acquired varying definitional nuances depending on geography, social class, and ethnicity. Within the gay world, "queen" tended to be more affirmative whereas "faggot" was more insulting. Different words reflected different degrees of effeminacy. For example, *The Lavender Lexicon* defined "nelly" merely as "An effeminate, affected homosexual who makes public display of his homosexuality, . . ." and "faggot" as ". . . the one who parades his homosexuality on the streets with off-the-shoulder sweaters, jackets, and wears makeup. Usually is scorned by all except his own crowd. Usually this is confined to the younger groups but sometimes continues a lifetime. This type of homosexual is not allowed in most establishments because of the fear that their presence will bring retaliation by police. This is probably the stereotyped homosexual."[12] Notably, this definition of "faggot," written by a gay person in the early 1960s, seethed with bitterness. The definitions imply that a "faggot" was swishier than a "nelly." "Swish" thus represented a continuum of male effeminacy rather than a specific model of male effeminacy.

The *Oxford English Dictionary* defines "swish" as a type of sound and a style of movement. Swish is "A hissing sound like that produced by a switch or similar slender object moved rapidly through the air or an object moving swiftly in contact with water; movement accompanied by such sound." This definition reflects the fact that many *ONE* correspondents described swishes as a sort of unwanted noise. "Swishing and *noisy* 'queens' ought to be stopped"; they went about "*screaming*, waving bent wrists in the public. . . . When they are arrested or beaten up, they *holler* and *shout* blaming [it] on the other fellow, of course they're never at fault," complained various *ONE* correspondents.[13] A correspondent wrote bitterly, "The flaming faggot who swishes up Lexington Avenue in New York City *screaming* and calling attention to his eccentricities sets back homosexuality. He is an object of scorn and the general public places all deviates in the same class. He is a menace and decent homos have cause to resent him."[14] As a verb, the *Oxford English Dictionary* defines swish as a type of movement involving repetitive back-and-forth motion, as in "to whisk (the tail) about."[15] This definition reflects the distinctive walk of many swishes. Stereotypically, swishes walked in an effeminate style, swaying hips from left to right.

The 1961 *ONE* survey revealed that 32 out of 388 male survey respondents (8.2 percent) described themselves as "feminine."[16] This figure is similar to other estimates homophile activists, *ONE* readers, psychiatrists, and journalists provided. In a 1958 televised panel discussion in New York City, for example, psychiatrist Albert Ellis, author Gerald Sykes, and Mattachine officer Tony Segura agreed with each other that 5 percent of homosexuals were "obvious."[17] Wardell Pomeroy, an associate of Alfred Kinsey, estimated at the 1964 Daughters of Bilitis Convention that 15 percent of gay men were "obvious," while 5 percent of lesbians were obvious through explicitly "butch" mannerisms.[18] A *ONE* survey respondent from Newburgh, New York, similarly estimated that 15 percent were obvious.[19] These estimates were unscientific to be sure, but collectively suggest that swishes probably made up somewhere between 5 percent and 15 percent of total gay men in these years.

Homophile sources reveal two basic criticisms of swishes. Many *ONE* correspondents argued that swish visibility tipped off police and vice squads to the camouflaged whereabouts of gay social life and thus posed a danger to their livelihoods. For *ONE*'s editors and other homophile activists, however, it was more a question of how the minority should be iconically represented. In their view, swishes represented a degrading stereotype as well as an outdated model of homosexual identity. Homophile leaders wanted to create an iconic image of gays and lesbians as serious, dignified, loyal Americans just as entitled to rights, protections, and benefits as any other American. Gender conformity was an essential part of this strategy, and swish visibility went against this strategy. "We are all familiar with the homosexual stereotype," wrote Marcel Martin in *ONE*, describing an archetypal swish in a sneering tone:

> He is a rather grotesque figure, a caricature of a woman at her best and man at his worst. Physically he is, first of all, effeminate, tall, willowy; his hair is blond and wavy, more than likely marcelled; his eyelashes are long and his eyebrows either plucked or accentuated with make-up; he has a soft pinkish complexion. One hand is always on a hip, the other dangles loosely from the wrist of an upheld arm. He walks with short mincing steps; he talks with a reedish voice in high pitched tones and, usually, with something resembling a lisp. His clothes are stylish, though gaudy (he has a passion for pink shoes, red ties, and mauve undershorts), and much too tight. He sells ribbons in department stores, but may rise to heights of an assistant floor walker; he also waves women's hair and decorates other people's houses. In character, he is mean, cruel, vicious, given to petty jealousies and has a passion for intrigue; he is a gossip and untruthful.[20]

Martin's conceptualization of the swish stereotype can be compared to African-American stereotypes such as the "Sambo," "coon," or "buck." A *ONE* contributor in 1957 compared swishes to the coon-based " 'Stepin Fetchit' caricature of the Negro. . . . Who can take them seriously?"[21] Echoing the strategies of 1950s black civil rights leaders, homophiles wanted to be taken seriously in the public sphere by replacing the swish stereotype with a positive iconic image of their minority along the lines of an idealized white-collar professional worker. They were going for a gay version of Sidney Poitier, who throughout the 1950s and 1960s defied prevailing racial stereotypes by portraying mature, smart, and well-spoken (as opposed to childlike, dumb, and inarticulate) African-American characters in mainstream Hollywood films. Mattachine activists wore suits and ties in some of the earliest gay street demonstrations during the mid-1960s, conveying a Poitier-like masculine seriousness.[22] Don Slater's image in *Life* magazine in 1964, with his white-collar shirt, tie, and neat hair, similarly conveyed an image of masculine respectability that homophile activists wanted to project.

Dorr Legg explained to a European homophile activist in 1955 that *ONE* magazine's antiswish bias was necessary to overcome prevailing gay stereotypes. He wrote, "In America popular belief virtually assumes that there are ONLY masculine women and feminine men who have homosexual tendencies. The 'man in the street' instantly classifies all homosexuals as 'swishes' with long fingernails, painted eyebrows, and exaggerated clothing or as 'butch' women with short hair, loud coarse voices, and smoking cigars! Thus, to correct this impression locally it is almost requisite that we eliminate references to such individuals. Not because they do not exist, not because they do not have their rights, but because there has been (in America) infinitely TOO MUCH emphasis already upon that particular issue."[23] Legg also believed that swishing was neurotic and anachronistic. He wrote in 1964, "Let us be rid of all of this nonsense. Let women be women, and proud that they are. Let men be men, and proud of their maleness, free of any shame that they should love another man. Let them stop their idiotic attempts at femininity and cut out the sex-changeling chitchat. It's out of date, you know."[24] Legg's attitude reflected the rise of the middle-class model of homosexuality as well as the influence of the Kinsey Reports on human sexuality, which similarly debunked older gender inversion models of homosexuality.

Legg's antiswish views reflected a pervasive pro-masculine bias in *ONE* magazine. Walt Whitman, for example, was a favorite *ONE* subject because he "made no connection between effeminacy and manly love," according to Jim Kepner. Whitman personified "an idealization of uninhibited association between men; the frank admiration of virility and masculine beauty; the love of fellow workers, and of strangers."[25] The ONE Institute offered an entire course devoted to Whitman and his poetry, and in 1954, *ONE* activist Chuck Rowland proposed plans for a gay community center in Los Angeles to be called the Walt Whitman Guidance Center.[26] Whitman was a homophile hero largely because he represented a robustly masculine homosexual heritage.

In postwar lesbian culture, butch lesbians, often referred to as "dykes," were not demonized as strongly as male swishes among gay men. No doubt many middle-class lesbians, especially those with professional careers, fretted about butches in a manner similar to gay male anxieties over swishes, but overall, *ONE* sources and published letters from women in *The Ladder* do not contain the same consistent scorn, vitriol, and anxiety over opposite-gender mannerisms. Homophile magazines occasionally published confessional-style essays from "reformed" butches who enthusiastically described the virtues of femininity. "Not too long ago, I was what is considered a 'butchy butch,' " wrote Frankie Almitra in *ONE* in 1959. "Crudely so. I went through the motorcycle jacket and [L]evi stage. I even carried the holy fact that I was a butch to the point of wearing my hair in a flat-top haircut. . . . I have walked down streets and had fingers pointed at me. I have been denied admittance to some of the nicer restaurants because of my appearance. I have lost job opportunities for which I was fully qualified."[27] In these confessionals, embracing femininity made everyday life easier.

Yet Joan Nestle and other lesbian scholars have described a certain heroic status given to butch lesbians, especially within working-class lesbian circles.[28] The Daughters of Bilitis preached moderation in butch mannerisms. The organization warned against excessive, over-the-top butchness yet also recognized that masculinity provided certain social advantages for many women in a patriarchal society—even among middle-class career women.[29] Barbara Stephens, a frequent contributor to *The Ladder*, wrote in 1957 that masculinity made her feel more powerful in the workplace: "We know how clothes affect the behavior of others towards us, and many a woman has confided to me: 'Padded shoulders make me appear stronger, tougher, more self-sufficient. People aren't so apt to push me around.' Or, 'a tailored suit makes me appear professional; people respect me as a "brain" instead of looking down on me as an ordinary "silly female. . . ." ' [These ideas] reflect the prevalent acceptance of 'masculine superiority' and the prestige of male occupations."[30] Even excess butchness could be acceptable if it were contained within lesbian circles, commented a reader of *The Ladder* in 1957. "I think Lesbians themselves could lessen the public attitudes by confining their differences to their friends and not force themselves deliberately upon public notice by deliberate idiosyncrasies of dress and speech."[31] The Daughters were also ambivalent toward butch-femme role-playing in lesbian culture. They recognized that such practices shaped an important amount of lesbian culture, but argued that lesbians should not feel pressured to assume either identity.[32]

The greater tolerance for butchness among lesbians compared to swishiness among gay men is partly explained by a discourse of masculine supremacy underlying American cold war political rhetoric. Historian K. A. Courdeleone has argued that cold war political rhetoric was imbued with sexualized language characterizing a "political culture that put a new premium on hard masculine toughness and rendered anything less than that soft and feminine and, as such, a real or potential threat to the security of the nation."[33] For men, loyalty to masculinity signified national loyalty itself. The magazine *Man's Day*, for example, published the 1956 story "Are American Men becoming Sissies?" which exemplified this politicized masculine toughness. The article stated, "physically weak men often become mentally and morally weak," and, "one reason the Red Chinese were able to brain-wash so many GI prisoners [in the Korean War] was because they were dealing mostly with soft garrison troops and raw recruits."[34] Most crises of the cold war, whether brainwashing in Korea or the Cuban missile crisis, provoked calls for masculine assertion in political and social life. Thus, lesbian masculinity, within certain limits, was less socially problematic because of this politicized masculine supremacy. Swishes, in contrast, violated 1950s norms by appearing to have relinquished their masculinity, a central pillar in the fight against communism. Swishes visibly represented the homosexual threat as well as other threats of weakness, passivity, emotionalism, unreliability, and broken willpower. Rather than defend swishes' rights to be swishes, homophile organizations usually ignored or condemned them.

Considerable antiswish sentiment emerged during ONE, Inc.'s effort to construct a Homosexual Bill of Rights in 1961.[35] Some comments reflected the anxieties about swishes as the prevailing gay stereotype, for example, "We would be more widely accepted if the public didn't think we were all swishes." Some gay men were terrified to be seen in public with a swish because it could expose them as a homosexual. "It is irritating to see a nelly faggot and it is death to be seen WITH one," commented a man from San Jose, California. Others commented, "Gay people that want to be noticed and recognized as gay are the cause of our social problems"; "Attempts should be made to educate and possibly eliminate the public 'swish' "; "The 'normal' homo resents these jerks as much as the heterosexual does, I believe"; and, "STAMP OUT QUEENS!"[36] Most survey respondents saw no irony in denying civil rights to swishes while demanding civil rights for themselves—to them, the civil rights of the majority of gay people depended on the secondary marginalization of this supposedly extreme faction. Some observers noted the hypocrisy, however. Author Donald Webster Cory, for example, criticized the homophile movement in 1962 for its "prejudice and intolerance toward the extreme effeminates."[37]

Some correspondents considered swishes immature. "All this la-di-da, limp-wristed exhibitionism is disgusting," griped Alex from Montana in 1957. "The homosexual who acts that way is suffering from infantilism; maturity of mind and body is both necessary."[38] These readers suggested that swishing was a youthful phase that "normal" (that is, passing or gender conformist) gay men eventually outgrew. John from Brooklyn reminisced nostalgically in a 1962 letter to *ONE* about his own swish "phase": "when I came out into Gay Life, which really isn't so gay, I was 14 years old, and in New York at the time [1954] you couldn't wear enough paint, or dress feminine enough, or swish too much, as I came out with a loud crowd, I know now that being loud was only a release although I most certainly do not regret it one bit. . . . I also did it to attract the male eye, and I sure did, I was the Honey and they were the bee."[39] John described swishiness as an important part of his "coming out" to gay life, as well as an effective strategy to find sexual partners—the traditional method of gay male recognition. But by stating that it had merely been a youthful phase, he reinforced the idea that older swishes were stuck in a permanent adolescent rebellion.

'Curing' Swish

Homophile writers held many of the same attitudes about swishes that heterosexuals held about homosexuals more generally. Politicians, police officials, and other public commentators, for example, argued that gay people were a dangerous menace that deserved to be ostracized. Many of the passing gay men quoted in the previous section made the same claims against swishes.

Some homophile writers, however, were more sympathetic toward swishes. Jim Kepner, for example, described how he overcame his own prejudices against swishes in a 1954 *ONE* magazine article. Despite his intent to defend swishes, the article has a distinct tone of condescension: "They had stood at one time as a threat in my sub-conscious," he wrote, "but after a few meetings, I marveled to see develop my understanding and sympathy for their unique problem. I even started swishing more myself and found it to be rather fun. It's your trademark, part of your tribal lore."[40] Even though swishing could be fun, Kepner characterized it as a "problem" that passing gay people should view with "sympathy" and "understanding."

Similar to the misbegotten notion that homosexuality was curable through psychoanalysis or aversion therapy, some passing gay people believed that swishes could be "cured" of their feminine mannerisms. Swishes could be taught to act masculine in order to pass as heterosexual more effectively. Reflecting a social constructionist view—the idea that gender identity is not fixed biologically but rather performed according to specific social and cultural standards—some postwar gay men viewed their masculinity as an intricate performance rather than innate behavior. Masculinity thus could be taught to swishes in order to reduce the hostility they encountered from society at large and from other gay men.

Even poor Tom Lee in *Tea and Sympathy* suffered through a masculinity lesson when his roommate took pity on him and tried to teach him how to walk "like a man."

The 1955 *ONE* article, "The Margin of Masculinity," described the process of learning masculine mannerisms in intricate detail. The author admitted teaching a swish how to act more masculine might seem silly, but a "preponderant accumulation" of effeminate mannerisms "can attract suspicion, ridicule, and public scorn. This in turn can affect the homosexual's business or professional career and limit his circle of friends. It follows that the elimination (or even skin deep correction) of these traits would do much to defeat frustration and at the same time broaden the potential scope for existence in a hostile society." He advised:

> First, watch your hands. . . . Avoid the limp wrist as you would the plague. Bend the hand forward if you must; but never let the wrist tilt it toward the back of the forearm. . . . Learn to control the little finger. The "fairy finger" I've heard it called. Brawny truck drivers can stop at their diners and while sipping coffee hoist their little fingers to the ceiling—and get away with it. But you can't Johnnie. . . .
>
> Learn the masculine manner of smoking, Johnnie. This too is an exacting accomplishment, but like handling matches, it is important. . . . Never remove a cigarette from your mouth with a two fingered Boy Scout salute. . . . Catch it between the thumb and second finger, making sure that the little finger doesn't spring out of formation as you do. If, while lowering it, you want a real Dead-End-Kid effect, hold it in such a way that the lighted end is cupped by the hand.
>
> Next, Johnnie, learn the upright posture of masculine males. When standing at ease, under no circumstance allow the weight of your body to rest on a single leg while the knee of the other dips inward. . . . Rest your weight equally on both legs, knees rigid. . . .

According to the author, performing masculinity was no simple matter. It required paying close attention to every detail of body movement and posture.

> Your posture while seated can be as telling as at any other time. . . . Crossing the legs is a universal posture of both sexes. But the womanly way is to hook one knee over the other and swing the free-hanging leg to and fro, toe sharply pointed. The

masculine way is to prop the ankle of one leg on the knee of the other; and to drop the elevated knee to such a level that the leg is almost parallel to the floor. When you lean back in this position, your arms can rest on the arms of the chair or you can lace your fingers on your diaphragm. When leaning forward, grasp the instep or ankle of the raised foot with the hand that's nearest to it; and prop the elbow of the other arm on the knee, while the hand either hangs forward and down (palm toward chair, fingers touching and slightly curved) or swings to join the other hand in the neighborhood of the ankle.[41]

This elaborate, detailed description shows that passing as heterosexual was a complex effort that required skill, precision, practice, and acute attention to one's body and speech mannerisms. Passing was not passive. Passing as heterosexual in the 1950s represented a reconciliation between the history of homosexuality as gender inversion with the new realities of the McCarthy era and its middle-class emphasis on masculine supremacy in the face of communist peril. It was not a denial of one's authentic self, but rather a practical survival tactic that allowed individuals to become more comfortable with their gay identities by avoiding the political, social, and economic penalties of visibility.

The lengths gay men went to achieve gender conformity was further demonstrated in a letter written by a Hollywood magazine editor identified as H. D. in 1954. In Washington, D.C., and Los Angeles, he organized "group hypnotherapy" sessions to adjust gay people's gender mannerisms in order to help people "in the work-a-day world." Each session met twice a week for four to six weeks. H. D. emphasized that no effort was made to change anyone's sexual behavior or desires. He admitted the process had limitations, but the groups were "[a] blessing for those of us who have obvious mannerisms which make it difficult to integrate into acceptable conduct recognized by society. The hissing 'S' used by males, the use of well-defined words which stamp the male homo, the exaggerated walk, and compulsion to use cosmetics and feminine attire, can all be banished through hypnotherapy." H. D. described hypnotizing a prominent architect and repeating phrases such as, "You will henceforth always maintain your wrist in a firm position, and your hand will not flutter or be held limp. You will forever cease to pat your hair, nor will you walk with a feminine gait, but rather with a purposeful, masculine stride." In another case, he claimed success in removing the words "honey," "dear," and "gracious" from a man's vernacular speech.[42]

Another solution for learning proper masculine behavior could be found in physique magazines. These magazines encouraged robust masculinity through body and muscle development. Many physique magazines had obvious gay overtones and large gay readerships. Bob Mizer, the gay publisher of the popular *Physique Pictorial*, for example, shared the opinion with Dorr Legg, Jim Kepner, and other homophile writers that male homosexuality and effeminacy had no inherent connection. According to a 1960 *Physique Pictorial* editorial, ". . . homosexuality was the standard way of life among the rugged Greek warriors, and according to researchers of our own current times is no rarity among such masculine occupations as truck drivers, cowboys, military men, policemen, and many others. Bodybuilding, and the creation of a rugged powerful body[,] will almost always remove the stigma of 'sissy' from any young man, because big muscles and femininity are incongruous."[43] Physique magazines such as *Physique Pictorial* gave gay men practical advice on "fitting in" more effectively through exercise, diet, and weight training. Their unsubtle eroticism also created an idealized gay male aesthetic that reinforced masculine hegemony by using imagery such as soldiers, cowboys, and motorcycle gangs. By using bluntly masculine iconic representations of male homosexuality, physique magazines furthered the impression that swishes were out of step with postwar gay culture.

Swish Perspectives

In the early 1960s, a growing number of *ONE* readers were criticizing the homophile movement's antiswish bias. A Greenwich Village man, for example, wrote in 1963, "It seems from many letters in your columns that many gay people are prejudiced against the Swish. Well, I am one and want to live. . . . The gay world must realize that there are variants within the sex variant group. I'd rather be an honest, loud-spoken swish than a sugar-coated phoney."[44] For many, swishing simply felt natural and authentic. Isaac wrote from Chicago in 1964, "I was deeply hurt and resentful that you gave editorial prominence to a statement that the 'infernal display of effeminacy' displayed by many homosexuals should be abolished. Anyone who really knows effeminate homosexuals knows that the effeminacy is as natural to them and as integral to their personalities as is the homosexual act itself which the editorial defends. Effeminacy serves as an integrating, tension-releasing, often enjoyable part of many homosexual's lives. If effeminate homosexuals are considered an embarrassing burden to the homosexual movement, I think you have rejected a great many of your friends."[45] Mr. C. of Newburyport, Massachusetts, defended his effeminacy as a matter of individualism, "I have no intention of submerging my individuality for a lot of weak-kneed conformists who if they were honest with themselves would admit they admire me for having the courage to be a non-conformist, but it is easier for them to join the mob and agree with general condemnations than to stick their necks out."[46] Mr. C.'s comments echo broader postwar debates about the nature of conformity and the individual in society, and his use of terms "weak-kneed conformists" and "mob" was a stinging critique of the homophile movement's antiswish bias.[47]

Several self-identified swishes wrote letters to *ONE* in a camp linguistic style. Camp writing can be considered the literary equivalent of effeminate body mannerisms because both swishing and camp writing appropriated the voice, vocabulary, and linguistic patterns of female impersonators. Swish, gender inversion, and cross-dressing are intrinsic components of camp. According to David Van Leer, "Camp is the best-known gay linguistic style, occupying within male homosexual culture roughly the same position as 'playing the dozens,' or 'signifyin'' within African American culture. A complex of loosely defined theatricalisms, camp imitates the hyperbolic of musicals and popular movies as well as other visual extravagances like overstated décor and fashion, and especially cross-dressing. In its verbal forms, it favors quotation, mimicry, lip-synching, gender inversion, trenchant put-downs, and bad puns. Between World War II and Stonewall [1969], such theatricalisms were epitomized by the stylized performances of drag queens."[48] Letters written in a camp style stand out from the majority of letters written to *ONE*. Campy letters used a less formal tone, detoured into lengthy tangential discussions, and contained rapier witticisms and an absurdist sense of humor. To write a campy letter was to reject the hegemonic masculinity underlying the majority of *ONE's* contents and letters. It signified defiance against the prevailing antiswish bias.

A 1964 *ONE* magazine subscription cancellation from Leslie, a self-identified "queen" who had "always been one of the girls," exemplified the camp style. Leslie lived in a small town in Montana, and he made no effort to pass as heterosexual. His family disapproved of his affairs with men but otherwise loved him dearly. He explained, "most of the straights of both sexes in this town accept me socially and invite me to their homes though I have noticed that wives keep a wary eye on me and never, never leave me alone with their husbands. A few 'squares' here do not accept me and I couldn't care less." A campy passage described a recent car purchase, the tone evoking a drag queen:

The reason I have failed to renew my subscription to your splendid magazine ONE is due to TV and car payments. You see, my credit is just too good here and I have splurged. Foolish? Yes it is. But look, angels; how could I refuse to purchase the beautiful blue and white Ford Station wagon when the tall, handsome, blonde salesman, after looking around to be sure that none of the other people in the showroom were watching us, put his arm around me, pulled close and whispered, "Just think of how much fun we could have in that car, baby." That did it. Almost swooning with rapture and desire, I looked into his blue eyes and weakly murmured "I'll buy it." Did he keep his word? Yes, he did. There was a hot time in the old town that night.[49]

Clearly, Leslie refused to apologize for his swish visibility or accommodate the "few squares" who did not accept him.

ONE magazine's feature stories, with a few exceptions, avoided the informal tone, incongruous juxtapositions, and ambiguous gender pronouns that characterized campy writing. When such writing did appear, ONE usually received angry letters complaining that swishes were taking over the magazine and jeopardizing its success. Campy essays from James Barr Fugaté, for example, including "In Defense of Swish" and "Camping in the Bush," elicited many complaints. Many readers howled in protest when ONE ran advertisements for swishy menswear (including rhinestone-embedded undergarments) in 1954 (see Figures 17 and 18, Win-Mor Clothing advertisements). One reader complained, "The feminine attire worn by the male model, I find disgusting and against every principle of your fine work."[50] Campy writing or swishy imagery in ONE was usually restricted to brief asides or comic relief, but even these contents provoked reader complaints.[51]

Perhaps the campiest writing to appear in ONE was the December 1953 short story, "Jingle, You Belles You!" The story was a satirical exploration of workplace discrimination against gay people. It featured a cartoonishly masculine department store manager, "a big butch ex-All American three-quarter-back from way back," searching for a suitable Santa Claus for the store's annual Christmas display. The manager's hostility toward gay people was described in an unambiguously camp style: "He swore if he ever saw as much as *one* real fairy in Fairyland he'd mow them through garden supplies, knife them through kitchenware and end up doing simply frightful things to them in Danish Pottery." A flamboyantly swishy Santa arrived, "the kindest, gentlest, sweetest Santa that ever minced down from the Pole. It weighed at least two hundred pounds

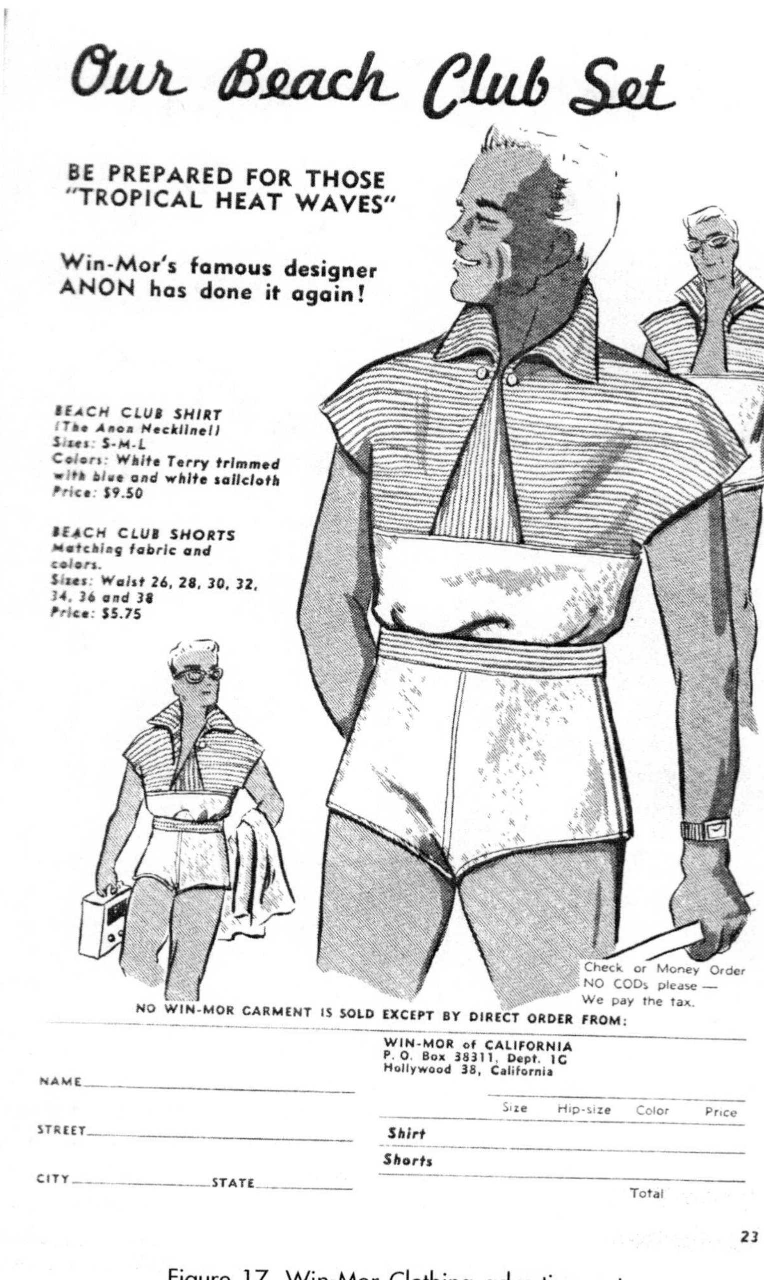

Figure 17. Win-Mor Clothing advertisement.

*his page is dedicated
to those who appreciate
the ultimate in original design,
fine quality in fabrics
and superb craftsmanship.
The designs are
created by the fabulous ANON
exclusively for
"WIN-MOR of California".
We offer these
originals
for your discriminating approval.*

"MOON-GLOW"
Nights of comfort in sheer nylon
with jeweled satin trim.
COLORS—Black Magic or White.
SIZES—Small, medium and large.
(Also available in jersey)
PRICE—The Top .... $ 8
　　　　　The Bottom $14
　　　　　Both $21

"DREAM"
Here is our answer to the gay 90's
nightshirt. They used flannel — we
use nylon and satin!!
COLOR—Foam White only.
SIZES—Small, medium and large.
PRICE—$12

"EASE"
In satin studded with rhinestone.
COLOR—Black Magic or White.
SIZES—Small, medium and large.
(Also available in Jersey or
sheer nylon)
PRICE—$4

Figure 18. Win-Mor Clothing advertisement.

before pillows and was as graceful as a feather in a breeze." Word spread among the department store's mostly gay employees that the store Santa was a swish, causing amusement. Slaussey, the bigoted manager, failed to notice at first. Like Leslie's letter, the story's tone evoked a drag queen.

> Santa—sitting before whole fields of parents and progeny— wasn't just doing a dollar an hour job to draw unemployment compensation after New Year's. That one was nothing less than holding court. It had dozens of tiny lavender bows in the white beard, brilliant sequins sewed all over the costume, gilt sprinkled in wig and eyebrows, and the biggest pinkie ring ever to be borrowed from Accessories. Those full lips were "Carmen's Kiss! The *Latest* Red Menace!" and the immense cheeks simply *burned* with rouge. There was carefully applied eye shadow and, believe it or not, a diamond beauty mark. Somehow, and you won't believe this either, the whole effect was just right.

The store Santa proved popular with customers, but Slaussey flew into a rage and chased "it" around the store. After a slapstick incident on an escalator, Slaussey caught the Santa and fired him for his swishy mannerisms. But then a gaggle of horrified parents and screaming children complained to the store management and within ten minutes, Santa, "serene as a queen [was] restored to her rightful throne by divine intervention." The store's corporate offices censored Slaussey. Justice and fairness prevailed.[52]

At first glimpse, "Jingle, You Belles You!" seems like a mere silly story, but it humorously dealt with the serious issue of job discrimination against gay people. The swishy Santa achieved one of the homophile movement's major goals: the right to work and earn a paycheck in one's desired profession. In this sense, the story was consistent with the magazine's broader political goals. Ultimately, however, "Jingle, You Belles You!" was a remarkable fluke, a road not traveled by *ONE* in its defense of unabashed swishiness. The lack of similar stories over the years indicated how *ONE's* editors curtailed camp writing in the magazine just as they urged minimizing swishy body mannerisms.

Facing the usual ostracism from mainstream society as well as prejudice from other gay people, some swishes internalized a deep sense of self-loathing. James, from Philadelphia, for example, described how his inability to control his swishy mannerisms had crippled his self-esteem. James had been a lonely child growing up in Anaheim, California. He buried himself in intellectual pursuits as a teenager. At seventeen he suffered a "nervous collapse" caused by the growing pressure of his same-sex desires, which had cast him "into the black sea of self-doubt." James joined the Army hoping that military service would awaken a latent heterosexuality, but the experience left him more miserable and confused. After his military service, a psychiatrist bluntly told James that he was gay and must get used to the idea. This helped James accept his homosexuality.[53]

But James knew there was a deeper problem. Not only was he gay, but his style, behavior, and mannerisms announced his homosexuality in a way that seemed beyond his control. "The real problem was that people immediately recognized me for what I was, and ridiculed me. Men called me a 'blazing faggot.' I saw others whom I recognized as the definition of this slur, and detested them for being so obvious. . . . I began to search the mirror carefully. . . . At first I saw only what I had always seen. A young, blond, five foot ten of slight build, sensitive face, and a neat appearance. Then I saw the gestures, the chiseled [sic] features, the dancer's grace, the tricky, secretive smile. I DID blaze!" At first, James vowed to tone down his effeminate mannerisms. "I changed from fashionable to conservative baggy clothes. I cropped my neatly combed hair—even dyed it mouse-brown. I took on gruff ill manners." But, like Tom Lee in *Tea and Sympathy*, his efforts to butch himself up failed. "My attempt at a heavy swaggering walk turned out stumbling stagger. I was undergoing the most hellish experience of my life, not to become straight, but not to seem gay. It evidently did not work." James abandoned his efforts to act masculine and pass as heterosexual. He returned to his "fashionable suits" and walked in a manner that felt natural to him. He vowed to ignore any hostility his behavior provoked. Yet as he penned the letter, the struggle still burned within him. "So reads the history of a blazing faggot who would give his right arm to be but a tiny spark. . . . The straights disown me as out of their world. My own kind are afraid of the possible stigma of being seen with me." The lack of trustworthy published information on homosexuality made navigating his gender crisis all the more treacherous, uncertain, and confusing. "What can I do? . . . I have never had someone to advise me. I have always had to stumble along by trial and error. Is there a way to erase twenty-two years in order to build an entire new character that is unnoticeable? Unnoticeable yet attractive to its peers? Or is there a secret way to find one person who will accept me as is—face value—and not care what the world thinks?"[54]

Like Leslie from Montana, James praised *ONE* in his letter, but *ONE*'s consistent antiswish rhetoric surely contributed to his gender anxiety. Despite calm assurances from passing gay men that swishy behavior could be eliminated with practice, hypnosis, or weightlifting,

James's letter hinted at the trauma of such a process. The letter challenged the homophile argument that swishing—whatever its causes, origins, or basis—could be contained within private gay spaces and kept out of public sight. Wearing a heterosexual mask certainly allowed many gay men to participate more fully in American life, but James's case demonstrates why some gay men preferred the social inconveniences of swishy behavior over a charade that felt unnatural, abnormal, and dishonest—as dishonest as the movie adaptation of *Tea and Sympathy*, which pretended that homosexuality had nothing to do with the story. In the end, the "loud," "screaming" swishes who refused to apologize for their behavior may have suffered the wrath of other gay people, but embracing swish identity—like accepting gay identity itself—also brought self-acceptance that could easily outweigh the negative reactions. Such swish assertion and pride in the face of this hostility was yet another manifestation of the growing civil rights impulse.

Clearly, though, swish self-acceptance came at a high cost. Swishes—all gay people for that matter, but especially swishes—found themselves caught in an awkward transitional moment in the history of gender in the United States. Before World War II, scientific experts encouraged society to believe that sexual identity and gender behavior were deeply connected. In recent decades, however, gender theorists such as Judith Butler and R. W. Connell have emphasized that gender and sexuality have no inherent biological connection. Gender behavior is a social construction, a product of society and culture rather than biology. The shift in thinking that disconnected gender from sexuality happened over many years, but perhaps the most decisive moment was the 1948 publication of Alfred Kinsey's *Sexual Behavior in the Human Male*. The male Kinsey Report refuted the idea that gay men were inherently effeminate by reporting unexpectedly high levels of male homosexual behavior in American society. Kinsey's research reshaped thinking about the relationship between gender and sexuality in the 1950s and early 1960s. To use Dorr Legg's words, Kinsey's research made swishing seem "out of date."

While this transitional moment was difficult for self-identified swishes, homophile movement activists and writers embraced the moment as an opportunity to reinvent the public image of gay men away from gender inversion and toward a middle-class model of gender conformity—a model conveniently suited to "passing as heterosexual" that avoided the penalties of gay visibility. Yet these homophile efforts could not entirely undo the important role of effeminacy as a visible marker of gay identity among previous generations of gay men. To an important extent, the widespread animosity toward swishes after World War II was generational. We are reminded that gay culture does not pass from parent to child as do the cultures of racial or religious minorities. Each generation therefore feels more necessity and freedom to reinvent the image and meaning of homosexuality in a way that makes sense at a particular historical moment. In the mid- to late 1960s, a new generation would once again reinvent the social, cultural, and political meaning of lesbian and gay identity within the context of contemporary movements such as the counterculture, the militant Black Power movement, and the antiwar movement. In this new era of "louder" outspoken activism, the swish's dignity was somewhat restored. But even in the more liberated 1970s, effeminacy remained a source of contentious debate and bitter division within gay politics and the gay community. The secondary marginalization of swishes lingered, and, unfortunately, lingers still.

Conclusion

When I began reading the letters written to *ONE* editors, I was expecting horrifying tales of suicides, homophobic violence, and involuntary lobotomies. Instead, I was surprised by the upbeat tone of so many letters. Even in the bleakest descriptions of antigay discrimination, a sense of humor, irony, and resilience often prevailed. I searched for the phrase "the closet," but instead found only "coming out."

Some *ONE* correspondents did succumb to a victim mentality. Early in my research, for example, I came across several letters written in 1955 by Howard, a man who resided in Santa Barbara, California. Howard was miserable, lonely, and afraid—the stereotypical 1950s gay man from a post-Stonewall perspective. He wrote letter after letter, page after page woefully detailing his misery and loneliness. "PLEASE HELP ME, YOU ARE MY LAST HOPE, MY ONLY HOPE," he wrote. Dorr Legg eventually lost his patience. He sternly told Howard to stop wallowing in misery and "awaken from the self-pity." When Howard wrote back asking for more assistance, Legg responded that unless Howard included a $100 check made out to "ONE, Incorporated" in his next letter, Legg would cease replying to his letters.[1]

When I first read this exchange between Howard and Dorr Legg, I felt sorry for Howard and thought Legg was cruel in cutting him off so rudely. As I delved deeper into the letters, however, I realized that Howard's profound misery was atypical. From Legg's perspective, yes, it's a cruel world out there, but he continually urged readers not to complain, but to *do* something about their situation—as much as possible, anyway. He urged them to use their anxiety for constructive purposes and not succumb to paralysis and victimhood. The letters overall convey such a tone, despite exceptions.

Wearing a heterosexual mask was an important dimension of this civil rights impulse. Rather than negate their sense of lesbian or gay identity, the mask in fact bolstered it by enabling gay people to survive each day while they searched for, and increasingly found, one another. The

223

mask allowed gay people sufficient camouflage to construct a national community and a stronger sense of collective identity and culture. Of course, gay people would have preferred not to wear the mask, and some gay people (such as swishes) refused to wear it. But on the whole, the mask allowed the gay minority to take important strides forward by eluding the repressive forces designed to ruin their lives and destroy gay social bonds.

Virulent anticommunist and antigay sentiments remained fixtures of American politics throughout the 1950s. In 1960, the election of youthful, optimistic John F. Kennedy seemed to signal a new direction for U.S. politics. However, as the nation suffered through the Bay of Pigs fiasco, the Cuban missile crisis, and troop escalations in Vietnam, Kennedy's policies reinforced the anticommunist status quo and continued to exclude gay people from public life. *ONE* correspondents seemed unimpressed with Kennedy. They saw hypocrisy in his famous inaugural declaration, "ask not what your country can do for you—ask what you can do for your country." Gay people's efforts to serve their country in the military, in government, and in education were clearly not welcome. A *ONE* correspondent from Virginia wrote in 1961, "Does [Kennedy] mean 'The question for each of us who is not a sexual pervert is, "What can I do for my Government?"' . . . Have any of you [at *ONE*] thought of writing to President Kennedy and asking what homosexuals *can* do for their Government?"[2] Lesbians, in contrast to gay men, were more hopeful about Kennedy because of his pledge to improve women's status in the United States.[3]

Kennedy's November 1963 assassination initiated the political and cultural changes collectively referred to as "the sixties." Historian Jon Margolis has described 1964 as "the last innocent year," noting, "if some people had smoked marijuana, dressed exotically, embraced Eastern mysticism, written or painted erotica, and spoken openly about sex in earlier years, it was in 1964 that this kind of behavior burst out of its Bohemian ghetto; all of a sudden, more than a few middle-class suburbanites were studying Zen, puffing pot, and taking Allen Ginsberg seriously."[4] Americans saw major challenges to the status quo in the months immediately following the Kennedy assassination: sweeping civil rights legislation, exponential military escalation in Vietnam, a free speech showdown in Berkeley, and an "invasion" by the long-haired Beatles. In 1964, the 1960s arrived.

In the same year, the national gay minority stepped further out of the shadows and into the media spotlight. *Life* magazine published its lengthy article "Homosexuality in America," which included photographs of *ONE's* Don Slater and the Mattachine Society's Hal Call.[5] Other mainstream magazines followed with their own analyses of American gay culture. According to Edward Alwood, the press "carried more stories about homosexuals in 1964 than in the previous three years combined. The number was even greater for 1965, and the trend continued into 1966."[6] This unprecedented media coverage was reinforced by several liberal Supreme Court rulings on obscenity during the 1950s and 1960s, including *ONE*'s landmark 1958 decision against the Los Angeles postmaster. These rulings ushered in a flood of mass-market paperback books and periodicals with homosexual themes.[7] Gay erotica now could be sold "above the counter." Once the boldest magazine on the newsstand, by 1965 *ONE* seemed quite tame.

Indeed, ONE, Inc., did not adapt well to the dizzying cultural changes of the mid-1960s. In 1965, a conflict between Dorr Legg and Don Slater tore the organization apart. Tension brewed for years over the direction of the organization. Legg believed the future of the organization was not in the magazine but in The ONE Institute and its educational programs. He wanted ONE to become the world's first "gay university." Slater, however, believed that the corporation's limited resources should remain devoted to the magazine. In April 1965, Legg lobbied enough support to expel Slater from ONE's board of directors. Shocked and enraged by his expulsion after so many years of dedicated service, Slater showed up at ONE's offices in the middle of night with a moving truck and hauled everything away—the library, the subject files, the circulation lists, everything. In the following months, two versions of *ONE* magazine circulated, a Slater version and a Legg version, leaving readers baffled and confused. A bitter court fight ensued over ONE, Inc.'s materials, records, and copyrights, and in 1967, a court divided the materials between Slater and Legg. Legg retained the name "ONE, Inc.," which allowed him to continue his education projects under the name The ONE Institute. *ONE* magazine ceased publication in 1967. Slater renamed his magazine *Tangents*, which lasted until 1970.[8]

The conflict between Legg and Slater, like so much else in the 1960s, had an important generational component. Legg was sixty-one years old in 1965. He saw himself as the guardian of the original homophile vision of assimilation and respectability. He dismissed much of the youthful activism of the 1960s as superficial and unserious, and he considered street protests obnoxious and ineffective.[9] Slater, in contrast, was almost twenty years younger than Legg. He was more sympathetic to the outspoken, militant 1960s political activism. He recognized that *ONE* was losing ground to a new generation of gay publications such as *Drum* that mixed political essays with erotic content.[10] By the late 1960s, the new style of raucous, youthful political activism easily drowned out homophiles such as Legg, who clung to his homophile principles until his death in 1994.[11]

"Gay liberation," the next phase of gay political activism, featured the same in-your-face visibility, militancy, and revolutionary sentiment as anti–Vietnam War protests, Black Panther rallies, radical feminist demonstrations, and countercultural gatherings. The chief accomplishment of gay liberation activists in the late 1960s and 1970s was to reimagine the concept of "coming out": no longer would gay people come out only to each other, but now they came out to everyone. The cumulative effect of millions of gay people voluntarily coming out to their families, employers, and peers led to greater acceptance of gay people in public life throughout the 1970s. In 1973, the American Psychiatric Association removed homosexuality from its list of mental illnesses, and in 1975, the federal government revoked its ban on gay employees. Openly gay people began winning elections to public office. By 1980, homosexuality had been decriminalized in nearly half the country. In this new historical context, millions of gay men and lesbians felt emboldened to remove the masks that had helped them survive the more paranoid, claustrophobic 1950s and early 1960s.

Several 1960s social movements influenced and shaped the character of gay liberation. New Left organizations such as Students for a Democratic Society politicized a generation of young activists by organizing civil rights and anti–Vietnam War demonstrations—demonstrations that provided models for gay liberation demonstrations. Unfortunately, gay people were not always welcome in New Left organizations, and certain New Left leaders did not take gay causes seriously. College-age lesbians and gay men disenchanted with the New Left turned their energies to gay liberation instead.[12]

Second-wave feminism, also known as women's liberation (or women's lib), provided organizing models for gay liberation as well as a significant political outlet for lesbians during the 1960s and 1970s. Many lesbians felt more empowered in women's rights organizations than in male-dominated gay liberation organizations. Lesbians increasingly conceptualized their oppression in terms of gender and patriarchy rather than sexuality. Unfortunately, as with the New Left, some feminist leaders believed that visible lesbian participation and leadership threatened the credibility of the women's movement. Betty Friedan, for example, discouraged lesbians from holding prominent positions in the National Organization for Women, the most visible mainstream feminist organization of the 1970s. Lesbians ostracized by mainstream feminist groups could join more radical organizations, lesbian-oriented groups, or gay liberation groups instead. The Daughters of Bilitis, the preeminent lesbian rights organization of the late 1950s and early 1960s, adapted better than ONE, Inc., or Mattachine to the new temper of 1960s activism by embracing "lesbian-feminism."[13]

Other social trends influenced gay liberation as well. The intro-duction of the birth control pill into American society in the early 1960s made nonprocreative sex less taboo. Many young people "dropped out" of society and experimented with countercultural lifestyles involving com-munes, drugs, and non-Western religions. The idea of a gay or lesbian "lifestyle" became more socially acceptable in such a context of social and sexual experimentation. Furthermore, the Vietnam War discredited the military-industrial complex among this baby boom generation, leading to a rejection of the nationalism/militarism/masculinity nexus that char-acterized 1950s political culture as a whole and formed the basis of gay discrimination policies. As protest over the war grew, the idea that homo-sexuals posed a national security risk seemed increasingly ludicrous.

The character of lesbian and gay politics had shifted long before the Stonewall riots in June 1969. These riots, sparked by a gay bar raid in New York City, symbolized the gay movement's new anger, visibility, youthfulness, and outspoken collective pride. The 1960s context inspired gay people to march in the streets, create hundreds of gay and lesbian activist organizations across the country, and most importantly, come out to family members, coworkers, and straight friends. The gay libera-tionist movement was not so much a rejection of homophile principles (as Justin David Suran has argued) as it was an adaptation to the new cultural and political climate.[14] The homophiles, after all, had painstak-ingly created gay communication networks during the 1950s and 1960s and had created the country's first openly gay press. By 1969, dozens of gay publications, organizations, businesses, cultural, and political groups had spread news of the riots across the country. Without this existing network of gay organizations and activists, news of the Stonewall riots might not have traveled beyond Greenwich Village.[15]

The violence of the Stonewall riots reflected the broader 1960s con-text as well. After the 1967 "summer of love," violence became increas-ingly associated with 1960s activism. Chicago police ruthlessly beat up demonstrators at the 1968 Democratic convention, for example, and some members of the peaceful Students for a Democratic Society recon-figured themselves as the bomb-toting Weathermen. Black Panthers were having regular shoot-outs with police. Robert Kennedy and Martin Luther King Jr. were brutally assassinated in 1968. The 1968 Tet Offensive rained red blood onto America's television sets during the evening news, and the Manson family, characterized as a "hippie" cult by the press, savagely murdered celebrities in order to trigger an apocalyptic race war.

Disturbingly, as more gay people asserted their visibility by "coming out" to the heterosexual world, homophobic vigilantes increasingly used violence to keep gays "in their place"—that is, hidden. The newfound visibility of masses of lesbians and gay men made them easier targets of random violence. Perhaps the most famous victim was Harvey Milk, the openly gay member of the San Francisco Board of Supervisors gunned down in 1978 by Dan White, a disgruntled, politically conservative former Supervisor. Despite killing San Francisco mayor George Moscone in the same shooting spree, White, to the dismay of San Francisco's gay community, served only five years in prison.[16] Such antigay violence has been at the core of gay activism since the early 1970s. Homophile activists, in contrast, said almost nothing about such random violence during the 1950s and early 1960s. Passing as heterosexual provided many levels of protection, including degrees of protection from homophobic gay bashings and murders. In the liberated 1970s, visibly gay people still lived with major risks and threats.

These risks were usually outweighed by the unprecedented freedoms of the 1970s, freedoms only imagined in the 1950s. Compared to the 1970s, the 1950s seemed like a bleak period to the gay liberation era scholars who characterized life before Stonewall as a dark age for homosexuals. But the devastating onset of the AIDS crisis in the 1980s and the Reagan administration's years-long refusal to acknowledge the crisis—a dark age for gay men if ever one existed—compels a more complex understanding of how gay people experienced the 1950s. The 1950s were not so much a dark age, then, as an age of anxiety. The 1950s offered new ways to identify as gay and participate in gay culture as well as experience specific dangers associated with such participation. The good and the bad were inextricably linked. The political oppression of gays after World War II, ironically, reflected the significant growth of a national gay community in these same years.

For most heterosexual-identified Americans, homosexuality was one of many postwar anxieties alongside atomic destruction, communist infiltration, racial integration, delinquent teenagers, status anxiety, and even Momism. The worries about homosexuality were not merely social and political, but also personal. The release of the Kinsey Report on male sexuality in January 1948 had suddenly cast doubt on the heterosexuality—and hence manhood—of more than one-third of American men. The female Kinsey Report in 1953 observed that nearly one-fifth of American women had had lesbian experiences at some point in their adult lives. These were startling statistics. Undoubtedly, personal unresolved sexual anxieties lay at the heart of many self-professed patriots' antigay crusades. The sexual ambiguity of several leading anticommunist and anti-homosexual crusaders during the 1950s, such as Joseph McCarthy, Roy Cohn, and J. Edgar Hoover, demonstrates how gay purges under the guise of national security allowed certain "confirmed bachelors" in positions of power to protect themselves by convincing the public—and perhaps themselves—that they were heterosexual (whether or not they were). By persecuting others, they perversely protected themselves. These anxieties about sexuality in the 1950s were a fundamental component of the postwar red scare and of postwar American culture more broadly.

Alfred Kinsey was deeply troubled that politicians and morality crusaders frequently cited his data as justification for homosexual crackdowns. They completely missed the point. For Kinsey, the abundance of homosexuality in human sexual behavior pointed toward the inherent diversity and profound individuality of all living things, something he initially encountered during his gall wasp research as a young man. Homosexuals were not aberrant freaks, but simply part of the natural order of things. To repress homosexual desires, in Kinsey's view, was to repress a fundamental aspect of being human.[17]

In the spring of 1956, Alfred Kinsey visited ONE, Inc.'s offices in downtown Los Angeles. This was a big event for *ONE*'s staff; *ONE* repeatedly venerated Kinsey as a saint of gay freedom. For two hours, Kinsey, Dorr Legg, Don Slater, Jim Kepner, and other members of *ONE*'s staff discussed a range of topics while sipping coffee from paper cups. Kepner described *ONE*'s postal harassment and ongoing court battles over obscenity; Kinsey sympathized by describing his own postal harassment over a shipment of European research materials being detained at the border. Kinsey did criticize ONE, Inc.'s efforts, however, to do too many things at once. He advised them to focus on one thing, such as the magazine, and do it well (no doubt to Legg's chagrin). Kinsey praised *ONE* magazine as an invaluable tool to help gay people accept themselves and overcome the stigma and shame that society imposed on them. The conversation was vibrant and lively, and everyone was impressed by Kinsey's intellectual vitality.

A few months later, Kinsey died of heart problems and pneumonia. Kepner wrote in *ONE*, "To the staff and the readers of *ONE*, his death is an immeasurable loss, deeply and personally felt. Here was a precise, yet bold scientist, daring the fury of those committed to antiquated bias, adding more light to the sex question than any predecessor, yet one who'd barely begun the work he'd outlined."[18] With Kinsey gone, others had to pick up his torch of sexual tolerance and spread the flame. Thousands and millions of gay people in subsequent years and decades preserved Kinsey's spirit by asserting their right to life, liberty, and the pursuit of happiness and by fostering a more enlightened, tolerant, and tolerable society to live in. Years later, we can be reassured that Kinsey's humane message has not been drowned out by the fear-driven cacophony of intolerance, bigotry, and scapegoating that so routinely surges through U.S. politics and culture.

Appendix

Categories of *ONE* Correspondence

Table 2. Breakdown of sample of 812 letters to *ONE* by categories

Category	Description	Number of Letters (812)	Percentage of Letters
1. Job	Firings, anxiety about losing job	102	13%
2. Legal	Arrests, lawyer requests, legal questions	83	10%
3. Rights	Calls for rights and action	83	10%
4. Reports	Descriptions of local gay life	68	8.4%
5. Family	Family and marriage issues	64	7.9%
6. Lonely	Lonely, isolated people	59	7.2%
7. Moving/ Traveling	Descriptions or thoughts of moving and traveling	52	6.4%
8. Religion	Mentions churches or religion	47	5.8%
9. Post Office	Incidents and anxieties about postal harassment	41	5.1%
10. Theory of homosexuality	Musings over nature, origins of sexual identity	24	3.0%
11. "Swish"	Discussion of male effeminacy	17	2.1%
12. Life story	Detailed autobiography	16	2.0%
13. Nervous breakdown	Mentions or describes nervous breakdown	14	1.7%
14. Coming Out	Letter represents first admission of homosexuality	10	1.2%

This table displays tabulations of several recurring topics in the letters. Some letters fell into several categories and other letters did not fall into any category, therefore the percentages do not add up to 100 percent. In this chart, I excluded letters in the regional files because they pertained primarily to *ONE*'s distribution. Thus, the total letter sample for these calculations is 812.

Notes

Introduction

1. W. L. [William Lambert, aka Dorr Legg], "Case History," *ONE* IX, 8 (August 1961), 19–21.

2. Ibid., 20.

3. Ibid.; 2004 conversation with Stuart Timmons, former executive director of ONE National Gay and Lesbian Archives.

4. A short sample of monographs that apply "the closet" to gay people in the 1950s includes Vito Russo, *The Celluloid Closet* (New York: Harper Colophon, 1981); Eve Kosofsky Sedgwick, *Epistemology of the Closet* (Berkeley: University of California Press, 1990); Annette Friskopp and Sharon Silverstein, *Straight Jobs, Gay Lives: Gay and Lesbian Professionals, the Harvard Business School, and the American Workplace* (New York: Scribner, 1995), 40; Arlene Stein, *Sex and Sensibility: Stories of a Lesbian Generation* (Berkeley: University of California Press, 1997), 14; Gilbert H. Herdt, *Same Sex, Different Cultures: Gays and Lesbians across Cultures* (Boulder, CO: Westview, 1997), 155; Jeffrey Escoffier, *American Homo: Community and Perversity* (Berkeley: University of California Press, 1998), 65–78; Patricia Juliana Smith, ed., *The Queer Sixties* (New York: Routledge, 1999), xiv; William N. Eskridge, *Gaylaw: Challenging the Apartheid of the Closet* (Cambridge, MA: Harvard University Press, 1999), 59–60; John M. Clum, *Still Acting Gay: Male Homosexuality in Modern Drama* (New York: St. Martin's Press, 2000), 74; Patrick Dilley, *Queer Men on Campus: A History of Non-Heterosexual College Men, 1945–2000* (New York: RoutledgeFalmer, 2002), 55–82; Steven Seidman, *The Social Construction of Sexuality* (New York: Norton, 2003), 61–62.

5. Major studies of the homophile movement include John D'Emilio, *Sexual Politics, Sexual Communities: The Making of a Homosexual Minority in the United States* (Chicago: University of Chicago Press, 1983); Stuart Timmons, *The Trouble with Harry Hay* (Boston: Alyson Books, 1990); Marcia M. Gallo, *Different Daughters: A History of the Daughters of Bilitis and the Rise of the Lesbian Rights Movement* (New York: Carroll and Graf, 2006); Martin D. Meeker, *Contacts Desired: Connecting to the Gay Male and Lesbian World from the 1940s into the 1970s* (Chicago: University of Chicago Press, 2006); James T. Sears, *Behind the Mask of the Mattachine: The Hal Call Chronicles and the Early Movement for*

Homosexual Emancipation (New York: Harrington Park Press, 2006); C. Todd White, *Pre-Gay L.A.: A Social History of the Movement for Homosexual Rights* (Urbana: University of Illinois Press, 2009).

6. Athan Theoharis, *Seeds of Repression: Harry Truman and the Origins of McCarthyism* (Chicago: Quadrangle, 1971); John Lewis Gaddis, *Now We Know: Rethinking Cold War History* (Oxford, UK: Oxford University Press, 1997).

7. Major studies of McCarthyism include Daniel Bell, ed., *The Radical Right* (Garden City, NY: Doubleday, 1963); Michael Rogin, *The Intellectuals and McCarthy: The Radical Specter* (Cambridge, MA: MIT Press, 1967); Theoharis, *Seeds of Repression*; David Caute, *The Great Fear* (New York: Simon and Schuster, 1978); Stanley Kutler, *The American Inquisition* (New York: Hill and Wang, 1982); Ellen Schrecker, *No Ivory Tower: McCarthyism and the Universities* (New York: Oxford University Press, 1986); Richard Fried, *Nightmare in Red: The McCarthy Era in Perspective* (New York: Oxford University Press, 1990); Griffin Fariello, *Red Scare: Memories of the American Inquisition, an Oral History* (New York: Norton, 1995); Ellen Schrecker, *Many Are the Crimes* (Boston: Little, Brown, 1998); M. J. Heale, *McCarthy's Americans: Red Scare Politics in State and Nation, 1935–1965* (Athens: University of Georgia Press, 1998); Ted Morgan, *Reds: McCarthyism in the Twentieth Century* (New York: Random House, 2004); M. Stanton Evans, *Blacklisted by History: The Untold Story of Joseph McCarthy and His Fight against America's Enemies* (New York: Crown Forum, 2007).

8. Brett Beemyn, "A Queer Capital: Lesbian, Gay, and Bisexual Life in Washington, D.C., 1890–1955" (Ph.D. diss., University of Iowa, 1997); Randolph W. Baxter, " 'Eradicating This Menace': Homophobia and Anti-Communism in Congress, 1947–1954" (Ph.D. diss., University of California, Irvine, 1999); Bradley Usher, "Federal Civil Service Employment Discrimination against Gays and Lesbians, 1950–1975: A Policy and Movement History" (Ph.D. diss., New School for Social Research, 1999); Robert Dean, *Imperial Brotherhood: Gender and the Making of Cold War Foreign Policy* (Amherst: University of Massachusetts Press, 2001), 63–168; David K. Johnson, *The Lavender Scare: The Cold War Persecution of Gays and Lesbians in the Federal Government* (Chicago: University of Chicago Press, 2004).

9. Johnson, *Lavender Scare*, 166; Dean, *Imperial Brotherhood*, 66.

10. U.S. Congress, Senate, *Committee on Expenditures in the Executive Departments, Interim Report Submitted to the Committee on Expenditures in the Executive Departments by Its Subcommittee on Investigations: Employment of Homosexuals and Other Sex Perverts in Government*, 81st Congress, 1950. Report reprinted in *Government versus Homosexuals* (New York: Arno Press, 1975).

11. Athan Theoharis, *Chasing Spies: How the FBI Failed in Counterintelligence but Promoted the Politics of McCarthyism in the Cold War Years* (Chicago: Ivan R. Dee, 2002), 177–197.

12. Johnson, *Lavender Scare*, 2–5.

13. George to *ONE*, 24 April 1955, 1955–1956 Folder, ONE Social Service Correspondence, ONE National Gay and Lesbian Archives, Los Angeles, CA (hereafter ONE Archive).

14. Elaine Tyler May, *Homeward Bound: American Families in the Cold War Era* (New York: Basic Books, 1988), 10–15.

15. On the postwar American family, see May, *Homeward Bound*; Arlene Skolnick, *Embattled Paradise: The American Family in an Age of Uncertainty* (New York: Basic Books, 1991); Joanne Meyerowitz, *Not June Cleaver: Women and Gender in Postwar America* (Philadelphia: Temple University Press, 1994); Elaine Tyler May, *Barren in the Promised Land: Childless Americans and the Pursuit of Happiness* (New York: Basic Books, 1995); Jessica Weiss, *To Have and To Hold: Marriage, the Baby Boom, and Social Change* (Chicago: University of Chicago Press, 2000).

16. Elizabeth Lapovsky Kennedy and Madeline Davis, *Boots of Leather, Slippers of Gold: The History of a Lesbian Community* (New York: Routledge, 1993); Esther Newton, *Cherry Grove, Fire Island: Sixty Years in America's First Gay and Lesbian Town* (Boston: Beacon Press, 1993); George Chauncey, *Gay New York: Gender, Urban Culture, and the Making of a Gay Male World, 1890–1940* (New York: Basic Books, 1994); Daneel Buring, *Lesbian and Gay Memphis: Building Communities behind the Magnolia Curtain* (New York: Garland, 1997); Brett Beemyn, ed., *Creating a Place for Ourselves: Lesbian, Gay, and Bisexual Community Histories* (New York: Routledge, 1997); The History Project, *Improper Bostonians: Lesbian and Gay History from the Puritans to Playland* (Boston: Beacon Press, 1999); Gary L. Atkins, *Gay Seattle: Stories of Exile and Belonging* (Seattle: University of Washington Press, 2003); Nan Boyd, *Wide Open Town: A History of Queer San Francisco to 1965* (Berkeley: University of California Press, 2003); Stein, *City of Sisterly and Brotherly Loves*; Tracy Baim, ed., *Out and Proud in Chicago: A Visual History of Chicago's Gay Movement* (Chicago: Agate Surrey, 2008).

17. Daniel Hurewitz, *Bohemian Los Angeles and the Making of Modern Politics* (Berkeley: University of California Press, 2007).

18. Allan Bérubé, *Coming Out under Fire: The History of Gay Men and Women in World War Two* (New York: Plume, 1991); Robert Cook, *Sweet Land of Liberty? The African-American Struggle for Civil Rights in the Twentieth Century* (New York: Longman, 1998).

19. Samuel Bernstein, *Mr. Confidential: The Man, the Magazine, and the Movieland Massacre* (London: Walford Press, 2006); Steven Watts, *Mr. Playboy: Hugh Hefner and the American Dream* (Hoboken, NJ: Wiley Press, 2008).

20. Alfred Kinsey, Wardell Pomeroy, and Clyde Martin, *Sexual Behavior in the Human Male* (Philadelphia: Saunders, 1948); Alfred Kinsey, Wardell Pomeroy, and Clyde Martin, *Sexual Behavior in the Human Female* (Philadelphia: Saunders, 1953); James H. Jones, *Alfred C. Kinsey: A Public/Private Life* (New York: Norton, 1997); Jonathan Gathorne-Hardy, *Sex the Measure of All Things: A Life of Alfred C. Kinsey* (Bloomington: Indiana University Press, 1998); Miriam G. Reumann, *American Sexual Character: Sex, Gender, and National Identity in the Kinsey Reports* (Berkeley: University of California Press, 2005).

21. Grace Metalious, *Peyton Place* (Boston: Northeastern University Press, 1956); Ruth Pirsig Wood, *Lolita in Peyton Place: Highbrow, Middlebrow, and Lowbrow Novels of the 1950s* (London: Routledge, 1995); Michael Paller, *Gentlemen*

Callers: Tennessee Williams, Homosexuality, and Mid-Twentieth Century Drama (New York: Palgrave Macmillan, 2005).

22. Recently published books on the 1950s that include the word "anxiety" in their titles include Gary Donaldson, *Abundance and Anxiety: America, 1945–1960* (Westport, CT: Praeger, 1997); Jessica Wang, *American Science in an Age of Anxiety: Scientists, Anticommunists, and the Cold War* (Chapel Hill: University of North Carolina Press, 1999); Allan M. Winkler, *Life under a Cloud: American Anxiety about the Bomb* (Urbana: University of Illinois Press, 1999); Daniel Horowitz, *The Anxieties of Affluence: Critiques of American Consumer Culture, 1939–1979* (Amherst: University of Massachusetts Press, 2004); Haynes Johnson, *The Age of Anxiety: McCarthyism to Terrorism* (Orlando, FL: Harcourt, 2005).

23. George Cotkin, *Existential America* (Baltimore, MD: Johns Hopkins University Press, 2003), 54–87; see also Paul Tillich, *The Courage to Be* (New Haven, CT: Yale University Press, 1952); Rollo May, *The Meaning of Anxiety*, rev. ed. (New York: Norton, 1977).

24. William Eskridge, for example, has written in *Gaylaw*, "Once homosexuality became a topic of widespread public as well as private discourse" following World War II and the publication of both Kinsey Reports, "the 'closet' emerged as an apt metaphor" (58). He cites two pieces of evidence for this supposed emergence: the first is an obscure 1949 novel called *Lucifer with a Book* in which a college student hides a forbidden painting in a closet and the second is an article from *ONE* magazine containing the quote, "For where among us breathes there not a man—or woman—who does not have his own Achilles heel—his own private skeleton in the closet?" Clearly, both of these passing, incidental references to closets were not the specifically gay modern appropriation of the closet, but rather the much older and more generic phrase "skeleton in the closet" from which the modern gay usage was derived. If "the closet" was in broad use during these years as Eskridge claims, we can reasonably expect that the phrase would appear in letters and other primary sources more frequently than these few generic references rooted in the older meaning. In addition, on page 99 of his otherwise superb study of gay people and the law, Eskridge cites a different *ONE* article as evidence that the phrase "coming out of the closet" was routinely used in the 1950s, but the article he cites ("Coming Out" from the June 1962 issue) contains no reference to "the closet" whatsoever and describes "coming out" explicitly in terms of "coming out to gay life" as is consistent with the letters. There is a tendency among oral history subjects to retroactively apply the phrase "the closet" to the 1950s, giving the false impression that the phrase was in common usage in these years. I searched diligently for the phrase "the closet" in the letters and other primary sources, but it simply was not there.

25. Dwayne to *ONE*, 10 August 1960, 1960 Folder, ONE Social Service Correspondence.

26. Historians have made this same observation about American gay life before World War II. See Chauncey, *Gay New York*, 6–7, 374–375; David K. Johnson, "The Kids of Fairytown: Gay Male Culture on Chicago's Near North Side in the 1930s," in Beemyn, ed., *Creating a Place for Ourselves*, 110–111.

27. Martin Meeker has written that the Mattachine Society metaphorically wore a "mask of respectability" as a means to negotiate a homophobic society as well as cultivate the bonds of the gay minority. My interpretation builds off Meeker's use of the "mask" metaphor by applying it more broadly to ordinary gay men and lesbians, who employed a similar negotiating strategy in everyday situations such as their job and family lives. See Martin Meeker, "Behind the Mask of Respectability: The Mattachine Society and Male Homophile Practice, 1950s–1960s," *Journal of the History of Sexuality* X, 1 (April 2001), 78–116. William Eskridge in *Gaylaw* also has an excellent discussion of the mask metaphor despite his incorrect assertion that large numbers of gay people started using the closet metaphor in the 1950s.

28. John Loughery, *The Other Side of Silence* (New York: Holt, 1998), 221.

29. This occupational data is derived from a 1960 survey distributed in *ONE* magazine. Because the survey asked specifically about occupation, it offers more useful data than voluntary statements of employment found in the letters. The survey data is stored at the ONE Archive.

30. Letters, *ONE* IV, 3 (March 1956), 25.

31. Steve Valocchi, "The Class-Inflected Nature of Gay Identity," *Social Problems* XLVI, 2 (1999), 207–224.

32. Meeker, *Contacts Desired.*

33. Estelle Freedman has argued that a "sex-crime panic" in the late 1930s targeting homosexuals under aggressive new "sexual psychopath laws" represented the first nationally coordinated crackdown against homosexuals. Indeed, this sex-crime panic had an important national dimension, but was merely a prelude to the cold war era crackdowns. The crackdowns in the late 1940s and 1950s were dramatically broader, better coordinated, and more specifically focused on homosexuals (whereas the main targets in the 1930s were child molesters and serial rapists). Only five states adopted sexual psychopath laws during the late 1930s, compared with twenty-five states from 1949 to 1955. On sex crime panics, see Estelle Freedman, " 'Uncontrolled Desires': The Response to the Sexual Psychopath, 1920–1960," *Journal of American History* LXXIV, 1 (June 1987), 83–106; George Chauncey, "The Postwar Sex Crime Panic," in William Graebner, ed., *True Stories from the American Past* (New York: McGraw-Hill, 1993), 160–178; Stephen Robertson, "Separating the Men from the Boys: Masculinity, Psychosexual Development, and Sex Crime in the United States, 1930s–1960s," *Journal of the History of Medicine and Allied Sciences* LVI, 1 (January 2001), 3–35; Neil Miller, *Sex-Crime Panic: A Journey to the Paranoid Heart of the 1950s* (Los Angeles: Alyson Books, 2002).

34. Based on the statistic from Alfred Kinsey's *Sexual Behavior in the Male* (1948) that 4 percent of the U.S. male population considered themselves "exclusive" homosexuals (that is, a "six" on Kinsey's scale of sexual orientation), Dorr Legg concluded from 1960 census data that approximately 3.5 million Americans were exclusively homosexual. Legg noted that if homosexuals or bisexuals who ranked a "four" or "five" on the Kinsey scale (indicating a homosexual preference although not exclusive homosexual behavior) were also counted, then at least 10 million homosexuals lived in the United States during the 1950s and early

1960s. Dorr Legg, "The Methods of Sociology," unpublished essay, undated [ca. early 1960s], Values Folder, ONE Institute Lecture Notes, ONE Archives; Kinsey, Pomeroy, and Martin, *Sexual Behavior in the Human Male*, 610–666.

Chapter 1
ONE Magazine and Its Readers

1. Ned to *ONE*, 7 December 1961, ONE General Correspondence.

2. Letters, *ONE* IV, 7 (October-November 1956), 38.

3. Ned to *ONE*, 26 August 1962, ONE General Correspondence.

4. Ronald to *ONE*, 14 October 1954, 1953–1954 Folder, ONE Social Service Correspondence.

5. Daniel to *ONE*, 14 April 1961, ONE General Correspondence.

6. Trent to *ONE*, 3 March 1963, ONE General Correspondence.

7. Jonathan Katz, *Gay American History: Lesbians and Gay Men in the U.S.A.* (New York: Harper Colophon Books, 1976), 408.

8. James T. Sears, *Behind the Mask of the Mattachine: The Hal Call Chronicles and the Early Movement for Homosexual Emancipation* (New York: Harrington Park Press, 2006); Martin D. Meeker, *Contacts Desired: Connecting to the Gay Male and Lesbian World from the 1940s into the 1970s* (Chicago: University of Chicago Press, 2006); Stuart Timmons, *The Trouble with Harry Hay* (Boston: Alyson Books, 1990); John D'Emilio, *Sexual Politics, Sexual Communities: The Making of a Homosexual Minority in the United States* (Chicago: University of Chicago Press, 1983), 57–91.

9. Marcia M. Gallo, *Different Daughters: A History of the Daughters of Bilitis and the Rise of the Lesbian Rights Movement* (New York: Carroll and Graf, 2006); Meeker, *Contacts Desired*, 77–140.

10. D'Emilio in *Sexual Politics, Sexual Communities* and Meeker in *Contacts Desired*, for example, focus disproportionately on the Mattachine Society and the Daughters of Bilitis; other works, such as Timmons's *The Trouble with Harry Hay*, Sears's *Behind the Mask of the Mattachine*, and Gallo's *Different Daughters*, focus exclusively on one or the other. Not until 2009, however, did the first book-length study of ONE, Inc., come out: C. Todd White, *Pre-Gay L.A.: A Social History of the Movement for Homosexual Rights* (Urbana: University of Illinois Press, 2009); see also Rodger Streitmatter, *Unspeakable: The Rise of a Gay and Lesbian Press in America* (Boston: Faber and Faber, 1995), 17–50.

11. Eric Marcus, *Making History: The Struggle for Gay and Lesbian Rights, 1945–1990, An Oral History* (New York: HarperCollins, 1992), 41.

12. "How ONE Began," in Marvin Cutler, ed., *Homosexuals Today, 1956* (Los Angeles: ONE Press, 1956), 64–71.

13. White, *Pre-Gay L.A.*, 49; D'Emilio, *Sexual Politics, Sexual Communities*, 110; Manuela Soares, "The Purloined *Ladder*: Its Place in Lesbian History," in Sonya Jones, ed., *Gay and Lesbian Literature since World War II* (New York: Haworth Press, 1998), 29.

14. Dale Jennings, "To Be Accused Is to Be Guilty," *ONE* I, 1 (January 1953), 10–12; "Are You Now or Have You Ever Been a Homosexual?" *ONE* I, 4 (April

1953), 5–13; "You Are a Public Enemy," *ONE* I, 5 (May 1953), 3–7; "And a Red Too," *ONE* I, 9 (September 1953), 2–3; Marlin Prentiss, "Are Homosexuals Security Risks?" *ONE* III, 12 (December 1955), 4–5; Lyn Pedersen, "Miami's New-Type of Witchhunt," *ONE* IV, 4 (April-May 1956), 8–12; Robert Winslow, "Inquisition," *ONE* IV, 5 (June–July 1956), 31–33.

15. Dorr Legg Interview, 1994, videotape VV0465, ONE Oral History Collection.

16. Ibid.; Wayne Dynes, "W. Dorr Legg," in Vern Bullough, ed., *Before Stonewall: Activists for Gay and Lesbian Rights in Historical Context* (New York: Harrington Park Press, 2002), 94–102.

17. Kepner commonly wrote for *ONE* under pseudonyms such as Lyn Pedersen and Dal McIntire, although sometimes he published in his own name. Many of Kepner's *ONE* essays are compiled in Jim Kepner, *Rough News, Daring Views: 1950s' Pioneer Gay Press Journalism* (New York: Haworth Press, 1998).

18. White, *Pre-Gay L.A.*, 65–69; Jim Kepner Interview, undated [1989–1991], videotape VV0005 ONE Oral History Collection.

19. Martin Duberman, *Stonewall* (New York: Dutton, 1993), 151.

20. Lewis Gannett and William Percy III, "Jim Kepner," in Bullough, ed., *Before Stonewall*, 124–134.

21. Joseph Hansen, "Don Slater," in Bullough, ed., *Before Stonewall*, 105.

22. Paul Welch, "Homosexuality in America," *Life*, 26 June 1964, 66–74; Meeker, *Contacts Desired*, 151–195.

23. *ONE* IV, 8 (December 1956), 1; *ONE* III, 5 (May 1955), 1.

24. *ONE* I, 12 (January 1953), 20; *ONE* III, 3 (March 1955), 16.

25. Ann Carll Reid to Jody Shotwell, 19 July 1954, ONE General Correspondence.

26. White, *Pre-Gay L.A.*, 83–84.

27. "Backstage at ONE," *ONE Confidential* IV, 7 (July 1959), 1, 3.

28. James Barr [Fugaté], *Quartrefoil* (New York: Greenberg, 1950); Susan Stryker, *Queer Pulp: Perverted Passions from the Golden Age of the Paperback* (San Francisco, CA: Chronicle Books, 2001), 103.

29. James Barr [Fugaté], "Queer Happenings on Capitol Hill," *ONE* II, 4 (April 1954), 12.

30. Ben to James Barr [Fugaté], 20 May 1954, James Barr [Fugaté] Folder V, ONE Subject Files.

31. James Barr [Fugaté] to Dorr Legg, 3 December 1954, James Barr [Fugaté] Folder III, ONE Subject Files.

32. Dorr Legg to William, 24 May 1954, ONE General Correspondence.

33. Cutler, ed., *Homosexuals Today, 1956*, 65, 70.

34. Bob Waltrip, "The Friday Night Quilting Party," *ONE Confidential* IX, 10 (October 1964), 5–6.

35. *ONE* V, 5 (May 1957), 18–19.

36. *ONE* III, 4 (April 1955), 1. On Albert Ellis, see David Allyn, *Make Love, Not War: The Sexual Revolution: An Unfettered History* (Boston: Little, Brown, 2000), 18–19.

37. *ONE* III, 4 (April 1955), 2–4.

38. Ibid., 6–7.

39. Norman Mailer, "The Homosexual Villain," *ONE* III, 1 (January 1955), 8–12. Mailer later expressed regret over writing the article. In *Advertisements for Myself* (1959), Mailer wrote that the article was "beyond a doubt the worst article I have ever written, conventional, empty, pious, the quintessence of the Square. . . . I writhed at what the gossip would be, for every reader who saw my piece there would be ten or a hundred who would hear that Mailer was writing for a faggot magazine. It would be taken for granted I was homosexual—how disagreeable! I used to wish *ONE* Magazine would fail, and be gone forever." Norman Mailer, *Advertisements for Myself* (New York: G. P. Putnam's Sons, 1959), 221; comments reprinted in "Tangents," *ONE* VII, 12 (December 1959), 11, 28.

40. *ONE* III, 4 (April 1955), 6–7.

41. Albert Ellis, "Are Homosexuals Necessarily Neurotic?" *ONE* III, 4 (April 1955), 8–12.

42. Letters, *ONE* III, 7 (July 1955), 18–20.

43. Marcus, *Making History*, 50.

44. Dal McIntire, "Tangents," *ONE* III, 4 (April 1955), 15–17.

45. Clarkson Crane, "Passing Stranger," *ONE* III, 4 (April 1955), 24–27.

46. *ONE* III, 4 (April 1955), 28–36.

47. Marlin Prentiss, "The Feminine Viewpoint," *ONE* III, 4 (April 1955), 37.

48. *ONE* III, 4 (April 1955), 47.

49. Streitmatter, *Unspeakable*, 25.

50. *ONE* VIII, 8 (August 1960), 4–5.

51. Daniel Simonowski, "Spies in the Closet," public lecture, 2 December 1984, Los Angeles, CA, videotape VV0457, ONE Oral History Collection; FBI Surveillance Newsclip, VV 0051, ONE Oral History Collection; *ONE Confidential* I, 2 (August 1956), 5–6. On FBI surveillance of homosexuals, see Athan Theoharis, *Chasing Spies: How the FBI Failed in Counterintelligence but Promoted the Politics of McCarthyism in the Cold War Years* (Chicago: Ivan R. Dee, 2002), 170–197.

52. William N. Eskridge Jr., *Gaylaw: Challenging the Apartheid of the Closet* (Cambridge, MA: Harvard University Press, 1999), 77.

53. Ibid; Joyce Murdoch and Deb Price, *Courting Justice: Gay Men and Lesbians v. the Supreme Court* (New York: Basic Books, 2001), 27–50; *ONE Confidential* I, 1 (March 1956), 12–19; *The Ladder* II, 5 (February 1958), 10–13.

54. In 1964, ONE, Inc., organized a "gay tour" of Europe for interested members. About fifteen members went on the tour. The itinerary included visits to London, Copenhagen, Zurich, Amsterdam, and Rome. In many of these cities, the tour members visited the offices of European homophile organizations. *ONE Confidential* IX, 12 (December 1964), 3–4.

55. *ONE* VIII, 1 (January 1960), 16–17.

56. Dorr Legg, ed., *Homophile Studies in Theory and Practice* (San Francisco, CA: GLB Publishers and ONE Institute Press, 1994); White, *Pre-Gay LA*, 62–92.

57. *ONE Confidential* I, 1 (March 1956), 2.

58. Ward to *ONE*, 21 June 1964, ONE General Correspondence.

59. D'Emilio, *Sexual Politics, Sexual Communities*, 81–87; 89–91.

60. Though D'Emilio's interpretation is still standard for most historians, I join several other scholars who have challenged D'Emilio's bleak assessment

of the homophile movement, including Meeker, Gallo, White, and Marc Stein in *City of Sisterly and Brotherly Loves: Lesbian and Gay Philadelphia, 1945–1972* (Philadelphia: Temple University Press, 2004).

Chapter 2
Newsstand Encounters: ONE Magazine's Volunteer Agents and Public Visibility

1. B. D. to *ONE*, 13 September 1954, [Washington,] D.C. Folder, ONE Regional Correspondence.

2. Randall to *ONE*, 2 March 1955, [Washington,] D.C. Folder, ONE Regional Correspondence; Dorr Legg to Randall, 8 March 1955, [Washington,] D.C. Folder, ONE Regional Correspondence.

3. James T. Sears, *Rebels, Rubyfruits, and Rhinestones: Queering Space in the Stonewall South* (New Brunswick, NJ: Rutgers University Press, 2001), ix. The quotations are from longtime gay activist Frank Kameny, who wrote the book's forward.

4. C. Todd White, *Pre-Gay L.A.: A Social History of the Movement for Homosexual Rights* (Urbana: University of Illinois Press, 2009), 40.

5. Dorr Legg to Elaine, 19 May 1953, California Folder, ONE Regional Correspondence.

6. Dorr Legg Interview, 1994, videotape VV0465, ONE Oral History Collection.

7. Dorr Legg to Charles, 7 January 1954, California Folder, ONE Regional Correspondence.

8. For example, Harvey (Cleveland, Ohio) to *ONE*, 1 July 1953, Ohio Folder; Roy (Riverside, California) to *ONE*, 20 July 1953, California Folder; Larry (New York City) to *ONE*, 17 October 1953, New York Folder; Gerald (Miami, Florida) to *ONE*, 2 December 1953, Florida Folder; James (Battle Creek, Michigan) to *ONE*, 1 January 1954, Michigan Folder; Michael to *ONE*, 30 March 1954, Connecticut Folder; Doug (Chicago) to Dorr Legg, 17 August 1954, Illinois Folder; Edgar Sandifer (Jackson, Mississippi) to *ONE*, 17 September 1954, Dealers Folder; Bobby (Cleveland, Ohio) to *ONE*, 26 September 1954, Ohio Folder; Louis (Flint, Michigan) to *ONE*, 20 January 1955, Michigan Folder; John (Denver, Colorado) to *ONE*, 8 March 1955, Colorado Folder; Robert (Seattle, Washington) to *ONE*, 21 March 1955, Washington Folder; Irving (St. Johnsbury, Vermont) to *ONE*, 29 September 1955, Dealers Folder; Greg (Hilo, Hawaii) to *ONE*, 5 October 1955, Dealers Folder; Walton (Birmingham, Alabama) to *ONE*, 11 January 1956, Dealers Folder; Peter (Ft. Smith, Arkansas) to *ONE*, 18 January 1956, Dealers Folder; Brian (Denver, Colorado) to *ONE*, 21 January 1957, Colorado Folder; Paul (Tulsa, Oklahoma) to *ONE*, 13 June 1958, Oklahoma Folder; Ben (London) to *ONE*, 7 September 1958, England Folder; Art (Omaha, Nebraska) to *ONE*, November 1958, Nebraska Folder; James (Boston) to *ONE*, 8 August 1959, Massachusetts Folder; Art (Denver, Colorado) to *ONE*, 29 December 1959, Colorado Folder; K. E. (El Centro, California) to *ONE*, 17 December 1961, California Folder; Keith

(Louisville, Kentucky) to *ONE*, 21 March 1966, Kentucky Folder, ONE Regional Correspondence. ONE's General Correspondence files also include many more examples. Furthermore, the distribution records currently housed at the ONE Archive are incomplete, indicating that many more volunteer agents existed whose efforts cannot be documented here.

9. William to Dorr Legg, 5 December 1953, ONE General Correspondence.

10. Dorr Legg to Conrad, 18 November 1953, California Folder, ONE Regional Correspondence.

11. Eleanor to Guy, 12 May 1953, California Folder, ONE Regional Correspondence.

12. Eleanor to Dorr Legg, 30 November 1953, California Folder, ONE Regional Correspondence.

13. Eleanor to *ONE*, 18 January 1954, California Folder, ONE Regional Correspondence.

14. Allen Ginsberg interviewed by Allen Young, in Winston Leyland, ed., *Gay Sunshine Interviews*, vol. 1 (San Francisco, CA: Gay Sunshine Press, 1978), 119.

15. Dorr Legg to Conrad, 7 December 1953, California Folder, ONE Regional Correspondence.

16. Conrad to Dorr Legg, 20 December 1953, California Folder, ONE Regional Correspondence.

17. James to *ONE*, 20 February 1956, Missouri Folder, ONE Regional Correspondence.

18. Eric Marcus, *Making History: The Struggle for Gay and Lesbian Rights, 1945–1990, An Oral History* (New York: HarperCollins, 1992), 53.

19. Anonymous to Jody Shotwell, 23 March 1955, ONE General Correspondence.

20. *ONE* XI, 1 (January 1963), back cover; other cities were added to this list based on sales receipts. ONE Regional Correspondence and reader comments in ONE Regional Correspondence, ONE Social Service Correspondence, and ONE General Correspondence.

21. Dorr Legg to Andrew, 9 September 1955, Wisconsin Folder, ONE Regional Correspondence.

22. Dorr Legg to Joel Warner, 4 January 1954; Billy Glover to *ONE*, undated, California—Los Angeles Folder, ONE Regional Correspondence.

23. Central Magazine Sales, Ltd., distribution list, 1964, Maryland Folder, ONE Regional Correspondence.

24. John Jensen (Lucian Press) to *ONE*, 13 March 1961, California—Los Angeles Folder, ONE Regional Correspondence.

25. James L. Baughman, *The Republic of Mass Culture: Journalism, Filmmaking, and Broadcasting in America since 1941* (Baltimore, MD: Johns Hopkins University Press, 1997), 1, 64.

26. Mary Ellen Zuckerman, *A History of Popular Women's Magazines in the United States, 1792–1995* (Westport, CT: Greenwood Press, 1998), 204.

27. John D'Emilio and Estelle B. Freedman, *Intimate Matters: A History of Sexuality in America* (Chicago: University of Chicago Press, 1997), 280.

28. Marcus, *Making History*, 41.

29. Dal McIntire [Jim Kepner], "Tangents," *ONE* V, 9 (December 1957), 22; see also Daniel Harris, *The Rise and Fall of Gay Culture* (New York: Hyperion, 1997), 88.

30. *Bernarr MacFadden's Vitalized Physical Culture*, April 1953, 13. ONE, Inc., investigated Guy Mathews and found his "Dr." credentials lacking. *ONE* II, 4 (April 1954), 16–23.

31. Herbert Cohen to *ONE*, 23 May 1955, New York Folder, ONE Regional Correspondence.

32. Dorr Legg to Frank Kameny, 6 June 1961, ONE General Correspondence.

33. Ted's Book Shop to *ONE*, 19 July 1955, Missouri Folder, ONE Regional Correspondence.

34. Jerry to *ONE*, 10 June 1956, Missouri Folder, ONE Regional Correspondence.

35. Lawrence to *ONE*, 10 October 1964, ONE General Correspondence.

36. Marjorie Heins, *Not in Front of the Children: "Indecency," Censorship, and the Innocence of Youth* (New York: Hill and Wang, 2001), 60–88; Joyce Murdoch and Deb Price, *Courting Justice: Gay Men and Lesbians v. the Supreme Court* (New York: Basic Books, 2001), 27–50, 65–88; Paul S. Boyer, *Purity in Print: Book Censorship in America from the Gilded Age to the Computer Age* (Madison: University of Wisconsin Press, 2002), 270–290.

37. "Suggestive Magazine Quiz Opens, Held Up," *Los Angeles Times*, 26 November 1957, Censorship—1950s Folder, ONE Subject Files.

38. Brian to *ONE*, 12 May 1954, ONE General Correspondence.

39. Herbert Cohen (Periodical Distributors of Greater New York) to Robert Gregory, 23 May 1954, New York Folder, ONE Regional Correspondence.

40. *ONE Confidential* III, 1A (1958), 8; Alexander News Company to *ONE*, 23 August 1954, Minnesota Folder, ONE Regional Correspondence; Al to *ONE*, 5 May 1960, ONE General Correspondence.

41. Clipping in Censorship—1950s Folder, ONE Subject Files.

42. Neil to *ONE*, 20 February 1965, ONE General Correspondence.

43. "*Perversion for Profit 2/2*," accessed via the Internet 15 August 2011, http://www.youtube.com/watch?v=_GMMOBRqtLk. See also Edwin A. Roberts, *The Smut Rakers* (Silver Springs, MD: National Observer, 1966), 100–117.

44. John Tebbel and Mary Ellen Zuckerman, *The Magazine in America, 1741–1990* (New York: Oxford University Press, 1991), 244–246; David Abrahamson, *Magazine-Made America: The Cultural Transformation of the Postwar Periodical* (Cresskill, NJ: Hampton Press, 1996), 72; Dorr Legg to International Committee for Sexual Equality (Amsterdam, The Netherlands), 22 February 1955, Holland Folder, ONE Regional Correspondence. Legg reported 4,000 newsstand sales and 1,500 subscriptions in this letter, a ratio consistent with other estimates that appear in the documents over the years.

45. George to *ONE*, 24 April 1955, 1955–1956 Folder, ONE Social Service Correspondence.

46. Roger to *ONE*, 1 March 1956, ONE General Correspondence.

47. *ONE* IV, 4 (April–May 1956), 44.

48. For example, Bob to *ONE*, 7 April 1961, ONE General Correspondence.

49. Jeffrey Alan Jones used the phrase "The Circuit" to describe "a series of tea-rooms in downtown Lexington," Kentucky. In Los Angeles, it was known as "The Run." Jeffrey Alan Jones, "Hidden Histories, Proud Communities: Multiple Narratives in the Queer Geographies of Lexington, Kentucky, 1930–1999" (Ph.D. diss., University of Kentucky, Lexington, 2001); Daniel Hurewitz, *Bohemian Los Angeles and the Making of Modern Politics* (Berkeley: University of California Press, 2007), 48–49.

50. Swasarnt Nerf, *Gay Girl's Guide*, 49. Dorr Legg, in ONE Institute lecture notes, also wrote at length about the importance of public squares for gay male contacts.

51. Frank Golovitz, "Gay Beach," *ONE* VI, 7 (July 1958), 6.

52. On lesbian public space, see Elizabeth Lapovsky Kennedy and Madeline D. Davis, *Boots of Leather, Slippers of Gold: The History of a Lesbian Community* (New York: Routledge, 1993); Lillian Faderman, *Odd Girls and Twilight Lovers: A History of Lesbian Life in Twentieth-Century America* (New York: Columbia University Press, 1991), 159–187; Daneel Buring, *Lesbian and Gay Memphis: Building Communities Behind the Magnolia Curtain* (New York: Garland, 1997), 131–148.

53. *The Ladder* II, 6 (March 1958), 19; *The Ladder* IV, 5 (February 1960), 14–17; *The Ladder* VI, 5 (February, 1962), 6–11; *The Ladder* VIII, 5 (February 1964), 12, 14–19; Alison Klinger, "Writing Civil Rights: The Political Aspirations of Lesbian Activist-Writers," in Ellen Lewin, ed., *Inventing Lesbian Cultures in America* (Boston: Beacon Press, 1996), 62–80; Yvonne Keller, "Pulp Politics: Strategies of Vision in Pro-Lesbian Pulp Novels, 1955–1965," in Patricia Juliana Smith, ed., *The Queer Sixties* (New York: Routledge, 1999), 1–25; Jaye Zimet, *Strange Sisters: The Art of Lesbian Pulp Fiction, 1949–1969* (New York: Viking Studio, 1999); Susan Stryker, *Queer Pulp: Perverted Passions from the Golden Age of the Paperback* (San Francisco, CA: Chronicle Books, 2001).

54. *The Ladder* IV, 7 (April 1960), 23.

55. Zsa Zsa Gershick, *Gay Old Girls* (Los Angeles: Alyson Books, 1998), 132.

56. Gallo, *Different Daughters*, 96–97.

57. F. Valentine Hooven III, *Beefcake: The Muscle Magazines of America 1950–1970* (Cologne, Germany: Taschen, 1995), 54. The docudrama film *Beefcake*, adapted from this book, contains a superb newsstand scene.

58. Letters, *ONE* VI, 11 (November 1958), 30.

59. *ONE* IX, 1 (January 1961), 32.

60. N. Angle, *On the Corner: Stories from Twenty Years at a Chicago Newsstand* (New York: Exposition Press, 1957), 50.

61. Samuel to *ONE*, 31 January 1958, 1958 Folder, ONE Social Service Correspondence.

62. Bob to *ONE*, 23 April 1962, 1962 Folder, ONE Social Service Correspondence.

63. *ONE* VI, 10 (October 1958), 30.

64. *ONE* X, 11 (November 1962), 31.

65. O. E. to *ONE*, 7 October 1957, 1957 Folder, ONE Social Service Correspondence.

66. Jim to Robert Gregory, 29 May 1957, New York Folder, ONE Regional Correspondence.

67. California Folder, ONE Regional Correspondence.

68. Al to *ONE*, 5 May 1960, ONE General Correspondence.

69. Al to *ONE*, 31 July 1960, ONE General Correspondence.

70. Peter to *ONE*, 21 January 1962, ONE General Correspondence.

71. Frank Kameny Folder, ONE General Correspondence, especially Frank Kameny to Dorr Legg, 5 April 1961; James T. Sears, *Lonely Hunters: An Oral History of Lesbian and Gay Southern Life, 1948-1968* (Boulder, CO: Westview Press, 1997), 201.

72. *ONE Confidential* I, 1 (March 1956), 8.

73. Oscar to *ONE*, 20 February 1965, ONE General Correspondence.

74. Roy to *ONE*, 20 January 1963, ONE General Correspondence.

Chapter 3
Imagining a Gay World:
The American Homophile Movement in Global Perspective

1. In the correspondence examined in this study, there were *ONE* subscriptions from Algeria, Argentina, Australia, Brazil, Canada, Ceylon [Sri Lanka], Colombia, Denmark, El Salvador, Finland, France, Germany, Honduras, India, Indonesia, Israel, Italy, Japan, Kenya, the Netherlands, New Zealand, Norway, Peru, the Philippines, Saudi Arabia, Singapore, South Africa, Sweden, Switzerland, the United Kingdom, and Uruguay.

2. *ONE* III, 8 (August 1955), 24; Manfreddo to *ONE*, 17 December 1954, European Magazine Subs Folder, ONE Regional Correspondence; Dorr Legg to H., 27 September 1954, Mexico Folder, ONE Regional Correspondence; Austria Folder, ONE Regional Correspondence.

3. Letters, *ONE* VII, 2 (February 1960), 30-31.

4. Exceptions to this trend include Nicholas C. Edsall, *Toward Stonewall: Homosexuality and Society in the Modern Western World* (Charlottesville: University of Virginia Press, 2003); David S. Churchill, "Transnationalism and Homophile Political Culture in Postwar Decades," *GLQ* XV, 1 (2009), 31-65.

5. Daniel Robinson and David Kimmel, "The Queer Career of Homosexual Security Vetting in Cold War Canada," *Canadian Historical Review* LXXV, 3 (1994) 319-345; Barry Adam, "Winning Rights and Freedom in Canada," in Aart Hendriks, Rob Tielman, and Evert van der Veen, eds., *The Third Pink Book: A Global View of Lesbian and Gay Liberation and Oppression* (Buffalo, NY: Prometheus Books, 1993), 26-27.

6. Evan to *ONE*, 29 April 1958, Canada Folder, ONE Regional Correspondence; *ONE Confidential* III 1A (1958), 8.

7. D. T. to *ONE*, 24 February 1958, Canada Folder, ONE Regional Correspondence.

8. England Folder, ONE Regional Correspondence; Dan to Bill, 30 August 1960, 1962 Folder, ONE Social Service Correspondence; Sanford to *ONE*,

7 October 1960, ONE General Correspondence; Alexander to the Mattachine Society, 9 October 1953, Mattachine Foreign Correspondence 1953–55 Collection, ONE Archives.

9. Edsall, *Toward Stonewall*, 291.

10. Ibid., 293; Peter Wildeblood, *Against the Law* (New York: Julian Messner, 1959); Peter Wildeblood, *A Way of Life* (London: Weidenfield and Nicolson, 1956); Peter Wildeblood to *ONE*, 1 May 1956, ONE General Correspondence.

11. Peter Wildeblood to *ONE*, 1 May 1956, ONE General Correspondence.

12. Peter Wildeblood to *ONE*, 10 June 1956, ONE General Correspondence.

13. Scottish Home Department, "Report on the Committee on Homosexual Offences and Prostitution" (London: Her Majesty's Stationary Office, 1957); also published as *The Wolfenden Report* (New York: Lancer Books, 1964).

14. England Folder, ONE Regional Correspondence; Homosexual Law Reform Society Progress Reports, in Mattachine Society SF 1957–1968 Collection, Box 103–224.

15. Robert Aldrich, *Colonialism and Homosexuality* (London: Routledge, 2003), 235–238, quotation on 238.

16. Dorr Legg to C. E., 5 March 1963, 1963 Folder, ONE Social Service Correspondence; Dorr Legg to Gregory, 19 July 1961, Australia Folder, ONE Regional Correspondence.

17. Brian to *ONE*, 15 December 1964, ONE General Correspondence; anonymous to *ONE*, 23 March 1965, 1965 Correspondence Folder, ONE General Correspondence.

18. Marcia M. Gallo, *Different Daughters: A History of the Daughters of Bilitis and the Rise of the Lesbian Rights Movement* (New York: Carroll and Graf, 2006), 148.

19. M. S. to *ONE*, 21 March 1965, ONE General Correspondence.

20. Dr. W. A. to *ONE*, 13 November 1964, R Folder, ONE General Correspondence; Gordon Isaacs and Brian McKenndrick, *Male Homosexuality in South Africa: Identity Formation, Culture, and Crisis* (Cape Town: Oxford University Press, 1992).

21. Marvin Cutler [Dorr Legg], ed., *Homosexuals Today 1956* (Los Angeles: ONE, Inc., 1956), 154.

22. Peter.to *ONE*, 21 January 1963, ONE General Correspondence.

23. Edward to *ONE*, 11 August 1962, ONE General Correspondence.

24. Marc to the Mattachine Society, 9 October 1953, Mattachine Foreign Correspondence 1953–1955.

25. Robert Anderson, *Tea and Sympathy* (New York: Random House, 1953); George Chauncey, "Tea and Sympathy," in Mark Carnes, ed., *Past Imperfect: History According to the Movies* (New York: Holt, 1995), 258–261.

26. "Tea and Sympathy," *Der Kreis*, May 1954, 35–36.

27. John Lauritsen and David Thorstad, *The Early Homosexual Rights Movement (1864–1935)* (New York: Times Change Press, 1974); Charlotte Wolff, *Magnus Hirschfeld: A Portrait of a Pioneer in Sexology* (London: Quartet Books, 1987); Hubert Kennedy, *Ulrichs: The Life and Works of Karl Heinrich Ulrichs Pioneer of the Modern Gay Movement* (Boston: Alyson Books, 1988); Erwin Haeberle, "Swastika, Pink Triangle, and Yellow Star: The Destruction of Sexology and the

Persecution of Homosexuals in Nazi Germany," in Martin Duberman, Martha Vicinus, and George Chauncey, eds., *Hidden From History: Reclaiming the Gay and Lesbian Past* (New York: Signet, 1989), 365–379.

28. Cutler, ed., *Homosexuals Today 1956*, 109–176.

29. Paul to the Mattachine Society, 27 July 1953, Mattachine Foreign Correspondence 1953–1955. Italics added.

30. *ONE Confidential* II, 3 (August 1957), 13–13a.

31. Cutler, ed., *Homosexuals Today 1956*, 136.

32. *The Circle* [Der Kreis] to *ONE*, 26 May 1956, Germany Folder, ONE Regional Correspondence.

33. Rudolph [aka Karl Meier or Rolf] to Dorr Legg, 30 September 1960, Der Kreis Folder, ONE Regional Correspondence.

34. Cutler, ed., *Homosexuals Today 1956*, 171; ONE Archive Periodicals Collection.

35. Cutler, ed., *Homosexuals Today 1956*, 109–176.

36. Isaac to *ONE*, 17 November 1955, Denmark Folder, ONE Regional Correspondence.

37. Neilson to *ONE*, 7 August 1961, Denmark Folder, ONE Regional Correspondence; Cutler, ed., *Homosexuals Today 1956*, 150–152; Leila Rupp, "Transnational Homophile Organizing: The International Committee for Sexual Equality," paper delivered at the American Historical Association conference, Boston, Massachusetts, January 2011, 19–22.

38. *The Circle* [Der Kreis] to *ONE*, 26 May 1956, Germany Folder, ONE Regional Correspondence.

39. Jack Argo to *ONE*, 8 April 1955, Germany Folder, ONE Regional Correspondence.

40. Rudolph Burkhardt [Karl Meier], "Der Kreis," in Cutler, ed., *Homosexuals Today 1956*, 167.

41. Rupp, "Transnational Homophile Organizing," 8.

42. Cutler, ed., *Homosexuals Today 1956*, 142–46; Holland Folder, ONE Regional Correspondence.

43. Alex to *ONE*, 4 June 1956, Holland Folder, ONE Regional Correspondence.

44. Rupp, "Transnational Homophile Organizing," 13–14.

45. Dorr Legg to Rolf and Charles, 15 May 1958, Der Kreis Folder, ONE Regional Correspondence.

46. "Rudolph" to *ONE*, 29 May 1958, Der Kreis Folder, ONE Regional Correspondence.

47. "Rudolph" to Dorr Legg, 20 October 1964, Der Kreis Folder, ONE Regional Correspondence.

48. Mark McLelland, *Queer Japan from the Pacific War to the Internet Age* (Lanham, MD: Rowan and Littlefield, 2005), 70.

49. Ibid., 131.

50. Ibid., 133, 160.

51. Letters, *ONE* VII, 7 (July 1959), 31.

52. Bernardino del Boca di Villaregia ("Han Temple Org—Nawa Sangga") to *ONE*, 15 June 1956, European Magazine Subs Folder, ONE Regional Correspondence.

53. Robert Lindner, *Must You Conform?* (New York: Rinehart and Company, 1956), 66–72.

54. *Los Angeles Mattachine Society Newsletter*, II, 11 (December 1954).

55. Jim Kepner, "I Remember Chuck," unpublished essay, Chuck Rowland Folder, ONE Subject Files.

56. Aside from *The Keval* and *Homosexuals Today 1956*, ONE Press published only two additional books during the 1950s and 1960s: James Barr Fugaté's play *Game of Fools* and the bizarre science fiction novel *AE: The Open Persuader*.

57. Harry Otis, *The Keval and Other Gay Adventures* (Los Angeles: ONE, Inc., 1959); Harry Otis Oral History, 7 March 1982, videotape VV0454, ONE Oral History Collection.

58. Edward Said, *Orientalism* (New York: Vintage, 1979).

59. Churchill, "Transnationalism and Homophile Political Culture in the Postwar Decades," 48–57.

60. Otis, *The Keval*, 9.

61. Ibid., 38.

62. Ibid., 17.

63. Ibid., 58.

64. Ibid., 73.

65. Rudi Bleys, *The Geography of Perversion: Male-to-Male Sexual Behavior outside the West and the Ethnographic Imagination, 1750–1918* (New York: New York University Press, 1995); Robert Aldrich, *Colonialism and Homosexuality*.

66. Albert to *ONE*, 9 September 1964, ONE General Correspondence; 8 March 1965, 1964 Folder, ONE Social Service Correspondence.

67. Otis, *The Keval*, 34–35.

68. Ibid., 56.

69. On gay tourism, see Gordon Waitt and Kevin Markwell, *Gay Tourism: Culture and Context* (New York: Haworth Press, 2006).

70. Otis, *The Keval*, 69.

71. Otis, *The Keval*, 69–70.

72. Peter Drucker, " 'In the Tropics There Is No Sin': Sexuality and Gay Lesbian Movements in the Third World," *New Left Review* 218 (July-August 1996), 75–100; Andrew J. Rotter, "Gender Relations, Foreign Relations: The United States and South Asia, 1947–1964," *The Journal of American History* LXXXI, 2 (September 1994), 518–542; Said, *Orientalism*.

73. Letters, *ONE* IV, 6 (August-September 1956), 45. The writer's comment "not to be confused" refers to "tea-rooms," the American slang term for public restrooms where gay men have anonymous sex with one another.

74. Otis, *The Keval*, 60.

75. McLelland, *Queer Japan*, 160.

76. Rajiv to *ONE*, 20 November 1958, 1958 Folder, ONE Social Service Correspondence; *ONE* VII, 2 (February 1959), 29–30.

77. Ibid.

78. Robert Aldrich, *Colonialism and Homosexuality*, 285; see also Ruth Vanita, ed., *Queering India: Same-Sex Love and Eroticism in Indian Culture and Society* (New York: Routledge, 2002), 1–9.

79. Pablo to *ONE*, 30 May 1963 and 1 August 1963, ONE General Correspondence.

80. Bob Basker Interview, 1 July 1996, videotape VV0468, ONE Oral History Collection.

81. Pablo to *ONE*, 30 May 1963 and 1 August 1963, ONE General Correspondence.

82. Daniel Schluter, *Gay Life in the Former USSR: Fraternity without Community* (New York: Routledge, 2002); Igor S. Kon, "Gay and Lesbian Situation in Russia," unpublished paper, undated (1995 or later based on references), Russia Folder, ONE Subject Files.

83. Bret Hinsch, *Passions of the Cut Sleeve: The Male Homosexual Tradition in China* (Berkeley: University of California Press, 1990), 162–171.

84. See especially Hendriks et al., *The Third Pink Book*.

Chapter 4
ONE Magazine Letter Archetypes

1. William Eskridge, *Gaylaw: Challenging the Apartheid of the Closet* (Cambridge, MA: Harvard University Press, 2002), 66, 87.

2. Dorr Legg lecture notes, "Arrest: Consequences" Folder, ONE Institute lectures.

3. Eskridge, *Gaylaw*, 89–91.

4. Daniel Hurewitz, *Bohemian Los Angeles and the Making of Modern Politics* (Berkeley: University of California Press, 2007), 115–149; Nan Alamilla Boyd, *Wide Open Town: A History of Queer San Francisco to 1965* (Berkeley: University of California Press, 2003), 104. Other prominent case studies of gay police crackdowns intertwining with local politics include John Gerassi, *The Boys of Boise: Furor, Vice, and Folly in an American City* (New York: Collier Books, 1966); Fred Fejes, "Murder, Perversion, and Moral Panic: The 1954 Media Campaign against Miami's Homosexuals and the Discourse of Civic Betterment," *Journal of the History of Sexuality* IX, 3 (1999), 305–347; Neil Miller, *Sex-Crime Panic: A Journey to the Paranoid Heart of the 1950s* (Los Angeles: Alyson Books, 2002).

5. Eskridge, *Gaylaw*, 63, 78.

6. Athan G. Theoharis, *Chasing Spies: How the FBI Failed in Counterintelligence but Promoted the Politics of McCarthyism in the Cold War Years* (Chicago: Ivan R. Dee, 2002), 170–197.

7. David Johnson, *The Lavender Scare: The Cold War Persecution of Gays and Lesbians in the Federal Government* (Chicago: University of Chicago Press, 2004), 79–80, 84–92; Randolph W. Baxter, " 'Eradicating This Menace': Homophobia and Anti-Communism in Congress, 1947–1954" (Ph.D. diss., University of California, Irvine, 1999), 190–197.

8. John to *ONE*, 27 January 1961, 1961 Folder, ONE Social Service Correspondence.

9. Ibid.

10. Carl to *ONE*, 9 November 1964, ONE General Correspondence.

11. Joseph Styles, "Outsider/Insider: Researching Gay Baths," *Urban Life* VIII, Number 2 (July 1979), 139–152; George Chauncey, *Gay New York: Gender, Urban Culture and the Making of the Gay Male World 1890–1940* (New York: Basic Books, 1994), 217–218; Ira Tattelman, "Speaking to the Gay Bathhouse: Communicating in Sexually Charged Spaces," in William L. Leap, ed., *Public Sex/Gay Space* (New York: Columbia University Press, 1999), 75.

12. Dorr Legg to Carl, 11 November 1964, ONE General Correspondence.

13. Carl to *ONE*, 22 November 1964, ONE General Correspondence.

14. Eskridge, *Gaylaw*, 88; Dorr Legg lecture notes, Arrest: Consequences Folder, ONE Institute lectures.

15. Christopher to *ONE*, 8 October 1963, 1963 Folder, ONE Social Service Correspondence.

16. For example, see Will Fellows, *Farm Boys: Lives of Gay Men from the Rural Midwest* (Madison: University of Wisconsin Press, 1996).

17. Christopher to *ONE*, 8 October 1963, 1963 Folder, ONE Social Service Correspondence. Italics added.

18. On Cohn and his tendency to persecute gay people, see Sidney Zion, *The Autobiography of Roy Cohn* (Secaucus, NJ: Lyle Stuart, 1988); Nicholas Von Hoffman, *Citizen Cohn* (Toronto: Bantam, 1988); Michael Cadden, "Strange Angel: The Pinklisting of Roy Cohn," in Marjorie Garber and Rebecca Walkowitz, eds., *Secret Agents: The Rosenberg Case, McCarthyism, and Fifties America* (New York: Routledge, 1995), 93–105.

19. Carroll to *ONE*, 8 October 1963, 1963 Folder, ONE Social Service Correspondence.

20. Warren to *ONE*, 23 June 1964, 1964 Folder, ONE Social Service Correspondence.

21. Estelle Freedman, " 'Uncontrolled Desires': The Response to the Sexual Psychopath, 1920–1960," *Journal of American History* LXXIV, 1 (June 1987), 83–106.

22. Warren to *ONE*, 23 June 1964, 1964 Folder, ONE Social Service Correspondence.

23. Neil Miller, *Sex-Crime Panic: A Journey to the Paranoid Heart of the 1950s* (Los Angeles: Alyson Books, 2002).

24. Warren to *ONE*, 23 June 1964, 1964 Folder, ONE Social Service Correspondence.

25. Ibid.

26. Lawrence to *ONE*, 1 January 1955, ONE General Correspondence.

27. Al to *ONE*, 31 July 1960, ONE General Correspondence.

28. Al to *ONE*, 8 June 1962, ONE General Correspondence.

29. For an insightful review of *They Walk in Shadow*, see *The Ladder* III, 7 (April 1959), 18–20.

30. Lori to *ONE*, 30 December 1960, 1961 Folder, ONE Social Service Correspondence.

31. Ibid.

32. Daniel to *ONE*, 12 September 1963, 1963 Folder, ONE Social Service Correspondence.

33. Theodore to *ONE*, 5 February 1958, 1958 Folder, ONE Social Service Correspondence.

34. Joey to *ONE*, 27 October 1962, 1962 Folder, ONE General Correspondence.

35. Anonymous to *ONE*, 25 December 1961, 1961 Folder, ONE Social Service Correspondence.

36. Randolph to *ONE*, 10 December 1963, 1963 Folder, ONE Social Service Correspondence.

37. Clark to *ONE*, 30 July 1961, ONE General Correspondence.

38. Dal McIntire, "Tangents," *ONE* VI, 4 (April 1958), 19.

39. Clark to *ONE*, 30 July 1961, ONE General Correspondence.

40. Al to *ONE*, 12 November, 1960, ONE General Correspondence.

41. On the history of gay tourism in the United States, see Gordon Waitt and Kevin Markwell, *Gay Tourism: Culture and Context* (New York: Haworth Press, 2006), 58–63.

42. E. A. to *ONE*, 25 July 1959, 1959 Folder, ONE Social Service Correspondence.

43. Simon to *ONE*, 23 August 1956, ONE General Correspondence.

44. Dorr Legg to Simon, 10 September 1956, ONE General Correspondence.

45. Dorr Legg to Arthur, 28 September 1965, ONE General Correspondence.

Chapter 5
'Branded Like a Horse':
Homosexuality, the Military, and Work

1. Allen Drury, *Advise and Consent* (Garden City, NY: Doubleday, 1959); see also Parker Tyler, *Screening the Sexes: Homosexuality in the Movies* (New York: Holt, Rinehart, and Winston, 1972), 67–69; Vito Russo, *The Celluloid Closet: Homosexuality in the Movies* (New York: Harper and Row, 1981), 120–122, 141–143.

2. Peter Hegarty, "Homosexual Signs and Heterosexual Silences: Rorschach Research on Male Homosexuality from 1921 to 1969," *Journal of the History of Sexuality* XII, 3 (July 2003), 400–423.

3. Survey 166, ONE Institute "Homosexual Bill of Rights" Survey, 1961.

4. On World War II's influence on the black civil rights movement, see Robert Cook, *Sweet Land of Liberty? The African-American Struggle for Civil Rights in the Twentieth Century* (New York: Longman, 1998), 71–82.

5. These statistics exclude the regional correspondence files because those letters were largely focused on *ONE*'s distribution. Thus, this 13 percent figure is based on the 812 letters used in this study from the social service and general correspondence files. See the appendix and bibliography for further explanation.

6. Minutes, "Committee on Social Service—Initial Meeting of 2/25/58," 1958 Folder, ONE Social Service Correspondence.

7. "A Survey of Job and Related Problems Faced by Homosexuals," undated, prepared by Social, Educational Research and Development, Inc., of Silver

Spring MD, 4, 11. A copy of the report is in Employment—Gays (II) Folder, ONE Subject Files.

8. "The Deviate and His Job," *Chicago Area Mattachine Society Newsletter* II, 1 (March 1955).

9. Lonnie to *ONE*, 11 August 1960, ONE General Correspondence.

10. Ray to *ONE*, 12 December 1957, ONE General Correspondence.

11. Greg to *ONE*, 21 September 1962, ONE General Correspondence.

12. Maria De La O, "Lesbians in Corporate America," in Karla Jay, ed., *Dyke Life: A Celebration of the Lesbian Experience* (New York: Basic Books, 1995), 265–281; Trisha Franzen, *Spinsters and Lesbians: Independent Womanhood in the United States* (New York: New York University Press, 1996), 45; Gillian Dunne, *Lesbian Lifestyles: Women's Work and the Politics of Sexuality* (Toronto: University of Toronto Press, 1997), 92–126; M. V. Lee Bladgett, *Money, Myths, and Change: The Economic Lives of Lesbians and Gay Men* (Chicago: University of Chicago Press 2001), 111.

13. Manuela Soares, "The Purloined *Ladder*: Its Place in Lesbian History," in Sonya Jones, ed., *Gay and Lesbian Literature since World War II* (New York: Haworth Press, 1998), 31.

14. "Toward Understanding," *ONE* VIII, 2 (February 1960), 24–25.

15. Ibid. See also William Parker, "Homosexuals and Employment," distributed by the Lincoln-Omaha Council on Religion and Homosexual, Employment—General Folder, ONE Subject Files, 11; Christian Arthur Bain, "A Short History of Lesbian and Gay Labor Activism in the United States," in Gerald Hunt, ed., *Laboring for Rights: Unions and Sexual Diversity across Nations* (Philadelphia, PA: Temple University Press, 1999), 59.

16. For example, Joel to *ONE*, 12 November 1957, 1958 Folder, ONE Social Service Correspondence; A. V. to *ONE*, 26 June 1960, 1960 Folder, ONE Social Service Correspondence.

17. *The Ladder* VI, 8 (May 1962), 10, 23; M. P. Feldman, "Aversion Therapy for Sexual Deviations: A Critical Review," *Psychological Bulletin* LXV, 2 (February 1966), 65–79; Martin Weinberg and Alan Bell, *Homosexuality: An Annotated Bibliography* (New York: Harper and Row, 1972).

18. John Colin Williams, "Discharges from the Military: An Examination of Labeling Theory" (Ph.D. diss., Rutgers University, 1970), 213.

19. Allan Bérubé, *Coming Out under Fire: The History of Gay Men and Women in World War Two* (New York: Plume, 1990), 201, 262–270; Williams, "Discharges from the Military," 48, 74–79.

20. Williams, "Discharges from the Military," 40–41.

21. *The Ladder* I, 9 (June 1957), 18.

22. Williams, "Discharges from the Military," 41–42.

23. File 706, Box 2213, Confidential Decimal File, July 1955–June 1956, RG 159 (Records of the Inspector General's Office), National Archives and Records Administration (College Park, MD). I thank Margot Canaday for sharing this document with 'me.

24. Memo, Bureau of Naval Personnel, 6 October 1953, Military—1950s Folder, ONE Subject Files.

25. Williams, "Discharges from the Military," 37–38.

26. Elson to *ONE*, 30 August 1960, ONE General Correspondence.
27. Jesse to *ONE*, 27 January 1961, 1961 Folder, ONE Social Service Correspondence. On antihomosexual lectures in the military, see Bérubé, *Coming Out under Fire*, 263–264.
28. Wayne to *ONE*, 29 May 1959, ONE General Correspondence.
29. Sean to *ONE*, 19 December 1963, ONE General Correspondence.
30. Dorr Legg to Sean, 4 February 1964, ONE General Correspondence.
31. Williams, "Discharges from the Military," 43–47.
32. File 706, Box 2213, Confidential Decimal File, July 1955–June 1956, RG 159.
33. "Discharge for Homosexual Acts or Tendencies," Air Force Regulation No. 35–66, 23 July 1956, Department of the Air Force, 13. Italics in original.
34. Dan to *ONE*, 23 August 1960, 1960 Folder, ONE Social Service Correspondence.
35. Edward to *ONE*, 8 March 1960, ONE General Correspondence.
36. Rosalyn Baxandall and Linda Gordon with Susan Reverby, eds., *America's Working Women: A Documentary History* (New York: Norton, 1995), 270–276.
37. Gordon to ONE, Inc., 10 May 1970, 1970 Folder, ONE Social Service Correspondence.
38. Jack to *ONE*, 9 November 1964, ONE General Correspondence.
39. Timothy to *ONE*, 27 March 1958, 1958 Folder, ONE Social Service Correspondence.
40. Leisa D. Meyer, *Creating G.I. Jane: Sexuality and Power in the Women's Army Corps during World War II* (New York: Columbia University Press, 1996), 171.
41. Ronald to *ONE*, 26 March 1963, 1963 Folder, ONE Social Service Correspondence.
42. Meyer, *Creating G.I. Jane*, 171; Williams, "Discharges from the Military," 48.
43. Letters, *ONE* IX, 3 (March 1961), 29.
44. *The Ladder* II, 3 (December 1957), 17–18.
45. Tim to *ONE*, 24 June 1961, 1961 Folder, ONE Social Service Correspondence.
46. Tim to *ONE*, 2 July 1961, 1961 Folder, ONE Social Service Correspondence.
47. Ibid.
48. Ibid.
49. Ibid.
50. Ibid.
51. Tim to *ONE*, 24 June 1961, 1961 Folder, ONE Social Service Correspondence.
52. Carroll W. Pursell Jr., ed., *The Military-Industrial Complex* (New York: Harper and Row, 1972), 204–208; Sam C. Sarkesian, ed., *The Military-Industrial Complex: A Reassessment* (Beverly Hills, CA: Sage, 1972); Stuart W. Leslie, *The Cold War and American Science: The Military-Industrial-Academic Complex at MIT and Stanford* (New York: Columbia University Press, 1993).
53. Tom Engelhardt, *The End of Victory Culture: Cold War America and the Disillusioning of a Generation* (New York: Basic Books, 1995), 119; see also

Chicago Area Mattachine Society Newsletter II, 3 (May 1955); William H. Whyte, *The Organization Man* (Garden City, NY: Doubleday Anchor Books, 1956), 191–192, 206–207; Williams, "Discharges from the Military," 214.

54. Mattachine Pioneers Panel, 1 June 1986, VV0059, ONE Oral History Collection.

55. "A Decade of Progress in the Homophile Movement," *ONE* VII, 2 (November 1962), 6.

56. John to *ONE*, 23 February 1959, 1959 Folder, ONE Social Service Correspondence.

57. John to *ONE*, 2 March 1959, 1959 Folder, ONE Social Service Correspondence.

58. John to *ONE*, 20 March 1959, 1959 Folder, ONE Social Service Correspondence.

59. Dorr Legg to James, 23 March 1959, 1959 Folder, ONE Social Service Correspondence.

60. Williams, "Discharges from the Military," 257.

61. Andy to President Dwight Eisenhower, carbon copy sent to *ONE*, 21 March 1960, 1960 Folder, ONE Social Service Correspondence.

Chapter 6
Classroom Anxieties: Educators and Homosexuality

1. Robert Anderson, *Tea and Sympathy* (New York: Random House, 1953), 26–27.

2. David Gerstner, "The Production and Display of the Closet: Making Minnelli's *Tea and Sympathy*," *Film Quarterly* L, 3 (Spring 1997), 13–26.

3. Ruth Fassbinder, "And Gladly Teach: Lesbian and Gay Issues in Education," in Louis Diament, ed., *Homosexual Issues in the Workplace* (Washington, DC: Taylor and Francis, 1993), 119.

4. Jackie Blount, *Fit to Teach: Same-Sex Desire, Gender, and School Work in the Twentieth Century* (Albany: SUNY Press, 2005); Karen M. Harbeck, *Gay and Lesbian Educators: Personal Freedoms, Public Constraints* (Malden, MA: Amethyst Press, 1997).

5. Blount, *Fit to Teach*, 59, 77.

6. *Los Angeles Herald-Examiner*, 15 January 1954, Homosexual Scandals Folder, ONE Subject Files. The article noted that the principal paid a $150 fine and served five days in jail.

7. Herb to *ONE*, 14 August 1963, P Folder, ONE General Correspondence.

8. D. O. Cauldwell, *Private Letters from Homosexuals to a Doctor* (Girard, KS: Haldeman-Julius Publications, 1949), 6. Other examples include Edward to *ONE*, 8 March 1960, ONE General Correspondence; Survey 249, ONE Institute "Homosexual Bill of Rights" Survey, 1961; Letters, *The Ladder* IV, 7 (April 1960), 25.

9. Eric Marcus, *Making History: The Struggle for Gay and Lesbian Rights, 1945–1990, An Oral History* (New York: Harper Collins, 1992), 40.

10. Sarah to *ONE*, 23 August 1964, P Folder, ONE General Correspondence.

11. Wendy to *ONE*, 4 June 1964, ONE General Correspondence.

12. Canada Folder, ONE Regional Correspondence.

13. Ed to *ONE*, 30 January 1963, ONE General Correspondence.

14. Franklin to *ONE*, 23 January 1961, ONE General Correspondence; see also Robert to *ONE*, 24 March 1963, ONE General Correspondence; and John to *ONE*, 5 December 1961, ONE General Correspondence.

15. *ONE Confidential* V, 2 (February 1960), 1.

16. "The Successful Homosexual," *ONE* VII, 5 (May 1959), 6.

17. Harbeck, *Gay and Lesbian Educators*, 188–189.

18. Dorr Legg to John, December 1961, 1961 Folder, ONE Social Service Correspondence.

19. Harbeck, *Gay and Lesbian Educators*, 197–207.

20. Pete to *ONE*, 19 February 1965, 1965 Folder, ONE Social Service Correspondence.

21. Marcus, *Making History*, 45.

22. Lillian Faderman, *Odd Girls and Twilight Lovers: A History of Lesbian Life in Twentieth-Century America* (New York: Columbia University Press, 1991), 164–166; Elizabeth Lapovsky Kennedy and Madeline D. Davis, *Boots of Leather, Slippers of Gold: The History of a Lesbian Community* (New York: Routledge, 1993), 35, 146–150.

23. At the time, the word "provost" indicated executive leadership of the University of California, Santa Barbara. The university later adopted the word "chancellor" for the same position.

24. "Biographical Information," Clark G. Kuebler Case, Miscellaneous Correspondence, Biography, 1955 Folder, Office of the Chancellor, Chancellor's Records, Box 1, University Archives, University of California, Santa Barbara (hereafter, UCSB Archives). See also "Report Card," 23 August 1954, *Time* online, accessed via Internet on 8 June 2007, http://www.time.com/time/magazine/article/0,9171,823504,00.html.

25. Henry Machirella and Sidney Kline, "West Coast Educator Faces Court on Cop Morals Charge," *Los Angeles Daily News,* 7 November 1955, Entrapment Folder, ONE Subject Files.

26. See clippings in Clark Kuebler, Clippings Folder, Office of the Chancellor, Chancellor's Records, Box 1, UCSB Archives.

27. "Memo to Staff," 7 November 1955, Clark Kuebler, Clippings Folder, UCSB Archives.

28. Widely quoted in clippings, see also University of California Academic Senate Record, Northern Section II, 3 (7 November 1955), accessed via Internet on 7 June 2007, http://content.cdlib.org/xtf/view?docId=hb796nb4kn&brand=calisphere&doc.view= entire_text. Italics added.

29. Quoted in UP-AP wire story about Kuebler's arrest in many newspapers, 5 November 1955; see clippings at UCSB Archives.

30. According to Harry Otis, Lexington Avenue was considered "fashion row" in the 1930s and was commonly associated with gay men. "Harry Otis: A Very Gay Life," 7 March 1982, VV0454, ONE Oral History Collection. A letter from

1954 also mentions a high level of gay male visibility on Lexington Avenue. See Letters, *ONE* II, 5 (May 1954), 28.

31. Machirella and Kline, "West Coast Educator Faces Court on Cop Morals Charge"; *Chicago Tribune*, 7 November 1955, Entrapment Folder, ONE Subject Files.

32. "Educator Upheld in Morals Case," 11 November 1955, *New York Times*; "Allegations against Cop in Kuebler Case Probed," 11 November 1955, *San Francisco Examiner*, Entrapment Folder, ONE Subject Files.

33. "Educator Upheld in Morals Case," 11 November 1955, *New York Times*.

34. Compiled from clippings in Clark Kuebler, Clippings Folder, UCSB Archives.

35. "College Head Explains His Resignation," 18 December 1955, *Long Beach Independent-Press-Telegram*, Entrapment Folder, ONE Subject Files.

36. Verne A. Stadtman, *The Centennial Record of the University of California* (Oakland: University of California Regents, 1967), 487. Accessed via Internet on June 7, 2007, http://content.cdlib.org/xtf/view?docId=hb4v19n9zb&chunk.id=div00969&brand=oac&doc.view=entire_text.

37. James Schnur, "Closet Crusaders: The Johns Committee and Homophobia, 1956–1965," in John Howard, ed., *Carryin' On in the Lesbian and Gay South* (New York: New York University Press, 1997), 132–133.

38. Gerard Sullivan, "Political Opportunism and the Harassment of Homosexuals in Florida, 1952–1965," *Journal of Homosexuality* XXXVII, 4 (1999), 63–65, 74.

39. James T. Sears, *Lonely Hunters: An Oral History of Lesbian and Gay Southern Life, 1948–1968* (Boulder, CO: Westview Press, 1997), 81.

40. Schnur, "Closet Crusaders," 141.

41. Sears, *Lonely Hunters*, 75.

42. Ibid., 59–75, 88–92.

43. Schnur, "Closet Crusaders," 137–141.

44. Sears, *Lonely Hunters*, 75.

45. Stacy Braukman, " 'Nothing Else Matters But Sex': Cold War Narratives of Deviance and the Search for Lesbian Teachers in Florida, 1959–1963," *Feminist Studies* XXVII (2001), 553–577.

46. Paul to *ONE*, 16 April 1959, ONE General Correspondence. The date on the letter was written as "1958," however, the date stamped on the letter at the time *ONE* magazine received it is 1959, and the events he is describing occurred after April 1958.

47. Harold to *ONE*, 23 January 1960, ONE General Correspondence.

48. Fred to *ONE*, 17 May 1962, ONE General Correspondence.

49. Dal McIntire, "Tangents," *ONE* VII, 3 (March 1959), 16.

50. Jonathan to *ONE*, 22 August 1963, ONE General Correspondence.

51. Sears, *Lonely Hunters*, 94.

52. Patrick to *ONE*, 19 March 1964, C Folder, ONE General Correspondence.

53. Clifford to *ONE*, 14 February 1965, 1964 Folder, ONE Social Service Correspondence.

54. Dorr Legg lecture notes, "Hx Marriage" Folder, ONE Institute lectures, ISHR Collection.

55. For example, Surveys 53, 249, ONE Institute "Homosexual Bill of Rights" Survey, 1961; Pete and Tom to *ONE*, 23 March 1963, 1963 Folder, ONE Social Service Correspondence.

56. Brandon to *ONE*, 21 December 1963, ONE General Correspondence.

57. John Howard, *Men like That: A Southern Queer History* (Chicago: University of Chicago Press, 1999), 69.

58. Patrick Dilley, "Which Way Out? A Typology of Non-Heterosexual Male Collegiate Identities," *Journal of Higher Education* LXXVI, 1 (January-February 2005), 71.

59. Bib 'N Tucker to *ONE*, 13 January, 1954, California Folder, ONE Regional Correspondence.

60. Meredith Eliassen, *San Francisco State University* (Charleston, SC: Arcadia Publishing, 2007), 37.

61. Ibid., 82; "Alumni and Friends," *San Francisco State Alumni Magazine* VII, 2 (Spring 2007), accessed via Internet on 26 August 2009, http://www.sfsu.edu/~sfsumag/archive/spring_07/alumni9.html.

62. Letters from college students that mentioned loneliness include Edward to *ONE*, 17 November 1958, 1958 Folder, ONE Social Service Correspondence; Robert to *ONE*, 30 November 1961, 1961 Folder, ONE Social Service Correspondence; G. T. to *ONE*, 18 April 1962, 1962 Folder, ONE Social Service Correspondence; Joey to *ONE*, 27 October 1962, 1962 Folder, ONE Social Service Correspondence; Randolph to *ONE*, 10 December 1963, 1963 Folder, ONE Social Service Correspondence; Nathan to *ONE*, 6 May 1963, 1963 Folder, ONE Social Service Correspondence; Max to *ONE*, 18 November 1964, 1964 Folder, ONE Social Service Correspondence.

63. Fred to *ONE*, 10 May 1961, ONE General Correspondence.

64. Harry Hay to Dorr Legg, 15 May 1958, ONE General Correspondence.

65. Brett Beemyn, "The Silence Is Broken: A History of the First Lesbian, Gay, and Bisexual College Student Groups," *Journal of the History of Sexuality* XII, 2 (April 2003), 206.

66. Survey 11, ONE Institute "Homosexual Bill of Rights" Survey, 1961.

67. Robert to *ONE*, 11 November 1964, P Folder, ONE General Correspondence. A letter from a sociology student at Nebraska State Teachers College expressed the same sentiment. See Henry to *ONE*, 2 February 1965, ONE General Correspondence.

68. James to *ONE*, 16 January 1962, ONE General Correspondence.

69. Dorr Legg lecture notes, Cruising Folder, ONE Institute lectures. Legg taught architecture at the University of Oregon during the 1930s and early 1940s, giving him firsthand experience negotiating academic culture as a gay man. Dorr Legg Interview, 1994, videotape VV0465, ONE Oral History Collection; Wayne Dynes, "W. Dorr Legg," in Vern Bullough, ed., *Before Stonewall: Activists for Gay and Lesbian Rights in Historical Context* (New York: Harrington Park Press, 2002), 97.

70. Nicholas to *ONE*, 10 April 1964, T Folder, ONE General Correspondence.

71. Richard to *ONE*, 6 July 1962, 1962 Folder, ONE Social Service Correspondence.

72. Dan to Dorr Legg, 17 July 1962, ONE General Correspondence.

73. Brandon to *ONE*, 21 December, 1963, ONE General Correspondence.

74. Nicholas C. Edsall, *Toward Stonewall: Homosexuality and Society in the Modern Western World* (Charlottesville: University of Virginia Press, 2003), 160.

75. Letters, *The Ladder* IV, 7 (April 1960), 25.

76. Survey 249, ONE Institute "Homosexual Bill of Rights" Survey, 1961.

77. Jess Luther, "The Force," *ONE* VII, 7 (July 1959), 17, 20.

Chapter 7
Family Anxieties: Parent and Family Responses to Homosexual Disclosures

1. Robert Anderson, *Tea and Sympathy* (New York: Random House, 1953), 50.

2. Arlene Skolnick, *Embattled Paradise: The American Family in an Age of Uncertainty* (New York: Basic Books, 1991), 72.

3. Elaine Tyler May, *Homeward Bound: American Families in the Cold War Era* (New York: Basic Books, 1988); Jessica Weiss, *To Have and To Hold: Marriage, the Baby Boom, and Social Change* (Chicago: University of Chicago Press, 2000).

4. Norm to *ONE*, 13 September 1962, 1962 Folder, ONE Social Service Correspondence.

5. Ron to *ONE*, 23 February 1965, 1964 Folder, ONE Social Service Correspondence.

6. Clifford to *ONE*, 14 February 1965, 1964 Folder, ONE Social Service Correspondence.

7. Bill to *ONE*, 24 January 1964, 1964 Folder, ONE Social Service Correspondence.

8. Marijane Meaker, *Highsmith: A Romance of the 1950s* (San Francisco, CA: Cleis Press, 2003), 25. Italics in original.

9. Simon to *ONE*, 23 August 1956, ONE General Correspondence.

10. Survey 138, ONE Institute "Homosexual Bill of Rights" Survey, 1961.

11. Marvin to *ONE*, 29 May 1958, 1958 Folder, ONE Social Service Correspondence.

12. "Dear Mom and Dad," *Denver Mattachine Society Newsletter* IV, 5 (May 1960), 10.

13. Ibid., 11. "Invert" was a word used for homosexuals primarily among turn-of-the-century sexologists such as Havelock Ellis. At the time, sexologists believed that homosexuality was explained by gender inversion. The term was somewhat archaic in the 1950s, but some heterosexual experts and gay people still used the term.

14. Ibid., 12.

15. Ibid., 12.

16. R. A. to *ONE*, 10 April 1958, 1958 Folder, ONE Social Service Correspondence. An edited version of the letter appeared in *ONE* VI, 8 (August 1958), 29.

17. *ONE* VII, 4 (April 1959), 31.

18. Laurie Heatherington and Justin A. Lavner, "Coming to Terms with Coming Out: Review and Recommendations for Family Systems-Focused Research," *Journal of Family Psychology* XXII, 3 (June 2008), 329–343.

19. Frances LaSalle, "Night for Decision," *The Ladder* II, 3 (December 1957), 10–15; see also Randy Shephard, "Familiar Strangers," *ONE* VIII, 5 (May 1960), 14–16.

20. Alfred Kinsey, Wardell Pomeroy, and Clyde Martin, *Sexual Behavior in the Human Male* (Philadelphia: Saunders, 1948), 650–651.

21. Ray Evans to Pete and Tom, 27 March 1963, 1963 Folder, ONE Social Service Correspondence.

22. Pete and Tom to *ONE*, 23 March 1963, 1963 Folder, ONE Social Service Correspondence.

23. Review of *A Minority: A Report on the Life of the Male Homosexual in Great Britain*, by Gordon Westwood, *ONE* VIII, 9 (September, 1960), 18–19.

24. Darden Asbury Pyron, *Liberace: An American Boy* (Chicago: University of Chicago Press, 2000).

25. James Barr Fugaté to Jody Shotwell, 23 October 1954, James Barr [Fugaté] Folder III, ONE Subject Files.

26. Eric Marcus, *Making History: The Struggle for Gay and Lesbian Rights, 1945–1990, An Oral History* (New York: HarperCollins, 1992), 75.

27. Lance to *ONE*, 11 March 1965, 1964 Folder, ONE Social Service Correspondence.

28. Letters, *ONE* XI, 5 (May 1963), 30.

29. Arthur to *ONE*, 18 June 1964, WES Folder, ONE General Correspondence.

30. Mrs. "Glen" to *ONE*, 20 August 1963, 1963 Folder, ONE Social Service Correspondence.

31. Ibid.

32. Steve to *ONE*, 8 September 1963, 1963 Folder, ONE Social Service Correspondence.

33. Reverend Bernard Newman, Abbot, St. George Monastery, Las Vegas, to Steve, 1964 Folder, ONE Social Service Correspondence.

34. John to *ONE*, 26 February 1962, 1962 Folder, ONE Social Service Correspondence.

35. Daryl to *ONE*, 24 November 1961, 1961 Folder, ONE Social Service Correspondence.

36. For example, see D. J. West, *Homosexuality* (Middlesex, UK: Penguin Books, 1968), 220–226.

37. Anne Fredericks, "One Parent's Reaction," *The Ladder* V, 11 (August 1961), 4–7.

38. Letters, *Physique Pictorial* VII, 1 (Spring 1957), 4.

39. See especially Edmund Bergler, *Homosexuality: Disease or Way of Life?* (New York: Hill and Wang, 1957).

40. Elaine Tyler May, *Barren in the Promised Land: Childless Americans and the Pursuit of Happiness* (New York: Basic Books, 1995), 18–19, 127–134.

41. Jessica Weiss, "Making Room for Fathers: Men, Women, and Parenting in the United States, 1945–1980," in Laura McCall and Donald Yacovone, eds., *A Shared Experience: Men, Women, and the History of Gender* (New York: New York University Press, 1998), 349–367; Skolnick, *Embattled Paradise*, 69–71.

42. Steven Mintz and Susan Kellogg, *Domestic Revolutions: A Social History of American Family Life* (New York: Free Press, 1988), 188.

43. Fred Brown and Rudolph Kempton, "Sex Answers and Questions: A Guide to Happy Marriage" (New York: McGraw Hill, 1950). The pamphlet was a condensed version of a book of the same name. A copy is filed in the Sex Education Folder, ONE Subject Files.

44. Peter Nardi, David Sanders, and Judd Marmor, *Growing Up before Stonewall: Life Stories of Some Gay Men* (London: Routledge, 1994), 50.

45. Philip Wylie, *Generation of Vipers* (New York: Rinehart, 1942).

46. Jessica Weiss, "Making Room for Fathers," in McCall and Yacovone, eds., *A Shared Experience*, 349–367.

47. "Flight from Masculinity," *Picture Week*, 3 January 1956, 32, Gender Identity and Roles I Folder, ONE Subject Files.

48. *San Francisco Examiner*, 2 June 1960. Clipping in Bachelors Folder, ONE Subject Files.

49. "Man Must Rule Home—Expert," *Los Angeles Times,* 11 November 1960, Gender Identity and Roles I Folder, ONE Subject Files.

50. Ted Berkman, "The Third Sex—Guilt or Sickness?" *Coronet* magazine, November 1955, 133. See also Skolnick, *Embattled Paradise*, 70.

51. Charlotte Patterson, "Family Relationships of Lesbians and Gay Men," *Journal of Marriage and the Family* LXII, 4 (November 2000), 1063.

52. Ibid.

Chapter 8
Homosexuals and Marriage under the Shadow of McCarthy

1. Robert Anderson, *Tea and Sympathy* (New York: Random House, 1953), 35.

2. Ibid., 123.

3. E. B. Saunders, "Reformer's Choice: Marriage License or Just License?" *ONE* I, 8 (August 1953), 11.

4. J. M. Underwood, "388 North American Male Homosexuals: A Sociological and Attitudes Study, Section Two," Unpublished Report, May 1969, 7–8. The report was based on the 1961 ONE Institute "Homosexual Bill of Rights" Survey questionnaires and is filed with the questionnaires at the ONE Archive in Los Angeles. The questionnaires were distributed in *ONE*'s April 1961 issue.

5. "DOB Questionnaire Reveals Some Facts about Lesbians," *The Ladder* III, 12 (September 1959), 12–13.

6. Elaine Tyler May, *Homeward Bound: American Families in the Cold War Era* (New York: Basic Books, 1988) 183–207; Jessica Weiss, *To Have and to Hold: Marriage, the Baby Boom, and Social Change* (Chicago: University of Chicago Press, 2000).

7. Dorr Legg lecture notes, Avoidance Folder, ONE Institute lectures.

8. "Toward Understanding," *ONE* VII, 6 (June 1959), 26.

9. *Denver Mattachine Society Newsletter* I, 5 (November 1957), 7.

10. Letters, *ONE* X, 10 (October 1962), 30.

11. Letters, *ONE* X, 12 (December 1962), 31.

12. H. Laurence Ross, "Modes of Adjustment of Married Homosexuals," *Social Problems* XVIII (1971), 388.

13. This was reported in several letters; see also Michael W. Ross, *The Married Homosexual Man* (London: Routledge, 1983), 121.

14. Clipping dated 9 January 1956 from unidentified newspaper, on file in Paul Coates Folder, ONE Subject Files.

15. *Denver Mattachine Society Newsletter* I, 1 (July 1957).

16. Ross, "Modes of Adjustment of Married Homosexuals," 390.

17. "Should Homosexuals Marry?" *The Ladder* III, 8 (May 1959), 21–23.

18. "DOB Questionnaire Reveals Some Facts about Lesbians," *The Ladder* III, 12 (September 1959), 12–13.

19. Marcia M. Gallo, *Different Daughters: A History of the Daughters of Bilitis and the Rise of the Lesbian Rights Movement* (New York: Carroll and Graf Publishers, 2006), 73.

20. Miriam Gardner, "Behind the Borderline," *The Ladder* V, 1 (October 1960), 7. On youthful marriages in the 1950s, see Weiss, *To Have and to Hold*, 15–48.

21. Gardner, "Behind the Borderline," 11.

22. Nancy Osborne, "One Facet of Fear," *The Ladder* I, 9 (June 1957), 6–7.

23. Marion Zimmer Bradley, "Some Remarks on Marriage," *The Ladder* I, 10 (July 1957), 15–16.

24. "DOB Questionnaire Reveals Some Facts about Lesbians," 14. On social pressures for women to bear children in the 1950s, see Elaine Tyler May, *Barren in the Promised Land: Childless Americans and the Pursuit of Happiness* (New York: Basic Books, 1995).

25. Bradley, "Some Remarks on Marriage," 14.

26. "Readers on Writers," *ONE* VI, 10 (October 1958), 25.

27. "Raising Children in a Deviant Relationship," *The Ladder* I, 1 (October 1956), 9; *The Ladder* I, 4 (January 1957), 4.

28. Daniel Rivers, "'In the Best Interests of the Child': Lesbian and Gay Parenting Custody Cases, 1967–85," *Journal of Social History* XLIII, 4 (Summer 2010), 917–943.

29. James to *ONE*, 25 November 1960, 1960 Folder, ONE Social Service Correspondence.

30. Vince to *ONE*, 23 April 1955, 1955–1956 Folder, ONE Social Service Correspondence.

31. Survey 205, ONE Institute "Homosexual Bill of Rights" Survey, 1961.

32. Dr. Alfred Blazer, "Men Who Can't Marry (And How to Detect Them)," *Pageant*, August 1954, 118–123. Clipping in "Gender Identity and Roles" Folder I, ONE Subject Files.

33. Marlon to *ONE*, 15 February 1961, 1961 Folder, ONE Social Service Correspondence.

34. *Los Angeles Daily News*, 10 November 1953, Homosexual Scandals Folder, ONE Subject Files.

35. Four newspaper clippings describe this incident: *Los Angeles Herald-Express*, 5 November 1953; *Los Angeles Daily News*, 10 November 1953 and 9 December 1953; and *Los Angeles Times*, 9 December 1953. See Homosexual Scandals Folder, ONE Subject Files.

36. Robert to *ONE*, 4 March 1965, ONE General Correspondence.

37. Louis to *ONE*, 20 January 1955, Michigan Folder, ONE Regional Correspondence. See also John Loughery, *The Other Side of Silence* (New York: Holt, 1998), 161.

38. For example, see John to *ONE*, 2 December 1957, ONE General Correspondence.

39. Laud Humphries found in the late 1960s that 54 percent of the men he surveyed that had gay sex in public restrooms were in opposite-sex marriages. Laud Humphries, *Tearoom Trade: Impersonal Sex in Public Places* (Hawthorne, NY: Aldine Publishing, 1970), 105.

40. Mr. A. V. to *ONE*, 26 June 1960, 1960 Folder, ONE Social Service Correspondence.

41. Survey 330, ONE Institute "Homosexual Bill of Rights" Survey, 1961.

42. "DOB Questionnaire Reveals Some Facts about Lesbians," 12.

43. Marijane Meaker, *Highsmith: A Romance of the 1950s* (San Francisco, CA: Cleis Press, 2003), 132.

44. Marjorie Garber, *Bisexuality and the Eroticism of Everyday Life* (New York: Routledge, 2000), 392–419; Ivan Hill, ed., *The Bisexual Spouse: Different Dimensions in Human Sexuality* (McLean, VA: Barlina Books, 1987).

45. Garber, *Bisexuality*, 251.

46. Shane Phelan, *Sexual Strangers: Gays, Lesbians, and Dilemmas of Citizenship* (Philadelphia, PA: Temple University Press, 2001), 115–138.

47. Garber, *Bisexuality*, 21.

48. "DOB Questionnaire Reveals Some Facts about Lesbians," 17–18.

49. Jess Stearn, *The Grapevine* (Garden City, NY: Doubleday, 1964), 127.

50. Underwood, "388 North American Male Homosexuals," 1.

51. According to U.S. Census data from 1950 and 1960, approximately two-thirds of total American adults older than age fifteen were married. Data accessed online on 18 September 2009, www.census.gov/population/www/socdemo/hh-fam.html.

52. Herman Lynn Womack to *ONE*, 26 July 1962, ONE General Correspondence. On Womack's case, see Joyce Murdoch and Deb Price, *Courting Justice: Gay Men and Lesbians v. the Supreme Court* (New York: Basic Books, 2001), 65–66.

53. Marcel Martin, *ONE* IX, 11 (November 1961), 7.

54. Randy Lloyd, "Let's Push Homophile Marriage," *ONE* XI, 6 (June 1963), 10.

55. Ibid., 5–6.

56. Ibid., 6–7.

57. Letters, *ONE* XI, 9 (September 1963), 29.

58. Jody Shotwell, "Gay Wedding," *The Ladder* VII, 5 (February 1963), 4–5. See also a description of a lesbian wedding in Roey Thorpe, "The Changing Face of Lesbian Bars in Detroit, 1938–1965," in Brett Beemyn, *Creating a Place for Ourselves: Lesbian, Gay, and Bisexual Community Histories* (New York: Routledge, 1997), 170. Jim Kepner witnessed a gay male wedding ceremony at the Mark Hopkins Hotel in San Francisco in 1942. Jim Kepner, *Rough News, Daring Views: 1950s' Pioneer Gay Press Journalism* (New York: Haworth Press, 1998), 2.

59. "Toward Understanding," *ONE* VII, 12 (December 1959), 24.

60. Surveys 191/192, ONE Institute "Homosexual Bill of Rights" Survey, 1961.

61. Curtis to *ONE*, 16 December 1959, ONE General Correspondence.

62. Surveys 191/192, ONE Institute "Homosexual Bill of Rights" Survey, 1961.

63. For examples of domestic themes see, "Steve Wengryn at Home," *Physique Pictorial* VIII, 1 (Spring 1958), 16–17; "A Visit from a Cousin," VIII, 1 (Spring 1958), 29; "Brother Cinder-Elmer," IX, 1 (Spring 1959), 30; "What's Cooking" and "Helpful Guest," X, 3 (January 1961), 23; "At Home," XI, 2 (November 1961), 4; and "The Cruel Stepbrothers," XII, 2 (November 1962), 21.

64. *Physique Pictorial* X, 4 (April 1961), 30–31.

65. For examples see, "That's Not Music! That's My Brother" and "Bathroom Athlete," *Physique Pictorial* V, 3 (Fall 1955, 15, 16); "Down on the Farm," VI, 1 (Spring 1956), 17; "T.V. Bachelors," VI, 2 (Summer 1956), 19; "A Stitch in Time," VII, 1 (Spring 1957), 16; "2: A.M. Daddy," VII, 1 (Spring 1957), 18; and "The Young Carpenters," VII, 3 (Fall 1957), 18.

66. *Physique Pictorial* X, 4 (April 1961), 30. On Art-Bob, see F. Valentine Hooven, III, *Beefcake: The Muscle Magazines of America 1950–1970* (Cologne, Germany: Taschen, 1995), 90–91.

67. *Physique Pictorial* VII, 1 (Spring 1957), 18.

68. Joanne Meyerowitz, *Women Adrift: Independent Wage Earners in Chicago, 1880–1930* (Chicago: University of Chicago Press, 1988), 95; Meaker, *Highsmith*, 28.

69. Bill to *ONE*, 7 September 1960, 1960 Folder, ONE Social Service Correspondence.

70. Darden Asbury Pyron, *Liberace: An American Boy* (Chicago: University of Chicago Press, 2000).

71. Dorr Legg lecture notes, Prostitution Folder, ONE Institute lectures.

72. Anthony Summers, *Official and Confidential: The Secret Life of J. Edgar Hoover* (New York: G. P. Putnam's Sons, 1993), 80–95, 240–258. Summers has made the most forceful case that Hoover was homosexual, but most historians agree that his evidence is flimsy, including David K. Johnson, author of *The Lavender Scare: The Cold War Persecution of Gays and Lesbians in the Federal*

Government (Chicago: University of Chicago Press, 2004), and Robert Dean, *Imperial Brotherhood: Gender and the Making of Cold War Foreign Policy* (Amherst: University of Massachusetts Press, 2001). See a review of Summers's book in the *London Times*, 7 March 1993, which finds the evidence questionable. Curt Gentry in *J. Edgar Hoover: The Man and His Secrets* (New York: Plume, 1991) similarly does not take the homosexual rumors very seriously in this more than 800-page biography of Hoover. But the rumors have been etched in the public imagination due to a 1993 PBS *Frontline* television special based on Summers's book.

73. Athan Theoharis, *J. Edgar Hoover, Sex, and Crime: An Historical Antidote* (Chicago: Ivan R. Dee, 2002), 23–55.

74. Gentry, *J. Edgar Hoover*, 190; Athan Theoharis and John Stuart Cox, *The Boss: J. Edgar Hoover and the Great American Inquisition* (New York: Bantam, 1988), 123.

75. Jack Lait and Lee Mortimer, *Washington Confidential* (New York: Dell, 1951), 34, 120.

76. *San Francisco Chronicle*, 23 May 1972, J. Edgar Hoover Folder, ONE Subject Files; Gentry, *J. Edgar Hoover*, 691–692.

77. Gentry notes parenthetically that Tolson "often hinted at a romance with a chorus girl during his early years in the capitol," but Gentry emphasizes, as with Hoover, Tolson's perpetual bachelorhood. Gentry, *J. Edgar Hoover*, 190.

78. *Frontline: The Secret File on J. Edgar Hoover*, written and directed by William Cran, 1993, produced by PBS.

79. Jim Egan, "Homosexual Marriage: Fact or Fancy?" *ONE* VII, 12 (December 1959), 9.

80. Ibid.

Chapter 9
"I shall always cherish Sunday"

1. Donny to *ONE*, 29 January 1964, 1964 Folder, ONE Social Service Correspondence.

2. Thaddeus Russell, "The Color of Discipline: Civil Rights and Black Sexuality," *American Quarterly* LX, 1 (March 2008), 101–128; Elijah G. Ward, "Homophobia, Hypermasculinity and the U.S. Black Church," *Culture, Health & Sexuality* VII, 5 (September-October 2005), 493–504; Horace Griffin, "Their Own Received Them Not: African American Lesbians and Gays in Black Churches," in Delroy Constantine-Simms, ed., *The Greatest Taboo: Homosexuality in Black Communities* (Los Angeles: Alyson Books, 2000), 116; Cathy J. Cohen, *The Boundaries of Blackness: AIDS and the Breakdown of Black Politics* (Chicago: University of Chicago Press, 1999), 35; George Chauncey, *Gay New York: Gender, Urban Culture, and the Making of the Gay Male World, 1890-1940* (New York: Basic Books, 1994), 244–266.

3. Patrick J. Egan and Kenneth Sherrill, "California's Proposition 8: What Happened, and What Does the Future Hold?" National Gay and Lesbian Task

Force Policy Institute, 2009, 2; Irene Monroe, "Proposition 8 and Black Homophobia," *Gay and Lesbian Review Worldwide* XVI, 1 (January-February 2009), 6.

4. M. V. Lee Badgett and Mary King, "Lesbian and Gay Occupational Strategies," in Amy Gluckman and Betsy Reed, eds., *Homo Economics: Capitalism, Community, and Lesbian and Gay Life* (New York: Routledge, 1997), 81.

5. For example, see Leroy to *ONE*, 6 April 1955, ONE General Correspondence; Marvin to *ONE*, 29 May 1958, 1958 Folder, ONE Social Service Correspondence.

6. Chauncey, *Gay New York*, 47–63; Timothy J. Gilfoyle, *City of Eros: New York City, Prostitution, and the Commercialization of Sex, 1790–1920* (New York: Norton, 1992); Kevin White, *The First Sexual Revolution: The Emergence of Male Heterosexuality in Modern America* (New York: New York University Press, 1993).

7. The male and female Kinsey Reports largely discredited gender inversion theories. See Stephanie Hope Kenan, "Scientific Studies of Human Sexual Difference in Interwar America" (Ph.D. diss., University of California, Berkeley, 1998), 14–15; Steve Valocchi, "The Class-Inflected Nature of Gay Identity," *Social Problems* XLVI, 2 (1999), 215.

8. Russell, "The Color of Discipline," 103.

9. Tim Retzloff, " 'Seer or Queer?' Postwar Fascination with Detroit's Prophet Jones," *Gay and Lesbian Quarterly* 8 (2002), 271–296.

10. *Denver Mattachine Society Newsletter* I, 2 (August 1957), 21.

11. Whether "sassies" was a misspelling of "sissies" or whether "sassies" was deliberately used as a slang word for gay men is unclear. I have found no evidence of the word "sassies" being used to describe gay men in these years in any other sources.

12. E. Patrick Johnson, "Feeling the Spirit in the Dark: Expanding Notions of the Sacred in the African American Gay Community," in Constantine-Simms, ed., *The Greatest Taboo*, 92–93.

13. See for example Wallace D. Best, *Passionately Human, No Less Divine: Religion and Culture in Black Chicago, 1915–1952* (Princeton, NJ: Princeton University Press, 2005), 188–189.

14. The text says "Dercular."

15. Parker Tyler, *Screening the Sexes: Homosexuality in the Movies* (New York: Holt, Rinehart, and Winston, 1972), 68–70.

16. Joseph Hansen, "Suicide and the Homosexual," *ONE* XIII, 5 (May 1965), 5–7.

17. Herbert Hendin, *Black Suicide* (New York: Basic Books, 1969), 5, 47–71; Herbert Hendin, *Suicide in America* (New York: Norton, 1995), 129–145.

18. See clippings in Suicide Folder, ONE Subject Files.

19. Emile Durkheim, *Suicide: A Study in Sociology*, translated by Donny A. Spaulding and George Simpson (Glencoe, IL: Free Press, 1951), 260.

20. *The Ladder* III, 2 (November 1958), 23–24.

21. For example, see Gary L. Atkins, *Gay Seattle: Stories of Exile and Belonging* (Seattle: University of Washington Press, 2003), 34–52.

22. Estelle Freedman, "'Uncontrolled Desires': The Response to the Sexual Psychopath, 1920–1960," *Journal of American History* LXXIV, 1 (June 1987), 83–106; George Chauncey, "The Postwar Sex Crime Panic," in William Graebner, ed., *True Stories from the American Past* (New York: McGraw-Hill, 1993), 160–178; Stephen Robertson, "Separating the Men from the Boys: Masculinity, Psychosexual Development, and Sex Crime in the United States, 1930s–1960s," *Journal of the History of Medicine and Allied Sciences* LVI, 1 (January 2001), 3–35.

23. Neil Miller, *Sex-Crime Panic: A Journey to the Paranoid Heart of the 1950s* (Los Angeles: Alyson Books, 2002), 77–88.

24. Warren to *ONE*, 23 June 1964, 1964 Folder, ONE Social Service Correspondence; Ronny to *ONE*, 15 September 1959, 1959 Folder, ONE Social Service Correspondence; Survey 226, ONE Institute "Homosexual Bill of Rights" Survey, 1961; *Miami News*, 12 April 1956, in Miami 1956 Folder, ONE Subject Files; *Daily Iowan*, 30 March 1956, Psychiatry and Gays Folder, ONE Subject Files; *ONE* XIII, 3 (March 1965), 3–6.

25. Sidney Bronstein to *ONE*, 29 January 1955 and 8 February 1955, Sidney Bronstein Folder II, ONE Subject Files.

26. Atascadero State Hospital Folder, ONE Subject Files; Atascadero Hospital Inmates, "The New Approach . . . Sex Offender to Good Citizen," in Pamphlets Collection, ONE Archives; Louis Frisbee, "Recidivism among Treated Sex Offenders: A Study of 1921 Male Discharges from a California State Hospital" (State of California's Department of Mental Health, 1963), in Mattachine Society San Francisco Collection, Box 103–224, ONE Archives; *San Francisco Mattachine Society Newsletter* 15, 15 August 1954; *San Francisco Mattachine Society Newsletter* 22, 15 March 1955.

27. Bronstein to *ONE*, 8 February 1955.

28. Murray Wexler, "The Relationship between Personality Organization and Electroshock: A Comparative Study of the Personality Characteristics of Psychotic Patients Who Improve or Do Not Improve from Electroshock Therapy" (Ph.D. diss., New York University, 1953), 107–108.

29. Wexler, "The Relationship between Personality Organization and Electroshock," 217; K. Freund, "Some Problems in the Treatment of Homosexuality," in H. J. Eysenck, ed., *Behavior Therapy and the Neuroses: Readings in Modern Methods of Treatment Derived from Learning Theory* (Oxford, UK: Pergamon Press, 1967); Lothar B. Kalinowsky, Hanns Hippius, and Helmfried E. Klein, *Biological Treatments in Psychiatry* (New York: Grune and Stratton, 1982); 269.

30. Electro-Shock Therapy Folder, ONE Subject Files; Irwin Spector, "A 'Cure' for Homosexuality," *Popular Psychology* (September 1972); Karl Bowman, "The Problem of Homosexuality," January 1953, reprinted from the *Journal of Social Hygiene*, Pamphlets Collection; M. P. Feldman and M. J. MacCullogh, "The Application of Anticipatory Avoidance Learning to the Treatment of Homosexuality," *Behavior Research and Therapy*, 2 (1965), 165–183; M. P. Feldman, "Aversion Therapy for Sexual Deviations: A Critical Review," *Psychological Bulletin* 65, 2 (February 1966), 65–79.

31. Marvin Cutler to Donny, 30 January 1964, 1964 Folder, Social Service Correspondence.

32. John Howard, *Men like That: A Southern Queer History* (Chicago: University of Chicago Press, 1999), 56.

33. Griffin, "Their Own Received Them Not," 116; Reginald Shepherd, "Coloring Outside the Lines: An Essay at Definition," in Smith, ed., *Fighting Words*, 27.

34. Marvin to *ONE*, 29 May 1958, 1958 Folder, ONE Social Service Correspondence.

35. *ONE* II, 6 (June 1954), 20; Survey 250, ONE Institute "Homosexual Bill of Rights" Survey, 1961.

36. Jim Kepner, "Gay Love, Christian Love, and the Bible," unpublished essay, Religion Binder, Jim Kepner Papers Box 103–127; Kepner, Editorial, *ONE* VIII, 12 (December 1960), 4–5. See also Henry George, "Pastoral Counseling for Homosexuals," (1951), reprinted from *Pastoral Psychology*, January 1951.

37. Letters, *ONE* VIII, 12 (December 1960), 30.

38. For example, see Kenneth Ross, "Letter to a Homosexual" (London: Society for the Promotion of Christian Knowledge, 1955), 8.

39. *The Ladder* VI, 4 (January 1962), 19.

40. Survey 129, ONE Institute "Homosexual Bill of Rights" Survey, 1961.

41. Survey 106, ONE Institute "Homosexual Bill of Rights" Survey, 1961; other examples include Survey 93, ONE Institute "Homosexual Bill of Rights" Survey, 1961; Edward to *ONE*, 8 March 1960, ONE General Correspondence.

42. Rev. Gene to *ONE*, 3 March 1963, R Folder, ONE General Correspondence.

43. Letters, *ONE* III, 3 (March 1955), 42.

44. Rev. L. to *ONE*, 30 April 1958, ONE General Correspondence.

45. Letters, *ONE* VI, 2 (February 1958), 30.

46. Marcia M. Gallo, *Different Daughters: A History of the Daughters of Bilitis and the Rise of the Lesbian Rights Movement* (New York: Carroll and Graf, 2006), 105–111.

47. Hal Call Folder, ONE Subject Files.

48. Survey 183, ONE Institute "Homosexual Bill of Rights" Survey, 1961.

49. Jim Kepner Interview, VV0005, ONE Oral History Collection; see also Survey 152, ONE Institute "Homosexual Bill of Rights" Survey, 1961.

50. Letters, *ONE* II, 6 (June 1954), 27.

51. C. F. to *ONE*, 9 June 1964, R Folder, ONE General Correspondence.

52. For examples, see Gary to *ONE*, 10 December 1960, ONE General Correspondence; Survey 245, ONE Institute "Homosexual Bill of Rights" Survey, 1961; *New York Mattachine Society Newsletter* 16 (September 1957).

53. Daniel to *ONE*, 19 February 1961, 1961 Folder, ONE Social Service Correspondence.

54. Daniel to *ONE*, 22 April 1961, 1961 Folder, ONE Social Service Correspondence.

55. Letters, *ONE* VIII, 12 (December 1960), 30.

56. Nick to *ONE*, 2 October 1962, T Folder, ONE General Correspondence.

57. J. L. to *ONE*, 24 January 1955, Florida Folder, ONE Regional Correspondence.

58. Mike to *ONE*, 13 February 1965, U Folder, ONE General Correspondence.

59. Rev. George to *ONE*, 6 September 1954, ONE General Correspondence.

Chapter 10
Unacceptable Mannerisms: Gender, Sexuality, and Swish in Postwar America

1. Thomas P. Adler, *Robert Anderson* (Boston: Twayne Publishers, 1978), 76.

2. Geoffrey Shurlock to Joseph Breen, 26 August 1955, *Tea and Sympathy* MPA Production Code Folder, Margaret Herrick Library, Academy of Motion Picture Arts and Sciences Archive.

3. On the adaptation of *Tea and Sympathy*, see George Chauncey, "Tea and Sympathy," in Mark Carnes, ed., *Past Imperfect: History According to the Movies* (New York: Holt, 1995), 258–261; David Gerstner, "The Production and Display of the Closet: Making Minnelli's *Tea and Sympathy*," *Film Quarterly* L, 3 (Spring 1997), 13–26; Jerold Simmons, "The Production Code: Under New Management: Geoffrey Shurlock, *The Bad Seed*, and *Tea and Sympathy*," *Journal of Popular Film and Television* XXII, 1 (Spring 1999), 2–10.

4. William Attwood, George B. Leonard Jr., and J. Robert Moskin, *The Decline of the American Male* (New York: Random House, 1958); K. A. Cuordileone, " 'Politics in the Age of Anxiety': Cold War Political Culture and the Crisis in American Masculinity, 1949–1960," *Journal of American History* LXXXVII (September 2000), 515–545; James Gilbert, *Men in the Middle: Searching for Masculinity in the 1950s* (Chicago: University of Chicago Press, 2005).

5. George Chauncey, *Gay New York: Gender, Urban Culture, and the Making of the Gay Male World, 1890–1940* (New York: Basic Books, 1994), 47–63.

6. Daniel Harris, *The Rise and Fall of Gay Culture* (New York: Hyperion, 1997), 35.

7. Steve Valocchi, "The Class-Inflected Nature of Gay Identity," *Social Problems* XLVI, 2 (1999), 207–224.

8. James Barr [Fugaté], "In Defense of Swish," *Der Kreis* (January 1955), 40.

9. For example, see Cathy J. Cohen, "Black Sexuality, Indigenous Moral Panics, and Respectability: From Bill Cosby to the Down Low," in Gilbert Herdt, *Moral Panics, Sex Panics: The Fight over Sexual Rights* (New York: New York University Press, 2009), 104–129.

10. Shane Phelan, *Sexual Strangers: Gays, Lesbians, and Dilemmas of Citizenship* (Philadelphia, PA: Temple University Press, 2001), 115–138.

11. *The Lavender Lexicon: Dictionary of Gay Words and Phrases* (San Francisco, CA: Strait and Associates, 1964).

12. *The Lavender Lexicon.*

13. Survey 330, ONE Institute "Homosexual Bill of Rights" Survey, 1961; Lou to *ONE*, 25 November 1958, 1958 Folder, ONE Social Service Correspondence. Italics added.

14. *ONE* II, 5 (May 1954), 28. Italics added.

15. *Oxford English Dictionary*, online edition (www.oed.com).

16. J. M. Underwood, "388 North American Male Homosexuals: A Sociological and Attitudes Study, Section Two," unpublished report, May 1969, ONE Archive.

17. *Denver Mattachine Society Newsletter* II, 8 (August 1958), 4–6.

18. *The Ladder* VIII, 10 (July 1964), 7–9.

19. Survey 253, ONE Institute "Homosexual Bill of Rights" Survey, 1961.

20. Marcel Martin, "The Homosexual Stereotype," *ONE* IX, 9 (September 1961), 7.

21. Peter Genung, "A Heterosexual Viewpoint," *ONE* IX, 10 (Oct. 1961), 26–27. Stepin Fetchit enjoyed a successful 1930s film career playing characters who reinforced racist stereotypes that blacks were stupid and childlike. On Stepin Fetchit, see Donald Bogle, *Toms, Coons, Mulattoes, Mammies, and Bucks: An Interpretative History of Blacks in American Films* (New York: Continuum, 1989), 38–44.

22. David K. Johnson, *The Lavender Scare: The Cold War Persecution of Gays and Lesbians in the Federal Government* (Chicago: University of Chicago Press, 2004), 199–206.

23. Dorr Legg to ICSE (International Committee for Sexual Equality), 22 February 1955, Holland Folder, ONE Regional Correspondence.

24. *ONE Confidential* VIII, 3 (March 1964), 1–2; Dorr Legg, "Counseling the Homosexual," unpublished draft, 51, ONE Institute/IHSR Collection.

25. David Russell and Dalvan McIntire, "In Paths Untrodden: A Study of Walt Whitman," *ONE* II, 7 (July 1954), 13, 15.

26. Whitman seminar documents in ONE/ISHR Collection; Walt Whitman Guidance Center pamphlet draft in Social Service Center Folder, ONE Social Service Correspondence. The Walt Whitman Guidance Center never got past the planning stages.

27. Frankie Almitra, "Why Not Compromise?" *ONE* VII, 5 (May 1959), 15–16.

28. Joan Nestle, *A Restricted Country* (Ithaca, NY: Firebrand Books, 1987); Elizabeth Lapovsky Kennedy and Madeline Davis, *Boots of Leather, Slippers of Gold: The History of a Lesbian Community* (New York: Routledge, 1993); Lillian Faderman, *Odd Girls and Twilight Lovers: A History of Lesbian Life in Twentieth-Century America* (New York: Columbia University Press, 1991), 159–187.

29. For example, "The Lesbian Partnership," *The Ladder* II, 5 (February 1958), 18–19.

30. Barbara Stephens, "Transvestitism, a Cross-Cultural Survey" *The Ladder* I, 9 (June 1957), 10–14.

31. *The Ladder* I, 8 (May 1957), 20.

32. Marcia M. Gallo, *Different Daughters: A History of the Daughters of Bilitis and the Rise of the Lesbian Rights Movement* (New York: Carroll and Graf, 2006), 22–24.

33. Cuordileone, " 'Politics in the Age of Anxiety,' " 516.

34. "Are American Men becoming Sissies?" *Man's Day*, July 1956, Gender Identity and Roles Folder, ONE Subject Files.

35. On the Bill of Rights meeting, see R. E. L. Masters, *The Homosexual Revolution* (New York: Julian Press, 1962), 119–128; "Homosexual Bill of Rights Sizzles and Fizzles," *The Ladder* V, 6 (March 1961), 8–25.

36. Surveys 166, 195, 162, 116, 194, and 401, ONE Institute "Homosexual Bill of Rights" Survey, 1961.

37. *The Ladder* VI, 7 (April 1962), 6.

38. Alex to *ONE*, 10 February 1957, ONE General Correspondence.

39. John to *ONE*, 26 February 1962, 1962 Folder, ONE Social Service Correspondence.

40. Damon Pythias [Jim Kepner], *ONE* II, 3 (March 1954), 7–11.

41. James Martin Douglas, "The Margin of Masculinity," *ONE* III, 5 (May 1955), 10–13.

42. Letter from H. D. to *ONE*, 26 October 1954, and letter from H. D. to Robert Gregory, 28 October 1954, 1953–1954 Folder, ONE Social Service Correspondence.

43. *Physique Pictorial*, 10 (June 1960), 13. On male physique magazines, see F. Valentine Hooven III, *Beefcake: The Muscle Magazines of America 1950–1970* (Cologne, Germany: Taschen, 1995); Harris, *The Rise and Fall of Gay Culture*, 86–110; Christopher Nealon, *Foundlings: Lesbian and Gay Historical Emotion before Stonewall* (Durham, NC: Duke University Press, 2001), 99–140.

44. "Letters," *ONE* 9 (February 1963), 30.

45. Isaac to *ONE*, 18 April 1964, ONE General Correspondence.

46. "Letters," *ONE* 6 (March 1958), 30.

47. William H. Whyte, *The Organization Man* (Garden City, NY: Doubleday, 1956); David Riesman with Nathan Glazer and Reuel Denney, *The Lonely Crowd: A Study of the Changing American Character* (New Haven, CT: Yale University Press, 1961).

48. David Van Leer, *The Queening of America: Gay Culture in Straight Society* (New York: Routledge, 1995), 20; on camp see Susan Sontag, "Notes on Camp," in Sontag, *Against Interpretation* (New York: Dell, 1969), 277–293; Jack Babuscio, "Camp and the Gay Sensibility," in Richard Dyer, ed., *Gays and Film* (New York: Zoetrope, 1982), 40–57; Mark Booth, *Camp* (London: Quartet Books, 1983); Andrew Ross, "Uses of Camp," in Ross, *No Respect: Intellectuals and Popular Culture* (New York: Routledge, 1989), 135–170; David Bergman, *Gaiety Transfigured: Gay Self-Representation in American Literature* (Madison: University of Wisconsin Press, 1991), 103–121; Esther Newton, *Mother Camp: Female Impersonators in America* (Chicago: University of Chicago Press, 1972), 36, 56, 104–111.

49. Leslie to *ONE*, 5 May 1964, W Folder, ONE General Correspondence.

50. "Letters," *ONE* II, 9 (November 1954), 25; see also Rodger Streitmatter, *Unspeakable: The Rise of the Gay and Lesbian Press in America* (Boston: Faber and Faber, 1995), 25.

51. For examples of reader complaints about swishy overtones, see published letters in *ONE* II, 5 (May 1954), 28; II, 9 (November 1954), 25; III, 4 (April 1955), 6–7; III, 9 (September 1955), 26; IV, 1 (January 1956), 28; IV, 3 (March 1956), 28; V, 7 (August-September 1957), 30; VI, 4 (April 1958), 29–30; VI, 5 (May 1958), 30; VI, 6 (June 1958), 30; VI, 7 (July 1958), 30; VI, 10 (October 1958), 30; VII, 2 (February 1959), 28; VII, 6 (June 1959), 29, 31–32; VII, 12 (December 1959), 30; VIII, 5 (May 1960), 29.

52. Saul K., "Jingle, You Belles You!" *ONE* I, 12 (December 1953), 15–17. Other stories with swishy overtones include Double IX, "The Undividable Heart,"

ONE IV, 7 (October–November 1956); and K. O. Neal, "The Junk Dealer," *ONE* VIII, 3 (March 1960).

53. James to *ONE*, 5 June 1963, 1963 Folder, ONE Social Service Correspondence.

54. Ibid.

Conclusion

1. Howard to Dorr Legg, 26 January 1955; Dorr Legg to Howard, 2 February 1955; Dorr Legg to Howard, 21 October 1957, 1955–1956 Folder, ONE Social Service Correspondence.

2. Will to *ONE*, 30 August 1961, ONE General Correspondence. Italics added.

3. Jess Stearn, *The Grapevine* (Garden City, NY: Doubleday, 1964), 288.

4. Jon Margolis, *The Last Innocent Year: America in 1964, The Beginning of the Sixties* (New York: Perennial, 1999), viii.

5. Paul Welch, "Homosexuality in America," *Life* (26 June 1964), 66–74, 76–80; see also Martin Meeker, *Contacts Desired: Connecting to the Gay Male and Lesbian World from the 1940s into the 1970s* (Chicago: University of Chicago Press, 2006), 151–161.

6. Edward Alwood, *Straight News: Gays, Lesbians and the News Media* (New York: Columbia University Press, 1996), 50; see also Bradley Usher, "Federal Civil Service Employment Discrimination against Gays and Lesbians, 1950–1975: A Policy and Movement History" (Ph.D. diss., New School for Social Research, 1999), 140.

7. Susan Stryker, *Queer Pulp: Perverted Passions from the Golden Age of the Paperback* (San Francisco, CA: Chronicle Books, 2001), 97, 109.

8. C. Todd White, *Pre-Gay L.A.: A Social History of the Movement for Homosexual Rights* (Urbana: University of Illinois Press, 2009), 116–174; "*ONE, Incorporated vs. Donald Rutherford Slater et al.*," *ONE Confidential* XII, 5 (May 1967), 1–12; Vern Bullough, ed., *Before Stonewall: Activists for Gay and Lesbian Rights in Historical Context* (New York: Harrington Park Press, 2002), 99–101, 109–113, 117–118, 121–123.

9. "The Madness Multiplies," *ONE* XIII, 5 (May 1965), 5–7, 10–12.

10. On *Drum*, see Marc Stein, *City of Sisterly and Brotherly Loves: Lesbian and Gay Philadelphia, 1945–1972* (Philadelphia, PA: Temple University Press, 2004), 231–240.

11. W. Dorr Legg, *Homophile Studies in Theory and Practice* (San Francisco, CA: GLB Publishers and ONE Institute Press, 1994). Other homophile stalwarts adapted better to the changing times. Jim Kepner wrote prolifically for the new generation of gay liberation publications, and Mattachine founder Harry Hay organized the free-spirited "Radical Faeries" in the 1970s.

12. Elizabeth A. Armstrong, *Forging Gay Identities: Organizing Sexuality in San Francisco, 1950–1994* (Chicago: University of Chicago Press, 2002); Ian

Lekus, "Queer and Present Dangers: Homosexuality and American Antiwar Activism during the Vietnam Era" (Ph.D. diss., Duke University, 2003); Justin David Suran, "Coming Out against the War: Antimilitarism and the Politicization of Homosexuality in the Era of Vietnam," *American Quarterly* LIII, 3 (September 2001), 452–488.

13. Marcia Gallo, *Different Daughters: A History of the Daughters of Bilitis and the Rise of the Lesbian Rights Movement* (New York: Carroll and Graf, 2006), 130–136.

14. Suran, "Coming Out against the War," 452–461.

15. Meeker, *Contacts Desired.*

16. Randy Shilts, The *Mayor of Castro Street: The Life and Times of Harvey Milk* (New York: St. Martin's Griffin, 2008).

17. James H. Jones, *Alfred C. Kinsey: A Public/Private Life* (New York: Norton, 1997); Jonathan Gathorne-Hardy, *Sex the Measure of All Things: A Life of Alfred C. Kinsey* (Bloomington: Indiana University Press, 1998).

18. Lyn Pedersen [Jim Kepner], "A Tribute to Alfred Kinsey," *ONE* IV, 6 (August-September 1956), 7, 7–12; Dorr Legg to Rudolph, 30 August 1956, Der Kreis (Zurich) Folder, ONE Regional Correspondence; *ONE Confidential* II, 7 (April 1958), 14–15.

Sources and Bibliography

Note on Primary Sources

At the time I conducted my research, the ONE National Gay and Lesbian Archive in Los Angeles held two separate correspondence collections. The collection used for this book was labeled "Old Correspondence" and consisted of four file-cabinet drawers of letters written from 1952 to 1965. I examined between 3,000 and 4,000 letters from this collection and extracted information from 1,083 letters written by 735 individuals. I used letters that contained personal information, thoughts, or opinions, and I ignored letters that focused solely on subscribing to the magazine. The second collection of ONE, Inc., correspondence filled more than a dozen file-cabinet drawers and represented thousands more people than the "Old Correspondence" collection. This second collection contained correspondence from 1952 into the 1990s, and the majority of these letters were written after 1965. I therefore examined only the "Old Correspondence" collection and left the other collection to future scholars.

The "Old Correspondence" collection comprised three smaller collections of letters: Social Service Correspondence, General Correspondence, and Regional Correspondence. The Social Service Correspondence was organized by year and consisted of approximately 30 percent of the total letters examined. These letters tended to be the longest and richest in detail. The General Correspondence was organized alphabetically and consisted of approximately 45 percent of the total letters examined. The General Correspondence letters provided information on the widest range of topics. The Regional Correspondence was organized by state or country and consisted of approximately 25 percent of the total letters examined, and these letters formed the basis of chapters 2 and 3.

I have changed the correspondents' names to preserve their anonymity. I have only used real names when those names were published in *ONE* magazine or another source. Despite the passage of several decades,

I cannot assume that every correspondent would want his or her name publicly disclosed. They wrote their letters believing that ONE, Inc., would protect their anonymity, and I must respect that wish. Altering their names complicates the letters' retrieval by other scholars. I have in my possession a master list of correspondents' names that I can share with scholars under special circumstances.

I also examined a small amount of Mattachine Society Correspondence stored at the ONE Archive. This collection contained many letters from foreign countries and was useful for chapter 3.

Other primary source materials stored at the ONE Archive provided contextual information about gay and lesbian life in the 1950s and early 1960s. Of particular importance was a collection of 388 survey questionnaires from male homosexuals gathered by ONE, Inc., in 1961. These questionnaires were distributed in *ONE Confidential* VI, 1 and 2 (January and February 1961) and in *ONE* IX, 4 (April 1961). The survey was intended to form the basis of a Homosexual Bill of Rights, the brainchild of Dorr Legg. Although the effort to construct such a document failed, One Institute students analyzed the questionnaire data throughout the 1960s. In 1969 J. M. Underwood wrote the most extensive report and analysis of the data, "388 North American Male Homosexuals: A Sociological and Attitudes Study," which is filed with the questionnaires at the ONE Archive. Because the collection was officially "unprocessed" at the time the research was conducted, access to these documents may be limited.

I also examined many internal documents of ONE, Inc., and *ONE* magazine, such as annual reports, financial statements, internal memos, inventories, documents of incorporation, and other business documents. At the time I examined these documents they were incomplete and highly disorganized. They have since been processed and catalogued properly.

Of the three main individuals behind *ONE* magazine (Dorr Legg, Jim Kepner, and Don Slater), I examined many of Legg and Kepner's personal papers. Kepner's papers included his extensive writings on gay history, diaries, and personal correspondence dating back to World War II. They also contained fascinating material on science-fiction fan culture in the 1940s. Legg's papers largely concerned ONE, Inc., especially the One Institute. His typed lectures were particularly useful. Legg's papers also included mimeographed handouts from One Institute courses as well as research papers written by One Institute students. Slater's papers were unavailable because of a legal dispute regarding their ownership.

Perhaps the ONE Archive's deepest trove of information was its vast subject file collection, filling several hundred drawers. Many of Jim Kepner's original subject file folders compiled during the 1940s,

1950s, and early 1960s remained intact. These folders included invaluable newspaper and press clippings of homosexual topics during these years. Throughout this book, I have cited the subject file folder in which I originally found this material. Some of this material has since been reprocessed into different collections.

I used the ONE Archive's library of rare books and oral history collection extensively. I also read every available issue of the following publications in the indicated years as well as many issues of the *Mattachine Review* and *Der Kreis*:

> *ONE* magazine (1953–1967)
> *ONE Confidential* (1956–1967)
> *The Ladder* (1956–1966)
> *Physique Pictorial* (1950–1965)
> *Mattachine Society Newsletters*:
>   Boston (1958–1961)
>   Chicago (1955–1960)
>   Denver (1957–1960)
>   Detroit (1959)
>   Los Angeles (1953–1957)
>   New York (1956–1961)
>   Philadelphia (1961)
>   Washington, D.C. (1956)

Some of the primary source material regarding *Tea and Sympathy* was stored at the Margaret Herrick Library, Academy of Motion Picture Arts and Sciences, Beverly Hills, California. I also used archival materials at the University of California, Santa Barbara, Special Collections, for chapter 6.

Selected Books, Articles, Dissertations, and Pamphlets

Abelove, Henry, Michéle Aina Barale, and David M. Halperin. *The Lesbian and Gay Studies Reader*. New York: Routledge, 1993.

Abrahamson, David. *Magazine-Made America: The Cultural Transformation of the Postwar Periodical*. Cresskill, NJ: Hampton Press, 1996.

Adam, Barry D. *Rise of a Gay and Lesbian Movement*. Boston: Twayne Publishers, 1987.

Adler, Thomas P. *Robert Anderson*. Boston: Twayne Publishers, 1978.

Aldrich, Ann. *We Walk Alone through Lesbos' Lonely Groves*. New York: Gold Medal Books, 1955.

Aldrich, Robert. *Colonialism and Homosexuality*. London: Routledge, 2003.

Allyn, David. *Make Love, Not War: The Sexual Revolution: An Unfettered History.* Boston: Little, Brown, 2000.

Altman, Dennis. *Homosexual: Oppression and Liberation.* New York: Avon Books, 1973.

Alwood, Edward. *Straight News: Gays, Lesbians, and the News Media.* New York: Columbia University Press, 1996.

Anderson, Elliott, and Mary Kinzie, eds. *The Little Magazine in America: A Modern Documentary History.* Yonkers: Pushcart Press, 1978.

Anderson, Robert. *Tea and Sympathy.* New York: Random House, 1953.

Angle, N. *On the Corner: Stories from Twenty Years at a Chicago Newsstand.* New York: Exposition Press, 1957.

Armstrong, Elizabeth A. *Forging Gay Identities: Organizing Sexuality in San Francisco, 1950–1994.* Chicago: University of Chicago Press, 2002.

Atkins, Gary L. *Gay Seattle: Stories of Exile and Belonging.* Seattle: University of Washington Press, 2003.

Attwood, William, George B. Leonard Jr., and J. Robert Moskin. *The Decline of the American Male.* New York: Random House, 1958.

Baim, Tracy, ed. *Out and Proud in Chicago: A Visual History of Chicago's Gay Movement.* Chicago: Agate Surrey, 2008.

Barr [Fugaté], James. *Game of Fools.* Los Angeles: ONE, Inc., 1954.

———. *Quatrefoil.* New York: Greenberg, 1950.

Baughman, James L. *The Republic of Mass Culture: Journalism, Filmmaking, and Broadcasting in America since 1941.* Baltimore, MD: Johns Hopkins University Press, 1997.

Baxandall, Rosalyn, and Linda Gordon with Susan Reverby, eds. *America's Working Women: A Documentary History.* New York: Norton, 1995.

Baxter, Randolph W. " 'Eradicating This Menace': Homophobia and Anti-Communism in Congress, 1947–1954." Ph.D. diss., University of California, Irvine, 1999.

Bayer, Ronald. *Homosexuality and American Psychiatry: The Politics of Diagnosis.* Princeton, NJ: Princeton University Press, 1987.

Beemyn, Brett. "A Queer Capital: Lesbian, Gay, and Bisexual Life in Washington D.C., 1890–1955." Ph.D. diss., University of Iowa, 1997.

———, ed. *Creating a Place for Ourselves: Lesbian, Gay, and Bisexual Community Histories.* New York: Routledge, 1997.

———. "The Silence Is Broken: A History of the First Lesbian, Gay, and Bisexual College Student Groups." *Journal of the History of Sexuality* XII, 2 (April 2003), 205–223.

Bell, Daniel, ed. *The Radical Right.* Garden City, NY: Doubleday, 1963.

Bell, David, and Gill Valentine, eds. *Mapping Desire: Geographies of Sexualities.* London: Routledge, 1995.

Bergler, Edmund. *1,000 Homosexuals: Conspiracy of Silence, or Curing and Deglamorizing Homosexuals?* Paterson, NJ: Pageant Books, 1959.

———. *Homosexuality: Disease or Way of Life?* New York: Hill and Wang, 1957.

Bergman, David. *Gaiety Transfigured: Gay Self-Representation in American Literature.* Madison: University of Wisconsin Press, 1991.

Bernstein, Samuel. *Mr. Confidential: The Man, the Magazine, and the Movieland Massacre*. London: Walford Press, 2006.

Bérubé, Allan. *Coming Out under Fire: The History of Gay Men and Women in World War Two*. New York: Plume, 1990.

Best, Wallace D. *Passionately Human, No Less Divine: Religion and Culture in Black Chicago, 1915–1952*. (Princeton, NJ: Princeton University Press, 2005).

Biggs, Earl R. *Sex, Science and Sin: A Study of the Normal and Abnormal Sex Activity of Our Time in Relation to Science, the Law and Religion*. Portland, OR: New Science Book Co., 1950.

Bieber, Irving. *Homosexuality: A Psychoanalytic Study*. New York: Basic Books, 1962.

Bilstein, Roger E. *The American Aerospace Industry: From Workshop to Global Enterprise*. New York: Twayne Publishers, 1996.

Bladgett, M. V. Lee. *Money, Myths, and Change: The Economic Lives of Lesbians and Gay Men*. Chicago: University of Chicago Press, 2001.

Blasius, Mark, and Shane Phelan, eds. *We Are Everywhere: A Historical Sourcebook in Gay and Lesbian Politics*. New York: Routledge, 1997.

Bleys, Rudi. *The Geography of Perversion: Male-to-Male Sexual Behavior outside the West and the Ethnographic Imagination, 1750–1918*. New York: New York University Press, 1995.

Blount, Jackie. *Fit to Teach: Same-Sex Desire, Gender, and School Work in the Twentieth Century*. Albany: SUNY Press, 2005.

Boag, Peter. *Same-Sex Affairs: Constructing and Controlling Homosexuality in the Pacific Northwest*. Berkeley: University of California Press, 2003.

Bogle, Donald. *Toms, Coons, Mulattoes, Mammies, and Bucks: An Interpretative History of Blacks in American Films*. New York: Continuum, 1989.

Booth, Mark. *Camp*. London: Quartet Books, 1983.

Boyd, Nan Alamilla. *Wide Open Town: A History of Queer San Francisco to 1965*. Berkeley: University of California Press, 2003.

Boyer, Paul S. *By the Bomb's Early Light: American Thought and Culture at the Dawn of the Atomic Age*. Chapel Hill: University of North Carolina Press, 1985.

———. *Purity in Print: Book Censorship in America from the Gilded Age to the Computer Age*. Madison: University of Wisconsin Press, 2002.

Bradley, Matt. *Faggots to Burn!* Hollywood, CA: Intimate Books, 1962.

Braukman, Stacy. " 'Nothing Else Matters But Sex': Cold War Narratives of Deviance and the Search for Lesbian Teachers in Florida, 1959–1963." *Feminist Studies* XXVII (2001), 553–577.

Brown, Fred, and Rudolph Kempton. "Sex Answers and Questions: A Guide to Happy Marriage." New York: McGraw Hill, 1950. (The pamphlet was a condensed version of a book of the same name. A copy is filed in the "Sex Education" Folder, ONE Subject Files.)

Brown, Ricardo J. *The Evening Crowd at Kirmser's: A Gay Life in the 1940s*. Minneapolis: University of Minnesota Press, 2001.

Buckley, Michael J. *Morality and the Homosexual*. Westminster, MD: Newman Press, 1959.

Bullough, Vern, ed. *Before Stonewall: Activists for Gay and Lesbian Rights in Historical Context*. New York: Harrington Park Press, 2002.

Buring, Daneel. *Lesbian and Gay Memphis: Building Communities behind the Magnolia Curtain*. New York: Garland, 1997.

Cahn, Susan K. *Coming on Strong: Gender and Sexuality in Twentieth-Century Women's Sport*. Cambridge, MA: Harvard University Press, 1994.

Caprio, Frank Samuel. *Variations in Sexual Behavior: A Psychodynamic Study of Deviations in Various Expressions of Sexual Behavior*. New York: Citadel Press, 1955.

Capsuto, Steven. *Alternate Channels: The Uncensored Story of Gay and Lesbian Images on Radio and Television*. New York: Ballantine Books, 2000.

Carnes, Mark, ed. *Past Imperfect: History According to the Movies*. New York: Holt, 1995.

Cauldwell, D. O. *Private Letters from Homosexuals to a Doctor*. Girard, KS: Haldeman-Julius Publications, 1949.

Caute, David. *The Great Fear*. New York: Simon and Schuster, 1978.

Chauncey, George. "Christian Brotherhood or Sexual Perversion? Homosexual Identities and the Construction of Sexual Boundaries in the World War One Era." *Journal of Social History* XIX (1985), 189–211.

———. *Gay New York: Gender, Urban Culture, and the Making of a Gay Male World, 1890–1940*. New York: Basic Books, 1994.

———. *Why Marriage? The History Shaping Today's Debate over Gay Equality*. New York: Basic Books, 2004.

Cleto, Fabio. *Camp: Queer Aesthetics and the Performing Subject: A Reader*. Ann Arbor: University of Michigan Press, 1999.

Clum, John. *Still Acting Gay: Male Homosexuality in Modern Drama*. New York: St. Martin's Press, 2000.

Cohan, Steven. *Masked Men: Masculinity and the Movies in the Fifties*. Bloomington: Indiana University Press, 1997.

Cohen, Cathy J. *The Boundaries of Blackness: AIDS and the Breakdown of Black Politics*. Chicago: University of Chicago Press, 1999.

Cole, Shaun. *"Don We Now Our Gay Apparel": Gay Men's Dress in the Twentieth Century*. Oxford, UK: Berg, 2000.

Connell, R. W. *Gender and Power: Society, the Person and Sexual Politics*. Stanford, CA: Stanford University Press, 1987.

Constantine-Simms, Delroy, ed. *The Greatest Taboo: Homosexuality in Black Communities*. Los Angeles: Alyson Books, 2000.

Cook, Robert. *Sweet Land of Liberty? The African-American Struggle for Civil Rights in the Twentieth Century*. New York: Longman, 1998.

Corber, Robert. *Homosexuality in Cold War America: Resistance and the Crisis of Masculinity*. Durham, NC: Duke University Press, 1997.

Cory, Donald Webster. *The Homosexual in America: A Subjective Approach*. New York: Castle Books, 1951.

Corzine, Harold Junior. "The Gay Press." Ph.D. diss., Washington University, 1977.

Cotkin, George. *Existential America*. Baltimore, MD: Johns Hopkins University Press, 2003.

Cross, Harold H. U. *The Lust Market*. New York: Citadel Press, 1956.

Cruikshank, Margaret, ed. *Lesbian Studies: Present and Future*. Old Westbury, NY: Feminist Press, 1982.

Cuordileone, K. A. " 'Politics in an Age of Anxiety,' Cold War Political Culture and the Crisis in American Masculinity, 1949–1960." *Journal of American History* LXXXVII, 2 (September 2000), 515–545.

Cutler, Marvin [Dorr Legg], ed. *Homosexuals Today, 1956: A Handbook of Organizations and Publications*. Los Angeles: ONE, Inc., 1956.

D'Emilio, John. *Sexual Politics, Sexual Communities: The Making of a Homosexual Minority in the United States*. Chicago: University of Chicago Press, 1983.

———, and Estelle B. Freedman. *Intimate Matters: A History of Sexuality in America*. Chicago: University of Chicago Press: 1997.

Dean, Robert. *Imperial Brotherhood: Gender and the Making of Cold War Foreign Policy*. Amherst: University of Massachusetts Press, 2001.

Deutsch, Albert, ed. *Sex Habits of American Men: A Symposium on the Kinsey Report*. New York: Prentice-Hall, 1948.

Diament, Louis, ed. *Homosexual Issues in the Workplace*. Washington, DC: Taylor and Francis, 1993.

Dickey, Brenda. "Attitudes toward Sex Roles and Feelings of Adequacy in Homosexual Males." *Journal of Consulting Psychology* XXV, 2 (1961), 116–22.

Dilley, Patrick. *Queer Men on Campus: A History of Non-Heterosexual College Men, 1945–2000*. New York: RoutledgeFalmer, 2002.

———. "Which Way Out? A Typology of Non-Heterosexual Male Collegiate Identities." *Journal of Higher Education* LXXVI, 1 (January-February 2005).

Ditzion, Sidney Herbert. *Marriage, Morals and Sex in America*. New York: Bookman Associates, 1953.

Doan, Laura L. *Fashioning Sapphism: The Origins of a Modern English Lesbian Culture*. New York: Columbia University Press, 2001.

Donaldson, Gary. *Abundance and Anxiety: America, 1945–1960*. Westport, CT: Praeger, 1997.

Drucker, Peter. " 'In the Tropics There Is No Sin': Sexuality and Gay Lesbian Movements in the Third World." *New Left Review* 218 (July-August 1996), 75–100.

Drury, Allen. *Advise and Consent*. Garden City, NY: Doubleday, 1959.

Duberman, Martin. *Stonewall*. New York: Dutton, 1993.

———, Martha Vicinus, and George Chauncey Jr., eds. *Hidden From History: Reclaiming the Gay and Lesbian Past*. New York: New American Library, 1989.

Dunne, Gillian. *Lesbian Lifestyles: Women's Work and the Politics of Sexuality*. Toronto: University of Toronto Press, 1997.

Durkheim, Emile. *Suicide: A Study in Sociology*. Translated by Danny A. Spaulding and George Simpson. Glencoe, IL: Free Press, 1951.

Dyer, Richard. *Gays and Film*. New York: Zoetrope, 1982.

Edsall, Nicholas C. *Toward Stonewall: Homosexuality and Society in the Modern Western World*. Charlottesville: University of Virginia Press, 2003.

Eliassen, Meredith. *San Francisco State University*. Charleston, SC: Arcadia Publishing, 2007.

Elkin, Henry. "Aggressive and Erotic Tendencies in Army Life." *American Journal of Sociology* LI, 5 (March 1946), 408–412.

Engelhardt, Tom. *The End of Victory Culture: Cold War America and the Disillusioning of a Generation*. New York: Basic Books, 1995.

Ernst, Morris L., and David Loth. *American Sexual Behavior and the Kinsey Report*. New York: Greystone Press, 1948.

Escoffier, Jeffrey. *American Homo: Community and Perversity*. Berkeley: University of California Press, 1998.

Eskridge, William N. *Gaylaw: Challenging the Apartheid of the Closet*. Cambridge, MA: Harvard University Press, 1999.

Esterberg, Kristin G. "From Accommodation to Liberation: A Social Movement Analysis of Lesbians in the Homophile Movement." *Gender and Society* VIII, 3 (September 1994), 424–443.

Evans, M. Stanton. *Blacklisted by History: The Untold Story of Joseph McCarthy and His Fight against America's Enemies*. New York: Crown Forum, 2007.

Eysenck, H. J., ed. *Behavior Therapy and the Neuroses: Readings in Modern Methods of Treatment Derived from Learning Theory*. Oxford, UK: Pergamon Press, 1967.

Faderman, Lillian. *Odd Girls and Twilight Lovers: A History of Lesbian Life in Twentieth-Century America*. New York: Columbia University Press, 1991.

———, and Stuart Timmons. *Gay L.A.: A History of Sexual Outlaws, Power Politics, and Lipstick Lesbians*. New York: Basic Books, 2006.

Fariello, Griffin. *Red Scare: Memories of the American Inquisition, an Oral History*. New York: Norton, 1995.

Fejes, Fred. "Murder, Perversion, and Moral Panic: The 1954 Media Campaign against Miami's Homosexuals and the Discourse of Civic Betterment." *Journal of the History of Sexuality* IX, 3 (1999), 305–347.

Feldman, M. P. "Aversion Therapy for Sexual Deviations: A Critical Review." *Psychological Bulletin* LXV, 2 (February 1966), 65–79.

Fellows, Will. *Farm Boys: Lives of Gay Men from the Rural Midwest*. Madison: University of Wisconsin Press, 1996.

Foucault, Michel. *The History of Sexuality. Vol. I, An Introduction*. Translated by Robert Hurley. New York: Vintage Books: 1978.

Franzen, Trisha. *Spinsters and Lesbians: Independent Womanhood in the United States*. New York: New York University Press, 1996.

Freedman, Estelle. " 'Uncontrolled Desires': The Response to the Sexual Psychopath, 1920–1960." *Journal of American History* LXXIV, 1 (June 1987), 83–106.

Fried, Richard. *Nightmare in Red: The McCarthy Era in Perspective*. New York: Oxford University Press, 1990.

Friedman, Mack. *Strapped for Cash: A History of American Hustler Culture*. Los Angeles: Alyson Books, 2003.

Friskopp, Annette, and Sharon Silverstein. *Straight Jobs, Gay Lives: Gay and Lesbian Professionals, the Harvard Business School, and the American Workplace*. New York: Scribner, 1995.

Fuss, Diana, ed. *Inside/Out: Lesbian Theories, Gay Theories*. New York: Routledge, 1991.

Gallo, Marcia M. *Different Daughters: A History of the Daughters of Bilitis and the Rise of the Lesbian Rights Movement*. New York: Carroll and Graf, 2006.

Garber, Marjorie. *Bisexuality and the Eroticism of Everyday Life*. New York: Routledge, 2000.

———, and Rebecca Walkowitz, eds. *Secret Agents: The Rosenberg Case, McCarthyism, and Fifties America*. New York: Routledge, 1995.

Gathorne-Hardy, Jonathan. *Sex the Measure of All Things: A Life of Alfred C. Kinsey*. Bloomington: Indiana University Press, 1998.

Geddes, Donald Porter, and Enid Curie, eds. *About the Kinsey Report*. New York: Signet, 1948.

Gentry, Curt. *J. Edgar Hoover: The Man and His Secrets*. New York: Plume, 1991.

Gerassi, John. *The Boys of Boise: Furor, Vice, and Folly in an American City*. New York: Collier Books, 1966.

Gershick, Zsa Zsa. *Gay Old Girls*. Los Angeles: Alyson Books, 1998.

Gerstner, David. "The Production and Display of the Closet: Making Minnelli's *Tea and Sympathy*." *Film Quarterly* L, 3 (Spring 1997), 13–26.

Gilbert, James. *Men in the Middle: Searching for Masculinity in the 1950s*. Chicago: University of Chicago Press, 2005.

Gilfoyle, Timothy J. *City of Eros: New York City, Prostitution, and the Commercialization of Sex, 1790-1920*. New York: Norton, 1992.

Gilmartin, Katie. " 'The Very House of Difference': Intersection of Identities in the Life Histories of Colorado Lesbians, 1940–1965." Ph.D. diss., Yale University, 1995.

Gluckman, Amy, and Betsy Reed, eds. *Homo Economics: Capitalism, Community, and Lesbian and Gay Life*. New York: Routledge, 1997.

Gordon, Michael, ed. *The American Family in Social-Historical Perspective*. New York: St. Martin's Press, 1983.

Graebner, William, ed. *True Stories from the American Past*. New York: McGraw-Hill, 1993.

Greenberg, David F. *The Construction of Homosexuality*. Chicago: University of Chicago Press, 1988.

Gross, Albert. "The Troublesome Homosexual." *Focus* XXXII, 1 (January 1953), 13–16.

Hack, Richard. *Puppetmaster: The Secret Life of J. Edgar Hoover*. Beverly Hills, CA: New Millennium Press, 2004.

Hansen, Joseph. *A Few Doors West of Hope: The Life and Times of Dauntless Don Slater*. Los Angeles: Homosexual Information Center, 1998.

Harbeck, Karen M. *Gay and Lesbian Educators: Personal Freedoms, Public Constraints*. Malden, MA: Amethyst Press, 1997.

Harris, Daniel. *The Rise and Fall of Gay Culture*. New York: Hyperion, 1997.

Hawes, Joseph M., and Elizabeth I. Nybakken, eds. *Family and Society in American History*. Urbana: University of Illinois Press, 2001.

Heale, M. J. *McCarthy's Americans: Red Scare Politics in State and Nation, 1935-1965*. Athens: University of Georgia Press, 1998.

Hegarty, Peter. "Homosexual Signs and Heterosexual Silences: Rorschach Research on Male Homosexuality from 1921 to 1969." *Journal of the History of Sexuality* XII, 3 (July 2003), 400–423.

Heins, Marjorie. *Not in Front of the Children: "Indecency," Censorship, and the Innocence of Youth*. New York: Hill and Wang, 2001.

Hendin, Herbert. *Black Suicide*. New York: Basic Books, 1969.

———. *Suicide in America*. New York: Norton, 1995.

Hendriks, Aart, Rob Tielman, and Evert van der Veen, eds. *The Third Pink Book: A Global View of Lesbian and Gay Liberation and Oppression*. Buffalo, NY: Prometheus Books, 1993.

Herdt, Gilbert H., ed. *Moral Panics, Sex Panics: Fear and Fight over Sexual Rights*. New York: New York University Press, 2009.

———. *Same Sex, Different Cultures: Gays and Lesbians across Cultures*. Boulder, CO: Westview Press, 1997.

Himelhoch, Jerome, and Sylvia Fleis Fava, eds. *Sexual Behavior in American Society: An Appraisal of the First Two Kinsey Reports*. New York: Norton, 1955.

Hinsch, Bret. *Passions of the Cut Sleeve: The Male Homosexual Tradition in China*. Berkeley: University of California Press, 1990.

History Project, The. *Improper Bostonians: Lesbian and Gay History from the Puritans to Playland*. Boston: Beacon Press, 1999.

Hoffman, Martin. *The Gay World: Male Homosexuality and the Social Creation of Evil*. New York: Bantam Books, 1968.

Hofstadter, Richard. *The Paranoid Style in American Politics and Other Essays*. Cambridge, MA: Harvard University Press, 1965.

Hooven, F. Valentine III. *Beefcake: The Muscle Magazines of America 1950–1970*. Cologne, Germany: Taschen, 1995.

Horowitz, Daniel. *The Anxieties of Affluence: Critiques of American Consumer Culture, 1939–1979*. Amherst: University of Massachusetts Press, 2004.

Horowitz, Helen Lefkowitz. *Rereading Sex: Battles over Sexual Knowledge and Suppression in Nineteenth-Century America*. New York: Knopf, 2002.

Hurewitz, Daniel. *Bohemian Los Angeles and the Making of Modern Politics*. Berkeley: University of California Press, 2007.

Howard, John, ed. *Carryin' On in the Lesbian and Gay South*. New York: New York University Press, 1997.

———. *Men Like That: A Southern Queer History*. Chicago: University of Chicago Press, 1999.

Humphries, Laud. *Tearoom Trade: Impersonal Sex in Public Places*. Hawthorne, NY: Aldine Publishing, 1970.

Hunt, Gerald, ed. *Laboring for Rights: Unions and Sexual Diversity across Nations*. Philadelphia, PA: Temple University Press, 1999.

Isaacs, Gordon, and Brian McKenndrick. *Male Homosexuality in South Africa: Identity Formation, Culture, and Crisis*. Cape Town: Oxford University Press, 1992.

Jay, Karla, ed. *Dyke Life: A Celebration of the Lesbian Experience*. New York: Basic Books, 1995.

————, and Allen Young, eds. *Out of the Closets: Voices of Gay Liberation.* New York: New York University Press, 1992.

Jezer, Marty. *The Dark Ages: Life in the United States, 1945–1960.* Boston: South End Press, 1982.

Johnson, David K. *The Lavender Scare: The Cold War Persecution of Gays and Lesbians in the Federal Government.* Chicago: University of Chicago Press, 2004.

Johnson, Haynes. *The Age of Anxiety: McCarthyism to Terrorism.* Orlando, FL: Harcourt, 2005.

Jones, James H. *Alfred C. Kinsey: A Public/Private Life.* New York: Norton, 1997.

Jones, Jeffrey Alan. "Hidden Histories, Proud Communities: Multiple Narratives in the Queer Geographies of Lexington, Kentucky, 1930–1999." Ph.D. diss., University of Kentucky, Lexington, 2001.

Jones, Sonya, ed. *Gay and Lesbian Literature since World War II.* New York: Haworth Press, 1998.

Jordon, Roger. *Hollywood's Sexual Underground.* Los Angeles: Medco Books, 1966.

Kaiser, Charles. *The Gay Metropolis, 1940–1996.* Boston: Houghton Mifflin, 1997.

Katz, Jonathan Ned. *Gay American History: Lesbians and Gay Men in the U.S.A.* New York: Harper Colophon Books, 1976.

————. *Gay/Lesbian Almanac: A New Documentary.* New York: Harper and Row, 1983.

————, ed. *Government versus Homosexuals.* New York: Arno Press, 1975.

————. *Love Stories: Sex between Men before Homosexuality.* Chicago: University of Chicago Press, 2001.

Kenan, Stephanie Hope. "Scientific Studies of Human Sexual Difference in Interwar America." Ph.D. diss., University of California, Berkeley, 1998.

Kennedy, Elizabeth Lapovsky, and Madeline Davis, *Boots of Leather, Slippers of Gold: The History of a Lesbian Community.* New York: Routledge, 1993.

Kennedy, Hubert. *Ulrichs: The Life and Works of Karl Heinrich Ulrichs Pioneer of the Modern Gay Movement.* Boston: Alyson Books, 1988.

Kenney, Moira Rachel. *Mapping Gay L.A.: The Intersection of Place and Politics.* Philadelphia, PA: Temple University Press, 2001.

Kepner, Jim. *Rough News, Daring Views: 1950s' Pioneer Gay Press Journalism.* New York: Haworth Press, 1998.

Kinsey, Alfred, Wardell Pomeroy, and Clyde Martin. *Sexual Behavior in the Human Female.* Philadelphia, PA: Saunders, 1953.

————. *Sexual Behavior in the Human Male.* Philadelphia, PA: Saunders, 1948.

Kutler, Stanley. *The American Inquisition.* New York: Hill and Wang, 1982.

Kwolek-Folland, Angel. *Engendering Business: Men and Women in the Corporate Office, 1870–1930.* Baltimore, MD: Johns Hopkins University Press, 1994.

Lait, Jack, and Lee Mortimer. *U.S.A. Confidential.* New York: Crown, 1952.

————. *Washington Confidential.* New York: Dell, 1951.

Lauritsen, John, and David Thorstad. *The Early Homosexual Rights Movement (1864–1935).* New York: Times Change Press, 1974.

Lavender Lexicon: Dictionary of Gay Words and Phrases, The. San Francisco, CA: Strait and Associates, 1964.

Leap, William L., ed. *Public Sex/Gay Space.* New York: Columbia University Press, 1999.

Legg, W. Dorr, ed. *Homophile Studies in Theory and Practice.* San Francisco, CA: GLB Publishers and ONE Institute Press, 1994.

Leibman, Nina C. *Living Room Lectures: Fifties Family in Film and Television.* Austin: University of Texas Press, 1995.

Lekus, Ian. "Queer and Present Dangers: Homosexuality and American Antiwar Activism during the Vietnam Era." Ph.D. diss., Duke University, 2003.

Leslie, Robert. *Casebook: Homophile.* New York: Dalhousie Press, 1966.

Leslie, Stuart W. *The Cold War and American Science: The Military-Industrial-Academic Complex at MIT and Stanford.* New York: Columbia University Press, 1993.

LeVay, Simon. *Queer Science: The Use and Abuse of Research into Homosexuality.* Cambridge, MA: MIT Press, 1996.

Levine, Martin, and Robin Leonard. "Discrimination against Lesbians in the Work Force." *Signs* IX, 4 (1984), 700–710.

Lewin, Ellen, ed. *Inventing Lesbian Cultures in America.* Boston: Beacon Press, 1996.

Leyland, Winston, ed. *Gay Sunshine Interviews, Volume I.* San Francisco, CA: Gay Sunshine Press, 1978.

Leznoff, Maurice. "Interviewing Homosexuals." *American Journal of Sociology* LXII, 2 (September 1956), 202–204

Lindner, Robert. *Must You Conform?* New York: Rinehart, 1956.

Lisagor, Nancy. "Lesbian Identity in the Subculture of Women's Bars." Ph.D. diss., University of Pennsylvania, 1980.

Loughery, John. *The Other Side of* Silence. New York: Holt, 1998.

MacCurdy, Frederick, et al. "Report on Study of 102 Sex Offenders at Sing-Sing Prison." Albany, New York: State of New York, 1950

MacKay, Anne, ed. *Wolf Girls at Vassar: Lesbian and Gay Experiences 1930–1990.* New York: St. Martin's Press, 1993.

Maggiore, Dolores J. *Lesbianism: An Annotated Bibliography and Guide to the Literature, 1976–1991.* Metuchen, NJ: Scarecrow Press, 1992.

Mailer, Norman. *Advertisements for Myself.* New York: G. P. Putnam's Sons, 1959.

Mann, William. *Behind the Screen: How Gays and Lesbians Shaped Hollywood, 1910–1969.* New York: Viking, 2001.

Marcus, Eric. *Making History: The Struggle for Gay and Lesbian Rights, 1945–1990, An Oral History.* New York: HarperCollins, 1992.

Margolis, Jon. *The Last Innocent Year: America in 1964, The Beginning of the Sixties.* New York: Perennial, 1999.

Marlowe, Kenneth. *The Male Homosexual.* Los Angeles: Sherbourne Press, 1965.

Marotta, Toby. *The Politics of Homosexuality.* Boston: Houghton Mifflin, 1981.

Masters, R. E. L. *The Homosexual Revolution.* New York: Julian Press, 1962.

May, Elaine Tyler. *Barren in the Promised Land: Childless Americans and the Pursuit of Happiness.* New York: Basic Books, 1995.

―――. *Homeward Bound: American Families in the Cold War Era*. New York: Basic Books, 1988.

May, Rollo. *The Meaning of Anxiety*. New York: Norton, 1977.

McCall, Laura, and Donald Yacovone, eds. *A Shared Experience: Men, Women, and the History of Gender*. New York: New York University Press, 1998.

McClellan, Grant S., ed. *Censorship in the United States*. New York: Wilson, 1967.

McLelland, Mark. *Queer Japan from the Pacific War to the Internet Age*. Lanham, MD: Rowan and Littlefield, 2005.

McCourt, James. *Queer Street: Rise and Fall of an American Culture, 1947–1985*. New York: Norton, 2004.

McPartland, John. *Sex in Our Changing World*. New York: MacFadden-Bartell, 1964.

Meaker, Marijane. *Highsmith: A Romance of the 1950s*. San Francisco, CA: Cleis Press, 2003.

Meeker, Martin. "Behind the Mask of Respectability: The Mattachine Society and Male Homophile Practice, 1950s–1960s." *Journal of the History of Sexuality* X, 1 (April 2001), 78–116.

―――. *Contacts Desired: Connecting to the Gay Male and Lesbian World from the 1940s into the 1970s*. Chicago: University of Chicago Press, 2006.

Menninger, William C. *Psychiatry in a Troubled World: Yesterday's War and Today's Challenges*. New York: Macmillan, 1948.

Metalious, Grace. *Peyton Place*. Boston: Northeastern University Press, 1956.

Meyer, Leisa D. *Creating G.I. Jane: Sexuality and Power in the Women's Army Corps during World War II*. New York: Columbia University Press, 1996.

Meyer, Richard. *Outlaw Representation: Censorship and Homosexuality in Twentieth-Century American Art*. Boston: Beacon Press, 2002.

Meyerowitz, Joanne J. *How Sex Changed: A History of Transsexuality in the United States*. Cambridge, MA: Harvard University Press, 2002.

―――, ed. *Not June Cleaver: Women and Gender in Postwar America, 1945–1960*. Philadelphia, PA: Temple University Press, 1994.

―――. *Women Adrift: Independent Wage Earners in Chicago, 1880–1930*. Chicago: University of Chicago Press, 1988.

Miller, Melody, Phyllis Moen, and Donna Dempster-McClain. "Motherhood, Multiple Roles, and Maternal Well-Being: Women in the 1950s." *Gender and Society* V, 4 (1991), 565–82.

Miller, Neil. *Sex-Crime Panic: A Journey to the Paranoid Heart of the 1950s*. Los Angeles: Alyson Books, 2002.

Mills, C. Wright. *White Collar: The American Middle Classes*. New York: Oxford University Press, 1993.

Mintz, Steven, and Susan Kellogg. *Domestic Revolutions: A Social History of American Family Life*. New York: Free Press, 1988.

Morgan, Ted. *Reds: McCarthyism in the Twentieth Century*. New York: Random House, 2004.

Mortimer, Lee. *Around the World Confidential*. New York: G. P. Putnam's Sons, 1956.

Mumford, Kevin J. *Interzones: Black/White Sex Districts in Chicago and New York in the Early 20th Century*. New York: Columbia University Press, 1997.

Murdoch, Joyce, and Deb Price. *Courting Justice: Gay Men and Lesbians v. the Supreme Court*. New York: Basic Books, 2001.

Nardi, Peter, David Sanders, and Judd Marmor. *Growing Up before Stonewall: Life Stories of Some Gay Men*. London: Routledge, 1994.

Navasky, Victor. *Naming Names*. New York: Viking Press, 1980.

Nealon, Christopher. *Foundlings: Lesbian and Gay Historical Emotion before Stonewall*. Durham, NC: Duke University Press, 2001.

———. "Invert-History: The Ambivalence of Lesbian Pulp Fiction." *New Literary History* XXXI, 4 (Autumn 2000), 745–764.

Negri, Vitali. *Psychoanalysis of Sexual Life*. Los Angeles: Western Institute of Psychoanalysis, 1949.

Nerf, Swasarnt. *Gay Girl's Guide: A Primer for Novices, a Review for Roues*, 3rd. ed. Np: Mimeographed, 1956.

Nestle, Joan, ed. *The Persistent Desire: A Femme-Butch Reader*. Boston: Alyson Books, 1992.

———. *A Restricted Country*. Ithaca, NY: Firebrand Books, 1987.

Neville-Rolfe, Sybil, ed. *Sex in Social Life*. London: Allen and Unwin, 1948.

"The New Approach . . . Sex Offender to Good Citizen." Emotional Security Program, Atascadero (California) State Hospital, 1955.

Newton, Esther. *Cherry Grove, Fire Island: Sixty Years in America's First Gay and Lesbian Town*. Boston: Beacon Press, 1993.

———. *Mother Camp: Female Impersonators in America*. Chicago: University of Chicago Press, 1972.

O'Neill, William L. *American High: The Years of Confidence, 1945–1960*. New York: Free Press, 1986.

Otis, Harry. *The Keval and Other Gay Adventures*. Los Angeles: ONE, Inc., 1959.

Paller, Michael. *Gentlemen Callers: Tennessee Williams, Homosexuality, and Mid-Twentieth Century Drama*. New York: Palgrave Macmillan, 2005.

Patterson, Charlotte. "Family Relationships of Lesbians and Gay Men." *Journal of Marriage and the Family* LXII, 4 (November 2000), 1052–1069.

Peiss, Kathy, and Christina Simmons with Robert Padgug, eds. *Passion and Power: Sexuality in History*. Philadelphia, PA: Temple University Press, 1989.

Phelan, Shane. *Sexual Strangers: Gays, Lesbians, and Dilemmas of Citizenship*. Philadelphia, PA: Temple University Press, 2001.

Pursell, Carroll W., Jr., ed. *The Military-Industrial Complex*. New York: Harper and Row, 1972.

Pyron, Darden Asbury. *Liberace: An American Boy*. Chicago: University of Chicago Press, 2000.

Reavis, John, Jr. *The Rejected*. San Francisco, CA: Pan-Graphic Press, 1961.

Reeves, Thomas. *The Life and Times of Joe McCarthy: A Biography*. New York: Stein and Day, 1982.

Retzloff, Tim. " 'Seer or Queer?' Postwar Fascination with Detroit's Prophet Jones." *Gay and Lesbian Quarterly* 8 (2002), 271–296.

Reumann, Miriam G. *American Sexual Character: Sex, Gender, and National Identity in the Kinsey Reports*. Berkeley: University of California Press, 2005.

Riesman, David, with Nathan Glazer and Reuel Denney. *The Lonely Crowd: A Study of the Changing American Character.* New Haven, CT: Yale University Press, 1961.

River, J. Paul de. *The Sexual Criminal: A Psychoanalytical Study.* Springfield, IL: Charles C. Thomas Publisher, 1950.

Rivers, Daniel. " 'In the Best Interests of the Child': Lesbian and Gay Parenting Custody Cases, 1967–85." *Journal of Social History* XLIII, 4 (Summer 2010), 917–943.

Roberts, Edwin A. *The Smut Rakers.* Silver Springs, MD: National Observer, 1966.

Robertson, Stephen. "Separating the Men from the Boys: Masculinity, Psychosexual Development, and Sex Crime in the United States, 1930s–1960s." *Journal of the History of Medicine and Allied Sciences* LVI, 1 (January 2001), 3–35.

Robinson, Daniel, and David Kimmel. "The Queer Career of Homosexual Security Vetting in Cold War Canada." *Canadian Historical Review* LXXV, 3 (1994), 319–345.

Rogin, Michael. *The Intellectuals and McCarthy: The Radical Specter.* Cambridge, MA: MIT Press, 1967.

Rose, Lisle A. *The Cold War Comes to Main Street: America in 1950.* Lawrence: University of Kansas Press, 1999.

Ross, Andrew. *No Respect: Intellectuals and Popular Culture.* New York: Routledge, 1989.

Ross, H. Laurence. "Modes of Adjustment of Married Homosexuals." *Social Problems* XVIII (1971), 385–393.

Ross, Kenneth. "Letter to a Homosexual." London: Society for the Promotion of Christian Knowledge, 1955.

Ross, Michael W. *The Married Homosexual Man.* London: Routledge, 1983.

Rotter, Andrew J. "Gender Relations, Foreign Relations: The United States and South Asia, 1947–1964." *The Journal of American History* LXXXI, 2 (September 1994), 518–542.

Rotundo, Anthony. *American Manhood: Transformations in Masculinity from the Revolution to the Modern Era.* New York: Basic Books, 1993.

Russell, Ina, ed. *Jeb and Dash: A Diary of Gay Life, 1918–1945.* Boston: Faber and Faber, 1993.

Russell, Thaddeus. "The Color of Discipline: Civil Rights and Black Sexuality." *American Quarterly* LX, 1 (March 2008), 101–128.

Russo, Vito. *The Celluloid Closet: Homosexuality in the Movies.* New York: Harper and Row, 1981.

Rutledge, Leigh. *The Gay Book of Lists.* Boston: Alyson Books, 1987.

Sadownick, Douglas. *Sex between Men: An Intimate History of the Sex Lives of Gay Men Postwar to Present.* San Francisco, CA: Harper San Francisco, 1996.

Sagarin, Edward. "Structure and Ideology in an Association of Deviants." Ph.D. diss., New York University, 1966.

Said, Edward. *Orientalism.* New York: Vintage, 1979.

Sarkesian, Sam C., ed. *The Military-Industrial Complex: A Reassessment.* Beverly Hills, CA: Sage, 1972.

Savitsch, Eugene de. *Homosexuality, Transvestism and Change of Sex.* London: William Heinemann Medical Books, 1958.

Schluter, Daniel. *Gay Life in the Former USSR: Fraternity without Community.* New York: Routledge, 2002.

Schrecker, Ellen. *Many Are the Crimes: McCarthyism in America.* Boston: Little, Brown, 1998.

———. *No Ivory Tower: McCarthyism and the Universities.* New York: Oxford University Press, 1986.

Sears, James T. *Behind the Mask of the Mattachine: The Hal Call Chronicles and the Early Movement for Homosexual Emancipation.* New York: Harrington Park Press, 2006.

———. *Lonely Hunters: An Oral History of Lesbian and Gay Southern Life, 1948–1968.* Boulder, CO: Westview Press, 1997.

———. *Rebels, Rubyfruits, and Rhinestones: Queering Space in the Stonewall South.* New Brunswick, NJ: Rutgers University Press, 2001.

Sedgwick, Eve Kosofsky. *Epistemology of the Closet.* Berkeley: University of California Press, 1990.

Seidman, Steven. *Romantic Longings: Love in America, 1830–1980.* New York: Routledge, 1991.

———. *The Social Construction of Sexuality.* New York: Norton, 2003.

Shilts, Randy. *The Mayor of Castro Street: The Life and Times of Harvey Milk.* New York: St. Martin's Griffin, 2008.

Simmons, Jerold. "The Production Code: Under New Management: Geoffrey Shurlock, *The Bad Seed*, and *Tea and Sympathy.*" *Journal of Popular Film and Television* XXII, 1 (Spring 1999), 2–10.

Shand-Tucci, Douglass. *The Crimson Letter: Harvard, Homosexuality, and the Shaping of American Culture.* New York: St. Martin's Press, 2003.

Sinfield, Alan. *Out on Stage: Lesbian and Gay Theatre in the Twentieth Century.* New Haven, CT: Yale University Press, 1999.

Skolnick, Arlene. *Embattled Paradise: The American Family in an Age of Uncertainty.* New York: Basic Books, 1991.

Smith, Geoffrey. "National Security and Personal Isolation: Sex, Gender, and Disease in the Cold-War United States." *International History Review* XIV, 2 (May 1992), 307–337.

Smith, Charles Michael, ed. *Fighting Words: Personal Essays by Black Gay Men.* New York: Avon Books, 1999.

Smith, Patricia Juliana, ed. *The Queer Sixties.* New York: Routledge, 1999.

Sontag, Susan. *Against Interpretation.* New York: Dell, 1969.

Stearn, Jess. *The Grapevine.* Garden City, NY: Doubleday, 1964.

———. *The Sixth Man.* New York: MacFadden Books, 1962.

Stein, Arlene. *Sex and Sensibility: Stories of a Lesbian Generation.* Berkeley: University of California Press, 1997.

Stein, Marc. *City of Sisterly and Brotherly Loves: Lesbian and Gay Philadelphia, 1945–1972.* Chicago: University of Chicago Press, 2000.

Storr, Anthony. *Sexual Deviation.* Baltimore, MD: Penguin Books, 1964.

Stouffer, Samuel Andrew. *Communism, Conformity, and Civil Liberties: A Cross-Section of the Nation Speaks Its Mind.* Gloucester, MA: Peter Smith, 1963.

Streitmatter, Rodger. *Unspeakable: The Rise of a Gay and Lesbian Press in America.* Boston: Faber and Faber, 1995.

Stryker, Susan. *Queer Pulp: Perverted Passions from the Golden Age of the Paperback.* San Francisco, CA: Chronicle Books, 2001.

Styles, Joseph. "Outsider/Insider: Researching Gay Baths." *Urban Life* VIII, Number 2 (July 1979), 139–152.

Sullivan, Gerard. "Political Opportunism and the Harassment of Homosexuals in Florida, 1952–1965." *Journal of Homosexuality* XXXVII, 4 (1999), 57–81.

Summers, Anthony. *Official and Confidential: The Secret Life of J. Edgar Hoover.* New York: G. P. Putnam's Sons, 1993.

Suran, Justin David. "Coming Out against the War: Antimilitarism and the Politicization of Homosexuality in the Era of Vietnam." *American Quarterly* LIII, 3 (September 2001), 452–488.

Sweet, Roxanna Thayer. *Political and Social Action in Homophile Organizations.* New York: Arno Press, 1975.

Tebbel, John, and Mary Ellen Zuckerman. *The Magazine in America 1741–1990.* New York: Oxford University Press, 1991.

Terry, Jennifer. *An American Obsession: Science, Medicine, and Homosexuality in Modern Society.* Chicago: University of Chicago Press, 1999.

Theoharis, Athan. *Chasing Spies: How the FBI Failed in Counterintelligence but Promoted the Politics of McCarthyism in the Cold War Years.* Chicago: Ivan R. Dee, 2002.

———. *J. Edgar Hoover, Sex, and Crime: An Historical Antidote.* Chicago: Ivan R. Dee, 2002.

———. *Seeds of Repression: Harry Truman and the Origins of McCarthyism.* Chicago: Quadrangle Books, 1971.

———, and John Stuart Cox. *The Boss: J. Edgar Hoover and the Great American Inquisition.* New York: Bantam, 1988.

Tillich, Paul. *The Courage to Be.* New Haven, CT: Yale University Press, 1952.

Timmons, Stuart. *The Trouble with Harry Hay.* Boston: Alyson Books, 1990.

Tyler, Parker. *Screening the Sexes: Homosexuality in the Movies.* New York: Holt, Rinehart and Winston, 1972.

U.S. Congress, Senate. *Committee on Expenditures in the Executive Departments. Interim Report Submitted to the Committee on Expenditures in the Executive Departments by Its Subcommittee on Investigations: Employment of Homosexuals and Other Sex Perverts in Government.* Eighty-first Congress, 1950.

U.S. Department of Health, Education, and Welfare, Social Security Administration, Children's Bureau. "The Adolescent in Your Family." Children's Bureau Publication 347, 1955.

Usher, Bradley. "Federal Civil Service Employment Discrimination against Gays and Lesbians, 1950–1975: A Policy and Movement History." Ph.D. diss., New School for Social Research, 1999.

Valocchi, Steve. "The Class-Inflected Nature of Gay Identity." *Social Problems* XLVI, 2 (1999), 207–224.

Van Leer, David. *The Queening of America: Gay Culture in Straight Society.* New York: Routledge, 1995.

Vanita, Ruth, ed. *Queering India: Same-Sex Love and Eroticism in Indian Culture and Society.* New York: Routledge, 2002.

Vidal, Gore. *The City and the Pillar.* New York: Grosset and Dunlap, 1948.

Von Hoffman, Nicholas. *Citizen Cohn.* Toronto: Bantam, 1988.

Waitt, Gordon, and Kevin Markwell. *Gay Tourism: Culture and Context.* New York: Haworth Press, 2006.

Walker, Lisa. *Looking Like What You Are: Sexual Style, Race, and Lesbian Identity.* New York: New York University Press, 2001.

Walker, Nancy A., ed. *Women's Magazines 1940–1960: Gender Roles and the Popular Press.* Boston: Bedford/St. Martin's, 1998.

Wang, Jessica. *American Science in an Age of Anxiety: Scientists, Anticommunists, and the Cold War.* Chapel Hill: University of North Carolina Press, 1999.

Ward, Elijah G. "Homophobia, Hypermasculinity and the U.S. Black Church." *Culture, Health & Sexuality* VII, 5 (September-October 2005), 493–504.

Watts, Steven. *Mr. Playboy: Hugh Hefner and the American Dream.* Hoboken, NJ: Wiley Press, 2008.

Waugh, Thomas. *Hard to Imagine: Gay Male Eroticism in Photography and Film from Their Beginnings to Stonewall.* New York: Columbia University Press, 1996.

Weinberg, Martin, and Alan Bell. *Homosexuality: An Annotated Bibliography.* New York: Harper and Row, 1972.

Weiss, Jessica. *To Have and to Hold: Marriage, the Baby Boom, and Social Change.* Chicago: University of Chicago Press, 2000.

West, D. J. *Homosexuality.* Middlesex, UK: Penguin Books, 1968.

Weston, Kath. *Render Me, Gender Me: Lesbians Talk Sex, Class, Color, Nation, Studmuffins. . . .* New York: Columbia University Press, 1996.

Westwood, Gordon. *Society and the Homosexual.* London: Victor Gollancz, 1952.

Wexler, Murray. "The Relationship between Personality Organization and Electroshock: A Comparative Study of the Personality Characteristics of Psychotic Patients Who Improve or Do Not Improve from Electroshock Therapy." Ph.D. diss., New York University, 1953.

White, C. Todd. *Pre-Gay L.A.: A Social History of the Movement for Homosexual Rights.* Urbana: University of Illinois Press, 2009.

White, Kevin. *The First Sexual Revolution: The Emergence of Male Heterosexuality in Modern America.* New York: New York University Press, 1993.

Whyte, William H. *The Organization Man.* Garden City, NY: Doubleday Anchor Books, 1956.

Wildeblood, Peter. *Against the Law.* New York: Julian Messner, 1959.

———. *A Way of Life.* London: Weidenfield and Nicolson, 1956.

Williams, John Colin. "Discharges from the Military: An Examination of Labeling Theory." Ph.D. diss., Rutgers University, 1970.

Winkler, Allan M. *Life under a Cloud: American Anxiety about the Bomb.* Urbana: University of Illinois Press, 1999.

Winski, Norm. *The Homosexual Explosion*. North Hollywood, CA: Challenge Publications, 1966.

Wolfenden, John, et al. "Report of the Committee on Homosexuals Offences and Prostitution." London: Her Majesty's Stationery Office, 1957.

Wolff, Charlotte. *Magnus Hirschfeld: A Portrait of a Pioneer in Sexology*. London: Quartet Books, 1987.

Wood, Ruth Pirsig. *Lolita in Peyton Place: Highbrow, Middlebrow, and Lowbrow Novels of the 1950s*. London: Routledge, 1995.

Woods, James D., with Jay H. Lucas. *The Corporate Closet: The Professional Lives of Gay Men in America*. New York: Free Press, 1993.

Wylie, Philip. *Generation of Vipers*. New York: Rinehart, 1942.

Yankowski, John S., and Hermann K. Wolff. *The Tortured Sex*. Los Angeles: Holloway House, 1965.

Zimet, Jaye. *Strange Sisters: The Art of Lesbian Pulp Fiction, 1949-1969*. New York: Viking Studio, 1999.

Zion, Sidney. *The Autobiography of Roy Cohn*. Secaucus, NJ: Lyle Stuart, 1988.

Zipter, Yvonne. *Diamonds Are a Dyke's Best Friend*. Ithaca, NY: Firebrand Books, 1988.

Zuckerman, Mary Ellen. *A History of Popular Women's Magazines in the United States, 1792-1995*. Westport, CT: Greenwood Press, 1998.

Index

293

160–61; childrearing and, 163–64;
conversion to heterosexuality and,
162, 167; homophile movement
and, 162; lesbians and, 162–64,
167; passing as heterosexual
and, 158, 162, 167; statistics of,
159–60
marriage (same-sex), 168–79; African-
Americans, 185–86; J. Edgar Hoover
and, 177–79; legal recognition of,
47, 157–58, 169–71; lesbians and,
168–69, 171, 173, 263n58; letters
from couples, 47–48, 148, 171–73;
statistics of, 168–69; visibility
and, 158, 169, 170, 172–173, 177;
wedding ceremonies, 171, 263n58
Martin, Del, 105
Martin, Marcel, 170, 207
Maryland. *See* Baltimore
masculinity: crisis in 1950s, 203–04,
209–10; lesbians and, 208–10;
nationalism and, 209–10, 227; *ONE*
and, 208; physique magazines and,
214; teaching of, 211–13
mask: closet and, 10–11; homophile
publications and, 11, *12*, *13*, 31;
as metaphor, 10–11, 79, 145–46,
223–24, 237n27
Massachussetts. *See* Boston;
Newburyport
masturbation, 112, 165
Mathews, Arthur Guy, 51, 243n30
Mattachine Midwest (Chicago),
103–04
Mattachine Review, 37, 61, 69;
circulation of, 20
Mattachine Society, 7, 19–20, 206,
207–08; Dorr Legg and, 21;
marriage and, 162; mask metaphor
and, 11, 237n27; religion and, 198.
See also Boston Area Mattachine
Society; Denver, CO, Denver
Mattachine Chapter; Mattachine
Midwest (Chicago)
May, Elaine Tyler, 7
Mayflower Hotel (Washington, D.C.),
177–78

McCarthy, Senator Joseph, 2, 4–5, 29,
67, 89, 117, 228; symbol of anti-gay
persecution, 6
McCarthyism, 5, 16, 67, 103;
homosexuals and, 4–6, 19, 54–55;
military discharges and, 102, 109;
ONE magazine and, 20; police
crackdowns and, 86, 132; teaching
profession and, 122, 132, 133
McIntire, Dal. *See* Kepner, Jim
Meaker, Marijane, 143, 167
medical profession. *See* hospitals;
mental hospitals; psychiatry,
psychology
Meeker, Martin, 237n27
Meier, Karl (pseud. Rolf), 69, 70–71;
visit to United States, 72
mental hospitals, 161, 191–94, 199;
criminal justice system and, 89–90,
192–93; letters from, 89–90
Mercer, J.D., 93
Metalious, Grace, 9
Metro-Goldwyn-Mayer, 203
Metropolitan Community Church, 200
Mexican-Americans. *See* Latino/as
Mexico. *See* Mexico City
Mexico City: homophile activism in,
74; *ONE* availability in, 34, 63
Meyer, Leisa, 113
Miami, FL, 55, 88; antigay hysteria in,
20, 36, 86, 115; letters from, 134,
200; *ONE* availability in, 49
Michelangelo, 21, 145
Michigan, 132; letters from, 127–28,
161. *See also* Detroit; Flint;
Highland Park
middle-class, 113, 184, 224;
homosexual identity and, 204, 221;
ONE magazine and, 14
Midwinter Meetings, 40, 71
military, 101–20, 150; antigay
policies, 107–13; Blue Angels, 115;
classifications of homosexuality,
107, 109; courts-martial, 110–12;
draft boards, 109, 117–18; G.I. Bill,
14, 102, 113; -industrial complex,
102, 114–19; Japan and, 78–79;